Democratic Humanism and American Literature

Democratic Humanism
and American Literature

Harold Kaplan

The University of Chicago Press
Chicago and London

The University of Chicago Press, Chicago 60637
The University of Chicago Press, Ltd., London

International Standard Book Number: 0-226-42422-7
Library of Congress Catalog Card Number: 71-184508

For Isabelle, Anne, and Claire

Contents

Among a democratic people poetry will not be fed with
legends or the memorials of old traditions. The poet will not
attempt to people the universe with supernatural beings, in whom
his readers and his own fancy have ceased to believe; nor will
he coldly personify virtues and vices, which are better received
under their own features. All these resources fail him; but Man
remains, and the poet needs no more. The destinies of mankind,
man himself taken aloof from his country and his age and standing
in the presence of Nature and of God, with his passions, his
doubts, his rare prosperities and inconceivable wretchedness,
will become the chief, if not the sole, theme of poetry
among these nations.

Alexis de Tocqueville

One key, one solution to the mysteries of human condition,
one solution to the old knots of fate, freedom, and foreknowledge,
exists; the propounding, namely, of the double consciousness.
A man must ride alternately on the horses of his private and
public nature, as the equestrians in the circus throw themselves
nimbly from horse to horse. . . .

Emerson

Apart from the pulling and hauling stands what I am,
Stands amused, complacent, compassionating, idle, unitary,
Looks down, is erect, or bends an arm on an impalpable certain rest,
Looking with side-curved head curious what will come next,
Both in and out of the game and watching and wondering at it.

Whitman

Preface

If America has had a distinctive culture, it has been based on politics. In this I agree with Tocqueville, whose insights originating in that assumption still startle us with their clairvoyance. A chapter heading in *Democracy in America*, "Of Some Sources of Poetry in Democratic Nations," could have given me a subtitle for this book. But to state my purpose, I should reverse Tocqueville's phrase to say that I search for the ethical intelligence of American democracy in the work of its classic writers. In politics we have our scriptural texts, and history has produced its generative myths, but the very nature of a liberal society suggests that the complex moral imagination required to express it can best be found in its imaginative writers. That perhaps accounts for the challenge originally felt by the writers of the literary renaissance of the nineteenth-century republic, and the way in which their work still meets deep response in us. In varying expressions, as distinct as the contrast between Mark Twain and Henry James, they committed themselves to their experience as Americans. Emerson, Thoreau, and Whitman were citizen-poets, as Whitman drew the design of that vocation, but so with very different, even opposing temperaments, were Melville and Hawthorne. As writers they were the freest critics of their civilization, but that criticism was reflected from a deeper allegiance or ethos expressed by their imaginations. To the extent that we have a moral tradition that supports democracy, it is more their creation than we yet appreciate.

One of my assumptions in writing this book is that a democratic culture places high value on a consciousness which is expansive, resists constraint, and seeks restlessly for the boundaries of all commitments. That is one way to describe the activity of the literary imagination and the dialectical structure of literary forms. These latter in their dramatic emphasis communicate a discipline of questioning more often than belief, and if the faith needed for action in the world is a matter of concern at all, it comes surrounded by such sophistication of judgment that to most observers it would appear useless for the purposes of political advocacy or allegiance. And yet the moral needs of liberal democracy are rare in this respect. The instrument for the exercise of freedom is the imagination itself. The imagination that dominates the American literary tradition, which is a romantic tradition, exists, or yearns to exist, outside whatever kingdom of necessity the real world imposes. For the American transcendentalists this impulse was almost a habit, even a mannerism. As Thoreau put it simply, "We need to witness our own limits transgressed, and some life pasturing freely where we never wander."

That sort of aspiration reflects the psychic temper of a revolutionary ancestry. The genie of freedom was liberated by the age of democratic revolutions, and for two hundred years the "transgression of limits" has been the troubled theme of Western liberal and agnostic thought. The effect has been that the development of modern literature has increasingly reflected a crisis in general culture. One need not recite the conventional wisdom on this theme, which would describe ever-increasing climaxes of rebellion that alternate with a demand, accumulating to the point of despair, for new shelters of belief and moral communication. In reading these American writers of an earlier period, it seemed to me that the task of stating a new and undefined freedom and reconciling it with culture was always implicit and sometimes in the foreground of their work. In the tradition as such, I think we have received something of rare value for our contemporary needs, namely, a debate over the survival of character and culture in a world more and more dominated by the one-sided ideal of liberation and personal transcendence, or by the equally one-sided appeal to the subordination and order of communities.

If the American writers of the nineteenth century form a bridge to the modern temperament, it is because in some respects "modernity" came to America at the beginning of its history. The early start was a compensation and so was the frontier, which supplied the best historical metaphor for both crisis and inspiration in a world without sovereign moral authorities. The American knew he was a man starting afresh, as though by his own choice, or he had that illusion, and so he could put all his moral energy into defining the terms of his freedom. Drawing from that cultural legend, the American classic writers seem like an avant garde for the modern consciousness because they faced the deep insecurity of a quarrel between man and his civilization. The earlier generations of the republic were close to the experience of cultural emigrants, leaving an old civilization behind and facing a wilderness. The democratic protagonist in this situation was Promethean, given magnificent opportunities to choose but severely warned of risk and cost to himself. The elements of the grand contest were these: the free man had to decide in what sense he was bound by nature or could master it; in what sense he was committed to his society and could reconcile his freedom with it. These were elements in equations of conflict, exceedingly complex, forming and transforming themselves in legend and myth and affecting the moral premises of democratic civilization.

The theme needs lengthier exposition, for which I refer to my first chapter, but here I could stress briefly what I find central in my discussion. The imaginative tradition represented by these writers presents us with a markedly subtle dialectic, its chief terms opposing cultural nostalgia, or the claim for order, against the idealization of nature and freedom. This dialectic kept either term from dominating the field, as in the old, inconclusive battles of conservative and liberal. At the same time one must be impressed by the relative absence or understatement of modes of resolution, those we might expect in a stronger tradition of religious and cultural unity, the ideal there being man at one with his nature and his civilization, and at one with his normative imagination or his conscience. In its more complex and interesting aspect, the dialectic was a form for maintaining the balance of opposed claims and compulsions, warding them off, so to speak, by dealing positively with ambivalence. A passage from my chapter on James comments on this effect. The context is a discussion of the misadventures of Daisy Miller, a "child of nature and freedom," as she becomes entangled in the mystifying trap of European "culture."

> The American theme which strikes response for many readers makes them perceive Daisy as a critical commentary on the extremes of cultural failure, a barren resourcelessness on one side, and an equally barren formalism on the other. This is valid, but the deeper complications of meaning should be stressed. A natural innocence has been violated and misjudged; the fresh impulse to live has gone unappreciated. Something deficient, in a kind of predestined failure, has been exposed in conventional forms of action and judgment. And yet the innocent,

unjudged life has no intelligible and negotiable being in itself; it must bend to the forms of action and knowledge. Without such forms it is either *vague*, as Daisy's mother is quintessentially vague, or it disintegrates in abuse as Daisy's fate proposes. To be merely natural is to be inadequate for human existence—this is the theme.

James, though it seems absurd to say so considering the specialized audience for his writing, was perhaps the most sophisticated and imaginative of all "democrats." Here in *Daisy Miller* and elsewhere in his work, the reader must achieve the balance of an extremely fine consciousness in the midst of quick and shifting contradictions. The task is to see beyond contradictions:

> The balance is always at strain, but the point of leverage nevertheless remains the educated moral judgment. This is then another democratic parable in the critical and neotragic development first illustrated by Hawthorne and Melville. In its first step, conventionally in fact, the theme criticizes the obtuse tyrannies of cultural forms and exhibits the primary value of the person, equipped with nothing much more than the strong impulse of life. But it is equally critical in its second step, as it exposes the resourcelessness of mere freedom and the destructiveness of nature. This is a consciousness that is revolutionary and conservative at the same time, because on its third level of understanding, it combines negatives and positives in order to safeguard freedom against the threat of order, and order against the threat of freedom. These are implicit judgments in the story, though freedom as a degenerate anarchy and order as a degenerate tyranny are lightly caricatured in the apolitical figures of Mrs. Miller and Mrs. Costello.

This passage expresses one way in which my interests in this book cohere and are emphasized. My use of such terms as democracy, dialectic, humanism, culture, nature, and consciousness is explained at greater length in my first chapter. But here a few more general observations on these terms might be helpful.

In the time since I began work on this book, two terms which have particular importance to me have become so widely used, not entirely to my regret, that they are now catch-words. I refer to "humanism" and "consciousness." Everywhere today we find Marxist, Christian, and existential humanists, scientific and literary humanists, but that development clarifies my own use of the word in a time when so many are either anticipating a social revolution or believe that we are experiencing one. Revolutions in the modern world are fought on behalf of man; there is no other sanction against existing institutions and doctrine. But that precisely is the traditional pattern in American civilization, which experienced a successful revolution at its start and received the mythology which goes with it.

There is less equivalence between a contemporary use for the word "consciousness" and my own. The numbered varieties of consciousness made popular by Charles Reich, "Consciousness II" and "Consciousnes III," are really descriptions of a spiritual and moral state needing redemption, and a contrasting state of grace. The term is used in a utopian sense to describe the unity of person, mind, and culture. My own use emphasizes the distancing of consciousness from action, even a division between it and what it contemplates. This consciousness is, as I have noted, a mode of criticism more than of belief, and it is the experience of individuals more than of communities.

The contemporary political ambiguity in the use of the word "democracy" is more serious. It too has been subjected to a utopian earnestness (or a cynical word-play), and in one half of the world and among strong factions of the West, it has come to mean something quite opposed to the traditional meaning of liberal democracy. The important and distinguishing political features of American democracy, as I stress them in this discussion, could be listed briefly. They are the individual franchise, the adversary system of elections, the bill of rights for expressive freedoms, and the contractual concept of the state, making it subject to the criticism of its members and their right of dissent.

Perhaps the most distinctive trait of this kind of democracy is the divorce of power from doctrinal authority. This was stressed originally by the enormously significant decision to separate religion from the state. But its implications were extended by the various safeguarding civil rights as well as the franchise. It was fundamental that moral authority would be vested in individuals who aggregated in the franchise. Doctrine, theory, and practice remained subordinate to this authority of the ballot. In other words a principle was politically valid only when verified by the massive choice of individuals. Theory becomes subordinate to choice; it has no ruling effects by itself. To say that an idea is true or right is one thing; to say that it must rule men is a very different thing, and that distinction is a fascinating and complex difficulty of democratic practice. The right becomes legitimate only when it acts through the consciousness and choice of men in the democratic consensus. The consensus refers here not merely to the power of the majority, but the judgment of the majority supported by the *consent* of the minority. The franchise on that level is morally unanimous, since it expresses a pacific agreement deeper than the issues of conflict. But it remains unanimous in that sense only insofar as it refrains from obligatory and uniform commitment to ideas, leaders, and parties.

The philosophic implication of the franchise is a humanism detached from all direct expressions of ideas and institutions. The man in the voting booth is the modest deity of this creed, and all terms of government and sanctions of public belief defer to him. He has no ideas, or rather he transcends his ideas in his role as voter. Ideas and values pass through him, but never define him. This is perhaps the best way to characterize the significance of a democratic humanism, as I treat it in this book and as it affects other manifestations of the democratic ethic.

This elusive premise of good faith suggests to me further the reasons why a major role should be given to literature in interpreting the ethical imagination of a democracy. The ideological justifications of democracy are likely to sound morally negative, and the ethical values of a free society are often expressed in implicit and immediate choices which by their nature resist formulation and often spend themselves as the energy opposing formal doctrine and ritual practice. A democracy thinks dialectically in precisely this sense, in that it defines its values as much by negatives as by positives. Democratic culture makes provision for including its "counter-culture," or "adversary culture," those terms in vogue today; it even allows for the possibility of going "beyond culture," in the sense that Lionel Trilling gave this phrase when he used it to describe a dominant activity of the modern literary consciousness. It is my purpose in these chapters to examine this paradox and to see what preparation there is for it in the literature of the liberal tradition. The unique and highly original ethical trait involved here is based on the capacity of a political society to use its negations against itself and survive.

Liberal democracy is founded on such discursive contradictions that it resists expression in ethical terms at all. The ultimate contradiction lies in the highly sophisticated principle that an ethic which binds society is directed against the didactic or conceptual tyranny of ethics. Freedom itself is a most disturbing premise, and in finding its own definition it moves at once into conflict with ideals of social order, or justice, or equality. It is also true that those who insist that an unqualified synthesis can be made of these values may find themselves the deepest temperamental enemies of democracy. That suggests a moral impasse which can become frustrating, as seems evident in contemporary politics, whether young, New Left, or reactionary. The task of understanding may require the kind of imagination which can view opposed values clearly and give them both a portion of assent. To understand or re-experience these conflicts is a primary need. There is a demand for ethical sophistication here like that invoked by Hegel in his theory of tragedy, which he based on what he called the intestinal division or quarrel of the ethical substance. Perhaps democracy requires a sense of tragedy, and the literary tradition seems to bear that out, as I observe at some length in later chapters. But democracy surely requires a culture of the intelligence, the highly developed consciousness, if only because it offers so little security in its institutions or in collective action.

What Emerson called the "double consciousness," what Whitman described as being "both in and out of the game," is a faculty precious to the liberal mind, whose awareness so closely resembles literary insight. A detachment of the mind meets democracy's deepest needs because in its most simple usable effect this detachment serves the capacity to form and re-form social combinations that do not require total commitment. The faculty of getting outside oneself in a given act or moment, of reducing commitments, is revealed, I believe, with singular clarity in the work of the American writers of the classic period. It is indeed a mode of self-transcendence, dangerously close to an intelligence which departs from both self and world, but its risks are also its opportunities, as we can see in the work of Emerson.

Emerson at the forefront of a tradition reminds us that his world was founded on the inspired creativity of man, as he expressed that power in "Man, the Reformer." Man's capacity to accommodate himself is the key to Emerson's metaphysics, not the pantheist God who never really appears on his pages. For Emerson the basic metaphor in any case is human. His traits as a writer were developed accordingly. He was the first of our dialecticians, and in that respect he was a spokesman for his democracy. Santayana called Emerson deeply subversive, and by that meant that Emerson offered up the world, as well as his own thought, to contradiction, even in the extreme case, to destruction. His instincts could not be called revolutionary, he was too mild and dispassionate for that, but his abiding prejudice was entirely on behalf of "new life."

What is man born for but to be a Reformer, a Remaker of what man has made; a renouncer of lies; a restorer of truth and good, imitating that great Nature which embosoms us all, and which sleeps no moment on an old past, but every hour repairs herself, yielding us every morning a new day, and with every pulsation a new life?

This system of "pulsation" required points of stable reference and a principle of defense. The strategy in Emerson's case was clear. First of all he expressed a radical humanism which asserted the sovereignty of man, the covert authority behind his own creeds and institutions. But at the same time Emerson maintained the source of his inspiration in transcendental spirit. This was a commitment to higher spheres, but it was as much the opportunity for freedom, an imaginative escape from the given world, and a liberation of conscience and judgment. Accordingly we might reconsider the word "transcendental," adapted from the thinking of Emerson and Thoreau, for its pertinent and rewarding use in democratic culture. Transcendentalism, when sufficiently divorced from spiritual authority figures, as it was in the case of Emerson, was an admirable philosophy for democrats insofar as it proposed that no practice, belief, or formal doctrine could demand complete allegiance, and that the authority of events or persons was always challengeable. Inspired by that which is beyond tangible authority, Emerson could say, "man shall treat with man as a sovereign state with a sovereign state." This irrational sovereignty was humanistic; it was seated really in the conscience, whatever spiritual signature it used.

Nevertheless the transcendental consciousness was an approach to values that are ostensibly esoteric and not easily the common idiom of democratic culture. In practical terms transcendentalism might translate itself simply into what Melville called "confidence." Confidence was needed in a morally eclectic society where the bonds between men seemed always new and exceedingly unstable. Confidence was the positive spirit of change in which a rapidly developing society learned to transfer its attention to the future. The Emersonian tradition, perhaps *because* of the vagueness associated with transcendental reassurance, was deeply in harmony with these active requirements of nineteenth-century America.

It was plausible that in the actual grim historical context some men would feel the moral shallowness of "confidence." Melville's temperament is the contrast and complement to that of Emerson, as observers have long noted and studied. But with Hawthorne, Melville belongs at the head of an equally important tradition, though one that has less notice in the surveys of what is characteristically American. No view of American literary culture can overlook the serious treatment of tragic themes and their relevant implications in democratic experience. The drama of personal moral freedom develops its dialectic of negation and affirmation, self-destruction and intrinsic faith, and there is the profoundest relationship between this quality of experience and tragic literature. Where I deal with tragedy, I stress Hegel's interpretation, as I have said, which describes the conflict of ethical terms, found irreconcilable on the plane of human action. In this sense tragedy is much closer to the imaginative needs of a democracy than the literary forms that lead to redemptive reconciliations and apocalyptic unities. Traditional tragedy featured a protagonist who was driven in his consciousness past the boundary of the institutions that protected him, the ideas that gave him security. Oedipus, Lear, Hamlet are models for such marginal experience. More directly, Prometheus and Antigone express "democratic" experience as they enact the tragic, rather than romantic, mode of rebellion, and project a tragically sophisticated understanding of freedom.

Romantic utopianism, addressed to the organic harmony of the person and the collective, is the opposite of the tragic consciousness, as a pragmatic and fatalistic realism is the opposite of the transcendental consciousness. These two forms of consciousness, both of them "alienated," which is a word that means a consciousness forced outside its norms of belief and its given commitments, are in my view dominant in the rich inheritance received by a democratic culture from its greatest writers.

It is not easy to express what they have in common, since there is so much that is implicit as a debate between the American transcendental and tragic humanists. Briefly, I could call it a species of independent or alienated good faith. An illustration is easiest from Hawthorne, since he was so explicit on the theme of "sympathy" as a moral communion based on the shared sense of suffering. *The Scarlet Letter* is a model for tragic writing in its expression of the tragic qualm, or the way in which all fixed forms of moral judgment have been shaken. It is a muted tragedy, a democratic morality superimposed on tragic experience, but the pattern is suggestive. Here one observes the failure of high moral judgments, the best that a community can define, and the fall of its best moral champion. The Puritan community itself, translated from a congregation of virtue to the audience for suffering, is led to feel kinship in a "triumphant ignomiy" which includes every-one and acknowledges the evident insecurity of all forms of human vir-tue or success. In an even greater climax of dramatic desolation like that which appears in the closing pages of *Moby Dick*, the only firm principle is an act of good faith, a gesture of solidarity, literally ex-pressed in that case as a communication from the dead. To make the correspondence with Emerson is hardly necessary, since in his dialec-tical rhapsody nothing is continuous but good faith in the midst of the dynamic contradictions and constant mutations of the world.

It is appropriate to say here, in concluding this preface, that my earlier book, *The Passive Voice*, which treated modern fiction of the age of Joyce, led naturally to the writing of this one. In studying and teaching American fiction of the nineteenth century, I was impressed by its humanist imperatives, which contrasted deeply with the tone of modern writing. My first book expressed my conviction that in its most creative phase modern literature had been brilliant but was sub-tly impoverished, and that it had undermined the ground of its own interest. The magnification of consciousness itself had become the sub-ject of fiction, whether confined to its "underground," or lifted to the heights of Olympian irony or esthetic detachment. That stress on the power of consciousness (or *knowing*, expressed in the myth of omni-science for the artist but carrying behind it the stronger cultural pres-tige of science), and a correlative deterioration in the quality of life, had led to a unique condition where intelligence was magnified to the degree that its subjects—people, experiences, things—were patronized. Something analogous might be described in modern philosophy which often seems to represent the glorification of mind accompanied by the trivialization of ideas. Or it might be expressed further, in a contem-porary idiom, as the preference for the medium over the message.

It struck me while reading Hawthorne that this patronizing of the human subject reflected what he meant by the "Unpardonable Sin." In any case I found myself drawn by the contrast and increas-ingly convinced that for a period of history American writing fulfilled its democratic ideals by transcribing insistently, within the direst view of human reality, or while most enchanted by transcendental commu-nications, a deep respect for the human protagonist, a proper univer-salization of the human interest. The nineteenth century in its general cultural outline has been usually a subject of deprecation in the modern mind. Its literary production, however, and I am thinking particularly of the great Russians as well as the Americans, makes it absurd to feel anything but intensely renewed respect and even envy. The literary achievement itself was remarkable, of course, but it may be also that both bodies of literature were prophetic, in the biblical sense. In our own time, moral judgments seem either eccentric, if not insane, or they are translated into practical or ideological politics. Accordingly the achievement of nineteenth-century humanism may be more than a haven of relief in bad times. The history of the last hundred years may contain a secret of great importance, the story of something lost but perhaps not irretrievable. It is there for the imagination at least to recover, and this in large part is the available gratification in reading the authors who are the subjects of this book, as it has been mine in writing it.

Acknowledgments

I express my appreciation for grants-in-aid received from the Dollard Study Grant, administered by Bennington College, and for a Ford Foundation Humanities Award. I particularly wish to acknowledge the benefit I received from teaching abroad at the Universities of Aix-Marseille, Clermont-Ferrand, Poitiers, and Dijon in France—experiences which were made possible by two Fulbright-Hays Lectureship grants. My foreign students and colleagues stimulated many of the interests which receive attention in this book.

My colleagues at Bennington College, Barbara Herrnstein Smith and Richard G. Tristman, Dean Robert E. Streeter of the Humanities Division, University of Chicago, and Professor Irving Howe, Hunter College of The City University of New York, read all or major sections of the manuscript with care and offered valuable criticism and encouragement.

1 / Democratic Humanism and American Literature

The Humanist Premise

A classic literature is profound in its suggestion of origins, and typically the writers who dominate a cultural tradition will point to its myths of genesis. The strongest root of narrative for the American imagination can most likely be traced to the story of Columbus and the discovery of a new world. In large outline this is the theme of an adventurous people rejecting an old life and finding a new one. Among the stories of the new settlement, the legend and the history of New England registers the keenest ring. There was more poetry, more religion, and in general more open imagination in the colonization of New England than in any other record of the prerevolutionary period. Because they made the most aggressive spiritual demands and expressed the most articulate sense of mission, those early Americans made the richest offering to the future. As George Santayana observed, they created a saga of spiritual adventure and migration, and permanently inscribed a moral aspiration in the myth of the frontier.

> It is notorious how metaphysical was the passion that drove the Puritans to those shores. . . . And their pilgrim's progress was not finished when they had founded their churches in the wilderness; an endless migration of the mind was still before them. . . . The moral world always contains undiscovered or thinly peopled continents open to those who are more attached to what might be or should be than to what already is.[1]

The thought occurs almost at once that in the historic sequence such motives would mingle with others less noble. Liberation in a new land has a large frame of reference, and if the Puritan settlers did

---

1. George Santayana, _Character and Opinion in the United States_ (New York: W. W. Norton and Co., 1934), p. 4.

nothing else, they supplied a conscience to accompany freedom, and this exciting but troubling conjunction is the stimulus for and preoccupation of much of the major writing of the American nineteenth century.

A few years ago Alfred Kazin discussed the "prophetic" strain of criticism in the proliferation of modern "American studies."

> Behind "American studies" is ... the common frustration of the utopianism, liberalism, radicalism that are so marked in our intellectual history. No one of any real intelligence goes into the "American field" without some prophetic instinct; after all, that is its greatest interest; we have no Shakespeares. But we do have this need to record our progress and to make it, seemingly, total. We have an insatiable utopian will, which whether based on what once seemed to be limitless land, or on eighteenth-century rational hopes, or nineteenth-century romantic Protestantism, or immigrants' passion, has always sought to marry nature to spirit, democracy to individual perfection, God to his "chosen country."[2]

This is generally discerning, but it is necessary to observe that critics with a "prophetic instinct" are appropriately reflecting the substance of American literature. They are certainly expressing more than mere cultural nationalism, as would be evidenced by examining the work of European critics of American writing. Santayana himself was by no means an assimilated American. The critic in the American field, when most deeply drawn into his study, is enacting the major role of criticism; he is interpreting and transmitting the active elements of a literary tradition, whether based on an "insatiable utopian will" or equally persistent disillusionments.

Utopianism, after all, had its monuments in our history. The second inspirational drama to extend the mythology of America took place when the American Revolution was fought and the testamental creed for an American "genesis" was produced in the Declaration of Independence. The word "independence" is sacred in an American lexicon and the task of fully examining its use and associated imagery in American writing has yet to be done. Like the Constitution produced several years later, the Declaration communicates a strongly self-conscious and intellectually principled historic event.[3] In this

2. "The Bridge," review in *The New York Review of Books* (July 15, 1965), p. 7.

3. This is a point developed with force by Hannah Arendt throughout her comparative study of revolutionary traditions, *On Revolution* (New York: The Viking Press, 1963). I am indebted to her for much that I express in the historical and political emphases of this chapter.

respect the American myth of genesis is rare in world history. It is in effect the memory of an act of willed self-creation. Accompanying it, therefore, we should expect the strongest manifestations of moral responsibility and strain, founded on hopeful determination but also on an implicit sense of guilt, for the Declaration was direct in its rejection of the old world and an old system of rule. This, as several students of American literature have pointed out, is basic to a stressed dramatic principle in the tradition. The appropriate narrative conceives the cycle of the "new start" not only in history but in life experience, and concerns itself deeply with patterns of death and rebirth and the ceremonies of individual and social purification. The Puritans, of course, prepared the tradition by rejecting the authority of the old church; this was the effect of their actions regardless of their claim that they were establishing a purified and right form for the church. The strongest moral traditions of America, the Puritan reform and the democratic revolution, both led to the simple postulate that there was a new place where living could reach perfection and an old place where living had failed historically. The transition, the Great Migration, meant in effect that it was possible to recreate man.[4] D. H. Lawrence proposed the idea more vividly than anyone else.

> That is the true myth of America. She starts old, old, wrinkled and writhing in an old skin. And there is a gradual sloughing off of the old skin, towards a new youth. It is the myth of America.[5]

The idea of man has philosophic centrality in any discussion which proceeds on this path, and more certainly than anything else the dominant American intellectual tradition is led by humanist aspirations. How does one define humanism then? In the American context the necessary assumptions were that man was both the first cause and the final end of his experiences and that he has in some unmentioned respect a dominance over his history, his present state, and his future. This is clearly expressed in the words of the Declaration of

4. The theme has had widespread influence and acceptance, particularly as expressed by R. W. B. Lewis in *The American Adam* (Chicago: University of Chicago Press, 1955) and Henry Nash Smith in *Virgin Land* (Cambridge: Harvard University Press, 1950). It is now almost a commonplace of cultural history, but as both Lewis and Smith make clear it has rich uses in the examination of variants and developments in the literary tradition. Convincing documentation was supplied in superb fashion by Howard Mumford Jones in *O Strange New World* (New York: The Viking Press, 1964).

5. D. H. Lawrence, *Studies in Classic American Literature* (New York: Boni, 1930), p. 79.

Independence, drawing as it does from social-contract theory and pro-
claiming that the assembly of men concerned were choosing their own
form of government and accordingly their own forms of living.

> We hold these truths to be self-evident: that all men are created equal;
> that they are endowed by their Creator with certain unalienable rights;
> that among these are life, liberty, and the pursuit of happiness; that,
> to secure these rights, governments are instituted among men, deriving
> their just powers from the consent of the governed.

"Inherent" and "unalienable" mean rights which precede the
organized state and transcend it. Although social-contract theory lost
credibility almost as soon as Americans began their political life, it
remains implicit in their institutions that the human personality is
somehow, in some primary reserve, independent of history and any
doctrinal or formal authority. John Adams wrote directly to this point.

> I say *rights*, for such they [men] have, undoubtedly, antecedent to all
> earthly government—*rights*, that cannot be repealed or restrained by
> human laws—*rights* derived from the great Legislator of the universe.[6]

Like his cousin, Samuel Adams supported revolutionary faith by offering the simple ideological first assumption that all human institutions
were humanly invented, or that somewhere in their genesis the act of
consent was operative.

> When men enter into society, it is by voluntary consent; and they have a
> right to demand and insist upon the performance of such conditions and
> previous limitations as form an equitable *original compact*.[7]

6. John Adams, "Dissertation on the Canon and the Feudal Law," *Works*
(Boston: Little, Brown, 1851), 3:449.
   Unencumbered as he was by a belief in the "great Legislator," Thomas Paine
was able to assert even more boldly that human rights and freedom were ordained in
the right of existence.

> An inquiry into the origin of rights will demonstrate to us that *rights* are
> not *gifts* from one man to another, nor from one class of men to another; for who
> is he who could be the first giver, or by what principle, on what authority, could
> he possess the right of giving? A declaration of rights is not a creation of them,
> nor a donation of them. It is a manifest of the principle by which they exist . . .
> for every civil right has a natural right for its foundation, and it includes the
> principle of a reciprocal guarantee of those rights from man to man. As, there-
> fore, it is impossible to discover any origin of rights otherwise than in the ori-
> gin of man, it consequently follows, that rights appertain to man in right of his
> existence only, and must therefore be equal to every man ("Dissertation on
> First Principles of Government," *The Complete Writings of Thomas Paine*,
> ed. Philip S. Foner [New York: The Citadel Press, 1945], 2:582–83).

7. "The Rights of the Colonists," *Old South Leaflets* (Boston: Directors of the
Old South Work, 1906), 7:417.

The deeper source of this fecund idea in the American tradition was clearly shown by Perry Miller and others who traced the "covenant" thinking of the Puritan ancestors. The Mayflower Compact was the first sacred document in American history, preceding both the Declaration and the Constitution. The people of that early community acknowledged their relationship through a contract in which they agreed to "covenant and combine ourselves together into a civil body politic," and in which they promised to obey and submit to the "general good," as defined by "just and equal laws." The contract had its appreciable significance in that it conditioned both freedom and obedience. One freely chose a government and one submitted to it. At once, however, a limit was put upon the power of institutions and even the sanctity of laws by tracing that first act of choice. Similarly, the prologue is familiar: "We do by these present, solemnly and mutually in the presence of God and each and one another. . . ." "Mutually" and "in the presence of one another" are words with ritual significance, revealing a moral experience as the basis of a free society. Laissez faire was not the principle of justification; the start was a positive act of moral communication. At the same time, as Hannah Arendt has pointed out, the Americans making their compacts avoided the deification of the "general will," or the people's absolute sovereignty, which the French, in a rival democratic tradition, emphasized in their Revolution.[8]

It seems clear that this claim of antecedent rights and the primordial contract implies a radical humanism, that is to say, humanism as a first premise. Man was indeed now "the great Legislator" on his own behalf. The free individual and his interests predate and sanction society; that is the crux of the matter, though such a belief would arouse evident intellectual difficulties with the naturalist and historicist anthropology of the nineteenth and twentieth centuries. It would be a useful hypothesis, I think, to say that the chief problems of American democratic culture have their source in that incipient conflict between the neutral scientific view of nature and the Enlightenment's implicitly ethical conception of natural rights. The test of a secular humanism would be its confrontation with an uncompromising secular naturalism. The word "nature," accordingly, assumed rich and troubling implications in American writing, as it did with the romantic and postromantic generations of Europe.

This particular conflict in the history of ideas activates the Emer-

8. Arendt, *On Revolution*, pp. 34–52.

sonian passion, and in Emerson's mind a radical humanism triumphed by becoming transcendental faith. Emerson's philosophic idealism was profound enough and the natural expression of his temperament, but in reading him one is brought to guess that it was not his idealism which led to absolute affirmations in his own "Song of Myself," but the reverse; the need to support his faith in the morally autonomous individual invited the broadest claim on the spiritual substance of the world.

> We lie in the lap of immense intelligence, which makes us receivers of its truth and organs of its activity. . . . If we ask whence this comes, if we seek to pry into the soul that causes, all philosophy is at fault. Its presence or its absence is all we can affirm.[9]

Emerson plausibly understood that human freedom required a suprarational affirmation. But such a belief in higher revelations drove the source closer to a personal human consciousness; the free man was like a tablet from God. The instrument of divinity was in fact man's freedom.

> And now at last the highest truth on this subject remains unsaid; probably cannot be said. . . . When good is near you, when you have life in yourself, it is not by any known or accustomed way; you shall not discern the footprints of any other; you shall not see the face of man; you shall not hear any name—the way, the thought, the good, shall be wholly strange and new. It shall exclude example and experience.[10]

Tocqueville at about this time was pointing out that "man," in himself, was the major object of reverential contemplation in democratic nations. His point was made in the midst of some bleak speculation on the barrenness of the sources of poetry in a democracy. Gods and heroes were irrelevant in an egalitarian world, whereas "an aristocratic people will always be prone to place intermediate powers between God and man." But in losing the resources of the hierarchies of the past and their lively and inspiring distinctions, a democratic people turns to its own singular and heroic subject.[11]

9. R. W. Emerson, "Self-Reliance," *The Selected Writings* (New York: Random House, The Modern Library, 1950), p. 156.

10. Ibid., p. 158.

11. "I am persuaded that in the end democracy diverts the imagination from all that is external to man and fixes it on man alone. . . . The destinies of mankind, man himself taken aloof from his country and his age and standing in the presence of Nature and of God, with his passions, his doubts, his rare prosperities and inconceivable wretchedness, will become the chief, if not the sole, theme of poetry among these nations" (Alexis de Tocqueville, *Democracy in America* [New York: Knopf, 1951], 2:73, 76).

Tocqueville's prophetic speculation that a democratic literature "diverts the imagination from all that is external to man and fixes it on man alone" is not difficult to verify in the record. One could begin with these words from Thoreau, a writer ordinarily conceived as capable of sounding the depths of misanthropy.

> I think that we are not commonly aware, that man is our contemporary—that in this strange, outlandish world, so barren, so prosaic, fit not to live in but merely to pass through—that even here so divine a creature as man does actually live. Man, the crowning fact, the god we know. . . .
>
> I think that the existence of man in nature is the divinest and most startling of all facts. It is a fact which few have realized.
>
> I can go to my neighbors and meet on ground as elevated as we could expect to meet upon if we were now in heaven.[12]

The initial surprise of finding this entry in Thoreau's journal would be lessened if we reflect that he went to the woods in order to find that "elevated ground" on which to meet his neighbors. That is not a paradox but a manifestation of the same drive toward anthropocentric revelations which inspired Emerson.

Democratic Universalism

Emerson came close to the roots of an informal democratic ideology when he said, "I have already shown the ground of my hope, in adverting to the doctrine that man is one." The rich literary manifestations that seemed to follow his announcement in "The American Scholar" suggest its inspirational force. And just as Emerson spoke, Tocqueville was noting that the impulse to propound the oneness of man was the strongest common trait of writers in a democracy.

> The general similitude of individuals, which renders any one of them taken separately an improper subject of poetry, allows poets to include them all in the same imagery and to take a general survey of the people itself.[13]

As Tocqueville understood, the key to the American moral and philosophic imagination lay in the historic elimination of hierarchical structures. Egalitarian principles opposed themselves to the hierarchical metaphysics of heaven and earth, of gods, angels, and men, and to the hierarchies of society for rank, trade, and class. Class and degree in ideas, in values, ultimately in the distinction between good and evil

12. *The Journal of Henry David Thoreau*, ed. Bradford Torrey and Francis H. Allen (New York: Dover Publications, 1962), 2:207-8.

13. Tocqueville, *Democracy in America*, p. 74.

and between salvation and damnation, would finally be threatened in the extreme secularization of thought to which Emerson and Whitman carried the premises of democracy. With these two in particular, the need to affirm the unity of experience and the equality of men led to a style of oracular inspiration. Sentences were their units in a grand catalog of separate but equally fervent pronouncements; a series replaced structure. As fiction writers and in temperamental contrast, Hawthorne and Melville expressed acutely dramatic sensibilities, but were almost compulsively attracted to the vein of allegory and symbolism.

Universalist ideas were to be a source of tension in both the imaginative and moral life of the American people. But basically they were moral inspirations, not empirical definitions, and as such they were generous and expansive principles of action. "America should speak for the human race," Emerson said. "It is the country of the Future." These ideas have been constants. Lincoln observed with clarity that the Declaration of Independence was universalist doctrine. The immigrants coming from every country of Europe did not feel the link of blood and ancestry with the men who wrote the Declaration but did feel the link of profound moral sentiment.

> They feel that the moral sentiment taught in that day evidences their relation to those men, that it is the father of all moral principle in them, and that they have a right to claim it as though they were blood of the blood, and flesh of the flesh, of the men who wrote that Declaration, and so they are.[14]

As Thomas Paine put it, it was a blessed accident that America provided a new place, relatively empty of people and a civilization, in which the universal idea of man could be put into practice and humanity could make progress in transcending the traditional hostile distinctions of nation, religion, and class.

> In such a situation man becomes what he ought. He sees his species, not with the inhuman idea of a natural enemy, but as kindred; and the example shows to the artificial world that man must go back to nature for information.[15]

14. "Speech in Reply to Douglas at Chicago, July, 1858," *Abraham Lincoln, His Speeches and Writings*, ed. Roy P. Basler (New York: The World Publishing Co., 1946), pp. 401–2.

15. The fuller sense of Paine's remarks is in the following: "As America was the only spot in the political world where the principles of universal reformation could begin, so also was it the best in the natural world. . . . The scene which that country presents to the eye of the spectator has something in it which generates and encourages great ideas. Nature appears to him in magnitude. . . . Its first settlers were emigrants from different European Nations, and of diversified professions of religion, retiring

The subsequent history of the American Indian may make this sound dreadfully hollow. It was easy to forget the Indians; they were a sparse population, and for the first immigrants they presented nothing that resembled a civilization. For more romantic myth-makers, the Indian was available as the model of universalist man, the "noble savage." In this way the theme of contradiction was struck at the outset, democratic idealism being born in the toils of its own negations. Even when the deepest faith was summoned by later, more sensitive writers, the strain of conscience is felt as a moral fierceness in their work. Thoreau's affirmations of innocence and freedom were voiced as though to lift the burden of all the hypocrisy and social crimes which he recognized, as illustrated by Negro slavery. The somber shadows in Hawthorne sufficiently attest his interest in a burdened conscience, explicitly applied in his case to bad historical memories.

These were pronouncements from the embattled moral center of the American tradition. Linked with the opportunity of the frontier and the magnification of nature, as Paine observed, and freed of old allegiances, a cosmopolitan and universalist ideal became the focus of a distinctly American humanism. Critics have contemplated the interracial alliances in American fiction, but not many have stressed this cultural ideal as their source, perhaps because rightly enough they were preoccupied with the negative social criticism and the moral complexities expressed in such relationships.[16] The historic paradoxes in the actual treatment of the Negro and the American Indian by the white settlers have been so strong that there naturally has been little appetite for examining a rhetoric which seemed to become emptier and emptier in a contrast with the facts. But the classic affirmations of a moral ideal cannot be mistaken in the great friendships of Chingachgook and Natty Bumppo, Queequeg and Ishmael, Huck and Jim, Ike McCaslin and Sam Fathers, and others. The theme is so clear in American fiction that it deserves the title of an archetype—a situation dramatizing racial and cultural differences with the object of transcending them.

---

from the governmental persecutions of the old world, and meeting in the new, not as enemies, but as brothers. The wants which necessarily accompany the cultivation of a wilderness produced among them a state of society which countries long harassed by the quarrels and intrigues of governments had neglected to cherish. In such a situation man becomes what he ought . . ." (Thomas Paine, *The Rights of Man* [New York: E. P. Dutton, 1951], p. 152).

16. Daniel G. Hoffman in *Form and Fable in American Fiction* (New York: Oxford University Press, 1961) is a notable and valuable exception.

In an even wider aspect, the universalist ideal put its stamp on the major stylistic vein in American writing. The poets, as Tocqueville said, intended to include all men in the same imagery, and by its own momentum this imagery tended to become an organic metaphysics of nature and man. Not only the founding fathers but the Transcendentalists, and not only the latter but Hawthorne and Melville, with their seriously skeptical and tragic temperaments, were led to make parallelism and analogy the major resources in their writing. Symbolism is the dominant mode of the classic American writers because wherever else their thinking led them, they treated the same central idea, "the doctrine that man is one." It was Melville, speaking as though he were Emerson, who pronounced the following:

> O Nature and O soul of man! How far beyond all utterance are your linked analogies! Not the smallest atom that stirs or lives on matter but has its cunning duplicate in mind![17]

Beyond their stressed personal and idiosyncratic qualities of style, the classic American writers shared a common emphasis in metaphors, almost obsessed with the relationship between the part and the whole, the particular and the universal. They had an inexhaustible appetite for large-scale associations. It was, for instance, a natural response of Thoreau's mind to think of the Indian Ganges as he looked at the ice of Walden pond. The American writer was lifted by his sense of analogy through the ranges of time and place, all history and geography, and ultimately to transcendental or symbolic levels of meaning. This imagination was exceedingly ambitious, and the serious weight of the writing of that period can be measured accordingly.[18]

17. Melville was perhaps the most explicit and insistent universalist of all American writers. He rejoiced because "we are not a narrow tribe of men with a bigoted Hebrew nationality. . . . No: our blood is as the flood of the Amazon, made up of a thousand noble currents all pouring into one." The linked analogies of the world were evidence of its common ownership. "For the whole world is the patrimony of the whole world; there is no telling who does not own a stone in the Great Wall of China" (*The Writings of Herman Melville*, vol. 3, *Redburn* [Evanston and Chicago: Northwestern-Newberry edition, 1969], pp. 169, 292).

18. Thoreau, sitting in his hut and listening to the Fitchburg train, felt the world coming to him. "I am refreshed and expanded when the freight train rattles past me, and I smell the stores which go dispensing their odors all the way from Long Wharf to Lake Champlain, reminding me of foreign parts, of coral reefs, and Indian oceans, and tropical climes, and the extent of the globe. I feel more like a citizen of the world at the sight of the palm-leaf which will cover so many flaxen New England heads the next summer, the Manilla hemp and cocoa-nut husks. . . ." (*Walden* [Boston: Houghton Mifflin, 1960], p. 83). The catalog goes on, reminding us of Whitman's more explicit attempts to gather together the things and experiences of the world.

It should perhaps be stressed that the hunger for universality was not simply a need to reduce all things to one thing. What fascinated Emerson's mind, when he was not writing joyful recognitions of the oneness of the universe, was the multiplicity of the universe and, better still, the pluralistic variety of a unified system. *E pluribus unum*, the national slogan, could be used quite simply to describe a strong pattern of American writing in which everything possible was done to exploit the tension of the one with the many, the part with the whole, and to provide one or another form of resolution in that basic dialectic.

Melville in particular, invites multiplicity with a passion that ultimately persists on behalf of unity. The key to the important difference with Emerson is of course Melville's sense of the tragic contradictions in experience. But even on this basis he pushed the principle of contrast to its point of ambiguous fusion where the capacity for differentiation ceases. For instance, such a familiar oxymoron as Melville's phrase, an "abhorrent mildness," in describing the whiteness of the whale, is an instrument for conveying the obscure but meaningful totality of experience. So also the barrier between differences is crossed in his pungent phrase, "the colorless all-color of atheism." The same impulse operated in Hawthorne's imagination when he described Hester on the scaffold both as adulteress and as a model for the Virgin, carrying her child as the image of a sacred goodness.

Nature and Civilization

In a new land nature is an ideal and a problem. Civilization is a hope, or perhaps a bad memory. In any case, to the explorers and settlers the dichotomy is sharp and adjustment insecure, with the ambiguity remaining on both sides. It must be remembered that the man who came to the new continent was not a savage but a European, and not of the dregs of Europe but of a civilized order strained to the pitch of modernity and historic change in those days. As Santayana put it for the settling of New England, the theme of the great adventure and its inspiration was this: "they founded their churches in the wilderness." The immigrants' purpose was transcendentally civilized, but they came to a wilderness. This disparity marks another major theme of dramatic contradiction in the American experience.

In such a case the imagination is apprehensive but strong: experience was an adventure in unexplored space and unspent time. Whatever occurred there invoked a uniquely strained self-assertion and a uniquely threatened security. Two temperamental points of view were possible, as in any crisis of change. One man facing a new world and leaving an old one might be filled with courage and the heightened desire for life. Another might look back and long for familiar places and reassuring certainties. R. W. B. Lewis, taking his terms from Emerson, described this classic division of spirit in the American past as that between the "party of Memory" and the "party of Hope."[19] But more than a matter of temperament, it was a division of allegiances and principled faith.

The terms used might better be the "party of nature" and the "party of civilization." It is not easy to measure the depth and extent of this historic conflict, not only in America but elsewhere in the modern history of the West. In the American tradition the dialectic of nature and culture derived directly from the European Enlightenment and was then extended under the dominant literary influence of romanticism. But as Charles Sanford suggested in his book, *The Quest for Paradise*, the discovery and settlement of America was antecedent to the eighteenth- and nineteenth-century critique of culture in Europe and was perhaps the stirring element in its development.[20] Hannah Arendt further proposed that Enlightenment concepts of the state of nature and their corollary, the theory of social contract, drew their stimulus for Europe from the American experience, rather than the reverse.[21] Arendt perceptively imagined the immediacy and tension of that actual contract made against the background of the wilderness, and the way it put its stamp upon American institutions. In writing about the signers of the Mayflower Compact, who signed while they were still on board ship, she observed,

> they obviously feared the so-called state of nature, the untrod wilderness, unlimited by any boundary, as well as the unlimited initiative of men bound by no law. This fear is not surprising; it is the justified fear of civilized men who, for whatever reasons, have decided to leave civilization behind them and strike out on their own. The really astounding fact in the whole story is that their obvious fear of one another was

19. Lewis, *The American Adam*, p. 7.

20. Urbana: University of Illinois Press, 1961.

21. "If Locke in a famous passage states, 'That which begins and actually constitutes any political society is nothing but the consent of any number of freemen capable of majority, to unite and incorporate into such society,' and then calls this act the 'beginning to any lawful government in the world,' it rather looks as though he was more influenced by the facts and events in America, and perhaps in a more decisive manner, than the founders were influenced by his *Treatises of Civil Government*" (Arendt, *On Revolution*, p. 168).

accompanied by the no less obvious confidence they had in their own power, granted and confirmed by no one and as yet unsupported by means of violence, to combine themselves together into a "civil Body Politick" which, held together solely by the strength of mutual promise "in the presence of God and one another," supposedly was powerful enough to "enact, constitute, and frame" all necessary laws and instruments of government.[22]

Such fervor suggests that at the time America was settled it must have seemed imperative to judge whether nature was a friendly spirit or brutal enemy, and whether the civilizations of Europe had been systems of decadent repression or, on the contrary, contained all the wealth of human achievement. In these respects more than others the intellectual tradition of America was founded on the strain of dual choices. To complicate these matters, attention must return to the fact that the deepest religious force in American origins was Calvinist. That surely proposed specific contradictions to the hopeful philosophy of the "state of nature." Ralph B. Perry's book *Puritanism and Democracy* remains notable for its comprehensive treatment of this double inheritance and its accompanying tensions. In sum, as he said, the practical teaching of Christianity was traditionally *against* nature. The drama of salvation which brought redemption to fallen man was a conversion of earth-born natural men, who since Adam had been stamped with innate depravity.[23] When it became necessary to overcome this prejudice it was appropriate to revive the prelapsarian Adam as hero. Original innocence vied with original sin; the issue became formidable in its philosophic and practical consequences. But whether fallen or innocent, man in the Edenic experience was dominant in the American secular and religious consciousness.[24]

The idea of "nature" had become an agent in the old drama of salvation or damnation. The biggest fact in American experience remained the opening of a new continent, an opening to the future. Should one then dread or expect much from life? Should one respect the old or admire the young? Should one worship the past or believe only in the future? Was old Europe the great human inheritance, or

22. Ibid., p. 166.

23. Ralph Barton Perry, *Puritanism and Democracy* (New York: Vanguard Press, 1944), p. 84.

24. See Lewis, *The American Adam*, and H. Nash Smith, *Virgin Land*, for their influential elaborations of the theme. Leo Marx's *The Machine in the Garden* (New York: Oxford University Press, 1964) is a later essay in this now traditional perspective of American criticism.

was that gift of civilization life-spoiling and corrupt, and was not the opening to the West the promise of a redemption? These choices tended to be irrationally exclusive in America, for Americans were afflicted by the myth of a great historic choice in which these things were imagined in contest. They felt an unusually keen challenge to define man and nature with the result that the American has always seemed to exist halfway in the process of being created. This indeed was to have the "complex fate" which Henry James described. Balzac put it less elegantly when he called Natty Bumppo "a magnificent moral hermaphrodite, born between the savage and the civilized worlds."

The parallel historic reality to consider in weighing these traditional choices was that America was founded in the revolutionary climax of Western history. It seems impossible to treat the idea of nature in the American tradition without at the same time considering the utopian and revolutionary criticism of civilization endemic in the West since the Renaissance and the Age of Discovery. The voyagers of the fifteenth and sixteenth centuries were inspired by medieval and Renaissance legends of what lay beyond the western ocean, sometimes figured as the island of Plato's Atlantis, or a new promised land in the religious vein, a rediscovered Eden. Columbus expressed himself accordingly, "God made me the messenger of the new heaven and the new earth, of which He spoke in the Apocalypse by St. John."[25] These apocalyptic expectations thus became secularized and utopian concurrently with the Age of Discovery. Suggestive inferences have been made for the historic relationship between the exploration of an expanding world and the Western cycles of revolution. As one writer put it,

> With the discovery of America, Edenic expectations entered the mainstream of history, assured of a prophetic fulfillment in the West. Without this westward-looking promise, the masses of Europe might never have stirred, the industrial revolution never begun, the social revolutions never launched.[26]

We do not question that the twin roots of American national history were the religious revolution, which broke the Catholic hegemony, and the secular Enlightenment, which finally broke the traditional political structures, monarchical and hierarchical, of Europe. Tocqueville himself said that America was the true offspring of Descartes, of

25. Cited in Sanford, *Quest for Paradise*, p. 40.

26. Ibid., p. 38. Sanford gives credit for the earlier investigation of this theme by Walter P. Webb, *The Great Frontier* (Boston: Houghton, Mifflin, 1952).

Luther, of Voltaire, and of John Locke. The importance of the fact that America existed and the support that fact gave to Enlightenment politics, which eventually became revolutionary politics, is expressed in the words of John Locke, who in order to illustrate the social contract said, "in the beginning all the world was America."

In discussing Jefferson's language in the Declaration of Independence, John Dewey remarked, "to put ourselves in touch with Jefferson's position we have . . . to translate the word "natural" into "moral.""[27] The important point to make is that the obsession with nature was the complement of the revolutionary criticism of human institutions, and that the development of America was deeply founded on both preoccupations. The intensity with which these commitments were made infuses the best writing produced by Americans in the classic period of the nineteenth century. An example which strikes a vibrant and explicit note is found in a minor masterpiece of Melville, "Benito Cereno." It has particular interest in the context of this discussion because it features an act of mutiny as the dramatic bridge between one extreme, a primitivist state of nature, and another extreme, a decadent state of civilization. On one side, Benito Cereno and his ship are the symbols of a broken empire. The signs of rejected authority are repeatedly stressed in the story: the empty scabbard worn by Cereno; his state of debilitation, which Captain Delano attributes to his class origin; the old flag of Spain which is used as a barber's apron by Babo. It is quite clear that one of the torments planned by Babo and the other Negroes is to confront Cereno at every stage with the evidence of his lost power and his failed historical glory.

These are easy perceptions in the mind of Captain Delano, that archetypal American whose prejudices would not be in favor of an old, inept, and tyrannical civilization. What is not so easy for him is to understand the "Negro" as treated in the story. At one point, Delano walks upon the sight of a young Negro mother naked and asleep, while her nursing baby crawls on her body to reach her breast.

27. John Dewey, *Freedom and Culture* (New York: G. P. Putnam's Sons, 1939), p. 156.

The normative use of the word "nature" drew its force from Enlightenment philosophy and from earlier Renaissance thinking, but as Sanford suggests these uses in turn may be traced to the discovery of the new world: "The vision of paradise in connection with discoveries in the New World was chiefly responsible for the great emphasis during the Renaissance upon nature as a norm for esthetic standards, for ethical and moral standards, for behavior, for social and political organization" (*Quest for Paradise*, p. 56).

The uncommon vigor of the child at length roused the mother. She started up, at a distance facing Captain Delano. But as if not at all concerned at the attitude in which she had been caught, delightedly she caught the child up, with maternal transports, covering it with kisses.

There's naked nature, now, pure tenderness and love, thought Captain Delano, well pleased.

But the final summary of events describes how the Negresses were the most inflamed for murder, and "had the Negroes not restrained them, they would have tortured to death, instead of simply killing, the Spaniard slain by command of the Negro Babo."

This is a characteristic reversal of values in Melville's work. The contrasting aspect of "naked nature," comes forward at the end of the story when Cereno fails to win back his will to live.

"You are saved," cried Captain Delano, more and more astonished and pained, "you are saved: what has cast such a shadow upon you?"

"The Negro."

There was silence, while the moody man sat, slowly and unconsciously gathering his mantle about him, as if it were a pall.

The shock of knowing the "Negro," as Cereno knew him, naked in nature, can make a moral sensibility collapse or, allegorically speaking, destroy a civilization. The ambiguities remain; the Negro in the aspect more familiar to Captain Delano "has a certain easy cheerfulness, harmonious in every glance and gesture, as though God had set the whole Negro to some pleasant tune." Or the Negro can be represented in the figure of Atufal, nobly strong and proud, a king's son in his own land. In such aspects the Negro is as attractive as human life itself.

But the mutiny leads to the discovery of interior mysteries, endlessly problematic in their challenge to life. This is best represented in the story by the final picture of Babo's grinning skull which, fixed on a pole in the Plaza, still looks across the city toward the monastery where Benito Cereno, after seeking spiritual and physical shelter, eventually dies. And so that skull will gaze, in mocking or threatening surveillance, over the moral strongholds of man.

As one reads this story for these wide implications, as Melville surely intended it to be read, there is a recognition of its significance, not only in his own work, but in the larger tradition of American thought and writing. There is no one-sided choice here of either a redemptive experience in nature or a renewed discovery of traditional moral civilization. We are at the climactic moment of change in the higher sense of the meaning of the word "revolution." Man faces in both directions and is appalled by what he sees: on the one hand a decadent, impotent, corrupt human culture; on the other hand an inexpressibly cruel violence in the natural instincts of rebellion.

It is a characteristic point in comment to say that Captain Delano, the representative American, lacks the sense of evil. On consideration this is not so; rather he senses evil everywhere, but always in a singular and exclusive application, first in Captain Cereno and then in the Negroes, and again, following fluctuating appearances, in Cereno. Delano's mind moves regularly between suspicion and good faith. He is incapable of making these coexist, or of seeing good and evil coexist in the same subject. When Cereno at the end of the story has collapsed in confronting the "Negro," Delano has already passed on to his phase of good cheer and confidence. These are plausible limitations on judgment; the story itself points to a more sophisticated moral understanding than either Cereno or Delano can express.

It is also clear in the story that Melville does not intend to define the blacks simply as unredeemed natural creatures. It is sufficiently obvious that the Negroes were victims of oppression by a highly developed white civilization. It is that fact of exclusion which stresses their raw and innate characteristics, whether exhibited as "pure love and tenderness" or as violence and cruelty. And implicitly what Melville sees is a kind of immutable tragedy in the meeting between nature and civilization at the margin of violence. To take slaves is to deal with men *as if* they were of nature and outside the civil bond. Melville does not force that observation and is, of course, not really interested in specific social criticism. As a matter of fact, later extenuations on behalf of the Negroes, either by the trial judges or the author, would be deeply unconvincing. It would be Delano again, on a higher plane, transforming dread truths into moral reassurances. But that should not prevent the reading of what is clear; the Negroes are being transported as slaves in Cereno's ship. The fact has explosive fatality and the story fulfills it.

In this view the story could be understood as a rendering of the sophisticated democratic consciousness. Sharply outlined as it is, the effect illustrates the pertinence of the word "classic" when we apply it to the achievement of Melville and his contemporaries. In its early scenes the story suggests the transience and corruptibility of institutions, or of civilization itself. But to give caution to revolutionary hopes, there is an understanding, on the level of Melville's persistent insight at least, of the deeply ambiguous forces drawn from nature. While Babo's skull is the onlooker, civilization is seen as a case of man transcending himself, fallible in what he might become but under threat from what he is. The theme here is the challenge from *both* terms, nature and civilization; beleaguered between them, but not entirely subject to either, the figure of man receives crucial attention.

The varying and complex qualities of American humanism rise from this confrontation of nature and civilization in "naked" or primordial terms. This is as true of Emerson as it is of Melville, though the first produced an inspirational humanism, more in harmony with the optimism of American beginnings, though tempered by an almost fatal detachment. That in itself was characteristic; everywhere Emerson's flights are accompanied by a critical consciousness, an alertness that wards off mere sentiment and bathos. Melville's mind was as fine, but its task was to transcend mere pessimism, and the result led him to what we can call a tragic humanism, in my judgment the more pertinent tradition in the American literary ancestry, history having done so much to jar with Emerson's tone. Surrounding and succeeding both Melville and Emerson, the volatility of mood in American writing can't be missed by any observer. The depths of naturalistic pessimism, the lyrical address to nature and liberation, the heights of revolutionary criticism, the retreats of conservative nostalgias, all these take their place in orchestrations of the great theme.

Tocqueville saw this insecurity of judgment enforced on Americans by their experience and spoke of it memorably. He said in his chapter "Of Some Sources of Poetry Among Democratic Nations":

> I need not traverse earth and sky to discover a wondrous object woven of contrasts, of infinite greatness and littleness, of intense gloom and amazing brightness, capable at once of exciting pity, admiration, terror, contempt, I have only to look at myself. Man springs out of nothing, crosses time, and disappears forever in the bosom of God; he is seen but for a moment, wandering on the verge of the two abysses, and there he is lost.[28]

Melville accepted the full vision described by Tocqueville, transformed in tragic insight and colored, prophetic as Tocqueville's passage is, in the tones of modern metaphysical writing, obsessed by the void. On the other hand it might be argued that Emerson overtly denied the premise and, denying any abyss in nature, voiced only an undramatic lyrical enthusiasm. But the quality of that enthusiasm is not simply

28. Tocqueville, *Democracy in America*, p. 76.

pantheistic; it is the response of Emerson's humanistic fervor (always partial to man, even in Emerson's strongest apostrophes to nature) and the expression of a greatly threatened need. His affirmation of life undertakes to embrace the nonabsolute contingent world, or that image of man wandering on the verge of two abysses. In a most characteristic statement he said:

> Life only avails, not the having lived. Power ceases in the instant of repose; it resides in the moment of transition from a past to a new state. . . . This one fact the world hates; that the soul *becomes*; for that forever degrades the past, turns all riches to poverty, all reputation to a shame, confounds the saint with the rogue, shoves Jesus and Judas equally aside.[29]

No words could better express the revolutionary readiness of Emerson's thought, and his enthusiasm is offered precisely for those uncertainties which the "world hates." It was in effect his intention to accommodate a moral civilization to that which is antithetical to its laws and institutions, namely, the innate restlessness and dissent of life, even the will for destruction. This was an adventure into the formless but immanent stream of experience, and though it might confound saint and rogue, or present the world with horribly superficial manifestations and fickle moods and choices, yet it was an order founded heroically on the terms of life itself, fully faced to its risks.

Imagination, Revolution, and Reality

One of the strongest effects in "Benito Cereno" is that of the ambiguity of appearances. All the agents and important symbols tend to promote mysteries and divide knowledge sharply between what is imagined, or misinterpreted, and the truth, which actually cannot be spoken, even if it can be realized. In the end this truth, which Cereno has been forced to experience, musters from him only the words, "the Negro," and after that, silence. In contrast Captain Delano believes in appearances, or wishes throughout the story to believe what he is told, despite apparent contradictions. In his case, it is not excessive imagination that is operating but the will to restrain imagination on behalf of a conventional understanding of conventional behavior. But this is an even greater restraint on the truth.

Surrounding Captain Delano, however, is a crumbling form, that of Cereno's rule, which has become artifice, and even Delano must be disturbed by this awareness. The pattern is breaking, implicit chaos is

29. Emerson, "Self-Reliance," *Writings*, p. 158.

coming through. This communicates itself at times to Captain Delano, and to the reader everywhere, as a profound sense of "unreality" in the experience.

> The living spectacle . . . has in contrast with the blank ocean which zones it, something of the effect of enchantment. The ship seems unreal; these strange costumes, gestures, and faces, but a shadowy tableau just emerged from the deep, which directly must receive back what it gave.

But this strain in the sense of reality is also enforced by the peculiar truth of the Negroes' revolt and the depth of their motives, and Babo's stubborn silence after he is captured is as expressive as Cereno's unwillingness or inability to speak beyond the surface of events.

The American protagonist, Tocqueville said, "springs out of nothing," and is found "wandering on the verge of the two abysses." It should be characteristic to see him pressed by a need to distinguish substance from shadow. Another remark by Tocqueville emphasizes this hunger to fill a void with the shapes of truth, or the contrasting temptation to fill it with the shapes of the imagination. In a democracy, he said,

> each citizen is habitually engaged in the contemplation of a very puny object: namely, himself. If he ever raises his looks higher he perceives only the immense form of society at large or the still more imposing aspect of mankind. . . . What lies between is a void.[30]

Hawthorne expressed this self-doubt and restlessness of the imagination when he made his confession of limitations in the preface to *The Scarlet Letter* and regretted his tendency to create only "moonshine images." Poe was defiantly determined to remain a Gothic fantasist and pile fantasy upon fantasy in his own willful definition of literature. Henry James made the dialectic of imagination and reality a major theme of his work, as in equally sophisticated fashion, did Wallace Stevens. It is clear that James understood his theme to be an American issue, perhaps the major dramatic problem in American history and culture. In a much quoted passage from his essay on Hawthorne, he described the *empty* reality which faced Americans as a serious if not fatal deprivation for artists. He meant and was interested in much more than that. In his fiction he describes Americans living in brilliant criticism of their American backgrounds and consequently ready to pursue the golden geese of the imagination. And like his teacher, Hawthorne, James proceeded to make the most of the theme, not restricting it to the familiar pattern of romantic disillusionment.

30. Tocqueville, *Democracy in America*, p. 77.

Ironically, writers in a later trend of American fiction returned to the romantic cycle in its reduced and weakened significance. Sherwood Anderson and Sinclair Lewis, admittedly lesser writers, made the hunger for experience the issue for embittered cultural criticism, spurred as they were by general interpretations of Freudian thought. Today the theme is popular again, as though the one enemy of life were the philistine repressions of middle America. James himself, however, wrote genuine tragedies of the imagination, that is to say, tragedies of freedom. "Reality" was the source of a moral education, and men who were the victims of their own magnified life-hungers and their own substitutive imaginations, found themselves disintegrated in character, living in that empty place of their isolation which Hawthorne's Wakefield, or his Ethan Brand, entered for different reasons. Such a victim of the imagination, though not an American, was Marcher in "The Beast in the Jungle"; another was that romantic pedant, the narrator in "The Aspern Papers." James's masterpiece in this vein is probably Gilbert Osmond, in *The Portrait of a Lady*, an example of the imagination become sterile and turned toward evil. In all these cases the saving sense of reality was embodied in living people, and to mistake it or abuse it was to abuse them.

However, James's observations on the actual poverty of the imagination in America, corroborated weightily by Hawthorne himself, and by Cooper, not to mention an army of cultural expatriates in the twentieth century, have led critics to make the frequent point that cultural deprivation has always been a factor in American experience, and that in crisis it has led to a heightened sense of disorientation between the real world and the world of ideas and ideals. Such a critic is Marius Bewley, who said characteristically,

> they [the deprivations in American culture] confronted him [the American novelist] with a society in which the abstract idea and the concrete fact could find little common ground for creative interaction.[31]

Van Wyck Brooks began his career years earlier with a similar pronouncement. Long before the writings of either Brooks or Bewley, Tocqueville observed the issue with his usual forehanded judgment, though as he stated it, it sounded deceptively like a direct contradiction in thought. He says, for instance, in his chapter entitled "Why the Americans Show More Aptitude and Taste For General Ideas Than

31. Marius Bewley, *The Eccentric Design* (New York: Columbia University Press, 1959), p. 18.

their Forefathers, The English," that democratic citizens generalize on the basis of equality and the ideal similarities of their fellow men,

> and thus it is that the craving to discover general laws in everything, to include a great number of objects under the same formula, and to explain a mass of facts by a single cause becomes an ardent and some-sometimes an undiscerning passion in the human mind.[32]

A few chapters later, explaining "Why the Americans Are More Addicted to Practical than to Theoretical Science," he notes that

> hardly anyone in the United States devotes himself to the essentially theoretical and abstract portion of human knowledge.[33]

The contradiction was not in Tocqueville but in the subject he was observing. What he may have meant to say was that the Americans pursued general ideas and practical matters with equal avidity but in striking isolation from each other, or perhaps, as American critics like Bewley and Brooks suggest, in despair of their being brought together.

Thus reinforced, the critical tradition seems to make the split between imaginative culture and experience a diagnostic scheme for explaining the limits or failures of American writing. This split, it seems to me, is just as likely to have been a creative stimulus. If there was unbalance on the side of the imagination, it led to the special flavors in the work of Hawthorne and Poe. They both reach a morbid intensity at the margins of consciousness; they are, after all, pioneering symbolists. On the other side it is easy to remember the keen awakening sense of actual experience in Thoreau's *Walden*, which was a long poem in praise of what the eyes can see and what a man can truly know.

> Let us settle ourselves, and work and wedge our feet downward through the mud and slush of opinion, and prejudice, and tradition, and delusion, and appearance, that alluvion which covers the globe, through Paris and London, through New York and Boston and Concord, through church and state, through poetry and philosophy and religion, till we come to a hard bottom and rocks in place, which we can call *reality*. . . . Be it life or death, we crave only reality.

In this determination there is the spirit of the pioneer. After all the task of the American was to master reality. He faced the term, his notion of the "real," as he was forced to face nature. Similarly his imagination could not create without being opposed by a criticism in his mind, the same criticism that applied to traditional beliefs and author-

32. Tocqueville, *Democracy in America*, p. 15.
33. Ibid., p. 42.

itative institutions. As Marius Bewley pointed out, from the beginning social forms, and therefore all forms, were seen as artifices in America, subject to the human power to reject as well as to create them. Bewley was accurate in his choice of a quotation from Hawthorne to support his point, the Hawthorne who felt that his creations had the same vivid and insubstantial effect as shapes in firelight.

> We who are born into the world's artificial system can never adequately know how little in our present state and circumstances is natural, and how much is merely the interpolation of the perverted heart and mind of man.[34]

In one of the more interesting phases of the American literary tradition, the search for the sense of the "real" led to an artful and perfected sense of the ambiguous, the real and the ambiguous becoming interchangeable terms. The work with the strongest claim to the status of a national epic introduces itself with "the image of the ungraspable phantom of life." Melville ended his own search, perhaps his own career as a writer of fiction, with the almost obsessive elaboration of what he called the "ambiguities." Hawthorne based his schematic fiction on the reversibility of value judgments, as well as the ambiguities of psychological experience, which was his chief realm of truth. The most subtle of all as a practitioner of the ambiguous, Henry James, carried his interest to the point where some of his critics and readers call it mystification of a perverse order.

It is an easily bridged distance from that point of sophistication to the simple demand for truth which is expressed in the stance of the boy-hero, Huck Finn. Huck's adventures and misadventures are based on an almost fatal need to be anchored in reality; the result is the comic and moral exposure of fictions, whether they are the conventional romanticizing expressed by Tom Sawyer or the more dangerous deceptions practiced by confidence men or embodied in social institutions.

Huck's enemy is not a specific society, but *any* society with organized patterns of action and belief. As he practices independence he increases the effect of unreality or absurd irrelevance in social forms. The criticism of formal doctrine (or of the collective imagination) on behalf of reality is a democratic exercise, the "real" being found in the immediate lives of individuals. Once the questioning of abstract collective generalizations begins, "reality" becomes a political and moral issue.

34. "The New Adam and Eve" *The Writings of Nathaniel Hawthorne*, vol. 5 (Boston: Houghton Mifflin, 1903).

This refinement of the idea of truth and the problem of knowing, moving as it does between two extremes of factualness and imaginative exercise, suggests T. S. Eliot's remark on the fineness of James's mind, so fine that no idea could violate it, and no "fact" either, one might say. A French critic who was struck by the wider pertinence of Eliot's notion has applied it richly to Emerson.[35] As the forerunner, Emerson suggests that we are observing a principle of the American tradition that can be called, as Philip Rahv did, a special American way of dealing with ideas.[36] This may be a condition of intellectual democracy; to fine and democratic minds all truths are partial, all theories have limited application. A "fine" mind is relativist, pluralist, complex, dialectical, and particularly democratic in the sense that all truths are elected on a conditional basis. In a wider reference, such a mind, no longer fine, is evasive and obfuscating, prone to rhetoric, equally prone to the pseudonymous fact. "You can fool all of the people some of the time. . . ." But fooling is based on the hunger for a better world. "All power to the imagination," student revolutionaries wrote on bulletin boards in France, in May, 1968. They knew that the real world is conservative.

At the heart of the revolutionary tradition there is romance. In that association the American classic writers confirm their debt to the literary influence of European romanticism. There were educated and literate people in the Colonies and the new States for more than a hundred years before the creative outburst which is called the American "renaissance." But English and continental literature could not have a great effect in America until their substance and temperament matched the American capacity for response. Dryden, Pope, and Johnson were widely read over here, but Wordsworth and Coleridge could teach what the Americans were ready to learn. As a new country inhabited by cultural immigrants, always conscious of the accepted wisdom in the old country, America was dependent on literary and intellectual innovation in Europe, most dependent in fact at the time when Emerson found the zest for declaring a cultural independence. It was when Europe had experienced the French Revolution and a cataclysmic sense of historic endings and beginnings that its own experience began to resemble that of the western republic. The interchange of ideas began

35. Maurice Gonnaud, *Individu et Société dans l'oeuvre de Ralph Waldo Emerson* (Paris: Didier, 1964).

36. Philip Rahv, *Image and Idea* (New York: New Directions, 1949), chap. 2.

which made it possible for American literature to assume confidence and follow its own sources of inspiration.

Recent contributors to the study of romanticism and to the old argument over whether the term has coherent meaning, have joined in locating the root of the romantic movement in modern political history and the seminal event of the French Revolution. Northrop Frye, who edited the volume of English Institute essays in which this finding is a major connecting thread, observed that "Romanticism . . . is not only a revolution but inherently revolutionary, and enables poets to articulate a revolutionary age.[37] The argument, as I interpret it and would like to extend it, goes as follows. Revolution is the dramatic extreme of liberation. It is moved by the passion of hope, and its intellectual instrument is what we call the imagination. But the imagination is subject to the anticlimaxes of disillusionment, just as the political romance faces counterrevolution, or the simple inertia of history, or something worse coming from within itself, expressed by the historic irony of the revolution "devouring its own children."

A revolutionary consciousness is formed by the assumption that civilization is subject to creative choice, or if the stress is deterministic, to an historic fatality which works for the good, as in Marxism. In either case "reality" gives up its resistance to the imagination. The ro-

37. Frye based himself on the documentation and conclusions offered by M. H. Abrams in his contribution to the same volume.

> The Romantic movement found itself in a revolutionary age, of which the French Revolution was the central symbol. . . . The fact of revolution was linked in many poetic minds with the imminence of apocalypse—the association of ideas that Mr. Abrams quotes from Coleridge as: "The French Revolution. Millennium. Universal Redemption. Conclusion." But the apocalyptic word did not remain revolutionary flesh for very long: anticlimax and disillusionment quickly followed. Mr. Abrams connects the frequent later Romantic theme of the plunging of hope into despair with this disillusionment, and shows that as the only place in which hope springs eternal can be the human mind, the theme of revolution fulfilling itself in apocalypse had to be transferred from the social to the mental world. . . . Such a feat was not a neurotic subjective substitute for revolution, but the articulating of a new kind of imaginative power—and also, of course, the bringing into literature of that new movement which we know as Romanticism (Northrop Frye, ed. *Romanticism Reconsidered* [New York: Columbia Univ. Press, 1963], pp. vi–vii).

Frye made this summation because he accepted its validity for himself and Abrams, as well as Lionel Trilling and René Wellek, the other contributors to the symposium. As a matter of intellectual consensus it in turn derives from the contemporary thinking of romantic critics, as Abrams points out: "it is Hazlitt's contention that the characteristic poetry of the age took its shape from the form and pressure of revolution and reaction" (ibid., p. 26).

mantic rhythm describes that enchanted hope in flight and falling; the arc communicates the pathos of imaginative freedom in collision with the real world. Frye illustrates with a different image from Schopenhauer. "In Schopenhauer the world as idea rides precariously on top of a 'world as will' which engulfs practically the whole of existence in its moral indifference."[38] This is perhaps the most characteristic temperamental note that can be applied to European romantic thought, though much of the selective illustration used by Frye comes from the more explicit pessimism of the twentieth century, as when he mentions Freud ("the conscious ego struggles to keep afloat on a sea of libidinous impulse") or Kierkegaard ("In Kierkegaard, all the 'higher' impulses of fallen man pitch and roll on the surface of a huge and shapeless 'dread' ").

Frye's use of the metaphor of a boat, drunkenly pitching in the sea, immediately calls up Melville as much as Rimbaud, and on the matter of precedence it could be argued that American romanticism was the first to invade the darker areas of metaphysical "dread" and take the crisis viewpoint of the vulnerable human enterprise. Frye's use of the symbolism of Noah's ark is specifically Melville's own view of the Pequod on the open ocean—"a fragile container of . . . values threatened by a chaotic and unconscious power below it."[39]

For good historical reasons it was this aspect of romantic thinking to which the classic American writers were most sensitive, namely, the idea of the fragility of human civilization against the background of nature and within the revolutionary cycles of history. I have proposed as my theme that this pervading insecurity, like that of the "open ocean," was the chief, perhaps the compelling stimulus in developing the characteristic humanism of this generation of writers. M. H. Abrams, contributing to the English Institute symposium, strengthens that judgment with these remarks on Wordsworth.

> Having given up the hope of revolutionizing the social and political structure, Wordsworth has discovered that his new calling . . . is to effect through his poetry an egalitarian revolution of the spirit (what he elsewhere calls "an entire regeneration" of his upper class readers) so that they may share his revelation of the equivalence of souls, the heroic dimensions of common life, and the grandeur of the ordinary and the trivial in Nature.[40]

So much in the larger tradition of romanticism has been opposed to the "equivalence of souls" and "the heroic dimensions of common life,"

38. Ibid., p. 22.   39. Ibid., p. 22.   40. Ibid., pp. 68–69.

as if to say that it was Coleridge rather than Wordsworth who left the most lasting impression on the subsequent literature, that it comes as a discovery to review this quite explicit democratic humanism in Wordsworth as he expressed it himself in the Supplementary Essay to the Preface of the 1815 edition of *Poetical Works*. It was his intention to establish "that dominion over the spirits of readers by which they are to be humbled and humanized, in order that they may be purified and exalted." As Abrams, who directs attention to this statement, goes on to say, Wordsworth's purpose in poetry was to achieve a revolutionary mode of sublimity, namely the mode of "sublimated humanity."[41] To find the best pupils of Wordsworth one must go to the American writers, and these, Whitman and Emerson as well as Melville and Hawthorne, developed the creed of a "sublimated humanity" to a point which might not be recognizable by Wordsworth himself, no doubt because of the undiluted democratic conditioning of the world in which they wrote.

Dialectical Democracy

Modern critics of American literature and the American cultural tradition use such words as "debate" or "dialogue" or "dialectic" with significant frequency. As Leo Marx pointed out in his own "dialectical" approach to the rich uncertainties of the subject,[42] it was Lionel Trilling who first applied that term directly, in his essay, "Reality in America."

> A culture is not a flow . . . the form of its existence is struggle or at least debate—it is nothing if not a dialectic.[43]

Since then, Richard Chase, R. W. B. Lewis, Marius Bewley, Daniel G. Hoffman, among others, have continued the discussion in this vein.[44] A critic of an earlier generation, Van Wyck Brooks, advanced the mode of locating a major antithesis, the split between ideals and practice, and thereby set an example of looking for the terms of cultural ambivalence.

41. Ibid., p. 68.

42. Leo Marx, *The Machine in the Garden* (New York: Oxford University Press, 1964).

43. Lionel Trilling, *The Liberal Imagination* (New York: The Viking Press, 1950), p. 9.

44. Richard Chase, *The American Novel and Its Tradition* (New York: Doubleday Anchor, 1957). Lewis, *The American Adam*. Bewley, *The Eccentric Design*. Hoffman, *Form and Fable in American Fiction*.

What side of American life is not touched by this antithesis? What explanation of American life is more central or more illuminating? In everything one finds this frank acceptance of twin values which are not expected to have anything in common: on the one hand, a quite unclouded, quite unhypocritical assumption of transcendent theory ("high ideals"), on the other a simultaneous acceptance of catchpenny realities. Between university ethics and business ethics, between American culture and American humour, between Good Government and Tammany, between academic pedantry and pavement slang, there is no community, no genial middle ground.[45]

The appropriateness of the term "dialectic" is another example of the concurrence of American experience with avant garde ideas of modern history. The great modern teachers of dialectic were Hegel and Marx, when they transformed the term as a mode of logic, and applied it to a "reality" which grows or changes in analogy with the growth of truth in the mind. The mind solves contradictions and moves toward conclusive insight, and so history grows toward the fulfillment of an ideal or whole truth. The word became, then, an historical and ontological term, used generally to describe a world which itself contains contradictions and which changes by the impact of conflicting forces.

Dialectic is the right word in a time of revolutionary instability, for it describes a state of mind as much, perhaps, as any overt phenomenon in history. The American cultural consciousness, founded on its legends of genesis, was an awareness poised between a rejected era of history and the outline of a bright future. To repeat the essential point, the unique event of American history was an act of rebirth in a new land which accompanied the cycles of revolution in modern history. Taking the form of a legend, this is an historic rite of passage, dedicated to the initiation of a whole people into revived and purified existence.

But history withheld perfection from this ambitious people, "the irony of history" taking its place alongside "the American dream" in the developing sequence of American self-consciousness. Certainly by the early part of the nineteenth century, the era of full literary expression of what was intrinsic in American experience, enough time had passed to reveal the reasons for a disillusionment as strong as the continuing hope. The time had come for writers to criticize a great experience and to deal with the quarreling of good and bad memories. The myth of a great change has to be in a sense a double myth which incorporates the two sides of the conflict inherent in change. We rec-

45. Van Wyck Brooks, *America's Coming of Age* (New York: The Viking Press, 1930), pp. 6–7.

ognize in the first important imaginative expressions of the American consciousness a quarrel of values so stressed that the optimistic myth of a new birth is now permanently interlocked with a tragic myth of something lost and forsaken.

The nostalgia for established forms, for a unifying intellectual and social tradition, for the color and detail, but above all the reassurance, offered by a complex history which survived tangibly—this was a force for dividing the mind and assailing the self-confidence of the settlers and their descendants. On the other hand, the dangers were balanced by the seductions of change, a new life, the absolute openness of a world of possibility.[46] In this sense to live at all was a great gamble, even for the relatively protected imaginations of the men of Concord. Life was a test or a challenge and, as Thoreau put it, one lived "to drive life into a corner, and reduce it to its lowest terms, and if it proved to be mean, why then to get the whole and genuine meanness of it, and publish its meanness to the world; or if it were sublime, to know it by experience." That urge to conquer experience and to judge life is indeed in the best writing of Emerson and Thoreau, and it leads in recurrent cycles to the apocalyptic and prophetic strain in American writing.

Unexplored nature was a bottomless depth (as Thoreau speculated in the case of the calm familiar surface of Walden pond). But to imagine the keenness of dialectical experience, add to this the profound sense of the instability of human institutions as expressed by the ideology of democracy itself.[47] Democracy was dialectical politics in the sense that it contained within itself the strain of alternatives not chosen, or the difficulty of a choice consciously made at the expense of

46. To add to these physical and social factors the impulse of strenuous Calvinism at the origin of American experience, is to understand better the Manichean dualism stamped in the American consciousness. For the Puritan, life was a drama with salvation or damnation received at its conclusion. The quarrel between the kingdom of light and the kingdom of darkness had lasted through the history of man on earth. Predestination did not soften the edges of conflict for the Puritan, and he was prepared for great reversals, like that which brought Dimmesdale, the saintly minister of *The Scarlet Letter*, to the scaffold for sinners.

47. Marius Bewley's work deserves particular attention both for his sense of the American dialectic and his perception that in large part its source was political, as manifested for instance in the following observation: "the division [in American experience] ... took on many different forms concurrently: it was an opposition between tradition and progress, between democratic faith and disillusion, between the past and the present and future: between Europe and America, liberalism and conservatism. ... At bottom the tension is political in character" (*The Eccentric Design*, p. 18).

another. The drafters of the Declaration established a clear principle of separation between the people and their institutions, affirmed by "inherent and unalienable rights" and by the premise that governments were *instituted* among men "deriving their just powers from the governed." This dramatized an incipient contest between men and their doctrines, moralities, sovereignties, and allegiances. A contest on behalf of what? That was beyond definition precisely because it had to be left open; it was the object of a search and continuous rediscovery. Its only covering term was the man with the franchise; therefore its supporting philosophy would be a species of humanism, so uncommitted to definition that perhaps only literature could give it comprehensible form.[48]

In politics, the men who constructed the nation placed a dialectical counter-valence into the institutions of government with the immensely significant rule of "checks and balances." They checked one another, but the ultimate check was that of rulers by the ruled, or the check of power by the act of consent. The innovation here in political institutions was what we might call the principle of ambiguous sovereignty. The state was not a final sovereign, true, but then was the democratic majority sovereign? Not unambiguously, for the designed difficulties of governing, the inertia of the past, the inheritance of laws and customs (the Constitution itself being the heaviest obstacle to change), the rights of individuals and minorities, all acted as restraints to the unlimited sovereignty of the people.

The effort of the American founders to act in restraint of power dramatized a unique historic willingness to distinguish between intrinsic values and society's institutions of authority. The ideal of free expression, which the American Bill of Rights supported with unprecedented guarantees, acknowledged that the monopoly of truth could not remain in the hands of power. It implied in fact that the expression of truth might often, if not usually, be inconsistent with the exercise of power. More precisely, the moral contradiction was implicit in the ratio of power and freedom. As John Adams put it,

> the jaws of power are always opened to devour, and her arm is always stretched out, if possible, to destroy the freedom of thinking, speaking, and writing.[49]

48. If I do not discuss the obvious relevance of the single distinctive American school of philosophy, pragmatism, it is because of the size of the subject and what it demands. However, Dewey in particular makes his sharp tribute to the Emersonian ancestry, as I indicate in the second chapter of this book.

49. Adams, *Works*, p. 457.

But Adams never questioned the legitimacy of power and nothing was further from his mind than a sentimental anarchism. As Hannah Arendt made clear in her book *On Revolution*, he was a particularly sophisticated thinker on the subject of the ethics of power and participated in forming a major and distinct political tradition in America.[50] Implicit in this tradition and its documents was a firm notion of the conditional nature of freedom, as well as of institutions. Politics was founded on a series of oppositions, as between ruler and ruled, between power and freedom, and upon a general area of contestation for partial truths, special interests, and fragmentary knowledge.

What is stressed in much of the early theory was the principle of a negative check, as if the functions of public morality and government were to restrain abuses, the substantive values of life being found elsewhere. To a large extent this was true of pragmatic bourgeois theories of government, but it is not a sufficient account of the American democratic tradition, nor could it explain that tradition's fervor and longevity.

One historian has recently cited several unfamiliar examples of theory at the time of the Revolution which affirm the conscious purpose of the American founders to establish the competition of values as a dominant principle of democratic institutions.

> Those who criticized such divisive jealousy and opposition among the people, said William Hornby of South Carolina in 1784, did not understand "the great change in politics, which the revolution must have necessarily produced. . . . In *these* days we are equal citizens of a DEMOCRATIC REPUBLIC, in which *jealousy* and *opposition* must naturally exist, while there exists a difference in the minds, interests, and sentiments of mankind"[51]

Even more interesting was the sophisticated view that virtue was not a necessary assumption for political behavior in the republic.

> William Vans Murray devoted an entire chapter of his *Political Sketches*, published in 1787, to a denial of the conventional view that republicanism was dependent upon virtue. . . . "The truth is," said Murray, "Montesquieu had never study'd a free Democracy." . . . The republics of antiquity had failed because they had "attempted to force the human

50. Arendt quotes Adams as follows: "Power must be opposed to power, force to force, strength to strength, interest to interest, as well as reason to reason, eloquence to eloquence, and passion to passion"(in *On Revolution*, p. 151). Marius Bewley, in *The Eccentric Design*, also makes particularly instructive use of Adams's thought.

51. Gordon S. Wood, *The Creation of the American Republic, 1776–1787* (Chapel Hill: University of North Carolina Press, 1969), p. 608.

character into distorted shapes." The American republics, on the other hand, said Murray, were built upon the realities of human nature. . . . They had been created rationally and purposefully—for the first time in history—without attempting to pervert, suppress, or ignore the evil propensities of all men.[52]

Behind this was the notion that self-interest could be translated into a public good. As another writer put it, the American democracy had introduced "into the very form of government, such particular checks and controls, as to make it advantageous even for bad men to act for the public good."[53]

But it seems clear that the thesis had a larger range, and that a concept of the good which *changes*, a frank ethical pluralism, was behind the unwillingness to let ethical sanctions be dominant in institutions and their acts. The greater ethic, beyond particular specifications of virtue, was in the effort to control a continuous process of change in a system which abjured violence.

"This revolution principle—that, the sovereign power residing in the people, they may change their constitution and government whenever they please—is," said James Wilson, "not a principle of discord, rancour, or war: it is a principle of melioration, contentment, and peace." Americans had in fact institutionalized and legitimized revolution.[54]

The last remark has the greatest significance, and from it may be drawn clarification for the moral strains and characteristic affirmations of the classic period of American writing.

The historic question was whether this "revolution principle" could really find peaceful ground. Observers could first of all note the obvious difficulties and contradictions. These were analyzed long ago by Tocqueville, whose book was founded on the subtly worked sense of contradiction and paradox in the institutions of the American republic in its first decades. Was democracy a theory of a polity or was it the justification of maximum individualism? Did the ideal of equality rule over the ideal of freedom in American civic and social life? Was majority rule a greater tyranny than that of kings and nobles, and how did one account for the strong conformist compulsions in a society championing freedom?

The genius of Tocqueville's book lay in his willingness to confront such paradoxes and pursue their plausibility. In one passage he emphasized the spirit of independence in the American democracy.

As social conditions become more equal, the number of persons increases who . . . owe nothing to any man . . . expect nothing from any man;

52. Ibid., p. 610.   53. Ibid., p. 611.   54. Ibid., p. 614.

they acquire the habit of always considering themselves as standing alone, and they are apt to imagine that their whole destiny is in their own hands.[55]

A few pages earlier, discussing the writing of history in democratic times, he says something exactly opposite.

> As it becomes extremely difficult to discern and analyze the reasons that, acting separately on the will of each member of the community, concur in the end to produce movement in the whole mass, men are led to believe that this movement is involuntary and that societies unconsciously obey some superior force ruling over them. . . . Historians who live in democratic ages, then, not only deny that the few have any power of acting upon the destiny of a people, but deprive the people themselves of the power of modifying their own condition, and they subject them either to an inflexible Providence or to some blind necessity. . . . In perusing the historical volumes which our age has produced, it would seem that man is utterly powerless over himself and over all around him.[56]

This latter is a brilliantly evocative passage, in the first place for its prophetic diagnosis of nineteenth-century determinism. Secondly it seems to evoke the characteristic breach between the people and their intellectual leaders in the American democracy. Finally this passage reflects the antithetic relationship between freedom and equality which Tocqueville made central in his work. He foresaw that these were destined to remain ambiguous and conflicting ideals of democratic culture. It was inevitable that equality would suggest not only equal rights and opportunities but the promise of perfect social equality administered through justice. Beyond this there was the hunger for order and uniformity. The tyranny of the majority was not only based upon the rule of an organized power but also on the inner revulsion from freedom itself and the need to have the communal order repeatedly sanctioned and made visible. This was a spirit of community so strong that it did not merely rest on external rules, but searched for absolute affinities in human nature and a safe spiritual home in nature. For these in turn safeguarded individualism, and in that respect the Transcendentalists, as spokesmen for this synthesis, were master dialecticians.

Conscience and Freedom

Emerson in particular seemed to understand the waves of effects set off by the immensely disturbing premise of individual liberty. He followed the radiating distinctions between the single man and the

55. Tocqueville, *Democracy in America*, p. 99.   56. Ibid., p. 87.

group, between a moment in time and the past or the future, between actions and judgments, and between the ineffable fragments of experience and the equally ineffable design of the whole. Purest in his sympathy for these alternatives, Emerson was led by his dialectic beyond any semblance of an integrated system of thought. (He was the first to know that he contradicted himself.) He appealed at last to mysteries, though they were not supernatural and not really spiritual, but grounded in the immediacy of actual experience.

> When good is near you, when you have life in yourself, it is not by any known or accustomed way . . . the way, the thought, the good, shall be wholly strange and new.[57]

This movement into the world of the endlessly new and strange was the basis of Emerson's faith in immanent values, as if to say, life is a stream of change but everything in that flux bears immediately the sign of its justification.

> These roses under my window make no reference to former roses or to better ones; they are for what they are; they exist with God today. There is no time to them. There is simply the rose.[58]

And from that he could go naturally to his noblest conclusion, a concrete or personalist humanism which was the anchor of the great miracle of being.

> History is an impertinence and an injury if it be anything more than a cheerful apologue or parable of my being and becoming.[59]

It becomes evident in a reading of the classic American writers that they were notable most of all for their moral sensitivity. They spoke as if prophets were needed in a time of troubles, when men questioned each other in their relationships. For if Emerson was concerned with preaching self-trust, his contemporaries, Hawthorne and Melville, to simplify issues for a moment, were equally concerned with what we might call the moral illuminations of self-distrust. It would clarify matters to say that in the work of these writers the dialectical values of freedom and community were internalized, in other words, put into the realm of moral criteria for which each man was responsible in his behavior. To think of a society as an antagonist to be held in check was easy. Also, experience and wisdom made it necessary to think of the individual as dangerous to himself; as free but at the same time

---

57. Emerson, "Self-Reliance," *Writings*, p. 158.
58. Ibid., p. 157.   59. Ibid., p. 157.

burdened by the bad conscience of freedom, never quite certain of the distinction between self-expression and selfishness, between creative ambition and agression, or between independence and a corrupting moral isolation. This way of working with positives and negatives is useful, I think, for if we say that in much of their work Hawthorne and Melville were preoccupied with the ordeal as well as the bad conscience of freedom, Thoreau and Emerson, in contrast, vividly exposed the bad conscience of conformity, that is, not simply the tyrannies but the corrupting transformations of community life.

It was reasonable to expect a deeply troubled record of the moral imagination in America, for a contradiction existed at the origin between two available conceptions of the human will. One was restrictive, an ideal of self-discipline, expressed by men who saw a difficult path through the world to salvation and who placed moral priority on the strength to master appetite and low natural desires. The other was, implicitly at least, pagan and permissive, a sanction for self-gratification in the "pursuit of happiness." Did the signers of the Declaration of Independence mean Americans to become hedonists when they raised "happiness" so high as a value? They didn't, of course, but that language and its implications became nevertheless a part of a mythology. There would have been less ambiguity if they had retained the old Lockean word "property" as part of the triad. To enjoy life had become a moral obligation. But this accompanied the deeper parallel tradition which associated pleasure with wrong-doing, so that a strong moral ambivalence existed at the root of an active history and culture.[60]

As we have considered the intellectual genesis of the American tradition, it seems to have been fated to be dominated by such opposed examples of a bad conscience. To think of that inheritance as divided between the secular doctrines of the Enlightenment and the religious estate of Calvinist Protestantism is to bring together ideas which, no matter in how many aspects they prove their historic continuity, still contain at their emotional center the most profound contradiction imaginable. The passions of Protestant Christianity were most deeply aroused by the vision of human fallibility and the overmastering power of God. For the intense Puritan, life on this earth was a phenomenon of experienced depravity as much as it was the proving

60. Hannah Arendt's discussion of the "terrible misunderstanding" which was latent in the phrase, "the pursuit of happiness," is illuminating in the context of her exposition of what the political thinkers of Jefferson's time meant by the more exact term, "the public happiness" (*On Revolution*, chap. 3).

ground of the elect. And further, no matter how strenuous in virtue and successful in achievement God's chosen were in manifesting his choice, they still surrendered dominance to him. In fact all acts of self-assertion, if properly covered by obeisance to him, could be transformed into acts of self-abnegation. But the daring fusion of the two ideas in Puritanism is itself a revelation of the dialectical stamp of earliest force on American ideas.

Similarly, the Enlightenment found an ultimate place of submissive inspiration in "nature," and Americans after the Enlightenment could believe in a predestined virtue and success in life, regardless of whether they were the children of Calvin or Rousseau. These complexities indicate that in the American tradition it was necessary to find supporting authority for free acts and thoughts, and that ultimately these authorities, whether God or nature, shared a kind of immutable or unreasoned power. If the individual was to be respected it was because the inspiration of nature, as Emerson would put it, or divine election, as his Puritan ancestors conceived it, spoke through him. But if these authorities were absolute they were also in the last analysis indeterminate and uncodable in any given case. What then if these finalities were themselves to be lost in the religious agnosticism and scientific naturalism of modern thought? By that hypothesis much of the special poignancy of nineteenth- and twentieth-century American writing can be understood. The ideals of freedom maintained their mythopoeic force in the tradition, but their philosophic sanctions or safeguards had been progressively undermined.

On this ground of a culture's existence, which, as Trilling put it, "is nothing if not a dialectic," the nineteenth-century American writers produced work which continues to grow more significant in a truly classic range. There is pathos in the story but more that is exhilarating, for their minds reached to the measure of their difficulties. It should be emphasized that they were *not* innocents abroad in their new world, since Emerson, Thoreau, and Hawthorne have so often been patronized this way. We think of Emerson and Thoreau as disciples of the romantic enthusiasm, but the truth is they had no enthusiasm that was not at the same time a criticism. Apparently nothing illustrated so well as democracy the failure of men to meet heroic standards of the good life. The point was that men like Thoreau and Emerson raised their standards in proportion to their disillusionment. One might call it an evangelical criticism. The real world would seem to reject their transcendental affirmations, yet these two keep a great intellectual dignity, and this is because they were dialecticians more than transcendentalists. Their writing had the energy of an auto-criticism, a procedure by which their ideas were open to experience and experience was felt vitally in their ideas. Their insights were incomplete revelations, admittedly, but beyond them appeared clear actualities of the earth and men.

Emerson particularly seemed to be aware that the ideal of a democratic culture was to provide for the unceasing criticism and affirmation of life. This alternation of emphasis, combined with his confidence (some would say his complacency) leads readers to a sense of thin monotony in his work; it is neither razor sharp nor hammer-blow strong. However, it *is* subtle and enormously intelligent, for he was a pioneer in thinking of yea and nay and all the alternatives of judgment as interlocked without losing their character as differences. They met somewhere, and to find that place out was the goal of his teaching.

The inward conflicts in Emerson's mind or Melville's mind are heightened in their significance by the contrasts which the two men present with each other, like the even more meaningful offsets that exist between Hawthorne and Thoreau. Thoreau preached self-sufficiency with a sublime sense of conviction, but Hawthorne seemed almost compelled to treat the death-in-life of moral isolation and the sickness of egotism. Emerson truly believed in the world as his home, and the poignance of Thoreau's dialogue with nature is still undiminished. But equally vivid in the minds of readers is Melville's vision of nature's cannibalism, the rawest taste of violence in all nineteenth-century literature (with the possible exception of Dostoevsky), accompanied by an equally convincing image of the shapeless, colorless phantom of nonmeaning which the Pequod pursued.

It is understandable that critics and historians, taking off from this sense of a debate or quarrel, would be confirmed in thinking of American culture as profoundly split in its values. To take one dominant example, R. W. B. Lewis, illustrating his thesis widely, described a dialogue between the American Adam of innocence and the American Adam of the fall, or tragic experience.

> . . . in the course of the dialogue, so the narrative figure of Adam—introduced as the hero of a new semidivine comedy—was converted into the hero of a new kind of tragedy, and grew thereby to a larger stature. It was the tragedy inherent in his innocence and his newness, and it established the pattern for American fiction.[61]

61. *The American Adam*, p. 6.

Earlier in this trend, Lionel Trilling also thought of two dominant schools in the nineteenth-century American tradition and emphasized their distinctions by illustrations from Henry James and Walt Whitman.

> . . . the real difference between them is the difference between the moral mind, with its awareness of tragedy, irony, and multitudinous distinctions, and the transcendental mind, with its passionate sense of the oneness of multiplicity.[62]

This has the strongest possible relevance as a way of distinguishing between opposed but complementary minds, between those making distinctions and those making affirmations, the mind of the tragedian or ironist and that of the rhapsodist of the organic universe, who fused all its parts.

There are many other ways to stress sharp principles of a dual American tradition, and one of the most observant was that of John Dewey who understood that American democracy was supported by the opposing legacies of Hobbes and Rousseau.[63] These names are effective symbols for the temperamental choices of both politics and literature in America for two centuries. Richard Chase, another perceptive analyst of this theme, finally concluded that inconsistency and incoherence were basic cultural factors that must be accepted by students despite their will to impose unity upon the subject.

> These facts suggest that there is no "focal center" in the American mind and that there is, instead, a dialectic or continuing dialogue between the Yea-sayers and the Nay-sayers. . . . this dialogue goes on within the minds of each of our most interesting and characteristic writers.[64]

This thought leads him rather far in his conclusions, to the point of considering contradiction or disorder as an esthetic rule by which the special quality of American writing can be understood.

> The English novel . . . follows the tendency of tragic art and Christian art, which characteristically move through contradictions to forms of harmony, reconciliation, catharsis, and transfiguration.
>
> Judging by our greatest novels, the American imagination, even when it wishes to assuage and reconcile the contradictions of life, has not been stirred by the possibility of catharsis or incarnation. . . . It has been stirred, rather, by the esthetic possibilities of radical forms of alienation, contradiction, and disorder.[65]

62. *The Liberal Imagination*, p. 11.   63. *Freedom and Culture*, chap. 2.

64. Richard Chase, Introduction to *Melville, A Collection of Critical Essays*, (Englewood Cliffs, New Jersey: Prentice Hall, 1962), p. 3.

65. Chase, *The American Novel*, p. ix.

On the whole this was a very much needed emphasis, and it gives students a criticism of the traditional judgment that American literature exhibits a deep cultural ambivalence and is the record of schizoid artists and abortive masterpieces. Debating Marius Bewley and others who have treated the dialectical elements of American thought and writing, Chase found that they put too much stress on the search for unity and the failure to find it, and thus distorted the actual quality of the work they were examining.

> Mr. Bewley is not alone in assuming it to be the destiny of American literature to reconcile disunities rather than to pursue the possibility it has actually pursued,—that is, to discover a putative unity *in* disunity or to rest at last among irreconcilables.[66]

His statement has immense importance for the understanding of the classic body of American writing, if we emphasize his "putative unity *in* disunity." How one rests at last among irreconcilables is the question of significant interest, and presumably something is brought into the field of conflict which offers a kind of unity, a "putative unity," without violating the realism which admits unreconciled oppositions. The problem is a democratic problem as well as a literary one, that is, it originates in the civilization these writers expressed, but not necessarily as the symptom of its failure. In such a context thinking will be as dramatic as experience, and writing will take the eccentric, alienated forms that Chase perceives in his general esthetic judgment, or it will shelter forms of resolution that Chase failed to notice, which are thematic and extend beyond disorder, and which reflect the ethic of democracy itself.

Chase's discussion, despite the major value of his assumptions and the exciting possibilities of his approach, took a wrong turn when he suggested that American writers developed an implicitly decadent taste for disorder and contradiction as such. "Irreconcilables" are in the foreground and the background of their work, but the record does not bear out the implications of intellectual adventurism or moral irresponsibility. What is most surprising and misplaced, I think, is Chase's reference to the absence of a tragic sensibility. The rebuttal seems clear in the fact that the only sizable tragic literature produced in the nineteenth century, apart from that of the Russians, was the achievement of American fiction writers.

Chase's theory of the "romance" novel is the key to the problem. The word romance, he says, signifies

66. Ibid., p. 7.

a tendency toward melodrama and idyll; a more or less formal abstract-
ness and, on the other hand, a tendency to plunge into the underside of
consciousness; a willingness to abandon moral questions or to ignore the
spectacle of man in society, or to consider these things only indirectly or
abstractly.[67]

I don't know of any writers of significance in the American nineteenth
century to whom these words could apply without contradiction except Poe. One could agree on the tendency toward melodrama and idyll,
and also the wish to consider "the spectacle of man in society" on a universalist rather than a local plane. It would be more clarifying to call
these the traits, not of romance, but of symbolistic and allegorical writing. But to emphasize a willingness to abandon the subject of man in
society and the most fundamental moral questions, is surely to lose the
major interests in the work of Hawthorne, Melville, James, Mark
Twain, and Cooper, It is precisely that spectacle and the moral issues
of man in society which are at the center of all the vital literature of
the American tradition. Chase supplied the corrective for his own
thought when he added,

> The very abstractness and profundity of romance allow it to formulate
> moral truths of universal validity. . . . The inner facts of political life
> have been better grasped by romance—melodramas, as they may be
> called—such as those of Dostoevski and Malraux—than by strictly
> realistic fiction.[68]

The judgment is exact.

In his first emphasis, however, Chase supported a finding which
was earlier produced by Lionel Trilling, remarking on the lack of a
class basis in the American novel.[69]

> Not that we have not had very great novels but that the novel in
> America diverges from its classic intention, which, as I have said, is the
> investigation of the problem of reality beginning in the social field. The
> fact is that American writers of genius have not turned their minds to
> society . . . the reality they sought was only tangential to society.[70]

It is difficult to appreciate what Chase and Trilling meant unless we
consider that they kept the realistic fiction of nineteenth-century

---

67. Ibid., p. ix.   68. Ibid., p. xi.

69. Trilling observes the following in his essay, "Art and Fortune": "In this
country the real basis of the novel has never existed—that is, the tension between a
middle class and an aristocracy which brings manners into observable relief as the
living representation of ideals and the living comment on ideas" (*The Liberal Imagination*, p. 260).

70. Ibid., p. 212.

France and England too much in the foreground of their minds with a correspondingly limited definition of the "social field." As for "classic intentions," it becomes clear after consideration that the Americans were closer in spirit to classic models, which meant they seriously treated social relations on a universal or cosmic scale. Chase cites a point made by Marius Bewley in his own review of the "split in American experience" and the effort "to discover a unity that . . . *was not there.*" Contradictions and divisions existed in Europe too, but in contrast to America "they were more ballasted by a denser social medium, a richer sense of the past, a more inhibited sense of material possibilities."[71] One might add that because of the very density of their social medium they were inhibited from confronting the ultimate issues of a social existence. For that, the naked metaphysical background of American experience was more of a stimulus.

A "Putative Unity"

Certainly from the beginning of American history the moral impulse was the strongest aspect of the way Americans expressed themselves. John Dewey was emphatic in declaring that the basis of American democratic practice was a moral passion, despite the stress by most critics, historians, and democratic apologists themselves on the thesis of bourgeois self-interest.[72]

> I have referred with some particularity to Jefferson's ideas upon special points because of the proof they afford that the source of the American democratic tradition is moral—not technical, abstract, narrowly political nor materially utilitarian. It is moral because based on faith in

71. Chase, *The American Novel,* p. 6 (citing Marius Bewley, "Fenimore Cooper and the Economic Age," *American Literature* [May, 1954]).

72. I think it can be asserted that nothing has done more to undermine the moral prestige of democracy (called bourgeois) in the nineteenth and twentieth centuries than its persistent linking with the quantitative egotism of capitalist economics and marketplace freedom. Adam Smith economics pretended to be a cold science, but the democratic beliefs intrinsic in American institutions were actually, at their inception, a secular religion. The difficulty or misunderstanding in part has come from the stress of the words "nature" and "natural rights" in early democratic theory. As Dewey saw it: "The words in which he [Jefferson] stated the moral basis of free institutions have gone out of vogue. We repeat the opening words of the Declaration of Independence, but unless we translate them they are couched in a language that, even when it comes readily to our tongue, does not penetrate today to the brain. . . . To put ourselves in touch with Jefferson's position we have therefore to translate the word 'natural' into *moral*" (*Freedom and Culture,* p. 156).

the ability of human nature to achieve freedom for individuals accompanied with respect and regard for other persons and with social
stability built on cohesion instead of coercion.[73]

It seems clear that this system of "cohesion" was to be based on
no formal moral doctrine, or political or religious prescript, but upon
an ideal of the moral unity of men which could not be enclosed or cut
off by partial allegiances. It was a paradoxical concept of moral kinship, based on the independence of the private conscience and on distinctions between private and public choices and acts. As such, what
flourished in the realm of both life-values and literary practices was
the search for a "putative unity" which was not contradicted in the
pluralist disorder of freedom. That this would be a difficult search goes
without saying, and that it should not find old forms of "harmony and
reconciliation" is equally apparent.

The old forms were in effect rejected when American society
moved toward the historic watershed of establishing freedom of conscience in the guise of the freedom of religious worship. This made the
premise for a culture that would be bound together in a unity that was
not based on a common religious creed which supplied, in Richard
Chase's meaning, "forms of catharsis and transfiguration." When the
time came widely in the world to establish purely secular states founded
on a moral civility and nothing else, Christian leaders of America were
ready to greet them appropriately. The early teacher of Emerson, William Ellery Channing, came quickly to bless the democratic revolutions in Europe (writing in 1832), not on behalf of religion but a universal humanism, which was after all the inevitable direction of his
Unitarian church.

> What is it, then, I ask, which makes the present revolutionary movement
> abroad so interesting? I answer that I see in it the principle of respect
> for human nature and for the human race developing itself more power-
> fully, and this to me constitutes its chief interest. . . . In this movement
> I see man becoming to himself a higher object. I see him attaining to the
> conviction of the equal and indestructible rights of every human being.[74]

73. Ibid., p. 162.

74. W. Ellery Channing, "Honor Due to All Men," *Unitarian Christianity and
Other Essays* (New York: The Liberal Arts Press, 1957), pp. 117–18. In this essay
Channing made the powerful point that the one basis for the doctrine of equality was
in the moral nature of men, which emphasized the will and the inspired imagination,
rather than extrinsic gifts, success and possessions: "I observe that there is one principle
of the soul which makes all men essentially equal, which places all on a level as to
means of happiness, which may place in the first rank of human beings those who are
the most depressed in worldly condition. . . . I refer to the sense of duty, to the power

Humanism in America was supported by the multiplicity and rivalry of creeds and the overriding principle of the free conscience. The Constitution in effect proposed that it was not the tie with God that was the foundation of human society but the tie with men, though they avow different Gods. To declare that no religion or formal doctrine should impose its rule on men was to appeal to some other basis of moral unity, which would be large enough to include all other distinctions.[75] "Every new mind is a new classification," Emerson said.

> But in all unbalanced minds the classification is idolized, passes for the end and not for a speedily exhaustible means, so that the walls of the system blend to their eye in the remote horizon with the walls of the universe. . . . They cannot imagine how you aliens have any right to see—how you can see. . . . They do not yet perceive that light, unsystematic, indomitable, will break into any cabin, even into theirs.[76]

What is that light and what is its source? Since it has multiple refractions and is always moving, it will not rest, Emerson implies, long enough for definition.

> Power ceases in the instant of repose; it resides in the moment of transition from a past to a new state, in the shooting of the gulf, in the darting to an aim.[77]

Perhaps obscurity must remain in what Emerson is saying. Light, which is the knowledge of value, is an intellectual mystery because it is coeval with life. "Life only avails, not the having lived," and more directly to this point, "thinking is the function, living is the functionary." Emerson's pregnant conclusion is this, "character is higher than intellect." This thought reverses the premise of traditional religious and moral codes, whether founded on reason or revelation. It is the purest humanism in its effort to say that all experiences are incarnate

---

of discerning and doing right, to the moral and religious principle, to the inward monitor which speaks in the name of God, to the capacity of virtue or excellence" (p. 113).

75. Jack Lively, in his book, *The Social and Political Thought of Alexis de Tocqueville* (London: Oxford University Press, 1962), discusses Tocqueville's stress on contradictions in the American system, namely, the uncertain balance between freedom and equality, and between freedom and order. He calls attention to Tocqueville's observation that the support for the balance was a recognized and specific moral capability. One might add that Tocqueville seemed to sense that Americans were consciously determined to found a system upon contradictory needs and interests, and that they were not simply the victims of those contradictions.

76. "Self-Reliance," *Writings*, p. 164.

77. Ibid., p. 158.

values, and that no life can be enclosed by the preconceptions of value. Was it giddy enthusiasm that prompted Emerson to say, in defiance of common sense, "a man is to carry himself in the presence of all opposition as if everything were titular or ephemeral but he"? We understand this better if we remember that "character is reality" and the single person is the moral starting place of all judgment and choice. If responsibility is within himself, so is the beginning of all loves and appreciations.

> Let us . . . hurl in the face of custom and trade and office, the fact which is the upshot of all history, that there is a great responsible Thinker and Actor working wherever a man works; that a true man belongs to no other time or place, but is the centre of things. Where he is, there is nature. He measures you and all men and all events. . . . Character, reality, reminds you of nothing else; it takes the place of the whole creation.[78]

The later chapters of this book regard the varying perspectives of a humanism which was developed as the corollary of freedom. It was a faith applied to the locus of contradictions in a culture which accepted great strains. The wars of actual experience, the debate of minds, the uncertainties of truth, the temptations of fantasy and feeling, the oppositions of civilization and nature, of order and freedom, all converge on the highly stressed American protagonist, a man acutely and dramatically aware of himself because he is never released from himself in a world where all contingencies are tentative and transitional.

The social issue, the demanding "contract" imposed by the American ancestors, appears as a striking example of ambivalence in the literature. Thoreau cancelled that contract, so to speak, and sometimes wrote as if he had been maddened by crowds and frustrated by all human relationships to the point of misanthropy. Hawthorne described the pathology of withdrawal, his theme was "forget yourself, forget yourself in the idea of another," and yet in his work the culmination of human relationships was tragic. But even if they wrote in the vein of tragedy, as Hawthorne and Melville did, and even if they were implicitly subversive, as Thoreau and Emerson were, these writers still met in a strangely unyielding, passionate search for moral good faith. The goal was an affective state which the nineteenth-century writers would call "sympathy," generated toward the phenomena of nature and toward men in the serial reversals and changes of life. Sympathy

78. Ibid., pp. 153–54.

as an affective principle worked against oppositions and denials: carried as far as the American writers carry it, it would challenge all estrangements. But it made unity not a dogma but a process in living.

The parallel in history suggests that the deepest moral theme of American democracy was the comradeship of men in the world, otherwise empty and threatening, a wilderness. The symbolic immigrant and pioneer was a man acquainted with metaphysical and psychological morbidities. He could know the primeval estrangement from nature, as he could know a primeval estrangement from himself, frightened by his own emotional depths, as the Calvinists were frightened by their religious terrors. The bareness of this dilemma leads us to understand Emerson and Thoreau more valuably than in a context provided by the pastoral naturalism of the English romantic poets, or by the spiritualism of German transcendentalists. Thoreau's withdrawal into the woods, we sense, was as much a move to test and dispel its terror as it was to confirm its hospitality. Thoreau was engaged in the spiritual pioneering which would domesticate nature and make it human. The Homer on his table, his bean field, his maternal pond, are all features of a humanistic pathos. He dramatizes the possibility of creating the human civilization out of the barest provision. The hunger for community in his case is such that he would invade the farthest margin of loneliness. For Thoreau the sense of community transcended society; it could be experienced outside it, just as it was the premise for society's existence.

His attack upon society was deeply consistent for it was directed against an external, substitute civilization which did not fill this need for community but diverted attention from it. His enlightened moral judgment told him (as it told Emerson) that human relationships were dead and evacuated of meaning, if they were not supported by the uncompromised sense of self. To withdraw, to show independence, were necessary acts of renewal for Thoreau, and in the cultural growth of democracy these renewals are a continuing ritual for the criticism and healing of the perennial mendacity of social life. What was an act of relief for Thoreau and the experience of pain for Hawthorne contribute to a rich combination of moral insight. It is to say that democracy supports itself in both the ideal of community and the ideal of isolation. And saying that is to say that both of these can become ordeals and privations, as is the case with values that are opposed but complementary.

There is finally no escape from the heretical and heterodoxical spirit of freedom. What is perhaps unique in the democratic social order is that it contains within itself an ethical imperative hostile to the traditional logic of collective order. This is in one aspect the revolutionary imperative to say no on behalf of the future. Another way of putting it is to recognize an ethical character which exists but is continually growing; exists, but is multiple and contradictory in the shape it takes among men. It resists definition, although definition is what it is always getting, particularly from collective doctrine and institutional laws and practice.

We deal here with a "putative unity," as Chase called it; it suggests the taking of risks and the talent for survival, and perhaps at the worst not much else. How far the demand goes is suggested by that frustrating book, Melville's *The Confidence Man*. A boatful of shabby impersonations, the sum being what? "Confidence" would require an almost unbearable sophistication of the moral temper. But this is perhaps democracy. No civilization does more to tempt the possibly unregenerate nature of man. There is an obvious and raucous good faith claimed on the political hustings, where the crudest appeals to emotional allegiance mingle with cynical laughter. But there are subtler paradoxes than that and more difficult passages through skepticism. The dialectic of democracy acknowledges that equality is guaranteed by the widespread worthlessness of men, and freedom by the futility of their adventures. A Sisyphean democracy, Camus, who so well understood Melville, might say. The genius of the system requires that one cannot rest with these conclusions but is driven on toward their opposites. In the end one rests somewhere "among irreconcilables," and that is where the obscure signs of ultimate good faith must be measured. In a sense, after Melville wrote *Moby Dick* he could write nothing further in the old style because he had transcribed the death of the hero. Monomaniacal in his effort to impose himself on the world, unforgiving for its lack of intelligible response, Ahab has demanded his unreconciled death. But meanwhile the survivor, Ishmael, bobs on the ocean and clings to his friend Queequeg's coffin, now become a life buoy.

Melville was obsessed by the deaths of ship's captains, and drew particular significance from each of them, Cereno, Ahab, and in his final writing, Captain Vere. He was transcribing the symbolic passage from hierarchical and paternal systems of order. These were unified systems of interest, requiring an authoritative personality, whose assertiveness as king, as father, as God, matched the dependency of his subjects. His death would be epochal and tragic, and it is perhaps the central event in the democratic imagination. Some of the most direct intuitions on this subject were expressed by D. H. Lawrence in his provocative but enduring book on the American classics. His lucid simplifications proceed as follows, "Mastery, kingship, fatherhood had their power destroyed at the time of the Renaissance."[79] This climax in history received its strongest increment in the story of America, enforced by the cycles of immigration and revolution. "Somewhere deep in every American heart lies a rebellion against the old parenthood of Europe." It is from this point that he launches into the strange new symbolic male relationship of Natty Bumppo and Chingachgook in the Leatherstocking tales, which he is explicit in calling a vital legend in the "myth of America."

> What did Cooper dream beyond democracy? Why, in his immortal friendship of Chingachgook and Natty Bumppo he dreamed the nucleus of a new society. That is, he dreamed a new human relationship . . . of two men, deeper than the deeps of sex. Deeper than property, deeper than fatherhood, deeper than marriage, deeper than love.[80]

One need not round out these matters with Lawrence's magnification of psychosexual relationships to see that his instincts are direct and revealing. The point to emphasize is that in moving toward a fraternal and egalitarian order, democratic culture has close ties with the complex fervor and guilt of regicide and patricide. The protagonist of democratic man must be conceived in ordealistic and morally unstable terms. As Louis Hartz observed in his major interpretation of the American liberal tradition, the American experience led to something new in the concept of community which involved giving up the traditional Platonism of organic forms and corporate wholes.[81] He was confirming Tocqueville in saying that men in America would not be held together by the knowledge that they were different parts of a structured whole but by their sense of similarity and equality.

This is an ideal of sibling similarity, the figure of a brother among brothers in a family without the authoritative father. As such the man of a democracy is seized by separate and conflicting needs which cannot be formed into an exact pattern of reconciliations. The formal unity of man is not a given truth, a starting premise, and it cannot

---

79. *American Literature*, p. 6.

80. Ibid., p. 78.

81. Louis Hartz, *The Liberal Tradition in America* (New York: Harcourt Brace, 1955), p. 55.

even be an ultimate ideal. In this sense democracy is a dramatically incomplete moral order where, repeatedly, ancient confrontations must take place, between man and nature, man and society, and man with himself. It is this seminal principle which Emerson recognized.

> What is man born for but to be a Reformer, a Remaker of what man has made; . . . imitating that great Nature which embosoms us all, and which sleeps no moment on an old past . . . ?[82]

But it seems apparent from the body of Emerson's work that it was not Nature from which he expected deepest reassurance. He made his claim on her, as was appropriate to his time and temperament, but the strongest resonance he has for succeeding generations comes from his great claim on mankind.

> The power which is at once spring and regulator in all efforts of reform is the conviction that there is an infinite worthiness in man, which will appear at the call of worth. . . . Is it not the highest duty that man should be honored in us?[83]

82. *The Complete Works* (Cambridge: The Riverside Press, 1903), 1:248.
83. Ibid.

2 / Emerson
The Double Consciousness

To reach Emerson, the modern reader must cross an intellectual barrier which is the effect of Emerson's recklessly confident homocentricity, adapting the whole of his thinking to the human interest. Any page of his work would illustrate this enthusiasm, so much a contrast it is to the human self-effacement of naturalist thought.

> There is nothing but is related to us, nothing that does not interest us—kingdom, college, tree, horse, or iron shoe—the roots of all things are in man.[1]

But what sort of humanism was it and what creative responsibility did it give to man, when Emerson could say,

> We lie in the lap of immense intelligence, which makes us receivers of its truth and organs of its activity.[2]

In another mood, equally reassuring, he says something exactly different.

> Nature is thoroughly mediate. It is made to serve. It receives the dominion of man as meekly as the ass on which the Saviour rode.[3]

Obviously the serenity of Emerson's spirit demanded that he acknowledge the power on both sides of the basic equation he was considering, the "Not-Me," which he called Nature, and the "Me" of personal being. Too much on one side would slip into the determinist authoritarianism of nature, and too much on the other would lay the trap of solipsism. The function of his thought, and we can understand him best this way, was to fight his way through such intellectual dangers on behalf of his basic affirmations. That gives his writing at times

1. "History," *Writings*, p. 131.
2. "Self-Reliance," *Writings*, p. 156.   3. "Nature," *Writings*, p. 22.

the fine tension of tightrope walking, and at others the loose consistency of careless inspiration.

But the inspiration was on behalf of a magnificent presumption in the original American experience. We might remind ourselves how much in American writing can be understood by the extremes which characterize the desire to surrender to nature and the will to dominate it, a curious reversibility of active and passive temperaments. Emerson's great statement on "Nature," the essay which is the keystone of his work, speaks with the elaborated self-confidence one conceives necessary for inhabiting a wilderness. Certainly in 1830 the memory of the adventure in the new land was fresh, intensified by the continuing existence of the open frontier. Emerson and Thoreau, each in his own way, must have heard the echoes of men at the frontier shouting to keep their courage up. And yet Emerson himself set foot in no wilderness, nor was Walden in any sense a meaningful simulation of one. Psychologically these men resembled expatriates who observed the American experience from the standpoint of a refined civilization, usually the most fruitful perspective of American writing. Paradoxically, the problem of nature became important when men were searching for the foundations of their lives in settled communities and not when they were directly facing the wilderness. The life of the pioneer and the immigrant had now become mythology as well as fact, and the struggle with nature was a morally inspiring legend. What was really at hand was the problem of human relationships in a culture struggling to create itself. The great theme of an accommodation to nature was most strongly urged by the need of the democracy to find its moral justifications, rather than by the primordial problem of safety and survival.

Emerson actually best portrays his role in the American literary tradition by his determination to find the inspiring support of civilization in the scheme of nature itself. This was not a new effort; the founding fathers had based the republic on the major premises of Enlightenment philosophy. Emerson was in a sense a democratic revivalist, a secular evangelist, ready to use the force of idealist philosophy and literary romanticism to reassert the metaphysical support of democracy. The early years of Emerson's career are parallel to the dominant years of conservative reaction in Europe and the restless returns to revolution in 1830 and 1848, as well as to the high years of the Jacksonian revolution in America. His revulsions from the latter are well marked in the journals. There was perhaps then an even more desperate case to be made on behalf of a morally designed and morally purposeful nature. This was an ethical inspiration which could certify freedom at a time when the democracy seemed most vulgar, corrupt, and violent in its behavior, and when a disillusioned reaction favored the return to aristocratic institutions. The classically American aspect of Emerson's thought is based on this precarious consciousness of his culture as well as the pathos of the search for moral justification.

The result was a paradoxical quality of thought which still puzzles interpretation. In his own time and even today Emerson's words might plausibly be interpreted as subversive enough to threaten *any* collective institution, but this jars with the actual tone of his writing and with a large part of the meaning he conveys. His urgency is not at all revolutionary, but rather that of the conciliator who would supply images of authority to replace those which had been overthrown. Emerson's thinking has the value of reassurance, not incitement. The significant fact is that at the time of the expansion in the West, his imagination was so little caught by it. Like Thoreau, he was determined to say to self-assertive adventurers that the Eldorado they longed for lay inward, and was available by an effort of consciousness rather than by the infernal aggrandizement of great actions.

If there is any quality that is entirely missing from Emerson's writing it is the dramatic sense of the personality forcing its will upon the world. Carlyle may have turned toward Frederick the Great in his hero worship, but Emerson's inclinations were quite definitely toward Plato and Jesus. It is obvious that he was intent on a pacific translation of the sacred egoism of his premises, to the point where individualism lost all its capacity to excite distrust and fear.

To invoke nature in a fond maternal figure of speech has its own poignancy, but to call that "lap" one of "immense intelligence" is a typical Emersonian address. To be the "organs of its activity" was to be discharged from insecure moral responsibility, particularly when it was understood that a deep moral law lies at the center and radiates everywhere. Surely, whatever its other values, this thought was a claim for confidence in the individual citizens of a free society. The principle was not only a release from the transient confusions and inconsistencies of behavior, it was a positive justification of them. Emerson's thinking converges precisely with the observations of Tocqueville produced in the same years of the century. Pantheism, the latter said, was the plausible outcome of democratic thinking because it

> teaches that all things material and immaterial, visible and invisible, which the world contains are to be considered only as the several parts

of an immense Being, who alone remains eternal amidst the continual change and ceaseless transformation of all that constitutes him.[4]

If democracy needed a god, it was obvious on the American continent that for religious and moral purposes, as well as for the limitless real estate in the west, each man could have a share in the divinity of nature. We remember Thoreau's poet blithely stealing and distilling the essence of the farms of his neighbors. The democracy of nature was quite unlike the omnipotence of God, traditionally marked by his kinglike quirks and prejudices, his favoritism, his jealous need for worship, his obscure but tyrannical will. A consistent pantheism is egalitarian in the long run; the inequalities of fortune and strength are readily seen to run themselves out in the natural cycles of dissolution and renewal.

The men of the American republic could sympathize with the egalitarianism of Emerson's thought as he pronounced his theory of correspondences and found the world composed rather simply by the principle of analogy and repetition. It was a metaphysical declaration of independence in which he asserted that all things were created equal. The unity of this world was not constructed from interrelated and subordinated functions but from the affinity of equal parts, each one sufficing to make a world in its essentials.

Equality was worse than nothing if it did not accompany the faith that men were not only equal but the centers of significant inspiration. Nature was the source of all inspired uses, which Emerson classified in his essay under four headings, Commodity, Beauty, Language, and Discipline. The last was the important function, served by all the others, and under this heading Emerson invoked the moral instruction of nature.

> The moral law lies at the centre of nature and radiates to the circumference. It is the pith and marrow of every substance, every relation, and every process. All things with which we deal, preach to us.[5]

Every practical utility, every sign of beauty, and every truth combined in their messages for right behavior.

If a system of freedom had not absorbed ethics into its "pith and marrow" it might be mere savagery. Emerson understood this, certainly, as he launched himself in the preaching of radical individualism and invaded the dangerous antithesis of freedom and order. It is the most impressive source of consistency in his work, after all, to find

4. Tocqueville, *Democracy in America*, 2: p. 31.
5. "Nature," *Writings*, p. 23.

that its primary energy was ethical, and this suggests how much in the first place he was a thinker on behalf of the intrinsic problems of democracy.

> It is not free institutions, it is not a republic, it is not a democracy, that is the end,—no, but only the means. Morality is the object of government.[6]

Ethics had an ultimate sovereignty. It ruled or should rule politics, and it was the evolutionary distillation of all religions. "Revolutions never go backwards," he says in "The Sovereignty of Ethics."

> It does not yet appear what forms the religious feeling will take. It prepares to rise out of all forms to an absolute justice and healthy perception. . . . America shall introduce a pure religion . . . all the religion we have is the ethics of one or another holy person.[7]

His concern clearly was with the point where politics and religion met, and that convergence was in the ethical response of men to the ethical communication of nature.

Here then were the essential elements. Stripped of old habits and prejudgments, men were gathered together in a new enterprise, in intimacy with each other and a generously inspiring nature. It would seem justified to think that, for Americans, "our whole history appears like a last effort of the Divine Providence on behalf of the human race." The corresponding effort of Emerson's mind was to explore the bases of the most sophisticated social ethic that the world had yet seen. It was to be an ethical order, but at the same time it was intended as a great human liberation from restraint. John Dewey understood, as might be expected, Emerson's ambition to knock down the barriers between creeds and morality, religion and actual life, and those systematic ethical abstractions which denied each man's ethical freedom.

> Against creed and system, convention and institution, Emerson stands for restoring to the common man that which in the name of religion, of philosophy, of art and of morality, has been embezzled from the common store and appropriated to sectarian and class use. Beyond anyone we know of, Emerson has comprehended and declared how much malversation makes truth decline from its simplicity, and in becoming partial and owned, become a puzzle of and trick for theologian, metaphysician and litterateur—a puzzle of an imposed law, of an unwished for and refused goodness, of a romantic ideal gleaming only from afar, and a trick of manipular skill, of specialized performance. . . .

6. "American Civilization," *Works*, 11: 309.
7. "The Sovereignty of Ethics," *Works*, 10: 207, 209, 212.

For such reasons, the coming century may well make evident what is just now dawning, that Emerson is not only a philosopher, but that he is the Philosopher of Democracy.[8]

Dewey was accurate in perceiving that Emerson's wish to reclaim and rejuvenate the truths of "theologian, metaphysician and litterateur" had a distinct democratic bias. Men who functioned by their choices had first to distinguish between what was secondary and what was primary. The institutionalization of culture was a greater threat to a viable humanist democracy than single tyrants and supernatural powers. Against traditional hierarchies, yes, but also against the abstract tyranny of "partial and owned truths," it was necessary to defend what Emerson called the "aboriginal Self." Here was the original place of equality, a high platform, and it was most important that it overlook all the circumstantial hierarchies and discriminations of actual living. The alternative to Emerson's mode of thought, if one wanted an absolute sanction for equality, was to offer it in heaven, as in the traditional divine promotion.

The democratic spirit of universal election is really at odds with the Christian eschatology in basic ways, and I think this fact is adequately communicated by the classic American writers. In reading Emerson, we are not surprised to come upon a remark such as this, "The simplest person who in his integrity worships God, becomes God." Whether this remains meaningful or not would perhaps depend on one's ties with the older God, who was interested in man but immeasurably beyond him; therefore to believe in this God was to endorse subordination as well as obedience as the ruling principles of life. Emerson's covert purpose was to get rid of the traditional revelation of God, the king and ruler of the universe, and bring credibility to new revelations. Men replaced kings when they became democratic: Emerson suggests that behind that revolution an even deeper one was going on in which men divided the metaphysical authority of God among themselves in order to justify their own freedom.

The Christian theme was man fallen away from God and needing salvation. In the actual practice of religion this was not so much to be reborn as to be elevated, as if in the grand hierarchy of creation one would be rewarded for acts of self-denial, the acceptance of instruction, the imitation of higher authority. Thus the pedigree of all men is poor and debased to start with and each must strive to gain entrance into

8. John Dewey, "Emerson," *Characters and Events* (New York: Henry Holt and Co., 1929), 1: 74.

the aristocracy of the saved, if only by practicing the conventions of the morally elect, the spiritual upper class, so to speak.

To give radical support to democracy, it was more plausible to affirm the high value of each man at the *start* of existence, rather than promise it in the conclusion, in the form of immortal salvation. Moral discriminations, made in the temperamental bias of democracy, move typically back to the sanctity of beginnings, the innocence of the intrinsic. Truth confronts falsehood, sincerity rejects imitation, purity opposes decadence; to regain the aboriginal self means to fight a battle with the conformist social self.

This led to at least two major paradoxical results in the effort to propound a democratic faith. One was to translate deeply secular and naturalistic assumptions into idealist or transcendental conclusions. To avoid the threat of primitivism it was necessary to affirm the predominant revelations of spirit. The other seeming contradiction was more fruitful and in the ethics of democracy more important. This was to move a new social gospel, revolutionary in its force, toward a practicing self-criticism, anarchistic in its implications. Democratic principles, when led as far as Emerson and Thoreau could take them, would suggest that democracy's own institutions were the enemies of its fecund spirit. The root of this faith was really an ideal of sublime statelessness, perfect in both freedom and equality, in which one believed transcendentally. But again it must be clear that Emerson used transcendentalism to support a secular and humanist faith, not to escape it. Its meaning turns on the following assumptions: that consciousness dominates matter, inspiration guides action, and the moral sense is a pure force lifted above all contingencies. These were apparently necessary discriminations in order to avoid being overwhelmed, in a secular system, by a merely vulgar and empirical intelligence. The latter he called the understanding, in the Coleridgean distinction he made between reason and understanding.

These ideas, which opposed themselves to a simpleminded utilitarianism, could have effective results in the democratic process. They offered a firm straightforwardness of judgment which led Emerson to say that in the conflict between institutions and the private conscience, the latter always took precedence; it surely is an indispensable democratic premise that men should remain the masters of their institutions. The inborn conflict became highly visible in Emerson's time. Theoretically, in an individualist and egalitarian democracy, institutions are the instruments of life, justified as utilities. But the demands of survival and progress turn instruments into necessities, usurping the role of true ends. There was all the more reason then to define true ends and maintain their dominance. However, if these were absolutes, they could not remain far removed, on the abstract or supernatural plane. Emerson knew with the strongest democratic instinct that he could not relax his respect for immediate existence, the single person, the particular thing, the "here and now" locus of reality. And yet there had to be a higher allegiance. The dialectic of Emersonian thought is particularly addressed to that difficulty. His style is an unresisting flow from the observation of particulars to intimations of the Over-Soul, as if searching for the inspired moment when the one divine fact was present. But as much as it served enthusiasm, the dialectic was a weapon of criticism. To take up the cause of the "aboriginal Self," whatever the transcendental support he could summon, meant to oppose himself to the whole enormous apparatus of instrumental and secondary considerations which support society. Despite his search for affirmations, Emerson dramatized a meaningful dualism in the issues of democratic thought which opposed the personal against the general, the immediate against the abstract, the content against the form, the ends against the means. That tension in his thought and writing makes it rich in the American tradition.

Precisely for that reason Emerson could not be called the champion of democracy in the simple sense. More often than not he was an unforgiving critic of the democratic process in his society. It is easy to obtain the impression from his writing that he was apolitical, or that he was concerned with the values that could not possibly be the provision of an organized state or any secular institution. One might variously label his thinking mystical, radically bohemian, anarchistic, or directly conservative and aristocratic, all terms to denote a revulsion from democratic civilization as it could be judged in his time.

In his early anti-Jacksonian responses he casually said "the spirit of political economy is low and degrading." Insofar as he had respect for elected officials, it was a respect won by actions which transcended their source of power, as in the case of Lincoln. What he felt about mere numerical democracy was pungently expressed in the Journals. "Majorities, the argument of fools, the strength of the weak."[9] This

9. Emerson adds in the following passage from the Journals, "One should recall what Laertius records of Socrates's opinion of the common people, that 'it was as if a man should object against a piece of bad money, and accept a great sum of the

is the impatience of an idealist, not a cynic. Such a man, without a trace of melioristic thinking, could not be expected to care for the democratic process, as distinct from its ideal assumptions. To believe in Man was apparently not the same thing as trusting a mass of men in action. Emerson was quite as sensitive to this problem as Tocqueville, as were for that matter the men at the Constitutional Convention.

> The Universal mind is so far from being measured in any finite numbers, that its verdict would be vitiated at once by any reference to numbers, however large. "The multitude is the worst argument," and, in fact, the only way of arriving at the Universal mind is to quit the whole world and take counsel of the bosom alone.[10]

In the heat of such revulsions from the democratic scene, Emerson labored for the moral justification of democracy. Where could a moral authority be found in such a debased conference of minds as the elective process implied? Was it not that very uncertain and inestimable moral authority which demanded Emerson's faith in the transcendental unity of the universe and the ethical inspiration of nature? At the same time, in the overwhelming complications of the problem, the public life of a democracy, its instrument of collectivities and majorities, bred the fiercer need for private autonomy.

The poet-idealist had a particular question to answer. How could a thousand ignoramuses deserve more consideration than one wise man? Loyalty deserved a higher sanction; indeed the highest had to be found. Democracy had lost a king, the profound symbol of an ethical ideal as well as functioning power; in his place, power was a machine, an unworshipped utility or, worse, an anonymous, abstract, and arbitrary master. "The world has been instructed by its kings," Emerson said.

> It has been taught by this colossal symbol the mutual reverence that is due from man to man. The joyful loyalty with which men have everywhere suffered the king, the noble, or the great proprietor to walk among them by a law of his own, make his own scale of men and things and reverse theirs, pay for benefits not with money but with honor, and rep-

---

same'" (*Journals of Ralph Waldo Emerson*, ed. E. W. Emerson and W. E. Forbes [Boston: Houghton Mifflin Co., 1910], 10: 397).

Such sharp revulsions suggest the basis for the Emersonian stress on "character," and the clinging to a Socratic idealism as a generalized faith. These were old defenses against the rule of numbers and opinions. Emerson was most a Platonist in seeking higher sanctions, or the purest sources of insight.

10. *The Journals and Miscellaneous Notebooks of R. W. Emerson*, ed. M. M. Sealts (Cambridge: Harvard University Press–Belknap Press, 1965), 5: 282.

resent the law in his person, was the hieroglyphic by which they obscurely signified their consciousness of their own right and comeliness, the right of every man.[11]

This is an irrepressible democratic response, democracy arguing with itself so to speak, and mediating the quarrel between the ideal of heroes and the ideal of free and equal mankind. As Perry Miller pointed out, "there was everything in Emerson's philosophy to turn him like Carlyle into a prophet of reaction and the leader-principle. But he did not go with Carlyle."[12]

Emerson "did not go with Carlyle" and that is the essence of his story. We can follow with sympathy what was after all the poignant stimulus of his writing. The struggle is fascinating. The "transcendental" escape hatch was perhaps no more than a kind of final resort. More typically the effort in Emerson is to establish new forms of measure, new sources of valuation; it was indeed an effort to define a new kingship. There need be no equivalence between public and private values; a man need not be the creature of his society; nor need a man live aggrandizingly, in such a way that his "greatness" is imposed upon others.

> We shall one day see that the most private is the most public energy, that quality atones for quantity, and grandeur of character acts in the dark, and succors them who never saw it.[13]

There is a gentle ardor in Emerson's thought that impresses everyone, and much of its effect comes from his effort to sail peacefully between the twin dangers of anomie and megalomania. How simply he states this in two sentences.

> The private life of one man shall be a more illustrious monarchy, more formidable to its enemy, more sweet and serene in its influence to its friend, than any kingdom in history. For a man, rightly viewed, comprehendeth the particular natures of all men.[14]

It is free for us to call Emerson a democrat if we remember this reserve. He refuses to worship forms of the "public energy," whether expressed as kings or majorities. He has a mystique appropriate to democracy, but it is never of the "people," but always of "man." That universal he draws from the "private life of one man," an oracle de-

11. "Self-Reliance," *Writings*, p. 155.

12. Perry Miller, "Emersonian Genius and the American Democracy," *New England Quarterly* 26 (1953): 27–44.

13. "Character," *Writings*, p. 379.

14. "The American Scholar," *Writings*, p. 59.

serving respect in his own right, but one who also provides the only communication available with the spirit in all men. This is the distinctive note of a struggle to escape the contradiction of the public power in a democracy. Emerson was eager to translate "the most private" into "the most public" energy, but the order of the phrases is of utmost importance, for to reverse them was to move into a very different kind of democracy, which the American republic was already beginning to exhibit. "Character acts in the dark," and that idea was meant to condition all public acts and ceremonies. "For a man, rightly viewed, comprehendeth the particular natures of all men."

The "right viewing" was the crux of the matter. For there was always the other danger, stressed by Emerson's own inclination to revere great men, a force proportionate to these reactions from the democratic scene. Could one really believe in human greatness and cultivate it, and still support the doctrine of equality, still expect that one's life would not be invaded by the greater and the greatest? One part of the answer was reassuring but perhaps glib. Greatness was not a matter of superficial achievement but of character. Those who were truly great achieved greatness not essentially by superior gifts, not by any explicit comparison of strength, but by the greater courage to *be* themselves. Greatness was the reward of self-confidence; to envy great men, to wish to be like them or, worse, to compete against them, would mean to submit to genuine inferiority. The admiration of great men was good, as their true greatness was good, but it should not lead to their elevation over others. Rightly understood it led to strengthened independence and at the same time a blessed and unstrained union. For all men are great, or can be, and all worlds of achievement are microcosmic analogies of each other; all kingdoms are personal and the individual reigns in each one among equals, who cannot be measured by a common standard or by their hierarchical relationships.

The moralists of Concord, Thoreau in particular, were determined to confront the democratic megalomania of success and to purge it of its evil. The motive to succeed could contradict the faith in individual autonomies, because the track led inevitably either to the domination or the imitation of others. Thoreau and Emerson recognized that in the contest for power and wealth no one was free. We cannot underestimate the force of this contradiction in their minds. Self-realization, the ideal of freedom, was apparently most difficult to attain in a free and competitive society. In that whirlpool of effort and communication men were forced to be insecure about what they were, particularly because of the insecurity of the standards for what they should be, the insecurity of the signs of recognition, the insecurity of *all* judgments in the free marketplace of judgments and ideas installed by liberal individualism. This was the familiar paradox that Tocqueville observed, that such a system should lead to a devouring moral dependency of one man upon others.

A free society was at war with its own premise. Would one be forced to an impossible choice? Men flocked toward unity and security, whatever the force that moved them, whether the traditional codes of submission or the brutal chaos of frontier freedom. Emerson's instinct was to go further into the sovereignty of the self, not to abdicate it. On one side this led him to make the easy resolutions of "idealist" thinking. But a closer reading of Emerson reveals that he sensitized his thought in its deepest grain with the principle of contradiction. Almost at once in his writing he discovered the need as well as the rewards of conducting a series of oppositions toward their precarious moments of balance, or intense occasions of insight. Stephen Whicher's study of Emerson gains credit for its emphasis on Emerson's dialectical perspectives, and he correctly observed the extension of the principle to a major tradition, with Emerson standing at the source.

> As with Whitman, Melville, and Henry Adams, we are dealing with a mind that makes any assertion of belief against the felt pull of its lurking opposite, the two forming together a total *truth of experience* larger than the opposing *truths of statement* of which it is composed.[15]

The clue to this mode of Emerson's thought comes very early. In January, 1822, when he was only nineteen, he addressed himself in his journal "to say something about Contrast."

> Contrast is a law which seems to exist not only in the human mind with regard to the objects of imagination as an associating principle, but also to obtain in the course of providence and the laws which regulate the World. . . .
> In this principle is lodged the safety of human institutions and human life.[16]

That last observation has the sharpest interest; he goes on to give the example of revolution, citing the overthrow of a "terrible murdering tyrant," and he imagines that particularly *then* "when the day of triumph burns with consuming splendor—here the mind pauses to an-

15. Stephen E. Whicher, *Freedom and Fate* (Philadelphia: University of Pennsylvania Press, 1953), p. 58.

16. *The Journals and Miscellaneous Notebooks*, 1:60–61.

ticipate change near at hand." This is a special conditioning of revolutionary enthusiasm, with powerful implications; one stands ready to foresee still another movement in history at the very time when justice and the "good" seem closest to achievement.

Of course the dialectical movement was in nature, or else it could not be so strong in human affairs.

> That great principle of Undulation in nature, that shows itself in the inspiring and expiring of the breath; in desire and satiety; in the ebb and flow of the sea; in day and night; in heat and cold; and, as yet more deeply ingrained in every atom and every fluid, is known to us under the name of Polarity.[17]

But whatever the support of nature, it is man who must first understand and meet the challenge of contradictions. Facing history, Emerson said, "It is the fault of rhetoric that we cannot strongly state one fact without seeming to belie some other." In that deft remark he pits his opposition to intellectual bigotry in the human sciences. Truth is an issue for party debate, or, so to speak, a continuing electoral contest that is never finally decided.

> Opposition is our belt and tonic. No opinion will pass, but must stand the tug of war. . . . We know the austere law of liberty,—that it must be reconquered day by day, that it subsists in a state of war, that it is always slipping away from those who boast it, to those who fight for it.[18]

It is affecting to think how much Emerson's ideas of nature or his metaphysics, were a kind of transcendental politics, in which it was necessary to assert the rights of man against the supervening authority of the universe.

> Morals implies freedom and will. The will constitutes the man. He has his life in Nature, like a beast; but choice is born in him; here is he that chooses, here is the Declaration of Independence, the July Fourth of zoölogy and astronomy.[19]

It is clear in some of these remarks that Emerson understood that the gravest contemporary threat to the justifications of freedom would come from a surrender to naturalistic determinism. This was behind his effort to demonstrate nature's moral meaning and divinity, but it also supported his concept of a dialectical natural process. The principle of polarity gave an outlet to man's power of opposition, his free-

17. "The American Scholar," *Writings*, p. 54.
18. *Journals*, 8:544.
19. "Character," *Works*, 10:91.

dom, as well as his ethical being. If necessary, Emerson was willing to move to a defiant humanism, leaving considerations of nature far behind.

> Man is not order of nature, sack and sack, belly and members, link in a chain, nor any ignominious baggage; but a stupendous antagonism, a dragging together of the poles of the Universe.[20]

The essay "Fate," in which these lines appear, needs stressing if we are to see what was behind the usual serenity of his mind and the blandness of some of his conclusions.

> For if Fate is so prevailing, man also is part of it, and can confront fate with fate. If the Universe have these savage accidents, our atoms are as savage in resistance.[21]

So savage and so strong in fact that the moral will recognizes itself as the order-making principle in the world.

> It puts us in place . . . where we belong, in the cabinet of science and of causes, there where all the wires terminate which hold the world in magnetic unity, and so converts us into universal beings. . . . The moral sentiment is alone omnipotent.[22]

Man "savage in resistance" is a rare chord in Emerson's expressed thought, but it suggests how much his work was a defense of freedom, which he could call a "stupendous antagonism." Behind all lyrical reassurance there remained the actual crisis which might return, forcing one to question how much affinity there really was between man and nature, or for that matter between man and man. Was it heroism or was it security that Emerson offered to the single person as he confronted the world? It is because of this uncertainty that at times we feel in Emerson the deeply felt threat and deeply wished relief which make him after all the spiritual cousin of Hawthorne and Melville. And we are led to see again the inner cohesion of nineteenth-century American literature, distinctive as it was for its sharp alternations of mood, moving from radical metaphysical reassurance to the most intense dramas of alienation.

But the question remains whether Emerson failed greatly in dealing with his own dialectical insights. In the end he was perhaps not tough-minded enough to make the most of his best intuitions. His urge to achieve resolutions, his persistent doubling back, as if to speak of

20. "Fate," *Works*, 6:22.

21. Ibid., p. 24.   22. "Character," *Works*, 10:95.

conflict were only a limitation of awareness, put him miles away not only from later writers, but from his own contemporaries, including Thoreau, who conceived a more dramatic and more immediately tangible world than he did. Emerson's debt to Coleridge and the German philosophers is easily acknowledged, but one begins to wonder in renewed perspective whether what he drew from them was both vitiating in his own writing and foreign to the real ground of the American imagination. What he owes to philosophic idealism perhaps filled his temperamental needs, but it drew the actual strain of conflict as well as a good deal of persuasiveness out of his teaching. So long as he pushed forward the belief in the Universal Spirit, he protected himself from the hazards of his dialectical vision and covered all bets. The passive, spectatorial genius of Concord could offer relief to the overstrained American experience, but could he really lead it, or express its characteristic inspiration?

Emerson was the first to stand at the crisis center of the American experience, dramatizing both the overwhelming presence of nature and the fast-growing threat of abstract society, the two converging upon the autonomous free man. He faced such dichotomies, he appealed implicitly to heroism and truthfulness of observation, and then made his way easily, like a shadow, into the benevolent harmonies of spirit. Problems exist but have no development in Emerson's writing; they are obliterated by the transcendental enthusiasm. In that sense he was a man of prayer and faith, the great conciliator. He would resolve all difficulties between the human protagonist and the universe even before they occurred. "The act of seeing and the thing seen, the seer and the spectacle, the subject and the object, are one."[23] Merely to contemplate the bravado of this statement is to sense the anxiety behind it. What if the subject and the object in this world were not one, but absurdly divided, each moving in its own sphere and with its own reasons? What if the spectacle were only an enigma and the seer a man painting his own dreams? Emerson came so close to this judgment that he reversed its implications recklessly: "Time and space are but psychological colors which the eye makes but the soul is light."

We remember the contrasting defiance of his words in the essay "Fate." "For if Fate is so prevailing, man is also part of it and can confront fate with fate." But in the same writing he quickly takes the sting out of this.

23. "The Over-Soul," *Writings*, p. 262.

But Fate against Fate is only parrying and defence. . . . The revelation of Thought takes man out of servitude into freedom. . . . The day of days, the great day of the feast of life, is that in which the inward eye opens to the Unity in things, to the omnipresence of law:—sees that what is must be and ought to be, or is the best.[24]

If Emerson by these words was the "Philosopher of Democracy" he was himself striking at democracy's virility by taking a wide circle around the points of conflict in the dialectic of freedom. Those unsympathetic to the pretensions of democracy might say that a faith as intentionally evasive as this was indispensable to support the ragged, illogical life of a free society.

The judgment against much of Emerson's writing is that he fails to pursue the implications of his best thinking, that he is neither a rock of resolute belief, nor a wholly inspired genius of the literary imagination. His tone is too sweet, too serene to cover the range his ideas invite; though he is eloquent, his words have often only a lyrical caress and uplift, and though he is concrete in his observations, he means to rejoice the eye and satisfy wonder, rather than orchestrate a conflict. Precisely at the moments when the intellectual and emotional demand upon him begins to build, one feels a fading away of moral force and the tone of an invulnerable detachment.

His desire for reconcilement in a universe of conflict led to the characteristic stress on a contemplative consciousness, for how else was unity to be conceived or even remotely approached? But the instrument for independence was also consciousness, extendable, withdrawing, penetrating, secretive, but always an invulnerable consciousness, an intelligence necessarily as large as the truth it comprehends, but as aloof from formal doctrine as it was from partial motives or single acts.

There will be an agreement in whatever variety of actions, so they be each honest and natural in their hour. For of one will, the actions will be harmonious, however unlike they seem. These varieties are lost sight of at a little distance, at a little height of thought.[25]

This is a confusing mode of operations, for it involves nothing less than a firm detachment from immediate concerns, even though one has just been urged to act spontaneously. The spontaneity is all right apparently, but it cannot be appreciated in its own terms, at its own moment, but rather "at a little height of thought." Does the harmony

24. "Fate," *Works*, 6:25.   25. "Self-Reliance," *Writings*, p. 152.

of the world depend then on an ascetic detachment from particular interests, even as one allows them full play? The bewildering extremes of Emersonian doctrine are here apparent. One acts with authentic response, but one simultaneously comforts oneself with detachment, aloof, considering, and cancelling discords at that safe "little height."

Whether because he secretly feared his own naturalist affirmations, or because he thought his main labor was to reassure even while he destroyed the traditional human shelters of belief, the typical effect of Emerson's thinking is quietistic. He is writing to give democracy its moral justification and relief of mind, not to send it on its way to stronger adventures. The ideal order which has embraced an ideal anarchy is led so safely away from the shock of conflict, that we begin to suspect it as one more specimen of obscurantist democratic rhetoric. A more disturbing conclusion is that a typical trait of passivity has been introduced into the practice of freedom. This strikes its note clearly at the very beginning of Emerson's work, in his essay on nature. "Standing on the bare ground I become a transparent eyeball." Perhaps nature has full sufficiency and needs no help in action; the function of man is to contemplate it. "I am nothing, I see all."

We may see this withdrawal into a subjective realm as a reflection of the moral problem of a democracy determined to believe in freedom without tragic modulations. Perhaps the ideal of freedom is forced to a split between action and thought. Society affirms that men may think what they like, but laws remain paramount and public opinion strong, and so while license is given ideas, they suffer a consequent diminution, and an even greater force operates for the conformity of acts. It is here that we can find a basis for the patronizing of intellect which is endemic in democracy. On the other hand the man of mind tends equally to show his contempt for the men of action, meretricious in their rhetoric, small-minded in their pragmatism. "The sensual man conforms thoughts to things; the poet conforms things to his thoughts." If Emerson was the poet of democracy, purest of all in his faith, he was also the closest to a contemplative mystic that American thought has produced.

"With consistency a great soul has simply nothing to do," he said. But that meant that Emerson was determined to lead the citizens of his democracy where only the soul, and the greatest of souls, can find consolation. He was a man who preached a divinity in natural acts, and then led his readers to an ultimate experience which was meditative. He praised a self-assertion which was absolute, and then persuaded his readers that the personal will was only exercised on behalf of circumstantial existence, that is, in the lesser world. He elevated the simplest intuition as the instrument of wisdom, only to lead his disciples to the acceptance of consciousness as higher than action. Elevating consciousness, the omniscient and "transparent Eyeball," he put a barrier against the complex intelligence, and strictly said that spiritual insight was not bound by the facts, the things, the persons of time and place in contingent reality. This was a democracy of spirit, a freedom and equality where soul engaged with soul in a sphere far removed from the painful historical battles where the idea of freedom was actually tested.

In one important aspect this was democracy founding its faith on mysteries beyond empirical challenge, in order to be as strong and superstitious as rival faiths. Nevertheless the uneasiness in reading Emerson remains, particularly for those who estimate him as a democratic moralist. Above all, democracy requires a god of battles and Emerson refused to carry his god into battle. The humanism of Emerson's faith at this point loses its conviction, because, being so absolute, it sacrificed the major part of the actual traits of humanity. His man-god has transcended mankind, and is finally as abstract as the toy wooden god of Melville's Queequeg, which he casually kept in his pocket and only took out for the assigned rites of meditation.

In what peculiar sense, then, is Emerson the spokesman for the rugged democracy of his time? He may have invented a kind of defense *against* freedom, which relaxes the nerves and can go so far as to be a kind of disengagement, which then becomes, absurdly, the chief characteristic of the free man.

> The lesson is forcibly taught . . . that there is no need of struggles, convulsions, and despairs, of the wringing of the hands and the gnashing of teeth; that we miscreate our own evils. We interfere with the optimism of nature; for whenever we get this vantage-ground of the past, or of a wiser mind in the present, we are able to discern that we are begirt with laws which execute themselves.[26]

Emerson truly longed for heroism and he had inspiriting things to say about it. But to protect heroism from the tragic circle around it, to protect himself from disappointment, he set absolute conditions against failure, and probably sacrificed any true claim to judge heroism. Whicher sharply describes this determination to have the best of his difficulties;

26. "Spiritual Laws," *Writings*, p. 192.

He could proclaim self-reliance because he could also advocate God-reliance; he could seek a natural freedom because he also sought a supernatural perfection . . . he could assert that the individual was the world because, thanks to the moral law, he knew that nothing arbitrary, nothing alien shall take place in the universe; the huge world, which he dared to defy, was really on his side and would not, as it were, spoil his game. The dual necessity, at once divergent and identical, to be free and invulnerable shapes much of his thinking.[27]

We are reminded of the magnificent obscurantism of Calvinist thought which could stress the omnipotence in the will of God and at the same time see the signs of this fatality (or divine election) working in the strenuous efforts of the individual to fulfill its commands. But why should a man not rest in the stream of circumstance, which would always be the enforcement of God's will? Why should he not surrender to his strongest impulses, which would again be the expression of God's omnipotent will? The alternatives of licentiousness and passivity were anathematic to both the Puritan and the American democrat. The secret of both strains of thought, at least for what they had in common, was perhaps the fact that they pioneered in emancipation and harshly challenged traditional human authorities. In terror of their presumption, they immediately countered by expressions of faith in an ultimate power, as absolute as could be conceived, but a power which acted *through* individuals and therefore guaranteed that their acts and experiences were not the reflection of chaos.

But this determination to provide spiritual comfort is not the whole story. Basically Emerson is a man of two moods, which are sometimes contradictory but at other points in his work reveal themselves as phases of a conflict which is undergoing resolution. As I have said, Emerson's role can be understood at its best as that of a dialectician treating the antithesis of freedom and order and the contradictions of man's life in nature. When he faces these directly and when his work rises beyond the anxious need to prove safety in freedom, he can stir the mind to a glimpse of daring conclusions. This is the quality of sophisticated insight which is the lasting heritage of his writing, the quality which without question was the one which attracted Nietzsche's significant praise.

The most interesting and sympathetic selection from his work would support the conclusion that Emerson was capable of a high moral realism, distinctly modern in its relevance and excitement. At

27. Whicher, *Freedom and Fate*, pp. 56–57.

that point it is no longer passivity or quietism which he proposes, but the adventure of the human consciousness which maintains its independence from circumstance, its autonomy in the midst of a universe which outside that consciousness is characterless and blind. In this respect Emerson does indeed address himself to heroism.

Reading his glorification of "Man Thinking" in "The American Scholar," one naturally asks, how does he conquer a danger by seeing through it, a difficulty by understanding it, as he says in those passages? The answer, if read carefully, is not by a mere aloofness of mind, but by a shift in what is most valued. Freedom is born in consciousness, freedom is first of all thought. This applies particularly well to the affirmations of democracy. Democracy is purest in its practice when it exercises the right of assent or dissent, whether these are given to the public error or the public wisdom. In the larger sense democracy is simply the sum of such independent attitudes and states of mind.

Much of Emerson's preaching is designed to form a public opinion which accepts the premise that the exercise of the free mind is more important than any effective result in action. The democrat is in this sense always an "idealist"; he must believe that mind has priority over events, because the latter are not only the opportunities but the limitations of freedom. Freedom is only justified by a belief in the redemptive power of the imagination, of hope, of ennobled purpose. If too high a value were put upon "realities," whatever they might be, the world as determined and actual becomes more important than the world as "potential," and the inspiration of democracy is undermined. To be conscious in this sense is to live open to the future, within the creative genius of change, and this is every man's privilege because it is intrinsic in life itself.

> It is a mischievous notion that we are come late into nature; that the world was finished a long time ago. As the world was plastic and fluid in the hands of God, so it is ever to so much of his attributes as we bring to it. To ignorance and sin, it is flint. They adapt themselves to it as they may; but in proportion as man has anything in him divine, the firmament flows before him and takes his signet and form. Not he is great who can alter matter, but he who can alter my state of mind.[28]

But this is not for the mere exercise of contemplation. Rather Emerson would propose that the reward of energy is the release of energy, the reward of freedom is *activity* in the flux of events. Why love

28. "The American Scholar," *Writings*, pp. 57–58.

mastery, Emerson might say, if it means a misguided effort to constrain the "unfinished world." As thinking has priority over thought, so acting has priority over acts. He said, in his praise of "Man Thinking," that men had made their greatest mistakes in worshipping their own creations rather than that force in themselves which is the source of manifold and contradictory achievement.

> The sacredness which attaches to the act of creation, the act of thought, is transferred to the record. . . . The writer was a just and wise spirit; henceforward it is settled the book is perfect; as love of the hero corrupts into worship of his statue. Instantly the book becomes noxious; the guide is a tyrant.[29]

"Instantly," we notice he says. In that sense he is a true revolutionary, demanding the utmost from men in their capacity to accept change. "The one thing in the world, of value, is the active soul."

In this perspective we can understand him when he says, "Character is higher than intellect. Thinking is the function. Living is the functionary."[30] Thinking transcends thought, but living is supreme over thinking. These are necessary democratic priorities. Every doctrine, every formal institution, must be challenged by the experiential drama which makes and remakes them. This value system puts what is concrete before the abstract, the functional before the static, the life before the theory, the man before the group. And if the world refuses these priorities, "Patience—patience," counsels Emerson, "if the single man plant himself indomitably on his instincts, and there abide, the huge world will come round to him."[31] And if it doesn't? Still more patience, for character is not only higher than intellect, it is, we might remember, the world itself, or without it, rather, there is no world. "It puts us in place . . . where we belong . . . there where all the wires terminate which hold the world in magnetic unity."[32]

We might summarize matters at this point. If character is created in the consciousness of a dilemma, Emerson was himself chief among characters. What he knew quite simply was the drama of the individual in a universe which no longer explained itself in a direct and authoritative revelation. There was on the one hand "Nature," a source of reassurance or terror. There was on the other side "Man," whose needs were clear and implored a defense. To make man the passive agent of "Fate," or determinist nature, would be to sacrifice his centrality with-

29. Ibid., p. 49.
30. Ibid., p. 54.

31. Ibid., p. 63.
32. "Character," *Works*, 10:95.

out having another locus for centrality, as in the traditional anthropomorphic image of God. On the other hand to give the human will unchecked dominance would expose men to the endless indeterminacy of free choice. It would then be, in the modern parlance, an absurd universe in which man's freedom would be equally absurd or ultimately irrelevant.

There is no doubt that Emerson hedged against these possible defeats in what he once called "the abyss of real Being." In so doing he was in greater harmony with his time and his antecedents than his contemporary, Melville, whose insights deserted the confident ideas of the Enlightenment. And yet Emerson's faith was often exposed at the barest point where alternatives converged, and where his forms of reassurance revealed a wrestling with "Fate and Freedom" in defense of the deeply challenged human position.

That being so, he owns his place as the first important intelligence of the American literary and philosophic tradition. The word that best describes his intrinsic mode of thought, to borrow from Kenneth Burke, is "dramatistic." By this I mean a keen sense of alternatives and reversals which is felt below his serial affirmations, a supreme ability to use the negative and survive. It is expressed, at an untypical extreme to be sure, when he describes "Man [as] a stupendous antagonism, a dragging together of the poles of the universe."

To accept the negative, means to submit thought to the polarities of conflict; in democratic language, to institutionalize dissent. It is true, as I have said, that Emerson felt temperamentally inclined to reassure his listeners, and yet his thought was radically subversive, as Santayana understood.

> What seemed, then, to the more earnest and less critical of his hearers a revelation from above was in truth rather an insurrection from beneath, a shaking loose from convention, a disintegration of the normal categories of reason. . . .[33]

This quiet enthusiast who either cast off social forms or made them only the emanations of creative individuals, like garments which express only their wearers, was the teacher of a truly revolutionary social order. The distrust of ideas and institutions was consistently to be implanted in the very structure of democratic institutions and beliefs.

33. George Santayana, *Interpretations of Poetry and Religion* (New York: Charles Scribner's Sons, 1900), p. 219.

To praise the practice of continuous dissent, and at the same time inspire secure and dispassionate faith, was an effort to teach a psychological miracle to men in a free society.

"Nothing is at last sacred but the integrity of your own mind." He repeats himself to make sure this extreme statement is caught.

> No law can be sacred to me but that of my nature. Good and bad are but names very readily transferable to that or this; the only right is what is after my constitution; the only wrong what is against it.[34]

This is not the expression of a senseless egomania; not a word or act in his life suggests that. There is not the slightest indication that Emerson anywhere recognized that his ideas might lead to savage anarchy. To be sure he was held by his faith in the personal soul and its harmonic communion with the "Over-Soul." But it would have been just as easy for Emerson to place the center of gravity for the "Over-Soul" in collectivities and large social and metaphysical combinations, as Hegel did. Instead, on behalf of the single person, Emerson made his consistent challenge to the rule of collective wisdom, the magic of abstractions, the ritual obedience of organized reason, the authority of the past.

The only way to understand Emerson's confidence is to see that he is speaking in a democratic context, so thoroughly embedded in it that he must have taken similar assumptions for granted on the part of his listeners. These assumptions were that truth being a genuine truth only in the singularity of insight or experience, no man would be impassioned to impose his truth upon others and make it a collective truth. Or more significantly, moral *externals* such as laws, governments, dogmas, were in constant flux and the absolute existed only in the intrinsic function of choice. "Power ceases in the instant of repose; it resides in the moment of transition from a past to a new state."[35] The homely illustration of his meaning would be to imagine the voter in the voting booth, where he is ritualized in value beyond his substantial choices and their results.

> These are the voices which we hear in solitude . . . the great man is he who in the midst of the crowd keeps with perfect sweetness the independence of solitude.[36]

34. "Self-Reliance," *Writings*, p. 148.

35. Ibid., p. 158.   36. Ibid, pp. 148, 150.

Surely this is a philosophy to support the franchise. All the forces which act in the world of values converge on the moment when the single man chooses.

> A man is to carry himself in the presence of all opposition as if everything were titular and ephemeral but he.[37]

That is an example of the magnificent "antagonism" on which man founds his being. It is a preaching of dissent as if dissent were wisdom. But its support is a myth of the absolute personality.

> You think me the child of my circumstances: I make my circumstances. . . . I—this thought which is called I—is the mould into which the world is poured like melted wax. The mould is invisible, but the world betrays the shape of the mould. You call it the power of circumstance, but it is the power of me.[38]

At this point the democrat becomes a transcendentalist. "For this self-trust, the reason is deeper than can be fathomed—darker than can be enlightened."[39] Self-reliance, a divine authority, cannot be defended by ordinary rationalizations. It justifies itself in the immanent being of men and their presence among each other, or not at all. A democracy in its last inspired argument affirms that a man is above his creeds and institutions, that they are subject to the sacred indeterminacy of his personal being: "history is an impertinence and an injury if it be any thing more than a cheerful apologue or parable of my being and becoming."[40]

This is insight applicable on a wider range than its spiritual affirmations. The political relevance is deep. Emerson in this way instructed democracy that it must exist without a formal ideology, which was perhaps easy in America, in the first half of the nineteenth century. But what was much more difficult, he would eliminate the rule of strength, of numbers, of wealth, of habit, of utility, or any of the other pretenders who moved into the vacuum of power in democratic society. What then was the standard of the good, the guide to belief?

There may be transcendental but little practical reassurance in that key pronouncement he made that the "good" will always be nameless and new when it appears:

37. Ibid., p. 148.
38. "The Transcendentalist," *Writings*, p. 90.
39. "The American Scholar," *Writings*, p. 58.
40. "Self-Reliance," *Writings*, p. 157.

you shall not discern the footprints of any other; you shall not see the face of man; you shall not hear any name; the way, the thought, the good, shall be wholly strange and new. It shall exclude example and experience.[41]

As a negative meaning this is clear, for it inspires the passion for dissent, the wish to say no to imposition from the outside. It is more difficult, however, to declare its positive argument. But this is the effect of its openness to multiple affirmations. The truth, the good, remain the objects of an exercise in which all men are invited to make their own effort. If we generalize, the form is freedom and the substance is—not zero—but everything. As a teacher it befitted Emerson not to fill in this space, for to do so would interfere with what he was inviting from others, the exercise of freedom. It was his disciple Thoreau who went further on the path of concrete existence, Thoreau who made the air he breathed his own and actively built his own world. There is no doubt that Emerson was a forerunner and a stimulus to other writers who committed themselves more solidly and produced more substantial works. But he outlined the area of achievement, he gave it a great encouragement, and that was because he had really only one subject, the eternally elusive and attractive subject of human freedom.

A strong faith and a great vagueness apparently characterize the speculative basis of freedom, where Emerson began. But this is consistent in the contrast with rival systems, less free, which are, correspondingly, highly articulate. To define the distinction one might say that these other schools of behavior, traditional, authoritative, formally positive, are eager to construct the living space for yet unborn men. Emerson's thought would leave this space open. The argument for leaving it open is a humanism in the distinct democratic sense. The space that is otherwise empty of assertions is for life and for the protean energy of man.

This was a difficult position for a man who was at heart a moralist. I think it helps define the sometimes puzzling limpness and vacuous quality of Emerson's writing. Perhaps it is a flaw of the liberal imagination, and surely no one was more liberal, in the exact sense, than Emerson. Liberalism cannot be apocalyptic in its gestures, and it is often vague when it would like to be most impassioned. The proper way to seize the fervor of Emerson's ideas is to look beyond his evangelical pronouncements for nature and the "Over-Soul"—to choose his criticism over his enthusiasm. His criticism constructs what I call

41. Ibid., p. 158.

a "living space" by discriminating against false generalities and false allegiances; it speaks for individual truths and lives. When he touches the strong center of personalist humanism in his writing, Emerson becomes vibrant, particularly for modern readers who have been bred in the intellectual climate of thinkers like Jaspers and Buber. Personality requires chiefly a defense, not a definition; to believe in a private inviolate realm of judgment is to build a bastion against externals. Even if one has little to say on behalf of the actual wealth of that private kingdom, one has it as a vantage point with which to make a continuous defense and keep the world under surveillance.

In a democracy, criticism is almost an act of ritual performance. It yields assent as much as dissent. The radicals of Concord were more daring in such criticism than any of the early revolutionaries because they realized that nothing was withheld from their attack, not history nor inherited belief, neither the institutions of the past nor those of the future, surely not the troubled institutions of democracy itself. Such total criticism is usually within the grasp of ascetic hermits, visionaries who live in the self-sufficient world of spirit. But Emerson hoped to spread his gospel in city and country, and it was to be one not of renunciation, but a curious ironic faith, ironic in the sense of purposeful detachment. Escaping the mere evocation of divine providence, a consolation he himself was tempted by excessively, his strongest form of reassurance was based on the equivocal variety and flux of the real world. The "vision of genius" was to see "polarity as the law of all being."[42] He put it with emphasis in his important essay on "Fate."

> One key, one solution to the mysteries of human condition, one solution to the old knots of fate, freedom, and foreknowledge, exists; the propounding, namely, of the double consciousness.[43]

The key to Emerson's thought in its most daring and creative vein lies in this consideration of the "double consciousness." To put consciousness first, as Emerson did, was to reject the tyranny of the

42. It supports my theme to find in his essay on polarities, "Compensation," that a "democratic" reasoning explores the dualism which "underlies the nature and condition of man." "Nature hates monopolies and exceptions. The waves of the sea do not more speedily seek a level from their loftiest tossing than the varieties of condition tend to equalize themselves. There is always some levelling circumstance that puts down the over-bearing, the strong, the rich, the fortunate, substantially on the same ground with all others" (*Writings*, p. 173).

This dialectic proposes that the world is various but that all things tend toward their unity. But similar things will also tend toward their variety.

43. "Fate," *Works*, 6:47.

actual world, but this was more by far than quietism. It was an argument against "necessity," misinterpreted as it usually is as the force behind whatever happens to have achieved existence. To have too much respect for the given world can make the issue of freedom seem irrelevant, or subordinate, as when the deficiencies or problems of a free society are demonstrated. But in the realm of the double consciousness, measurement of any sort, even judgment, cannot be confined to what is measurable. The dialectic distinguishes between the actual and the possible, the wish and the event, the motive and the act, distinguishes that is, by way of respecting these polarities. "Fate and freedom" were Emerson's terms for that dual dimension of experience. Nature as fate, a mechanism of objects and force, was the most direct threat to the hopes of democracy, as the philosophic and political career of the nineteenth century was to establish. On the other side, equally one-dimensional and distorted, there was the extreme logic of solipsism, a free consciousness self-condemned to isolation and futility. Perhaps Emerson understood there was no way of either reconciling or dismissing these perspectives, and wished only to establish their coexistence. Since his own bias was that of a philosophic idealist, this required some doing, and the difficult exercise is pictured in the image he used to illustrate the "double consciousness."

> A man must ride alternately on the horses of his private and public nature, as the equestrians in the circus throw themselves nimbly from horse to horse.[44]

One does not get intellectual clarity from this so much as a prophetic warning. The modern mind, and modern civilization, suffer these risks—the isolation of private worlds, the aggression of public ideologies and public power. The root of the difficulty, as Emerson thought, was religious or metaphysical, but the stake, the big risks, were in human relationships. The practical experience of democracy made this clear, that is, the kind of democracy which the Americans had established, which proposed a distinction between the private individual and the communal public, and aimed to protect their separate interests. The problem of democracy was how to give fairly proportioned faith to the rights of the one and the many, the part and the whole. These were some of the "old knots," and again the answer may be that they could not be untied, that freedom and order were not terms to be reconciled but rather opposed for the sake of the integrity

44. Ibid., p. 47.

of either term. Indeed this required a revolutionary form of consciousness. Insofar as human relationships were concerned, the double consciousness put men beyond the reach of certainties. But there was still the requirement of confidence and good faith.

> A man who has accustomed himself to look at all circumstances as very mutable, to carry his possessions, his relations to persons, and even his opinions, in his hand, and in all these to pierce to the principle and moral law, and everywhere to find that,—has put himself out of reach of all skepticism.[45]

Nothing less than that was his ambition, to be out of the reach of *all* skepticism, by resort to the highest moral law, which actually was not a law at all but the compulsion to cherish existence and defend it.

> The dread of man and the love of man shall be a wall of defense and a wreath of joy around all.[46]

One contemplates this assertion of the "double consciousness" with respect. Here, beyond both certainty and skepticism, was a moralizing irony, an assenting detachment. It was a sophisticated refuge of freedom and it was a humanism so generous that it transcended all human examples.

> The man has never lived that can feed us ever. The human mind cannot be enshrined in a person who shall set a barrier on any one side of this unbounded, unboundable empire. It is one central fire, which, flaming now out of the lips of Etna, lightens the capes of Sicily, and now out of the throat of Vesuvius, illuminates the towers and vineyards of Naples. It is one light which beams out of a thousand stars. It is one soul which animates all men.[47]

The double consciousness was a human power, but approximating the divine or what men had always considered divine. The power to transcend oneself as well as circumstance, to live in and at the same time beyond life's dimensions, is recognizably Christian and salvationary; but this principle Emerson was determined to use wholly on the human plane, leaving behind the distinctions between the secular and the divine.

In his depressed moments he might have confessed defeat. He reflects this in his essay "The Transcendentalist," as he speaks of the experience of being let down from the height of transcendental insight. "I was at my old tricks, a selfish member of a selfish society. . . . I ask,

---

45. "The Sovereignty of Ethics," *Works*, 10: p. 213.
46. "The American Scholar," *Writings*, p. 63.
47. Ibid., p. 59.

When shall I die and be relieved of the responsibility of seeing a Universe I do not use?"

He admits the fate of living in two worlds.

> The worst feature of this double consciousness is, that the two lives, of the understanding and of the soul, which we lead, really show very little relation to each other; never meet and measure each other: one prevails now, all buzz and din; and the other prevails then, all infinitude and paradise; and, with the progress of life, the two discover no greater disposition to reconcile themselves.[48]

But this incompatibility, perhaps this latent despair, may point to the most rewarding stimulus of his thought. He was determined to "ride alternately on the horses of his private and public nature," and he did. The effect for his modern readers is not to gain "infinitude and paradise," but to sense the utility and the sophistication of his dialectic. The simplest use was to make it possible for him always to give a second judgment of experience if the first did not suit. This moral reserve was a weapon of criticism and a mode of detachment whereby the practical compulsions of the world did not utterly overcome imaginative freedom. In Emerson's deepest meaning, it was a reserve of faith and enthusiasm, a justification of patience, a form of toleration for disillusioning experience.

This was freedom *and* faith, indeed a faith "beyond skepticism," though the skepticism was the guarantee, so to speak, of an exercised freedom. Contradiction, denial, failure, these were in consciousness, as well as the alertness of choice and hope. Emerson searched for the skill of his equestrian in order to survive; knowing him at his best, one feels the exuberance and poise of his mastery. Newton Arvin described this point of balance aptly,

> I have said that his thought—or better his feeling—moves back and forth between a trusting passiveness and an energetic activism; and for the most part this is true. But there are moments in his work when the dichotomy between the passive and active is transcended and what he expresses is a spiritual experience that partakes of both—an experience of such intensity, yet of such calm, that neither of the words, "active" or "passive," quite does justice to it.[49]

When Emerson expresses this particular gift of balance, himself the exponent of the double consciousness, we can understand John

48. "The Transcendentalist," *Writings*, p. 100.

49. Newton Arvin, "The House of Pain," *American Pantheon* (New York: Dell Publishing Co., 1967), p. 37.

Dewey's statement that "when democracy has articulated itself, it will have no difficulty in finding itself already proposed in Emerson." What Dewey meant is clear, I think. Emerson made the road open to the ultimate endowed critic of power and the established world, the enfranchised man. It is *his* consciousness which has been described, for it contains the judgment which respects itself and yet acknowledges the world. The chief thing, Emerson said, in his essay "Compensation," is that "the universe is alive." But immediately following that he asserts, "All things are moral." The present indicative of "All things are moral" is transcendental syntax, but these two appreciations are essential to the practice of freedom. Dewey, who understood him, put it this way,

> To them who refuse to be called "master, master," all magistracies in the end defer, for theirs is the common cause for which dominion, power and principality is put under foot. Before such successes, even the worshipers of that which to-day goes by the name of success, those who bend to millions and incline to imperialisms, may lower their standard, and give at least a passing assent to the final word of Emerson's philosophy, the identity of Being, unqualified and immutable, with Character.[50]

50. Dewey, *Characters and Events*, pp. 76–77.

Emerson said, as though he might be speaking to Thoreau, "Look in thy heart and write," and, "He that writes to himself writes to an eternal public." This assurance endowed them both with the oracular sincerity of egoists speaking to equals. A man communicates to others by discovering himself; by being deeply personal he becomes deeply universal. We admire Thoreau for the coolness with which he dealt with himself and his own experience, without embarrassment or hypocrisy. For us he is the classic poet of individualism, but I wonder if he is yet read with the understanding he will one day have. We know that his text is alive every time we touch it; in its contemporary relevance it burns.

With Thoreau, unlike Emerson, the spiritual mist seems to be absent, and his affirmations are never likely to sound pious. The swift irony of Thoreau's style, the dryness of his responses, his absolute sense of fact, all suggest that this was a man who wrested from his experience a confident sense of reality. His role as a major literary force can best be appreciated in the context of the later writing of Mark Twain, and of Hemingway and his generation. The esthetic rule of his writing could be called most simply the pleasure of truth-telling, and his battle with everything that was gross, superficial, and meretricious marks him out as a significant hero of the modern imagination. The most mistaken prejudgment in reading Thoreau is to expect the pastoral twilight, or to classify him vaguely as one who followed "nature" in search of a better world. This would be unjust to Emerson as well, but in Thoreau we sense a distillation of Emerson's strength.

In *Walden* the search for authentic experience is strong-minded almost to the extreme of monomania. "I went to the woods because I wished . . . to front only the essential facts of life," Thoreau says, and

he was willing to drive to that point past all the barriers of work, pleasure, and habit, past tradition and loyalty, past prestigious reason and
more prestigious faith. For it he was willing to upset and demolish a
whole civilization. The pertinent aspect of his writing is precisely the
challenge to civilization, and *Walden* was his most consistent and fully
developed act of civil disobedience.

We can understand that such motives would be strong in a young
society living close to the unoccupied half of a continent. Thoreau's
generation of Americans still lived in the world of the new, active in
making and doing, beginning and changing, and remembering clearly
the bare problem of survival. In another sense, the obsession with
"the essential facts of life" reflected the poverty of artifacts. Human
institutions had been placed suddenly like toys on the ground of a
wilderness. It would seem easy to get rid of them, or to build new ones
that were shaped roughly and naturally out of the actual landscape.
Forests were going down and fields were being planted in a world recently wild and unpredictable. The cities being built would seem as
impermanent as their progression was swift and their construction
new. Thoreau's work reflects this volatility of both sides of a traditional antagonism. *Walden* means to be persuasive in many ways, but
most deeply it would relieve the dramatic insecurity at the margin
between civilization and the wilderness. When Henry James, in the
significant later example, used Europe to represent an ideal unity of
man and his setting, of living values and actual things, he did so because the problem was his theme and Europe provided the legendary
or real standard. To find the organic unity of civilization and nature
had the urgency of a spiritual crisis for the classic American writers.
Emerson expressed this ordealist view of experience in a moment of
what might be called a frank address to the stimulus of his thought,
and the issue was the same for Melville as well as for Thoreau.

> In the present tendency of our society, in the new importance of the
> individual . . . society is threatened with actual granulation, religious
> as well as political. . . . Of course each poor soul loses all his old stays. . . .
> At first he is forlorn, homeless; but this rude stripping him of all support
> drives him inward, and he finds himself unhurt; he finds himself face to
> face with the majestic Presence, reads the original of the Ten Com-
> mandments, the original of Gospels and Epistles.[1]

Such notes help adjust the view of Emerson and Thoreau as
quietist and complacent in their inwardness. Thoreau in particular

1. Emerson, "Character," *Works*, 10:118–19.

developed the dramatic role of a protagonist in his work, and his mode of operation, differing from Emerson's, was to make the outer world so tangible, so solid in its responsiveness that the central effect of his writing is that of an unassailable health and a truly universal or metaphysical sense of security in the world. His directness, his will to consult the practical immediacy of living, is evident in the first chapter titles, "Economy" and "Where I Lived and What I Lived For." These headlined an effort to distinguish between large and small economic philosophies, comparing costs, work, desires, and real values. Economics was the knowledge of survival in the world, after all, but it was also a study of the way things and utilities were made to conform to needs. "Economy" was thus a way of studying the adaptations made between nature and civilization. Basically, as Thoreau put it, the distinction he searched for and the disjuncture he vividly felt was that between ends and means. He as well as Emerson had the keenest sense of civilization as a complex of beliefs and practices which had lost their enlivening justifications. In the first instance this was a reaction from the moral and spiritual shallowness of their society or, effectively the same thing, from the simpleminded absorption of its citizens in hard work. But their reaction was also a renewed response to the richest memory of the American tradition. An adventurous experiment in a new world renewed all the tests of truth and value. The practical and material curiosity of such a society is easily converted to "transcendental" questioning. On whatever ground of utility, or of moral and spiritual need, it is implicitly forbidden to take any value for granted, particularly since so few escaped earlier challenge by the temperaments of immigration and rebellion.

When Thoreau went to Walden it could be said that he was reenacting the antecedent myth of the new world's discovery. He was also reenacting the heroic model of the Declaration of Independence. (He points out that by accident he established residence on the Fourth of July. We can guess that a subterranean thought must have led to this "accident.") The radical spirit of independence questioned every allegiance to laws and institutions, and by such questioning transformed them all into secondary values. It was an oppressive superstition to regard them as ends rather than means, though that was a mistake to which all societies tended. But the advance into such questioning put the challenge to primary values. Thoreau was an honest rebel. He knew that his every negative provoked the greater need for first beliefs themselves. It was true that most men had let themselves be translated into the shell of social habits and utilities. The burden of proof was to show that real values originated apart from these. It was necessary to invite actual isolation, as Thoreau did, in order to demonstrate this and to renew the clear knowledge of what one "lived for."

Humanistic and democratic ideas in the West had been leading a long time to Thoreau's conclusion that society was only a tool. The historical relevance of his writing is found at his point of start, where he declared that men had become the tools of their tools. From that point he could deal with the reader in a truly adventurous open space of questioned values and rediscovered experiences. His book becomes in that basic sense a definition of the impulse to write literature. It may help us to understand what the forces of genesis were in the great age of nineteenth-century American writing.

Although we accurately think of Thoreau as an acid critic of his society, in retrospect we must recognize him as the spokesman for one of the strongest impulses the American historical experience itself bred. This was a hunger to know life in some absolute and immediate sense, not through intermediaries, not through a sense of the racial destiny or the collective interest, and certainly not through the ambitious postponements expressed by the traditional religion in which salvation arrived in the future after being well earned. Wasn't this immediate demand on life bred into the great Declaration's conjoined goals of life, liberty, and the pursuit of happiness? The American principles could be put this way; one must spend life, not save it as credit for another existence, and one must master one's own life and not surrender it to other masters. But the practices of these principles seemed strangely difficult and contradictory. Many straining individualists found themselves working hard for indefinitely postponed rewards, and many had translated the pursuit of happiness into the pursuit of wealth, a goal which apparently required saving rather than spending for the largest part of their lives.

It was an inspiration of genius that led Thoreau to choose the dominant metaphor of economics for his address to Americans. The most profound question he could ask was the relationship between cost and real values, and he ended his humane lesson in economics by demanding that all men question the cost of a thing by defining it as "the amount of what I call life which is required to be exchanged for it, immediately or in the long run." By his standard a major part of the hard labor of men was a cruel waste. The problem opened up would shock most men at the center of their lives. Thoreau's lesson in actual values would seem a simple one to teach until we remember that the economic system was as much an ethic and guide to behavior as it was a mechanism for distributing goods and work. The market price of things was a collective authority that could replace the old masters of traditional hierarchies. At the same time it seemed as resistant as nature in its immunity from any single man's arbitrary judgment.

However, price and cost were tyrants with the power to punish only so long as men were the victims of their own appetites. How relieving to discover that one could withdraw from low appetites and automatic conformities and be free. The invigorating effect of Thoreau's writing was to make most of the normal anxieties of men seem superficial. If you are near exhaustion, he says, and feel the quiet desperation of your life, it is because you are paying too heavy a price in labor for your life. Drop your burdens and receive your gift, for living only begins when working ends. It is true that most men would have second thoughts when they perceived the singularly ascetic content of that leisure which Thoreau offered. In his clear logic, most expressions of wealth and uses of property were complex ways of satisfying simple appetites, and the men concerned with them had not made much progress beyond the primitive goal of survival.

But that was a kind of ironic exaggeration. His real point and the one with the widest resonance, was a contribution to the critical wisdom of a free society. License, whether in the form of sensual or abstract greed, and liberation, spelled out in terms of a quantitative sum of literal pleasures, degraded the practice of freedom and finally contradicted it. An animal freedom was really its opposite, and it was this thought, not a conventional nineteenth-century moralism, which so thoroughly removed the pagan from Thoreau's spirit. And yet, as though fascinated by danger, he and Emerson advanced into nature to find their justifications. Again the speculation occurs that in their opposition to materialism the Transcendentalists were not searching for God, but trying to save the logic of a free society. If their practice did not lead to mere meditation, it put the emphasis on gratifications of the free mind, or consciousness, a subjective empire of experience which each man could hold, and not on overt and material satisfactions in society's offering. That required the sharp renunciation of the primitive images of freedom in the comprehension of most men.

The shock of Thoreau's words was greater because, as I have

said, they in part rested on the questions his audience had been taught to ask. What *was* making the most of one's life and how much effort was it worth? In the foreground of the commercial democracy this problem seemed for most people to have become forgotten, and yet everything in the social creed demanded an answer. The bitter possibility was that the American was doomed to constructing monuments of futility, more grotesque than the pyramids of the Pharaohs, though, as Thoreau said, "the grandeur of Thebes was a vulgar grandeur." One might speculate that these latter, the Egyptians, understood one thing: that a collective labor should have a collective significance, and that these efforts were linked to destiny (even if it was only the Pharaoh's immortality) or linked to a chain of imagined human interests. But the American seemed condemned to equally strenuous socialized labor which his own language of belief reduced to secondary significance. The individual man, by whom and for whom all values were supposed to be measured, was less and less visible in the growing industrial and agricultural enterprise. Surely these enormous tasks were achieved in the name of collective divinities. But where were they?

The truth was that most Americans were content to live with such contradictions. Many of them were strengthened by Protestant convictions and could be patient with rewards deferred. Their moral compulsions, at the same time, did not welcome the experience of spending rather than saving or of actually *using* their freedom in some immediate and sensuous vitality of living. The American Christian could make the assumption of his freedom and defer his happiness for heaven. But meanwhile both freedom and experience were understood as forms of potency, valued not so much in their use as in their promise. It was therefore natural and easy to create a commercial society. Money was the perfect abstraction for this freedom which was really power. The translation of money into power, the worship of power and the willingness to work for it, supported both the immense collective labor that had to be done as well as the ideal of freedom itself.

The question in the actual world, to anyone with a sensitive moral intelligence, was how wealth and power could be the goals of freedom without denying a realistic understanding of equality as well as the validity of freedom itself for all except a minority. The urgency in the thinking of Emerson and Thoreau is really admirable at that point of contradiction. They recognized that the practice of freedom required the severe examination of values—values to be discriminated from the debasing interests of power and ordinary appetites. The problem in their minds manifested itself in two ways. First, perhaps sensing the need for reassurance, they made the most emphatic claims for individual freedom that America had yet produced. But almost as a consequence, they found it necessary to turn their freedom toward the most quiet and subjectively emphasized experience. What world was there to conquer and enjoy at Walden? A singularly uncompetitive world of universally available sensations and inner visions. It could be contracted even further, as Thoreau said, to the corner of a cell and a glimpse of the blue sky, and its integrity would not be destroyed. Every stroke of his irony is laid against the normal bustle of life, against routine action and routine work. There was the Poet and there was the Farmer, and he knew which one really possessed the Farm. More than Emerson, Thoreau was determined to achieve Emerson's ideal consciousness, where "all mean egotism vanishes. I become a transparent eyeball; I am nothing; I see all."

But consciousness was life; in this state one could sit gloriously on a stump all day. "To be awake is to be alive. I have never yet met a man who was quite awake. How could I have looked him in the face?" Consciousness was blessed when it achieved the pure and immediate sense of being, together with its coordinates, the sense of order and wholeness. It was only a seeming passivity; this experience had the fullness of a complete action, satisfying every motive and every desire.

This stress upon consciousness rather than action as the locus of freedom deserves more attention than it has received from democratic theorists. It is easy to infer escapism and irrelevance for such an "academic" freedom, or an effort to evade the real difficulties of a free society. It is evident that Emerson and Thoreau were better justified in their understanding than that. An emphasis on the transcending mind or spirit could lead to quietism, but on the other hand it pointed accurately to the specific fortress which had to be defended. The man free in his consciousness *and* the expression of his thoughts could not only escape his oppressors with a tangible and independent personality, but he could escape being mastered by the practical concreteness of his own life. Thoreau's clearest image with this meaning was that of the farmer pushing his farm before him on a barrow, "a poor immortal soul . . . well nigh crushed and smothered under its load, creeping down the road of life."

This was an example of being overcome by the pressure of the inherited world, and Thoreau's revulsion from it was as important as his love for an ascertained reality, his need to be able to say throughout his life, "this *is*, and no mistake." Near the end of his life, when he should have been most oppressed by physical existence, Thoreau was most defiant, as he expressed it in a letter to his intellectual confidant, H. G. O. Blake.

> Zouaves?—pish! How you can overrun a country, climb any rampart, and carry any fortress, with an army of *alert* thoughts!—thoughts that send their bullets home to heaven's door,—with which you can *take* the whole world, without paying for it, or robbing anybody. See, the conquering hero comes! You *fail* in your thoughts, or you *prevail* in your thoughts only. Provided you *think* well, the heavens falling, or the earth gaping, will be music for you to march by. No foe can ever see you, or you him; you cannot so much as *think* of him. Swords have no edges, bullets no penetration, for such a contest.[2]

In another letter to an English friend and correspondent he placed a specifically American stress on this relation between freedom and the expansive imagination, deriving both, as Frederick Turner was to do later, from the existence of the open frontier.

> I dwell as much aloof from society as ever. . . . I am still immersed in nature, having much of the time a living sense of the breadth of the field on whose verge I dwell. The *great west* and *north west* stretching on infinitely far and grand and wild, qualifying all our thoughts. That is the only America I know. I prize this western reserve chiefly for its intellectual value. That is the road to new life and freedom,—if ever we are dissatisfied with this and not to exile as in Siberia and knowing this, one need not travel it.[3]

The view here is clear. Freedom properly understood was a spiritual function and conscious state, and only that understanding could give primacy to individual rights. Liberal democracy is founded on the rights of consciousness, and distinguishes itself accordingly from those societies which measure freedom, strangely indeed, by external scales of action and experience, or ignore it because they are in fact measuring something else—the real interests of men or the conditions for satisfying human wants. One can imagine Thoreau's response to that. What were "real" interests anyway, and what could possibly be the conditions for satisfying human wants? We remember how he strove to reduce them to a handful of beans and the shelter of his cabin, and even that was more than enough.

This was "transcendental" but it points, as I've said, to the emphasis on consciousness. I think it suggested the distinctive service of

2. *The Correspondence of Henry David Thoreau*, ed. Walter Harding and Carl Bode (New York: New York University Press, 1958), p. 558.

3. Ibid., p. 436.

the imagination, of free thoughts and speech, to Thoreau's audience in a free society. The question, however, directs itself to the limits of a subjective freedom. It might be put grossly this way: if no one prevents me from suffering, or living a worthless life, am I really free? This at least seems to be the question most often directed today at the open democracies. Their rivals in this respect are the contemporary Marxist states, and if these are not merely cynical in their favoring of the word "democracy," then the distinction between their use and that dominant in the American tradition must be studied. A familiar Marxist position proposes that freedom in society becomes a relevant issue only when a given series of conditions for satisfying human wants are achieved. As Engels put it, men would reach freedom only after the class conflict was finally settled, and society, led by the proletariat, had mastered the means of production and begun to provide abundance.

> Man's own social organization, hitherto confronting him as a necessity imposed by nature and history, now becomes the result of his own free action. The extraneous objective forces that have hitherto governed history pass under the control of man himself. Only from that time will man himself, more and more consciously, make his own history—only from that time will the social causes set in movement by him have, in the main and in a constantly growing measure, the results intended by him. It is the ascent of man from the kingdom of necessity to the kingdom of freedom.[4]

Thoreau paid his respects to "necessity," though he felt men were more troubled by *imagined* necessities. He calculated he could work six weeks of the year to provide his own needs, and so begin his life of freedom without waiting for the majestic series of events that Engels prescribed. The contrast with the views of Emerson and Thoreau is even more precisely expressed in the thinking of a modern Marxist like Herbert Marcuse, who added an authority borrowed from Freud to the scientific history and materialism of Marx and Engels. These authorities, as used by Marcuse, aim for objective sanctions; they *know* what human nature wants and what history makes necessary.

For instance, in arguing for the elimination of false tolerance (a repressive tolerance and false freedom), in liberal societies, Marcuse says this:

> I suggested that the distinction between true and false tolerance, between progress and regression can be made rationally on empirical

4. Friedrich Engels, *Socialism: Utopian and Scientific*, in Karl Marx and Friedrich Engels, *Basic Writings on Politics and Philosophy*, ed. Lewis S. Feuer (Garden City, N.Y.: Doubleday & Co., 1959), p. 109.

grounds. The real possibilities of human freedom are relative to the attainment stage of civilization. They depend on the material and intellectual resources available at the respective stage, and they are quantifiable and calculable to a high degree. . . . In other words it is possible to define the direction in which prevailing institutions, policies, opinions would have to be changed. . . . Consequently, it is also possible to identify policies, opinions, movements which would promote this . . . [change] and those which would do the opposite. Suppression of the regressive ones is a prerequisite for the strengthening of the progressive ones.[5]

Obviously Marcuse has no respect for subjective freedom whatever, since he would always be measuring it in terms of its "real" possibilities. If at any time an opinion or an action failed his measure, which as he says is "quantifiable and calculable to a high degree," it could be suppressed. An American Transcendentalist would have been horrified by this for many reasons, but dominantly I think for the violence it does to personal and intuitional judgment and the rights of consciousness. In the same essay, Marcuse attacks the tolerance which allows men to mistake their own interests and thereby construct a "false consciousness."

The conditions under which tolerance can again become a liberating and humanizing force have still to be created. When tolerance mainly serves the protection and preservation of a repressive society, when it serves to neutralize opposition and to render men immune against other and better forms of life, then tolerance has been perverted. And when this perversion starts in the mind of the individual, in his consciousness, his needs, when heteronomous interests occupy him before he can experience his servitude, then the efforts to counteract his dehumanization must begin at the place of entrance, there where the false consciousness takes form (or rather: is systematically formed)—it must begin with stopping the words and images which feed this consciousness.[6]

The contrast with Thoreau becomes particularly interesting, founded though it is on such a gap in time and in philosophic assumptions. Thoreau, too, did not wish to be tolerant of oppression, as witness his response to the slavery issue and the approaching Civil War. Nor did he have any scruple against revolutions.

All men recognize the right of revolution; that is, the right to refuse allegiance to, and to resist, the government, when its tyranny or its inefficiency are great and unendurable.[7]

5. "Repressive Tolerance," in Robert Paul Wolff, Barrington Moore, Jr., and Herbert Marcuse, *A Critique of Pure Tolerance* (Boston: Beacon Press, 1965), pp. 105–6.
6. Ibid., p. 111.
7. *Walden and Civil Disobedience*, ed. Sherman Paul (Boston: Houghton Mifflin, 1957), p. 238.

Probably today he would be as militant and impatient as he was with the American democracy of 1846. Nevertheless, he would find Marcuse's doctrine foreign and totally unacceptable, particularly for the calculated effort to "feed consciousness" in the supply and restraint of words and images. Determined as he was to keep his own mind free from the burden of conditions and necessities, he would hardly welcome an invasion in that sacred sphere by another consciousness, collective or otherwise. His hyperbole becomes strongest on behalf of his private, untouchable freedom, as when he remarks in *Walden* that a box not much larger than a coffin could be his home.

> I used to see a large box by the railroad, six feet long by three wide, in which the laborers locked up their tools at night; and it suggested to me that every man who was hard pushed might get such a one for a dollar, and, having bored a few auger holes in it, to admit the air at least, get into it when it rained and at night, and hook down the lid, and so have freedom in his love, and in his soul be free.[8]

The distinction that is important rests on the will to be free in the soul, an archaic word that still expresses better than any other the immunities and rights of the personality. In its place Marcuse uses language like "vital needs," "material and intellectual resources," and "better forms of life," which, he says, can be authoritatively defined. So, accordingly, can a "true" consciousness. But the rights of consciousness in Emerson's and Thoreau's radical view meant precisely that consciousness defined itself, and that consciousness was free because, and only because, no one else prescribed for it. There was substance in it, of course, products of teaching, example, persuasion, but these were subordinate to the final opportunity to say no or yes in the self-determination of consciousness. The possibility of being deluded had nothing to do with that, though as Emerson and Thoreau firmly said, the most certainly false consciousness was the one borrowed from others. If this is what tolerance or freedom meant, it required a barrier against all substantives which represent the good life or the happy man. Thoreau and Emerson had more than a means of resistance; they could escape into their own intuitions and transcendental inspirations. But is there as good an escape for others from Marcuse's advancing "quantifiables and calculables"? The question is most pertinent to the practice of democracy and suggests the value of rereading these older prophets.

In any case, analogies can be useful. The belief in a transcendental subjectivity points to what we may call a transcendental politics.

8. Ibid., p. 19.

This bars the state or community from acting as if its acts were inclusive, or as if there were a calculable general interest that could subsume individual lives. It forbids the assumption that a causal series in events can restrict the future, or that anywhere, at any time, consciousness can be fully rendered in behavior. Engels said something different: "the final causes of all social changes and political revolutions are to be sought not in men's brains, not in man's better insight into eternal truth and justice, but in changes in the modes of production and exchange." In the political sense this is explicitly what is meant by "materialism." But what the Marxist materialists intended was to put hope, or the apocalyptic emotions of revolution, into synthesis with the necessity in events, the laws of history. Hope thereby became absolute, irrefutable. The source was still romanticism, no doubt, but the romantic idealists were led in a different direction. In their political disillusionment, they transferred the theme of revolution from "the social to the mental world." That was the thesis of M. H. Abrams, and Northrop Frye, in the same discussion, added, "Such a feat was not a neurotic subjective substitute for revolution, but the articulating of a new kind of imaginative power."[9] The subject is most important and needs to be taken further. Romanticism in America found a context where that imaginative power seemed to have rich applications. The American Transcendentalists were devoted to it, but beyond the inspired moments of poetry; Thoreau was perhaps the most earnest of them all, in wishing only to live with the imagination in the daily world.

Alive as he was to the world, Thoreau maintained precedence for his interior mind. To *know* that the road to a new life was open was more important than traveling it. The curiosity of the reader bears upon this way of knowing. Rightly affirmed, it was not a lazy entertainment of fantasies, nor was it substantially mysticism. As a free consciousness it was first of all the positive experience of feeling open to the world, and perhaps the word that came closest to expressing it for Thoreau was "innocence." His daily ritual at the pond, his morning bath in its purifying waters, signified his effort to achieve "equal innocence with Nature herself." The word "innocence" for Thoreau was equivalent to religious grace, though it was the kind of grace present at the beginning of things rather than the end, a sharp and important distinction. "One world at a time," Thoreau is supposed to have said

9. Frye, *Romanticism Reconsidered*, pp. vi–vii.

on his deathbed, and the words remind us that his interest was reserved for the day of his birth, which he wished to celebrate all his life. To be innocent or in grace is to have gotten beyond all antitheses, whether between nature and man, body and mind, appearance and reality, ends and means. However, to sanctify man at his birth is a democratic preference, for thereby his rights and his justification in the eyes of others are absolute; they are moral finalities as well as starting points.

Innocence for Thoreau was the morning feeling when the power of living is undisappointed and unfrustrated, when desires and immediate experience are not distracted by foreboding, or bad memories, or self-doubt. Innocence meant an unspoiled readiness for life, and the faith in it, one could guess, gave necessary energy for the life of freedom. Could a democracy believe in itself without that belief in human innocence? This question remains the dramatic theme for understanding Thoreau and his contemporaries.

It was necessary to justify freedom against its destructive possibilities by a kind of immunity in the great system of things. Apart from idealist and pantheist postulates, that immunity from harm establishes itself by an injunction to love nature, knowing that one was loved by it in turn. Isn't all of *Walden* an example of personal freedom exercising itself in the harmonies of a great love? Not to be sure, in the love of men, for that was a kind of superficial manifestation, but in the deeper love of being itself. Thoreau's narration of his day's routine, his observations of nature, persistently seek to define an intimacy which is warm and protecting. At times his actions at the side of the pond and on its surface suggest the relationship of mother and child. The rise and fall of the pond was like breathing and "the heaving of its breast"; the pond has a mysterious equilibrium, always returning to tranquility after a jarring movement. That the pool is fed by an unknown source, that its waters nourish life in drinking as well as in the purification of bathing, are points that are suggestive enough. Resting, burrowing, feeding by his pond's side, plumbing its depth, he found a complete emotional and physical shelter, and that comfort in his natural home is the context of his claim for perfect independence.

One can refuse the governance of his fellow men and a dependence on them, if a deeper dependency is allowed and a deeper security guaranteed. For Thoreau every step away from involvement in society was a step toward affirming the natural community. This meant in effect that he was not rejecting but affirming the deepest community of men. If he withdrew to what we call isolation, it was because the community he knew was not community enough. There is indeed no question that the greatest threat to Thoreau's balanced wisdom, or his moral stability, came from his own misanthropic tendencies. How close these were to the surface is expressed I think in the vindictive edge to his essay "Civil Disobedience," and in some of his journal notes on the John Brown episode. The untypical violence of his excoriation of the man who dared to give his name to Flint's Pond strikes the note of what is the strongest revulsion in his experience.

> What right had the unclean and stupid farmer, whose farm abutted on this sky water, whose shores he has ruthlessly laid bare, to give his name to it? Some skin-flint, who loved better the reflecting surface of a dollar, or a bright cent, in which he could see his own brazen face; who regarded even the wild ducks which settled in it as trespassers; his fingers grown into crooked and horny talons from the long habit of grasping harpy-like. . . . I go not there to see him nor to hear of him; who never *saw* it . . . who never spoke a good word for it, nor thanked God that he had made it. Rather let it be named from the fishes that swim in it.[10]

But Thoreau didn't know this man, and his real offense was to affront the dignity of nature by "giving his name to it."

Much of what Thoreau says in this vein is a kind of astringent dose against democratic sentiment and a part of the larger effort to achieve a moral cleansing for himself and the members of his society. Like Emerson, Thoreau's confident idealism made him an ambiguous democrat. Neither one of them was eager to rule the state, but where it was instanced that righteousness did not govern it, they were not willing to reconcile themselves with the fact that it was the majority who ruled.

> But a government in which the majority rule in all cases cannot be based on justice, even as far as men understand it. Can there not be a government in which majorities do not virtually decide right and wrong, but conscience?[11]

In the passages of his journal which reflect Thoreau's embittered reactions to the hanging of John Brown, he pits that martyr of conscience against the "mass of men."

> Of course the mass of men, even the well-disposed but sluggish souls . . . cannot conceive of a man who is actuated by higher motives than they are. . . . He could not have been tried by a jury of his peers, because his peers did not exist.[12]

10. *Walden and Civil Disobedience*, p. 135.
11. Ibid., p. 236.　　　　　　　　12. *The Journal*, 12:409, 408.

Walden sufficiently indicates that Thoreau had a strong distaste for the collectivity of *men*, but that only pushed him further toward the magnification of *man*. Melville confessed the same divided feelings, but was explicit in refusing to call it an inconsistency. After all, the institutions of the American democracy admitted an implicit distrust of the "people," and this, when understood or balanced in the right perspective, a Thoreauvian perspective of individuals rather than elites, was simply the check and balance that this democracy demanded of itself.

It still must be said that Thoreau himself, insofar as his political attitudes converged in "Civil Disobedience," was decidedly not hospitable to the alternative demand made upon individuals. Since the individual conscience was absolute for Thoreau, it demanded absolute expression; his thinking took shape at the margin where radical individualism departed from an amenable relationship with collective action. The only sanction, as he saw it, for the rule of the majority was that it was "physically the strongest." Voting seemed an inadequate mode of expression for the aroused conscience. "Even voting *for the right* is *doing* nothing for it. It is only expressing to men feebly your desire that it should prevail." The forthrightness with which he expressed his ethical judgments has obscured the untenable basis of his politics, if the latter is defined as the mode by which individual ethical judgments communicate and agree for action. As George Kennan recently remarked, in discussing the strangely exact parallels between Thoreau's thinking and that of some elements of the contemporary "New Left," he left no provision for questioning the correctness of his own judgments; once they were formed he expected government to share and enact them, or else he withdrew his allegiance. As Kennan observed, "his essay, far from solving, never even faced the question of whose view was to prevail when the dictates of conscience conflicted as between one individual or another, between one minority or another, or between the conscience of an individual and the collective conscience of men charged with the responsibilities of government.[13]

It is true that Thoreau concerned himself with this problem even less than Emerson. Conscience, if it were the right conscience, would take care of itself, preferably by way of emancipating itself from the state. It is a natural development for passionate moralists in a democracy to become anarchists. Freedom, functioning under the ethical

13. George F. Kennan, *Democracy and the Student Left* (Boston: Little, Brown and Company, 1968), pp. 185–87.

imperative, seems to lead that way if the ethical sanction is really forceful. Here, in a contrast with Thoreau, the preoccupations of Hawthorne and Melville take on their deepest significance. They charged themselves, it may be said, with the clarification and refinement of the collective conscience, searching out the point where specific (and individual) judgments of right and wrong were superseded by a higher imperative. This acts on the tragic ground and invokes Hawthorne's familiar term, a "sympathy" which functions beyond the limits of ethical commitments and is the counterweight for ethical arrogance, a charge to which Thoreau made himself highly vulnerable. In this exact connection, I refer the reader to my discussion of *Billy Budd* (chapter 6 below) as it relates to the problem of "forgiving" the official act of the state while recognizing a transcendent value beyond its dealing.

It would be too much to suggest that Thoreau opened up a problem that Melville and Hawthorne proceeded to solve. However, the widened issues they shared become visible in Thoreau's writing, expressing the conflicts of conscience in a democratic society. Emerson himself knew them and had his own forms of compensation, preaching "patience" to conscientious individualists: "if the single man plant himself indomitably on his instincts and there abide, the huge world will come round to him." This was his pervasive tone, expressing a faith he was determined would survive "beyond skepticism."

One might be led to say of Thoreau that he was morally impatient, probably not a democrat, and less of a humanist than any of his contemporaries. That he was aware of a problem is expressed in a journal entry which was very likely influenced by his estrangement from Emerson.

> If I am too cold for human friendship, I trust I shall not soon be too cold for natural influences. It appears to be a law that you cannot have a deep sympathy with both man and nature. Those qualities which bring you near to the one estrange you from the other.[14]

This was a real danger, and Thoreau knew clearly not just the moral threat but what we can call the existential threat of human disaffection.

> I know of no redeeming qualities in me but a sincere love for some things, and when I am reproved I have to fall back on to this ground. This is my argument in reserve for all cases. My love is invulnerable. Meet me on that ground, and you will find me strong. When I am condemned, and

14. *The Journal*, 3:400.

condemn myself utterly, I think straightway "But I rely on my love for some things." Therein I am whole and entire. Therein I am God-propped.[15]

The important question is whether Thoreau made a distinction among "some things" he loved between the things of nature and the things which belong to man, and the answer is of course that he did not. He made the point himself in a letter to a correspondent.

> But I forget that you think more of this human nature than of this nature I praise. Why won't you believe that mine is more human than any single man or woman can be?[16]

Walden would be a clearer text for many readers if they were forewarned in this way that Thoreau's nature is nature "humanized" in the deepest sense possible. In a journal entry made later in the same year that he doubted his capacity to have sympathy for both man *and* nature, he answered himself clearly.

> Nature must be viewed humanly to be viewed at all; that is, her scenes must be associated with humane affections, such as are associated with one's native place, for instance. She is most significant to a lover. A lover of Nature is preeminently a lover of man. If I have no friend, what is Nature to me? She ceases to be morally significant.[17]

In this way, reading Thoreau we maneuver among paradoxes; in nature he found humanity, and by withdrawing from formal society he found a true community. Similarly he seemed to assert that by testing the deepest experience, he purified himself and restored innocence. Perhaps this was his greatest paradox, the proof that innocence was *in* experience, not something preceding it or following it or in contrast to it. To be innocent was to be immersed in reality as fully as Thoreau submerged himself in his morning bath. Nothing, except consciousness, is given reverence in *Walden* so much as fact, the categorical proofs of actual things in actual experience. If a spiritual assent is found in the woods, it is luminous only in proportion to its concrete manifestations.

Here was an idea of innocence that did not deny experience but welcomed it. Most warm, most vital in this thought is the preaching of a baptism in life itself. *Be present*, Thoreau said, at the rising of the sun, and meant that this would replace concern for the cause of its rising, or any other anxiety. "To improve the nick of time . . . to stand

15. Ibid., 1: p. 296.

16. *The Correspondence*, p. 45.   17. *The Journal*, 4:163.

on the meeting of two eternities, the past and the future, which is precisely the present. . . ." To leave past and future and win a victory over the present was a rare liberation. Such a moment of experience was the life deferred by a thousand modes of indirection. All the ways in which the belief in freedom heightens only anxiety, the ways in which happiness is merely the pursuit of happiness, a matter of fantasy and hopes deferred, are dismissed at one stroke.

This was a remedy for the neurosis of freedom, but also a direct attack on the time abstractions of social man. It was a "declaration of independence" from the hierarchies of cause and effect, purpose and function, the distribution of satisfactions according to work, talent, virtue, wealth, and rank, all of which were demands that troubled both the assurance of happiness and the assurance of human equality. A free society, in its most unsettling implications, placed a guarantee upon the intrinsic value of experience as well as each man's right to it. Men were expected to take full possession of their experience, despite the instability of their own sensations and the insatiability of the imagination. Would they be more gratified than frightened when it was announced that the moment had arrived? Too much was at stake, and rather than risk confrontation one might prefer the long postponement of a life's labor.

Americans could welcome a victory over experience because so much had been promised on its behalf. But would they take it on Thoreau's strange terms? For them mastery over experience would be more plausibly a matter of power over circumstances, over things, over other men. How puzzled his contemporaries must have been, if they read him, by Thoreau's double charge to master experience and at the same time give up the search for power and wealth. When Thoreau said reduce your wants rather than expand your strength to satisfy wants, he probably lost the major part of his audience. And yet much more keenly than they he wanted a victory of the personality over its own place and time in the world. By his own special means Thoreau was as much a champion of self-assertion as Captain Ahab. But probably because he felt the same threats, whether from himself, or the same phenomenal ultimate frustration which the white whale represented, his means, like those of Emerson, were a reductive strategy, to see, to touch, to think what was close—to centralize vision and master life in the full consciousness. Thoreau's writing exhibits its tension, its dark and light shading, when we understand the revulsion from self-aggrandizement which is fused with his celebration of independence. Loving freedom, he attacked the jostling pursuit of power and property, for how could this lead to anything but an unequal division of freedom? It was necessary to show by his life that a man could be a "failure" and be thereby a great individualist, freer and more independent than those who sought "success."

It is easier to see in this light that Thoreau was administering moral correctives to the practice of democracy. His method was to deal with extreme alternatives by the manipulation of paradox, to face contradictions directly by a mode of insight which is curiously close to irony and yet keeps its moral earnestness. All of *Walden* is a moral exercise of that sort; it is first a demonstration of how to pursue selfhood without engaging in the sordid competition for power. It is again a lesson in how to choose a reality of one's own, or how to accept the centrality of the self, without proposing continuous battle in the world. *Walden* affirms, it is *my* existence which is divine, not yours which I borrowed. This is an extreme assertion because the alternative in a democratic society was extreme, the acceptance of the abstract identity offered by institutions and crowds.

The presence of such contradictions in the world Thoreau knew determines the dominant tone of his writing. It is dry, acerbic, and calmly observant. It is not the tone of a man in an enthusiastic mood, but one educated beyond it and, furthermore, educated beyond his own skepticism, to another stage of sober belief. The cutting edge of Thoreau's style is his pervasive irony. This is intrinsic, an attribute of his actual belief and thought. The startling dual effect of Thoreau's system of values is to put the point of view alternately between self-inflation and its opposite. There is a kind of accordion effect between expansion and reduction as this protagonist considers himself in the universe. Perhaps the first view is necessarily reductive as in the caricature of vain pretensions transcribed in the first chapter of *Walden*. The analogy with the primitive seeking shelter in his cave and clothing himself with animal skins is wholesome. But then the view becomes so wide, taking in all civilized history and everything in nature, that the effect of this distance is both deeply reassuring and at the same time almost disinterested in its detachment. The imagination is one great weapon as Thoreau becomes his own hero, commanding space and time, and giving himself the largest landscape in which to see himself. But his second and his greatest weapon is the local sense of his own being, which becomes the anchor point of the wide, pluralist, uncatalogued world.

Let us settle ourselves, and work and wedge our feet downward through the mud and slush of opinion, and prejudice, and tradition, and delusion, and appearance, that alluvion which covers the globe, through Paris and London, through New York and Boston and Concord, through church and state, through poetry and philosophy and religion, till we come to a hard bottom and rocks in place, which we can call *reality*, and say, This is, and no mistake; and then begin . . .[18]

This magnificent declaration of purpose affirms that the world is large and contains many things, and that everywhere there is a thick crust of externals to preoccupy men, whether for good or evil, truth or mistake. It also affirms that the world is centered in one consciousness, and though multiplied by millions, that each is a "reality" and that each has the same right to the absolute possession of itself.

In other words there is as much humility as there is arrogance in Thoreau's examination of his life. It would be more accurate to say that he leaves both of these terms in their ordinary implications. Walden was a small place and Thoreau knew it; he did not intend or expect that it would become a place of pilgrimage. And yet he had no false humility because he meant, within the area he could easily enclose, to make an objective and detailed consideration of all that the world contains. His life at the pond was founded on a determination to share the world with equals, much as Whitman voiced this in his "Song of Myself." His experience was based on a moral warning to himself to refuse to carry more than he could bear, to refuse to swallow more than he could digest. Thoreau's form of intense self-assertion is simultaneously a doctrine of live and let live. In this respect he has the great advantage, like Emerson, of his philosophic idealism, which told him that the small space and power allotted to one man was infinite. Without encroaching on others it yet included all others.

There is pathos in this, as well as noble aspiration, those characteristic effects of democratic thought which arise from the determination to give one man his right to life, and yet prove that in taking full possession according to his own desires, he shares a world in common with many others. The first person in *Walden* has a kind of forceful idiosyncrasy of character that is unmistakable, and yet at the same time the Thoreauvian "I," much like Whitman's, is a literary and moral term which contains a magnified "We," representing mankind. This is a large symbolic identity, like a god's, which gives every ego particle its release from anonymity and isolation. Democratic thought

18. *Walden and Civil Disobedience*, p. 67.

in this way fights to maintain its balance and avoid implicit contradiction. It would like to destroy pretensions to dominance, and at the same time it would lift up all the small and insignificant selves of an egalitarian society to an absolute affirmation of their importance.

Such efforts to propound a synthesis of conflicting values could be bathetic or heavily casuistical. The remarkable effect of the Concord writers is their lightness of touch on this theme. How brightly ironic and gay is Thoreau's manner as he approaches the possible charge of self-love. A letter to one of his more intimate intellectual correspondents is particularly charming.

> Your words make me think of a man of my acquaintance whom I occasionally meet, whom you too appear to have met, one Myself, as he is called. Yet why not call him *Your*-self? If you have met with him & know him it is all I have done, and surely where there is a mutual acquaintance the my & thy make a distinction without a difference.[19]

But the deeper, more passionate sense of what was at stake is expressed in this passage from the journal.

> May I treat myself tenderly as I would treat the most innocent child whom I love; may I treat children and my friends as my newly discovered self. Let me forever go in search of myself; never for a moment think that I have found myself; be as a stranger to myself, never a familiar, seeking acquaintance still. May I be to myself as one is to me whom I love, a dear and cherished object. . . . As I regard myself, so I am. O my dear friends, I have not forgotten you. I will know you tomorrow. I associate you with my ideal self. . . . I love and worship myself with a love which absorbs my love for the world.[20]

"My love for the world," and the words "O my dear friends I have not forgotten you," could be footnote and parentheses through all the pages of *Walden*. In such respects the work of Thoreau was a democratic therapy as well as inspiration. The psychological strains of individual freedom required a source of strength, but this had to be an expansive strength which made no exclusions and yet still brought its focus on the protagonist self. In the largest range possible, Emerson and Thoreau based their affirmations on the system of nature, but it is quite evident how much these ideas were meant to support a religion of man. They drew the radii of the great circles of nature from the center of the single man. The movement of their affirmations is constantly outward from that center, and this principle dictates the law of their writing, the movement from a fact, a local experience, a per-

19. *The Correspondence*, p. 299.   20. *The Journal*, 2:314–15.

son, to a universalized meaning. If Thoreau himself roots downward in a single place, the things of his imagination travel widely, like the wavelets produced in the pond by a dropped stone.

This effect of radiated meanings is associated with organicism and symbolism, literary modes brought to marked development in the writing of Thoreau, Emerson, and Melville, and they seem accordingly characteristic ways of thinking in the literature of a democracy. The mode of symbolism suggests that everything is both itself and something larger, both concrete and an expansive essence. If the single man represented only himself, there could be no moral democracy, only the alternatives of anarchy or a mechanical gathering together in numbers. But as a man is both himself and symbolically every man, he can link himself with all men without losing his own completeness and independence. As Emerson said, facts (and men too) are the symbols of spirit, but they are in his sense symbols only because they partake of the common essence. This sort of symbolism is the expression of moral affinities and a moral communication.

We are dealing here with a profound unity of style and meaning, one that is rare in literary history for its clarity of implication. F. O. Matthiessen and Charles Feidelson have made powerful contributions to this topic, and examples are familiar in most readers' memories. But Thoreau's own quick and spontaneous manner is distinctive; his language marks a rhythm that moves from local observations to general insight, but in a way that seems truly unselfconscious, an organic but natural synthesis of his experience.

> We might try our lives by a thousand simple tests; as, for instance, that the same sun which ripens my beans illumines at once a system of earths like ours. If I had remembered this it would have prevented some mistakes. This was not the light in which I hoed them. The stars are the apexes of what wonderful triangles! What distant and different beings in the various mansions of the universe are contemplating the same one at the same moment! Nature and human life are as various as our several constitutions. Who shall say what prospect life offers to another? Could a greater miracle take place than for us to look through each other's eyes for an instant? We should live in all the ages of the world in an hour; ay, in all the worlds of the ages. History, Poetry, Mythology!—I know of no reading of another's experience so startling and informing as this would be.[21]

The passage ends strongly on behalf of its miracle, "to look through each other's eyes for an instant." The "various mansions of the uni-

21. *Walden and Civil Disobedience*, p. 6.

verse" have concentrated themselves in the immediate sensibility, and it is shared, one might say, between neighbors.

This is Thoreau's expression of the impulse of symbolistic writing in the American nineteenth century, a style of close communication and expansive reference, a mode of clothing abstractions and sublimating particulars. As I've remarked, it was a way of thought, perhaps the only viable one, to address to the problems of democracy. One could count, for instance, the contrasting intellectual bypaths and traps; these were the mechanical reasoning of interests or utilities, the abstractions of bureaucracy or convention, the dogmatics of partisanship, the libertarianism which drifted toward anarchy, the obscurantism of public opinion. To think symbolically, for Thoreau or Emerson, was to express relativity of vision even while concentrating on particulars. It served to raise consciousness from too much concentration on the here and now, or the grubbing, competitive self. It was a constant reminder that there are other earths under the sun and "distant and different beings." And yet a symbol could not be a general truth raised to monopolistic power, degrading itself, so to speak, as allegory. The high purpose was to develop the talent of the double consciousness, a quickness of spirit which avoided emotional and conceptual rigidities.

Addressing themselves with a spirit of reconciliation to the good relationships between the one and the many, the universe and its parts, Emerson and Thoreau translated symbolism into transcendentalism. But they were probably forced into too high a flight for their contemporaries in the busy and concrete world. All activist experience seemed to oppose the equality and unity of men, and more certainly the natural harmony of their lives in freedom. Experience would show that if men were equal at all, or if they were free in an unconditioned sense, or if they were at one with each other, it must be by way of some supramundane insight. Like priestly comforters, Thoreau and Emerson had to postulate a better world, though they put it into a higher consciousness which accompanied action in the real world and transcended its limitations. Was this private ritual of affirmations more irrational than other religions? Much less so really, because there was so little that was arbitrary in the definition of that reserved place for an intelligent and free consciousness. It was not meant as a paradisal retreat or a chance to ignore difficulty, but as an accompanying insight, a form of judgment which resembled ironic detachment, but without negative qualities, which affirmed rather than denied. Perhaps in the end it was simply the power of the imagination, a moral power which contemplated the largest circle of events and forbade an obsessive attention to partial truths. This power of the imagination we might call a rich capacity for tolerance or, to put it somewhat differently, a refusal to distort moral judgment by local and immediate interests or the more dangerous general aspirations which pretended to be absolutes. If they had lived longer, through their century and into the twentieth, they might have observed that ordinary ideologies were at fault. Moral, religious, or political, these were neither expansive enough in their universality, nor direct enough in their immediate revelations to deserve respect. Rational systems, political dogmas, always had this flaw. They could never include the whole truth of the world and they always abused the particulars of actual experience.

The moral imagination appropriate for a democracy transcended the limits of doctrine, and yet, and this was the genius of the Concord moralists, it enforced a return from the higher levels of vision. No principle could satisfy either Emerson or Thoreau if they could not find it expressed by "reality," and they knew what they meant by that word. It was democracy which sharpened the distinction between a law and life, between the state and individuals, between a dogma and an experienced truth. The suffrage suggested that important revelations were found in the sensibility of individuals. To have faith in individuals was to have faith in the real fragments of truth, and to have faith in natural reality was to have faith in individuals. To muster men at the ballot box was like mustering the particular facts for a system of knowledge. All of these particulars, the evidences of personal being, must be used to warrant the truth, and no principle, no idea, philosophically enticing as it might be, could be allowed to leave behind the sacred immediacy of personal experience and the sacred right to personal assent. It is an injustice, finally, to stress the transcendental enthusiasm of Emerson and particularly of Thoreau, for they were the champions of the existent world. Poet-citizens par excellence, they felt that all judgment flowed from immanent experience, and their injunction to readers has always been to inhabit the real world.

4/ Cooper, Poe, and D. H. Lawrence
The Myth of America

"Henceforth Be Masterless"

I have given much emphasis to one foreign observer's insights in proposing the themes for discussion in this book. Tocqueville has long renewed his vitality to generations of students, but a companion, in his capacity for suggestive excitement, arrived with the contrasting mind and temperament of D. H. Lawrence. Both of these men had just the right distance or distrust, combined with exceptional intelligence, to evaluate democratic culture with perceptions that read like prophecy. In the case of Lawrence, one must move beyond his prejudices, his sometimes eccentric and shallow judgments, as expressed in his comments on Hawthorne, for instance, in order to appreciate the remarkable achievement of his *Studies in Classic American Literature*.

The power of a critic like Lawrence comes precisely from the will to indulge both his prejudices and his sympathetic obsessions. As illustration, one of the most enriched endowments of criticism in literary history was manifested in D. H. Lawrence's chapters on Fenimore Cooper. To read these is to see Cooper magnified and transcending his faults. One cannot dispute the sense of a created myth in Cooper's fiction, apt and complete for American experience, but it is also difficult to deny the effect of a badly told myth, strong and suggestive in its outlines, but unenlivened by gifted invention or refinements of thought. We read as if subjected to one more session with the old tribal storyteller, expecting no new excitements and drawing pleasure from the cumbersome narrative because the awkwardness itself suggests the aboriginal source of myth.

What needs most to be noted was made vibrant in Lawrence's

reading, which brings Cooper marvelously to life. For Americans neither Poe nor Cooper are quite our own; there is something missing, as if they were translated writers, produced originally in another language. Appropriately, they both have found their best audiences abroad. But Lawrence makes us see how American they are, particularly Cooper, who stands at the center of Lawrence's serious thesis on American culture and literature. In his essay on Cooper's Leatherstocking novels, Lawrence writes a capsule history of America which goes as follows:

> Now the essential history of the people of the United States seems to me just this: At the Renaissance the old consciousness was becoming a little tight. Europe sloughed her last skin, and started a new, final phase.
> But some Europeans recoiled from the last final phase. They wouldn't enter the *cul de sac* of post-Renaissance, "liberal" Europe. They came to America.
> They came to America for two reasons:
> 1. To slough the old European consciousness completely.
> 2. To grow a new skin underneath, a new form. This second is a hidden process.
> The two processes go on, of course, simultaneously. The slow forming of the new skin underneath is the slow sloughing of the old skin. And sometimes this immortal serpent feels very happy, feeling a new golden glow of a strangely-patterned skin envelop him: and sometimes he feels very sick, as if his very entrails were being torn out of him, as he wrenches once more at his old skin, to get out of it. . . .
> So there he is, a torn, divided monster.[1]

By virtue of Lawrence's own revolutionary naturalism he was predictably sensitive to this "myth of America," as he called it. The old skin of European civilization was dramatically cast off, and here, enviably, was the great chance for a new birth of life, drawing only from life sources. It was not pagan utopia, or a success which interested Lawrence, but the agony of the change, and the conflictive life of the "torn, divided monster." America was an unresolved battle between nature and culture, and salvation was far off. The drama was best proposed, in Cooper, as the war between the red man and the white man, a war without appeasement or mercy. And if the Indians were now dead, they still act as unappeased ghosts within the "under conscious soul of the white American, causing the great American grouch, the Orestes-like frenzy of restlessness in the Yankee soul, the inner malaise which amounts almost to madness, sometimes."[2] This is not

---

1. *Studies in Classic American Literature*, pp. 76.
2. Ibid., p. 51.

a simpleminded or humanitarian guilt, in Lawrence's view. It is the ambivalent torn life of civilization itself which hates and would extirpate the natural creature. Cooper was important to Lawrence because Cooper "presented the Red Man to the white man," in the form to be sure of fairy tale and wish fulfillment, but nevertheless in a pattern which drew on historic truth.

The discovery of the "Red Man," that is, the discovery of the aboriginal world of America, was for Lawrence an historic event that dramatized his own sense of the ageless problem of culture. The problem was chiefly that of the white man, as Lawrence saw it, because it was in his soul that the war took place, a war featured by extreme ambivalence—"the desire to extirpate the Indian. And the contradictory desire to glorify him." For accepting this contradiction in his work, or rather for revealing it so clearly, Cooper was a remarkably apt figure to illustrate Lawrence's theme. He pictured him in "the Louis Quatorze" hotel in Paris, fascinated and pleased to associate with counts, cardinals, and English lords as *le grand écrivain Américain*. This was one dream of his life. The other was back home with Chingachgook and Natty Bumppo. Opposing each other, both visions exaggerated their dreamlike features. Impatient as Lawrence was with the genteel nostalgia covering Cooper's vision of the American woods, he did see in it "a kind of yearning myth," a prophetic half-truth announcing what had yet to be revealed. Lawrence's sense of Cooper's limitations is valid enough but his own expansion on the theme brings the actual myth involved beyond that of Natty Bumppo and Chingachgook in the American forest, to absorb the larger story Cooper actually told. This included the overcivilized Temples and the Effinghams, and in his own life included Mrs. Cooper, "a straight strong pillar of society, to hang on to," and "the culture of France to turn back to." The myth opposed culture, or "Europe," to the woods back home, and these terms played the functions of "yearning" imagination and disillusioning reality. But it didn't matter how these functions were assigned, for the myth was ambivalent and such roles were exchanged. As Lawrence put it, "if Cooper had had to spend his whole life in the backwoods, side by side with a Noble Red Brother, he would have screamed with the oppression of suffocation."[3] The implications open up accordingly and the myth that Lawrence reads from Cooper's work becomes a shared creation, an effort as it were on Lawrence's part to complete

3. Ibid., p. 75.

what was begun in Cooper, as if Lawrence himself were equipped to write America's epic story.

> The white man's spirit can never become as the red man's spirit. It doesn't want to. But it can cease to be the opposite and the negative of the red man's spirit. It can open out a new great area of consciousness, in which there is room for the red spirit too.[4]

Here Lawrence catches the largest perspective of his view of historic American culture, divided monster that it was. The striving for a new inclusive consciousness was compelled by severe contradictions in experience; this is the useful understanding of what is implicit in the American classics, which in every chapter of Lawrence's book he begins by patronizing and ends by respecting. In the primary aspect the new consciousness had to bridge again for mankind the chasm between civilization and nature. If Milord in Paris was an empty puppet of the imagination, the woods back home were strange and antagonistic.

> The American landscape has never been at one with the white man. Never. And white men have probably never felt so bitter anywhere, as here in America, where the very landscape, in its very beauty, seems a bit devilish and grinning, opposed to us.[5]

That was one quarrel in life that needed a new consciousness requiring the accommodation of man to the natural creature in himself. But there was another, more profound aspect of the opposition between the metaphoric white man and metaphoric red man which Lawrence touched, one that applied not only to the friendship of Natty and Chingachgook, but to the friendships of Queequeg and Ishmael and of Huck Finn and Jim. The new consciousness would express a democratic universality, specifically in the problem of racial intermixture. This meant, as Lawrence described it, a stripping away of old skins and identities in order to accept something deeper in the possible relations of men. Lawrence begins this passage of his discussion by describing a harsh, sacrificial, "self-murdering" quality in democratic experience. "Men murdered themselves into this democracy." This is intuitive and complex; it suggests the painful paradoxes of liberation when accompanied by the egalitarian ideal. The actual history was dramatically violent, and Lawrence's myth stresses the pangs of death as well as new birth: "sometimes the immortal serpent feels very happy . . . and sometimes he feels very sick." Cooper was as divided in mood himself in his view of the new America, and the clearest view of the ground for this ambivalence is present and can be studied in *The Pioneers*.

4. Ibid.   5. Ibid., p. 81.

It is significant that *The Pioneers* should have been written earliest in the Leatherstocking series. Cooper's imagination was seized first of all by the *old* Deerslayer, who, though he still follows the life in the forest, is now fighting for survival against the encroachment of civilization. This is featured in his contest with Judge Temple over his right to shoot deer in what has now become, incomprehensibly, owned and legally restricted land. But his physical attributes suggest the crisis of his "mythic" fate; he is tall and meager, emaciated but in good health, old but still greatly strong, and, above all, capable of enduring.

A complication of the story appears in the fact that Natty's direct enemy is not Judge Temple, an educated man of moral good will, but the comical mob, who are led as a posse against the wilderness men by "Squire" Richard Jones, Judge Temple's cousin. The latter expresses the narrow conservatism of the law, while the mob simply conveys Cooper's prejudices against the raw democracy, the social aggregate without culture or moral development. Temple, in contrast, is the aristocrat, indeed an English squire, and his function is to restrain excesses and resolve the contest between the townspeople and the men of the woods. The theme is a familiar one in American writing. Romantic extremes become assimilated, the aristocrat and the pagan hunter both oppose themselves to the middle ground, which presents the actual spearhead of advancing society. The frontier wilderness is most at odds with the frontier settlement; this is a democracy of merchants and farmers with a shabby morality and way of life, halfway between a real civilization and the redemptive purity of the woods, gaining advantages from neither. Young Edwards, who is disguised as a woodsman, the friend of Natty Bumppo, and supposedly an Indian half-breed, is really a gentleman, descendant of the Tory civilization of America. The disguise is not a disguise but a blending of values.

Natty is the hero who rescues a threatened culture, ironically enough, since he is the man, half-savage, in retreat from it. This is clear in the role he plays in the life of Major Effingham. What he brings from nature, his virility, his pure skills of survival, are put into the service of the Effinghams, Tories, and a dispossessed frontier nobility whose roots were in the old world. But the source of Leatherstocking's strength is out there, in that "quivering radiancy" of the landscape, which is problematic, dangerous, vivid, and pressing, and ultimately offers a religious revelation. Natty, in this phase of his life, is a holy man, if not a prophet. His isolation and celibacy, his self-reliance and unmistakable inner harmony affirm his mission. He speaks of the place he knows to the west, a great, good place on the height of a mountain. What do you see when you get there? Edwards, or young Effingham, asks. "Creation," is his answer, but then he adds he knows still a better place just beyond it that is "more nateral."

Apart from the rescue functions he performs (and these in repetition make the narrative sequence), Natty remains the unforgiving critic of the new society, not merely for the restrictions against the life of the free hunter, but for its ugly waste and defacement of nature. The pigeon shoot is a sign of this. Natty shoots with his single bullet and kills only one pigeon. The others from the town shoot the birds with a small cannon. Again he uses all his skill and takes a personal risk in spearing a single fish. The others use larger nets than they need and make it mass destruction. The issue is simple and highly stressed. Human society bears a guilt toward nature; in his social organization man abuses the natural law of competition in the wilderness. He also exceeds a mythic law of balance in nature. Retribution threatens, as when Ben Pump almost drowns in the fishing episode, but Natty saves him, maintaining his role as a moral example, possibly a redeemer of that misled civilization.

The greater case of abuse is illustrated in the degradation of the Indian. Indian John is a tragic remnant, living alone in his old land. His race has been wiped out by disease and the loss of the hunting grounds to the white man. He has fallen from glory, but he remains intrinsically noble, the spirit of natural freedom still glittering in his eyes. He has his own faith and morality, and he finally wards off the inept effort to convert him to Christianity. Natty is even less vulnerable; preaching, he says, makes the game scarce. Grant, the Christian minister, and his daughter are not impressive characters in the story; they are gentle and good, but weak and even morally obtuse. The daughter is cowardly in the woods, an antiquely feminine creature, and she is not worthy of Edwards, though she loves him. In contrast with Elizabeth Temple, she is horrified by the possibility that he might be half-Indian.

The fact that Indian John does in fact come so close to Christian conversion makes a point. The story dramatizes the halfway mark of uncertain resolution in the encounter between the Indian and white civilization. On one side the townspeople can deprecate the half-savagery of Natty and Edwards, who have shared the life of the Indian.

On the other side, from Natty's point of view, it becomes necessary to mourn the degeneracy of Indian John, once called Chingachgook, chieftain and friend of his youth. In this respect the death of Indian John is the focal scene of the story. He recalls his warrior youth, his people, and their vanished life in the land, and he then makes the historic indictment of the white men, with their two gifts of destruction for the Indian, rum and rifles. In his death John becomes pure Indian again, and the way he dies mocks the efforts of Grant to help him to a Christian death. It is a triumph of his own values, expressed by an invincible resignation; he accepts his death as the last expression of what is natural, and so masters it. Above all, "the truth lived in him."

It is important to remember that there are two agents of dispossession in the story. The Effinghams, victimized and outcast Tories, are the representatives of the English king, the old civilization destroyed in the Revolution. The guilt for dispossession adheres to the new American and points in both directions, the Indian wilderness and Europe. This comes to a focus with the humiliation of Leatherstocking as he is captured and put in the stocks for violating the town laws. The event is complicated by the fact that he has just saved Elizabeth Temple from wild animals. His affinity with nature is the only force that can placate it; he remains attached to the Temples, as if he were indispensable to their survival as well as their moral reeducation. Cooper didn't dare to write tragedy, though his theme could support it. It was necessary to come to terms with those forces from nature and civilization which made their claims and threatened retribution. In the interesting complications of the theme we discover that old Major Effingham had once saved Indian John's life, and that Chingachgook's tribe had then given him all the land of the area, adopting him meanwhile as a member of the tribe. The land guilt has been acknowledged, but the episode at the same time forecasts a reconciliation of white man and red man. Edwards, the surviving Effingham, had long ago been adopted as an Indian. The guilt of Judge Temple remains, but it is powerfully focussed toward both the Indians and the Effinghams. The symbolic meaning suggests that nature and the old civilization can join forces, but the new men of the new land, the Americans, will have to make their peace with both. This is done by Temple's own gestures of rescue and atonement, and finally by the marriage between his daughter and Edwards, heir of both the Indians and the European past. Thus Judge Temple acts the role of the mythic American in a more pertinent sense than Natty Bumppo; guilty and purged of guilt, he resolves in himself and his daughter's life the separate strands of conflict in early American history. It has been revealed that Natty, man of the woods, has been the loyal servant and retainer of aristocratic old Major Effingham. Two nostalgic ideals and two forms of guilt have united in this pattern. The romance may be too much, and Cooper may have wanted the best of this possible world, but the effects are still persuasive for a "myth of America." Only a romantic melodrama could make them so clear. This is emphasized with an exact symbolic gesture at the end. The grave of Indian John points toward the West. Next to him, the grave of Major Effingham has its foot toward the East. "They thought they had to journey different ways."

It is not surprising that D. H. Lawrence reacted strongly to Cooper's narrative. A European would be sensitive to the double tropism of the story, the clear division of loyalties between East and West. Apart from that he felt a strong affinity with Cooper's own ambivalent view of the new democracy, an ambivalence which Lawrence eventually carried to vivid extremes of hostility. Formal egalitarianism was more alien to Lawrence's temperament than any other social formalism. He was not one to accept an institutional world where the letter kills the spirit, and the imitative patterns of democratic life offended him to the depth. Observing, like other aristocrats of the spirit, including Cooper himself, the obtuse and vulgar values of democracy and the indifference of its institutions to rare individuals, authentic persons, he postulated that Cooper had to "dream beyond democracy."

> What did Cooper dream beyond democracy? Why, in his immortal friendship of Chingachgook and Natty Bumppo he dreamed the nucleus of a new society. That is, he dreamed a new human relationship. A stark, stripped human relationship of two men deeper than the deeps of sex. Deeper than property, deeper than fatherhood, deeper than marriage, deeper than love. So deep that it is loveless. The stark, loveless, wordless unison of two men, who have come to the bottom of themselves. This is the new nucleus of a new society, the clue to a new world-epoch.[6]

Was this really an experience going "beyond democracy" or was it a discovery of its own latent moral energy? Lawrence himself wasn't sure, I believe. He attacks its manifest attributes, but then comes back to terms that cannot be divorced from democratic values and assumptions. For instance, he protests against the mere negative freedom of

6. Ibid., p. 78.

those who were rejecting old masters, and declares that the new Americans could not know real freedom.

> Men are free when they are in a living homeland, not when they are straying and breaking away. Men are free when they are obeying some deep, inward voice of religious belief. Obeying from within. Men are free when they belong to a living, organic, *believing* community, active in fulfilling some unfulfilled, perhaps unrealized purpose. Not when they are escaping to some wild west. The most unfree souls go west, and shout of freedom. Men are freest when they are most unconscious of freedom.[7]

One is tempted to say that this is the voice of the irrepressible European, conditioned to imagine men living in civilized harmony, fully absorbed into their world and culture. The American tradition imagines rather, as I try to demonstrate in this book, that a free society cannot have a "religious" unity, that freedom is freedom when it meets the resistance of organized social life, that in fact men are freest when they are most conscious of it. Freedom, in other words, is a dialectical, not an organic state.

In that exact sense Lawrence was right in sensing that Cooper dreamt of human relationships "beyond democracy," if we mean by that term, as he seemed to, an order of institutions, rules, doctrine, and prejudice. The dialectic of "white culture" and "red nature" dramatized that liberation, though at considerable historic cost. The Indian was a challenge to any organic community; that is his meaning in Lawrence's own version of the myth. To know him as Natty Bumppo did, was to cross old barriers, to be prepared in some dangerous new sense to live "beyond" culture.

Lawrence came very close to recognizing this when he gave America the slogan, "Henceforth be masterless," though he contradicted this later by asserting that men cannot live without masters. To insist on being masterless meant probably to have neither a culture nor to achieve the fullness of life, not in Lawrence's terms of organic fulfillment in religious communities. But his own words on this dilemma describe the distinct quality of a masterless society. There were two choices.

> Men either live in glad obedience to the master they believe in, or they live in a frictional opposition to the master they wish to undermine. In America this frictional opposition has been the vital factor. It has given the Yankee his kick.[8]

7. Ibid., p. 9.   8. Ibid., p. 6.

The "Yankee kick" is something Lawrence senses and admires throughout his book, but never quite appreciates for what it was, precisely a part of the new moral landscape he proclaimed. He did, however, beginning with the enormously evocative friendship of Natty and Chingachgook, explore the primary responses of democratic man, person to person in a new setting of human immediacy.

> Natty and the Great Serpent are neither equals nor unequals. Each obeys the other when the moment arrives. And each is stark and dumb in the other's presence, starkly himself, without illusion created. Each is just the crude pillar of a man, the crude living column of his own manhood. And each knows the godhead of this crude column of manhood. A new relationship.[9]

It would be a mistake to read this reductively as sexual inversion and male narcissism, though that indeed is the lesson one school of critical thought seems to have taken from Lawrence's words, finding that they extend beyond the examples of Natty Bumppo and Chingachgook.[10] It meant more than that to Lawrence, as he returned to the theme. It was for him a new humanism, removed from all secondary and specialized loves, the worship of the godhead of man.

9. Ibid., pp. 78–79.

10. Leslie Fiedler's large treatment in *Love and Death in the American Novel* makes the strongest case, and the best answer to him that I have found appears in a reference in Daniel Hoffman's book on American fiction. It deserves full quotation. The bond of brotherhood, he says, ". . . has often been the closest relationship conceivable in the American imagination."

> Doubtless it is our residual puritanism which has made the power of sexual love less a force in our literature than the power of comradeship. Leslie Fiedler makes the most sensational statement of something approximating this thesis; he goes on to propose a "myth" of the infantile, immaculate, homoerotic love of a white and a colored man as the passionate theme of *Huckleberry Finn*, the Leatherstocking tales and *Moby Dick*. Seriously to entertain the notion of this as a major strand of American literature is surely to distort the cultural significance of the ties between Huck and Jim, Leatherstocking and Chingachcook, Ishmael and Queequeg. The two themes they actually exemplify are primitivism and egalitarianism.
> Among the ideals of the American Enlightenment, when the outlines of our culture were drawn with so firm a hand, romantic love would seem to have had little place. Egalitarianism, however, appears early as the basis of our national character. It is written into our eighteenth century political documents, and, as Crévecoeur observed even before those documents were drafted, it is in the spirit of our institutions and of our colonial laws. In a nation which has what Mr. Ellison calls "the white American's manichean fascination" with color, isn't the ideal expression of equality an absolute commitment to a member of another race—just because such a relationship is in reality so difficult to entertain? (Hoffman, *Form and Fable in American Fiction*, pp. 348–49.)

Beyond all this heart-beating stand the figures of Natty and Chingach-gook: the two childless womanless men of opposite races. They are the abiding thing. Each of them is alone, and final in his race. And they stand side by side, stark, abstract, beyond emotion, yet eternally to-gether. All the other loves seem frivolous. This is the new great thing, the clue, the inception of a new humanity.[11]

Lawrence suggests more than he explains, and what he suggests can only be illustrated by a long examination of more important writers than Cooper, in the book of the "childless, womanless" hero of *Walden* for instance, or in more exact parallel, in the relationship achieved by Ishmael and Queequeg against the background of the isolated and self-destroying Captain Ahab. Ahab opposing himself to the white whale is a true symbol of that liberation that goes "beyond democ-racy," but Queequeg and Ishmael may illustrate the first principles of a "new humanity."

"Old Things Need to Die"

A new birth of humanity was Lawrence's obsession in his own work, and he projected it into his general view of American writing. The myth he imagined was one of dying, as well as birth, and he plausibly chose Poe to illustrate the motif of the "old serpent" in its travail. "Old things need to die," he said in his very imaginative but sound reading of Poe, and "man must be stripped even of himself." The latter statement would have been even more remarkably apt for Melville, but it has its clear pertinence to Poe's tales of haunted with-drawal and intense struggle with death.

In the context of American criticism, Lawrence's discussion of Poe seems particularly rare and valuable. Most omnibus treatments of the classic nineteenth-century writers find little space for Poe. The general reaction implicitly follows that of Vernon Parrington in think-ing Poe somehow "outside the main current of American thought."[12]

11. *American Literature*, p. 86.

12. Parrington gives Poe two pages of his massive work, *Main Currents in Amer-ican Thought*, vol. 2 (New York: Harcourt, Brace). Of a later generation of influential critics, Richard Chase makes very rare incidental reference to Poe in his treatment of American romance fiction. Daniel Hoffman's excellent book on American romance in-dexes Poe only once. R. W. B. Lewis mentions him three times in his thematically designed study, though both he and Chase give sizable treatment to Brockden Brown. Charles Feidelson gives Poe relatively brief direct treatment in his *Symbolism and American Literature* (Chicago: University of Chicago Press, 1953), perhaps not what might be expected for the American who so much impressed the French generation of

Poe himself consciously aimed at transcending anything suggesting American provincialism, and his critical theories were notably not in harmony with the practice and temperament of most of his contemporaries. He considered himself a pure artist in a generation of moralists, specifically the Transcendentalists, whom he detested. He had some good words for Hawthorne, but they were emphatically not on behalf of Hawthorne's didactic and allegorizing impulses. Poe was right to feel his difference, and it is also natural that later critics find it easier to leave him out of the discussion than to make room for him in a literary context so featured by moral earnestness and by the ambition to judge life and instruct mankind. On the other hand it is not quite a paradox to find that Poe becomes more significant, not less, as one deals with the thematic substance of his work in relation to his contemporaries. In other words he is interesting as an historic imagination, consecutive and relevant in the discussion of the work of Thoreau and Hawthorne. And if his contemporaries had not colored so rich a canvas of allegories and moralities, he would be less interesting.

Against the background of Thoreau's writing, for instance, Poe's work receives sharper focus. A detailed contrast might not be rewarding, but the two men express temperamental alternatives in their work which dramatize the record of the American mind and imagination. *Walden* is an intense pursuit of the renewal and purification of life, and it makes a devoted search for what one might call the sensible state of innocence in a full range of appropriate effects. This is dominantly a celebration of health, of youth and beginnings, of daylight, of natural growing things, and above all, of calm security in the physical world.

> The indescribable innocence and beneficence of Nature,—of sun and wind and rain, of summer and winter,—such health, such cheer, they afford forever! and such sympathy have they ever with our race, that all Nature would be affected, and the sun's brightness fade, and the winds would sigh humanely, and the clouds rain tears, and the woods shed their leaves and put on mourning in midsummer, if any man should ever for a just cause grieve. . . . What is the pill which will keep us well, serene, contented? . . . For my panacea . . . let me have a draught of undiluted morning air. Morning air! If men will not drink of this at the

---

symbolist writers. It is characteristically a foreigner, though not a Frenchman, who offers the most suggestive basis for reading Poe in the context of his American contemporaries. I find Lawrence's treatment as stimulating and as important in its insight as his study of Cooper.

fountain-head of the day, why, then, we must even bottle up some and sell it in the shops, for the benefit of those who have lost their subscription ticket to morning time in this world.[13]

Poe's preoccupation with imaginatively selected morbidities is as strong as Thoreau's concern with health. The contrast suggests that Poe's was the temperament of decadence, which is a way of describing an imagination obsessed by sickness, decay, and death.[14] Thoreau makes the briefest reference to these topics, and when at the one time he questions a feeling of solitude in the woods, he calls it a "slight insanity." He goes on to say that such depressions, even in the most severely literal circumstance, were fantasies of a "diseased imagination."

> I have heard of a man lost in the woods and dying of famine and exhaustion at the foot of a tree, whose loneliness was relieved by the grotesque visions with which, owing to bodily weakness, his diseased imagination surrounded him, and which he believed to be real. So also, owing to bodily and mental health and strength, we may be continually cheered by a like but more normal and natural society, and come to know that we are never alone.[15]

Poe turned more or less consciously toward that kind of imagination when he proposed in "The Philosophy of Composition" that "melancholy is the . . . most legitimate of all the poetical tones," and that "the death . . . of a beautiful woman is, unquestionably, the most poetical topic in the world." The fascination in his mind was with death; though "Beauty" could heighten the melancholy in the poems, death itself and the fear which accompanied it were his favorite themes in the stories. If there was a psychic state for dying, it was dominated by fear, and Poe extended it to imaginative extremes, as if by pursuing it and magnifying it, one might come to the end of all secrets. Terror reached its climax in the fear of being buried alive, and Poe's repeated theme of premature burial goes beyond a Gothic titillation in its implications. To imagine being buried alive is to make the general fear of death tangible and expressive. One has moved into "absolute Night,"

13. *Walden and Civil Disobedience*, pp. 95–96.

14. To describe the conjunction of these themes, Lawrence borrows from Cooper an aphorism the latter received from a Frenchman. "L'Amérique est pourrie avant d'être mûre." Actually this wisdom seems to be standard European folklore, the latest attribution, I believe, going to Bernard Shaw. On the matter of this talent for decadence, Lawrence goes on to say, "America was not taught by France—by Baudelaire, for example. Baudelaire learned his lesson from America" (*American Literature*, p. 55).

15. *Walden and Civil Disobedience*, p. 94.

the world is a void, and yet there is *consciousness* of the void. This is the wholly concentrated effect of a passage like the following from "The Premature Burial."

> It may be asserted, without hesitation, that *no* event is so terribly well adapted to inspire the supremeness of bodily and mental distress, as is burial before death. The unendurable oppression of the lungs—the stifling fumes of the damp earth—the clinging to the death garments—the rigid embrace of the narrow house—the blackness of the absolute Night—the silence like a sea that overwhelms—the unseen but palpable presence of the Conqueror Worm—these things with the thoughts of the air and grass above, with memory of dear friends who would fly to save us if but informed of our fate, and with consciousness that of this fate they can *never* be informed . . . these considerations, I say, carry into the heart, which still palpitates, a degree of appalling and intolerable horror from which the most daring imagination must recoil. We know of nothing so agonizing upon Earth.[16]

In one sense this is the psychic extreme of loneliness. The situation is familiar if we invert the characteristic qualities of Thoreau's work. Thoreau penetrates all his writing with the countertheme for a "man lost in the woods and dying." Rather he is the man *found*, the woods are his home, the universe is real and solid, it is occupied to the full by a normal and natural society; realizing this, no man can ever be alone. To such a spirit, Poe's atmospheres and emotional effects would be perverse and masochistic.

The clear contrast with Thoreau and its pertinence to the larger tradition is supported by looking at Melville. There is sometimes the

16. Edgar Allan Poe, "The Premature Burial," *Tales of Mystery and Imagination* (London: J. M. Dent and Sons, 1908), p. 273.
The furthest Poe went in investigating this hypothesis that a kind of consciousness continues in the grave is expressed in the dialogue narrative called "The Colloquy of Monos and Una." After death there remains a form of sentience or consciousness, at first expressed as keenly perceptive and a "sensual delight." The point is made that in this condition there is a little pain, much pleasure, but no moral pain or pleasure at all. That is to say the sensations of sorrow and mourning are felt as intense and therefore pleasurable experiences, but they have no discriminated meaning whatever. From this point consciousness slowly decreases, though first reaching the climactic experience of a sixth sense, which is the abstract idea of time made sensible, the feeling of duration. When actual decay vanquishes the body, there is only this much left:

> Dust had returned to dust. The Worm had food no more. The sense of being had at length utterly departed, and there reigned in its stead—instead of all things—dominant and perpetual—the autocrats *Place* and *Time*. For *that* which *was not*—for that which had no form—for that which had no thought—for that which had no sentience—for that which was soulless, yet of which matter formed no portion—for all this nothingness, yet for all this immortality, the grave was still a home, and the corrosive hours, co-mates (ibid., p. 122).

note of a metaphysical terror in Poe, as if his protagonists were forced to look past all the margins of recognizable experience. In "Ms. Found In a Bottle," Poe delivers a description of the sea which approximates Melville's renewal of the "sense of the full awfulness of the sea which aboriginally belongs to it," that sea which will "forever murder and insult man."

> All in the immediate vicinity of the ship is the blackness of eternal night, and a chaos of formless water; but, about a league on either side of us, may be seen, indistinctly and at intervals, stupendous ramparts of ice, towering away into the desolate sky, and looking like the walls of the universe.[17]

In other respects his strong link with the "dark" interests of Hawthorne and Melville is more than superficial. He shared with them the drive of the imagination to reach some outer circle of mystery, to feel the awe of passing natural and psychic frontiers. He described this stimulus in some of his incidental notes on writing.

> These "fancies" have in them a pleasurable ecstasy, as far beyond the most pleasurable of the world of wakefulness, or of dreams, as the Heaven of the Northman theology is beyond its Hell. I regard the visions, even as they arise, with an awe which, in some measure, moderates or tranquillizes the ecstasy—I so regard them, through a conviction (which seems a portion of the ecstasy itself) that this ecstasy, in itself, is of a character supernal to the Human Nature—is a glimpse of the spirit's outer world.[18]

He felt the inner mystery as well, perhaps as much as Hawthorne. In the same set of notes, he imagines the project of writing a book called "My Heart Laid Bare," and he questions why there should be found no men with "sufficient hardihood to write this little book."

17. "Ms. Found In A Bottle," *Tales*, pp. 266–67.
The link between Poe and Melville is further suggested by the description of the captain in this story.

> Although in his appearance there is, to a casual observer, nothing which might bespeak him more or less than man, still, a feeling of irrepressible reverence and awe mingled with the sensation of wonder with which I regarded him. . . . But it is the singularity of expression which reigns upon the face—it is the intense, the wonderful, the thrilling evidence of old age so utter, so extreme, which excites within my spirit a sense—a sentiment ineffable. His forehead, although little wrinkled, seems to bear upon it the stamp of a myriad of years. His grey hairs are records of the past, and his greyer eyes are sybils of the future (p. 266).

18. Edgar Allan Poe, "Marginalia," *Selected Prose and Poetry* (New York: Holt, Rinehart and Winston, 1967), p. 436.

. . . to write it—*there* is the rub. No man dare write it. No man ever will dare write it. No man *could* write it, even if he dared. The paper would shrivel and blaze at every touch of the fiery pen.[19]

In these respects, Poe was a writer very much of his own time and people. He did not touch the profundities that Thoreau, Hawthorne, and Melville communicate, it is true. But apart from its rank in the pantheon, or its independent interest, his work becomes richer and clarifies its implications when viewed with his contemporaries. As an example, what is called Poe's literary necrophilia pertains in essence to a struggle between life and death. It is not an anomaly, but a singular demonstration of correspondence, that the cemetery art of Poe should be found in the context of the secular humanism of American writing, so often turned to proving the value of life. Thoreau's words in this respect are keys to insight for the tradition in which both he and Poe write.

> I went to the woods because I wished to live deliberately, to front only the essential facts of life, and see if I could not learn what it had to teach, and not, when I came to die, discover I had not lived. . . . I wanted to live deep and suck out all the marrow of life, to live so sturdily and Spartan-like as to put to rout all that was not life, to cut a broad swath and shave close, to drive life into a corner, and reduce it to its lowest terms.[20]

As a topic for the imagination, death is vivid as the frustration of that will to live. Extinction is most meaningful within the consciousness that is most alive. In "Morella" the narrator speaks of the gloomy inflated philosophizing of himself and his wife, the beautiful Morella (doomed to die like Berenice, Ligeia, and Eleonora),

> . . . the *principium individuationis*—the notion of identity *which at death is or is not lost forever*—was to me, at all times, a consideration of intense interest.[21]

The more powerful and characteristic treatment is expressed in *Ligeia* where the theme is quite simply the struggle against death. A beautiful loved woman fights passionately with her own death, and after succumbing returns to fight again to win possession of the body of her successor in the narrator's second marriage. That struggle is the single note of the story.

19. Ibid., p. 445.

20. *Walden and Civil Disobedience*, p. 62.   21. "Morella," *Tales*, p. 184.

Words are impotent to convey any just idea of the fierceness of resistance with which she wrestled with the Shadow. I groaned in anguish at the pitiable spectacle. I would have soothed—I would have reasoned; but, in the intensity of her wild desire for life,—for life—*but* for life—solace and reason were alike the uttermost of folly.[22]

This longing for elemental life is at the center of Poe's imaginative interests. That is the light struck by D. H. Lawrence to account for Poe's death obsession, and it served to complete Lawrence's pattern of the new birth myth of America. In the process by which the old civilized "European" consciousness is stripped away and the new man in a new skin takes on life, Lawrence aptly assigns the disintegrative effect to Poe.

He is absolutely concerned with the disintegration-processes of his own psyche. As we have said, the rhythm of American art-activity is dual.
1. A disintegrating and sloughing of the old consciousness.
2. The forming of a new consciousness underneath. . . .

Moralists have always wondered helplessly why Poe's "morbid" tales need have been written. They need to be written because old things need to die and disintegrate, because the old white psyche has to be gradually broken down before anything else can come to pass.
Man must be stripped even of himself. And it is a painful, some-times a ghastly process.[23]

Considered this way, Poe's theme is decadence, both cultural and natural. It is expressed in a series of dehumanizing and life-inhibiting experiences, climaxed by the nonlife or antilife which he imagines as the sentience of the tomb. The pursuit of esoteric knowledge and perverse sensations becomes in this aspect a deformation and implicit decay of life. The doomed women in Poe's stories are often gifted in addition to beauty with unusual intellectual power and learning. Or they are associated with men who are ("Berenice," "Eleonora"), and their fates are connected with dangerous adventures of knowledge. To move into such areas of consciousness is like opening the portals of death, which is the last esoteric mystery and outside the sphere of the human. It comes fatally between lovers, as described by the narrator in "Berenice."

In the strange anomaly of my existence, feelings with me, *had never been* of the heart, and my passions *always were* of the mind. Through the grey of the early morning—among the *trelissed* shadows of the forest

---

22. "Ligeia," *Tales*, p. 160.   23. *American Literature*, p. 93.

at noonday—and in the silence of my library at night, she had flitted by my eyes, and I had seen her—not as the living and breathing Berenice, but as the Berenice of a dream—not as a being of the earth, earthy, but as the abstraction of such a being—not as a thing to admire, but to analyze—not as an object of love, but as the theme of the most abstruse although desultory speculation.[24]

The working of the mind as magnified intelligence is the accompaniment of sickness, approaching madness, as well as approaching death. It emphasizes an exile from reality, the wandering among shades, some of which are contributed by the past, some by esoteric knowledge, others by the unmoored imagination. The burden of the past is a particular emphasis in this concept of a mind imprisoned within itself. The narrator in "Berenice" feels it.

... there are no towers in the land more time-honoured than my gloomy, grey, hereditary halls . . . it *is* singular that as years rolled away, and the noon of manhood found me still in the mansion of my fathers—it is wonderful what stagnation there fell upon the springs of my life—wonderful how total an inversion took place in the character of my commonest thought. The realities of the world affected me as visions, and as visions only.[25]

One sees a convergence of themes here which are heightened in visibility against the American literary background. The reference to "grey hereditary halls" and "the stagnation" of his father's mansion is highly characteristic and suggestive. That the past is a prison is one meaning of decadence. The esoteric intelligence turns to it by preference. Experience becomes equated with memory; it takes place indoors in the dank atmospheres of old castles and haunted chambers. The mind is charged and overactive with its inheritance, and this, like the ruined mansion of the Ushers, is superimposed upon an abyss. In a sense there is no real world at all, but only the dream images of a strange homeless intelligence which at the same time imagines its future as extinction. Life itself becomes a disease of the imagination, and the restless intellect moves into delirium as the prospect of death becomes more vivid.

This affinity of the introspective mind for death is matched by its affinity for crime. The feats of cerebration required to penetrate the mystery of crime and to solve it are conducted at the far margin of normal human life. Auguste Dupin is such a marginal person.

24. "Berenice," *Tales*, p. 179.   25. Ibid., pp. 175–76.

> It was a freak of fancy in my friend [Dupin] . . . to be enamoured of the Night for her own sake; and into this *bizarrerie*, as into all his others, I quietly fell. . . . At the first dawn of the morning we closed all the massy shutters of our old building; lighted a couple of tapers which, strongly perfumed, threw out only the ghastliest and feeblest of rays. By the aid of these we then busied our souls in dreams—reading, writing, or conversing, until warned by the clock of the advent of the true Darkness. Then we sallied forth into the streets.[26]

It is not sufficient to say that Poe is busy evoking an appropriate scene of mystery and suspense. It *is* mystery, but it should be noted that it is an entrance into a sphere beyond life, but bordering it, beyond humanity but partaking of it—just as the prematurely buried evoke those effects. For instance, when Dupin's deductions have followed themselves out, he forms this image of the murderer in "The Murders in the Rue Morgue."

> . . . we have gone so far as to combine the ideas of an agility astounding, a strength superhuman, a ferocity brutal, a butchery without motive, a *grotesquerie* in horror absolutely alien from humanity, and a voice foreign in tone to the ears of men in many nations, and devoid of all distinct or intelligible syllabification.[27]

To find that this "thing" is an escaped gorilla is something of an anti-climax and disappointment; the real mystery has been evoked in other terms, as expressed in the phrase "absolutely alien from humanity."

Like other manifestations of romantic Gothic, Poe's interest in crime detection was an interest in entering its sphere and savoring the experience. The clever captor, Dupin, is as glamorous an outsider and critic of mediocrity as the criminal himself. Dupin is an intellectual hero, almost demonic in his powers of reasoning, but turned to good pursuits in matching himself with criminals rather than against society. Actually, he has transcended both sides; he has defeated the criminals, who resemble the gorilla, a natural mystery, in their power of antisocial mystification. But he is also superior to the police, who represent conventional law and a conventional intelligence. He has found the right position for the authentic hero of the individualist creed; he is independent of the social order, but at the same time he maintains his moral superiority, like those ambiguous gunfighter heroes of Western movies who defeat the actual outlaws.

This Faustian intelligence, which is measured by its capacity to understand and detect crime, is an example of an immensely gifted

---

26. "The Murders in the Rue Morgue," *Tales*, p. 382.   27. Ibid., p. 402.

decadence. Morally exiled, self-alienated in their thoughts, as if to think itself were the sign of guilt, Poe's characters give no direct testimony of their origin. But they sometimes suggest a source for their oppression. The sentence from "Berenice" strikes a sustained note. "The noon of manhood found me still in the mansion of my fathers." If there is sickness, it is that of inheritance, or carrying the implication further, the sickness of a dying culture. It is almost too easy to juxtapose this with Thoreau's search for health and innocence in nature. Yet the dichotomy is always significant in romantic writing, and in the American context seems to transcend the bounds of literary convention. Lawrence felt it, accordingly, in sensing that Poe's stories were written to show how "old things need to die."

The fullest example of the way this theme works out is found in "The Fall of the House of Usher." The scene is another old mansion, "the melancholy house of Usher." Its proprietor, Roderick Usher, is deeply sick, both physically and mentally, but more obviously the latter. He lives alone, except for a sister, and they are the only survivors of a very ancient family and a past which reflects its splendor in the decaying house. They suffer from a "constitutional and family evil" but accompanying this patrimony of disease they have the highest refinements of intelligence and sensibility, In fact Roderick's disease seems to be largely the manifestation of an abnormal sensitivity— "the odours of all flowers were oppressive." In specific stress, however, his disease expresses itself as "an anomalous species of terror," a fear which is ever present but has no single or discernible source. He does express to the narrator a superstitious feeling about the house itself, that it or something in it is the source of his sickness and terror.

The fear arises from the past, but grows to its climax in the immediate fear of death. The sister is dying, and it is at this crisis that Usher has invited the narrator, a boyhood friend, to visit him and relieve his increasingly unbearable loneliness. They divert themselves with music, painting, and esoteric studies and conversation. Meanwhile the sister dies; Usher proposes to bury her in a vault within the walls, to protect her body from grave robbers, he says. After the burial, Usher's mental condition becomes worse; he seems close to madness as he wanders through the house, listening to distant sounds.

Finally he receives the signal he has feared and expected all his life; the deep vault below is heard opening. Usher expresses now what he has known from the beginning. He has heard the sound of the "buried alive." They had put her in her vault while still alive; he did not dare speak though he had sensed "her first feeble movements in the hollow coffin." Madeline herself, or her ghost, stands before the door now and enters, and in a final—or repeated—death agony, falls upon her brother, and "bore him to the floor a corpse and a victim of the terrors he had anticipated." The race of Usher is dead. The moment the narrator escapes, he looks back to see the whole house shake and fall to pieces and sink into the bordering lake.

It seems not too fanciful to suggest that the "deep and dank tarn" that "closed sullenly and silently over the fragments of the House of Usher" is an antonymous image for Walden pond. To further illustrate the contrast one might say that as the correlative for the building of Thoreau's sweet-smelling pine hut, the older house of decay had to fall and disappear. Poe's imagination is linked to that of Thoreau by the stages of an evolution; they divide a common myth in concentrating respectively on the old and the new, the dying and the just-born. Put alongside any page of *Walden* a passage like the following and one is helped to feel the contextual dynamism of Thoreau's images, or be more touched by the poignance of what he is celebrating.

> About the whole mansion and domain there hung an atmosphere peculiar to themselves and their immediate vicinity—an atmosphere which had no affinity with the air of heaven, but which had reeked up from the decayed trees, and the grey wall, and the silent tarn—a pestilent and mystic vapour, dull, sluggish, faintly discernible, and leaden-hued.[28]

The House of Usher, if we impose the allegory, is the house of civilization suffering from the neurosis of its history. It is, for instance, the habitation of life detached from the real world; the Ushers suffer from the overdeveloped intellect and imagination, in which "an excited and highly distempered ideality threw a sulphurous luster." For Usher it means finally "the tottering of his lofty reason upon her throne."

Poe's simplicity of treatment, or the lack of a conceptual theme, makes it easier to see the relevance of these effects in the wider context of a generation of writers and a consecutive tradition. The immediate parallel is with Hawthorne's division of mind and heart as moral agents, his sometimes equally "sulphurous" atmospheres, and his treatment of the mysterious suffering of those exiled from reality. Roderick Usher lives chiefly in a solipsistic nightmare. The void is the ultimate threat in Poe, not specific horrors, no matter how ingenious he is in inventing them.

28. "The Fall of the House of Usher," *Tales*, p. 130.

It was not that I feared to look upon things horrible, but that I grew aghast lest there should be *nothing* to see.[29]

Thoreau had said, as if in answer.

If you stand right fronting and face to face to a fact, you will see the sun glimmer on both its surfaces, as if it were a cimeter, and feel its sweet edge dividing you through the heart and marrow, and so you will happily conclude your mortal career. Be it life or death, we crave only reality.[30]

To long for the sword of the cutting truth is a powerful theme in the tradition of American writing. But so is the criticism of philistine realities, to which Poe contrasts the setting of "dark draperies" and the "encrimsoned light" of his haunted mansions. Poe's writing at every point is a demonstration against the commonplace; the only god of his imagination was "mystery." This extreme breach between what the ordinary world offers and what the imagination requires is implicitly a disease of civilization, a symptom of its birth and death pangs, as Lawrence would say.

It is appropriate therefore to bring Poe's typical protagonists into Lawrence's dramatic cast of "red man' and "white man" in the American psyche. Poe's subjects are, of course, "palefaces," rendered most directly, whether in Lawrence's meaning, or the later use by Philip Rahv to describe the culturally enervated extreme of a "pale-face-redskin" dichotomy in American writing.[31] Both Lawrence and Rahv develop important implications of a genuine myth which is associated with the meeting of the white and red races, and beyond that to the insecure existence of a transported civilization, surrounded by convincing images of natural man. The general reference is to a traditional conflict between an unmastered reality and an inadequate culture which dominates the American sensibility. The superrefinements of Roderick Usher's indoor life with books, painting, and music suggest "hypochondria," a "fervid facility," and "a ghastly and inappropriate splendour." These are not so much the marks of decay as of a great cultural insecurity and self-consciousness. Poe's contemporaries were closer in spirit to the new world frontier, and so captured the healthier energies of change, a sense of creativity as well as crisis in culture. Thoreau spoke with zest of a "busk" in which certain primitive peoples periodically threw away all their old possessions and so

29. "The Pit and the Pendulum," *Tales*, p. 223.
30. *Walden and Civil Disobedience*, p. 67.
31. *Image and Idea*, chap. 1.

purged themselves. Hawthorne wrote of a great bonfire in which civilization was reduced to its indestructible human sources, a capacity for good, a capacity for evil, and the similarly irreducible need to create more artifacts ("shams and appearances" Thoreau would say) to burn in the endless fires of innovation.

With Poe, whose touch is modern in that respect, civilization seems to express the last symptoms of crisis; in supreme cultivation it is haunted by a mental sickness, a species of fear in the anticipation of death, and of guilt in the retrospect of living. The emotions of guilt are stressed in "The Fall of the House of Usher," though the source is vague. It is stated that "sympathies of a scarcely intelligible nature had always existed between them," the twin brother and sister. The hint of incest need not be broader. The effect of guilt is more important than the cause. Did Roderick intend to bury his sister alive or was he responsible for a terrible mistake? The distinction again is unimportant; the guilt is pervasive and universal, it exists between the buried and the living.

This is emphasized in stories like "The Cask of Amontillado," where burying one's victim alive becomes the image of an ultimate crime, and "The Black Cat," where retribution arrives from the tomb. It is evident that Poe's imagination is searching for the incidents which convey the *extremes* of evil and of guilt, and these are made extreme by this absorption with the details of the grave. It is as if the acute moment of awareness exchanged between the murderer and his victim were held suspended for an eternity. Guilt in Poe is not subject to moral analysis and evaluation, it is true, but perhaps this is because it is absolute and defies rationalization. Notice a story like "The Imp of the Perverse" where the need to confess a crime is treated like an unexplained psychological obsession, rather than the product of an extended moral conflict. The confession in that story is simply made analogous to the impulse to jump felt by people at great heights. But perhaps guilt is not the word for what is involved, but a deep quarrel between life and death. The ravenous longing for life expressed by Ligeia, spokesman for the dead, and the guilty obsessions which assailed her living husband suggest a rhythm in experience deep enough to arouse speculation on many grounds, whether in the dramatic Freudian symbology, or in the cultural history which outlines a fatal conflict between the old and the new.

The theme in Poe must be correlated with Hawthorne's interest in the patrimony of evil and guilt, with Thoreau's celebration of the bath of innocence and his own hunger for life, or with Cooper's myth of the hero of the woods and open air, to speak only of Poe's contemporaries. To do so justifies a stress on a special American pattern for this drama of life-and-death antagonists. It is possible to see in Poe a distinctive magnification of the American myth of life, stressed as it was in the precarious ancestral experiences of revolution and immigration. The life-hunger of the immigrant implied an equal nostalgia for the "haunted ancestral halls" and the graveyards left behind. In Poe's case this was not nostalgia so much as an obsession dominated by a horror. What compulsion toward the grave was it that inhabited Poe's old houses and old families? Perhaps his world of the dead expressed the memory of an act of rejection-in-slaying which came to its climax in the revolution. Perhaps his stories evoke an old death-wish which pushed itself forward in the historic acts of American origin, a memory represented by such concentrated images of life-enfeeblement and decadence as Benito Cereno and Roderick Usher. Surely the war with England carried its abiding implications of regicide and parricide; all revolutions must, but this was a revolution more complete than others since it involved a really new start in a new place, that is to say, the vestiges of ancestry were rejected totally. To classify Poe's imagination in these terms, one could call it Tory, conservative in a morbid strain.

It is plausible to say, particularly when the strong legacy of Rousseau as well as of Calvin is understood, that the American myth embodied the rejection of the father civilization, Europe, to be replaced by nature, the mother, with her promise of permanent libidinal freedom. To review some of Thoreau's maternal imagery of the pond in *Walden* is only the beginning of research on this matter. The Oedipal strain is appropriately complicated, however, if a direct guilt toward nature is added, as in the complex legend of Cooper's Leatherstocking series. History recorded the ancestry of an uneasy conscience with crimes against the Indian as well as against the abused and wasted land. Lawrence's myth is complete in the description of such "grinning, unappeased demons." But the worst of these "unappeased demons" perhaps were in the memory of Europe.

This comes to something as blunt as Lawrence's remark, "Somewhere deep in every American heart lies a rebellion against the old parenthood of Europe." Lawrence made American civilization a climax of the historic change he saw in the Renaissance when "mastery, kingship, fatherhood had their power destroyed." It would be even more convincing to make this claim for the Protestant revolt and the democratic revolutions. Following his hint to take a Freudian perspective, the settlement of America, the revolt against England, and the establishment of a democracy could be seen as symbolic enactments of the crime of the primal horde. A paternal, authoritarian order dies and in its place is established a fraternal civilization, a collectivity of peers, brothers and equals. But these have morbid visions; if they are "free," they also feel guilty.

Cooper placed a heavily burdened conscience down in that New York clearing in the woods. Poe's imagery is much darker; it might be described as that of a man conscious of himself on the two sides of the wall of the tomb. Different as these writers were in mind and temperament, their work shares a pattern that contrasts life and death images, innocence and haunted evil, a fresh good conscience and the old echoes of guilt. It is appropriate to think of Henry James, whose tragic sense made it possible for him to condition the melodramatic extremes of Cooper and Poe. James brought Daisy Miller of Schenectady, New York, to Rome to die of the Roman disease, absorbed from the night air of the Colosseum exactly at the place where the Christian martyrs died. "The air of other ages surrounded one; but the air of other ages, coldly analyzed, was no better than a villainous miasma." Daisy's innocence was complexly oriented in the first place and contained an equally fresh and violent destructiveness, the consequence of her uneducated freedom. Accordingly this death of the new-world virgin on the soil of the old followed classic narrative in the complex tradition which Poe and Cooper represent.

In a final judgment one would have to put both Poe and Cooper on a secondary level among the American classic writers. But the notes to emphasize in their work are very much those which Lawrence chose. Together they might have written the epic American book which Lawrence envisioned. Their narratives contribute to an ordealistic view of democracy, Lawrence's view, in which Americans will always have to reckon with "unappeased ghosts," and "strange atonements." "Men murdered themselves into this democracy," he said, and that was an oracular remark which is not obscure in his context. Whatever the terms of conflict, white man and red man, innocence and guilt, culture and natural truth, the process was that of opening out to a "new great area of consciousness," sloughing the old one. This process required, as he said, two vibrations, and Poe had only one. But that one was profound enough in its absorption with the crisis of extinction, where everything leads in Poe's stories, even love, as in the stories of Ligeia and Berenice. Murder was the ultimate experience in this direction.

> Murder is not just killing. Murder is a lust to get at the very quick of life itself, and kill it—hence the stealth and the frequent morbid dismemberment of the corpse, the attempt to get at the very quick of the murdered being, to find the quick and to possess it.[32]

In Poe the point of view alternates between the murderer and his victim. The latter is found in his nightmare of a dying consciousness, between pit and pendulum. The former shares an equal loneliness, and is haunted by his remorse even before he kills. As Lawrence observed, what is involved is a lust for extremes, a "mystic violence." These are imaginative obsessions, one-sided but important. The American of Lawrence's myth takes half his shape in Poe's imagination. The violence is one emphasis; the structures which sheltered conscience are gone, experience is liberated to its extremes, the only value at stake is a heightened consciousness. At the same time, Poe's stories evoke a brooding, generalized moral sensitivity. This represents nothing in detail, however, but the readiness, even the desire, to feel guilt. In the largest sense these effects exhibit a dispersion of character, stressed by the absorption with various kinds of death—physical, moral, spiritual. It is relevant to recall Thoreau, a figure of proud, almost cruel self-sufficiency, who makes the remonstrance not merely of innocence, on which he so much insisted and which is really the aspect of a thoroughly purged conscience, but of the great will to live. And it is this hunger for life which is the implicit context for Poe's recital of the horrors of the tomb.

32. Lawrence, *American Literature*, p. 118.

5/ Hawthorne
The Need To Become Human

Hawthorne's mind mediated among terms of contrast, and it predisposed him to the writing of allegory. That could be demonstrated by the roles he assigns his three major characters in *The Scarlet Letter*. Chillingworth represents an excess of intellect, highlighted by an incompatibility with vital, natural force. The latter is poignantly implicit in the sensibility of Hester as Hawthorne first describes her. Although she is observed to be a woman of acute intelligence, she is rich in her latent sensuality and peculiarly open to the demands of life instincts. This is stressed by the relationship with Pearl, child of unlicensed passion, as well as the subordination of either moral remorse or personal bitterness that Hester feels for her original affair with Dimmesdale. Dimmesdale is the man of spirit, caught between the force of intellect and the force of passion, and appropriate to his role, it is for him that the deepest suffering of the conflict is reserved.

In its whole form the allegory transcribes divisiveness in human character and action. In his introduction to *The Scarlet Letter*, Hawthorne implicitly asserted that the divided self was his major theme. He was speaking of his vocation as a writer.

> The truth seems to be, however, that, when he casts his leaves forth upon the wind, the author addresses, not the many who will fling aside his volume, or never take it up, but the few who will understand him, better than most of his schoolmates and life-mates. Some authors, indeed, do far more than this, and indulge themselves in such confidential depths of revelation as could fittingly be addressed, only and exclusively, to the one heart and mind of perfect sympathy; as if the printed book, thrown at large on the wide world, were certain to find out the divided segment of the writer's own nature, and complete his circle of existence by bringing him into communion with it.

As his inhibitions begin to work, he calls this view of authorship indecorous in his next sentence, but experienced readers of his work would see that he has in fact spoken for himself as well as for his typical protagonists. They search to find out the "divided segments of their own natures." They are complete or incomplete in their "circle of existence" to the degree they have communion within their divided selves as well as to the extent they are communicants in the world. In this arena of division and conflict the aim is to achieve synthesis by that ultimate moral chemistry expressed in the word "sympathy." No one can understand Hawthorne's writing without examining this term; as he uses it, it is a moral and psychological state of grace and it supports the climaxes of recognition or insight required by his dramatic themes.

It could be put that Hawthorne was a Christian in exactly the sense that Emerson was not. Christianity emphasized a moral duality at the center of man's being and founded moral action upon a redemptive change of heart. Hawthorne felt a profound need to accept the existence of the traditional conscience. This was the source of his dramatic sensibility and of a moral temperament strikingly different from that of Thoreau or Emerson. Action was made tense, the introspective mind darkened by a war of dual selves, though one of these might remain hidden with a permanent veil over its face. This was an image for the unexplored complexity of human character. More than we can know, more than we can control lies within us. From this follows a grave susceptibility to moral isolation. The felt distance from others, so strong and brooding an effect in Hawthorne's writing, is a reflection of the breach within the self. But this divided consciousness is the necessary basis for the evolution of a moral identity. Young Goodman Brown wanders through the forest to hear the words "welcome to the communion of your race"; whether for good or evil, that ceremony of unification is the constant preoccupation of this most insistent moralist of American fiction.

It is under this heading that we can see Hawthorne as a formative writer of the democratic tradition. We take him into a comparison with Thoreau, for instance, and see that both focus their work upon the primordial drama of the self making a community. It is primordial in the metaphysical sense because they search out the bare first requirements for connected and meaningful existence. The self, the problematic hero of any democracy, knows itself by its capacity to make connection with the "external." This may not necessarily be a complex adjustment, defined in multiple relationships. The fact of connection, let us say the *act* of connecting, is itself the first need. In both Hawthorne and Thoreau the universe remains relatively unstructured, an illuminating fact for the predispositions of the new democracy. But how many examples of connecting affinities with nature are actually exhibited in Thoreau, repeating themselves, turning back upon variations in order to achieve greater assurance. In Hawthorne the affinities which are meaningful are with the community of men; they are moral affinities but they nevertheless become the foundation of the intelligible universe as such.

One fable which treats this theme as explicitly as possible is "The New Adam and Eve." Incidentally it describes the sense in which Hawthorne is only half a Christian. In a world in which all the people had died, life begins again with the creation of another Edenic couple in an empty modern city.

> They find themselves in existence and gazing into one another's eyes. Their emotion is not astonishment; nor do they perplex themselves with efforts to discover what, and whence, and why they are. Each is satisfied to be, because the other exists likewise.

One is reminded of the fatal last interview between Captain Ahab and Starbuck. "Stand close to me, Starbuck; let me look into a human eye . . . this is the magic glass, man." The image expresses a significant continuity of theme in the literature. It is in characteristic contrast that Hawthorne would use the look at oneself in the mirror to suggest the panic of solipsism, or the uncertainty of selfhood, as in the rites of privacy described for Dimmesdale in *The Scarlet Letter.* Thoreau was fascinated by the eye of Walden pond, or the sheet of transparent ice covering it. The pond is both mirror and glass in which one sees oneself, but also looks furthest into nature. This is the transcendental look through mirror, self, and nature, but it remains the gaze of introspection, a remarkable effort to break out of that moral and existential isolation which is Hawthorne's chief theme.

Hawthorne's Pillory

Democratic theory had its sharpest dialectical strain in the assumption that it could give moral support to both sides of the contested ratio of private freedom and the communal order. This is a contest between public and private spheres of living, and it is because Hawthorne gives it such clear emphasis that his stature in the American literary tradition has grown. But it is not only the torment of moral isolation which composes his theme in that respect. The concentration is as strong upon sins against privacy and violations of the autonomy of conscience. The vengeance of Chillingworth against Dimmesdale was diabolical because it was based on the witness of his secret inner life. This was conceived as a most cruel punishment—a humiliation of the soul.

On the other hand nothing was gained from Dimmesdale's self-sustained privacy except the inner death of the spirit. It is only when he can confess his sin publicly that his suffering can begin to act for relief. Not even a private admission to God or his direct acknowledgment of guilt to Hester is able to help him. Redemption must come precisely in his willingness to confront the public community. In a sense he turns the tables on Chillingworth's form of punishment. He challenges the stranger within himself with the confession of his secret sin, and so enters the public sphere with his full private being. The people are then confronted with a new moral responsibility, a test on their side to be observed together with the ordeal Dimmesdale is undergoing. In this great exchange of opportunities Hawthorne relates the ordeal of the private moral life to the instruction and growth of the public moral life, and does this so fundamentally that in the most imaginative view of society's problems one cannot overestimate the significance of the final scaffold scene in Hawthorne's novel.

All the major characters of *The Scarlet Letter* have been stressed in public roles which are brought to climax at the conclusion of the novel. Most obviously Dimmesdale is the public teacher, the standard bearer of morality. But he is simultaneously the sinner in private, whose crime deserved death if discovered. Chillingworth is a doctor and a healer, a man of largest wisdom in the community, but in his private life he is a poisoner who uses his wisdom for destruction. Similarly, to continue the effect of radical disparities, Hester has the public role of sinner, but this becomes a surface covering her actual sacrificial virtue, pronounced in her service to Dimmesdale, to Pearl, and to the community at large.

The conflict of public and private selves is the dramatic substance of Hawthorne's tragedy. For this reason the pillory, the place of public punishment, becomes the scene for the events with greatest weight of meaning. It is the place where public and person confront each other, the place of punishment and the place of revelation, as though by this ritual drama the individual and the community must come to final terms. It stands for the theatre of conscience, the nightmare place of revealed guilt, as when Dimmesdale mounts it alone at midnight when all the town is asleep, and the active protagonists of his private existence come forward as witnesses.

That contingency of the public life makes the "self" always problematic in Hawthorne's writing. It is never granted as an autonomous possession, and in fact it would seem that it can have no independent being at all, as illustrated by that thin but important story, "Wakefield." This describes the life of a man who leaves his wife and home and takes up residence in the next street, prompted first by a "morbid vanity" in wishing to know the effect of his absence. He remains "self-banished" for twenty years, giving up "his place and privileges with living men, without being admitted among the dead." Wakefield's way of self-banishment is desperate for its inanition, and the story is briefly told. On the one hand, to presume only the autonomy of the self is to release it to its demons, or build a private prison. On the other side, to submit passively and completely to a public order (illustrated in its extreme denatured form by the community of Shakers in "The Canterbury Pilgrims") is to turn equally against life. That dual fatality never fails to instruct Hawthorne's work, and it is what makes him the dramatic moralist that he is.

In the American context it was natural to make a sin of self-assertion, just as it was natural to make a crime of repression. The former ranks first in most readers' minds when looking at Hawthorne, but it must not be put out of balance. He was not jealous for the order of a community, like his ancestor judge of Salem. He was first of all a psychologist of complex moral behavior. As in his parable "Egotism and the Bosom Serpent," for instance, the consequence of morbid egocentricity is pure suffering, a self-affliction as well as an affliction upon others. Dimmesdale's greatest pain comes in his life of secrecy, made evident by his progressive wasting disease, in contrast to Hester's transvaluation of her vitality as a public servant. In more subtle aspects Chillingworth has refused to share not his own sin, but his relation to the others in theirs, as when he renounces, by concealing, his identity as Hester's husband. Accordingly he condemns himself equally to moral isolation, and in this isolation the very definition of evil begins to change and move toward unintelligible horrors.

As Hawthorne adequately illustrates in *The Scarlet Letter*, he can embrace without confusion the contrasting moral insight which protects the immunity of persons. That privacy, which can be violated, is exposed to danger when individual aggressors are active, but also when the community poses its weight in judgment and punishment, as in the case of Hester Prynne. In the first episode of *The Scarlet Letter*, the community is committing a brutality similar in theme to that of Chillingworth in his machinations against Dimmesdale, though not conceived in diabolism. When Hester is exposed to the public on the pillory, the author makes his own comment: "There can be no outrage, methinks, against our common nature,—whatever be the delinquencies of the individual,—no outrage more flagrant than to forbid the culprit to hide his face for shame." This is sensitive, but it is one manifestation of a stronger theme in the novel, which seriously challenges the right of the public to its moral rule over individuals.

It is important to remember that the sin which interested Hawthorne as much as any other was the sin of bigots acting as public judges. The scarlet letter he pretended to find in an unused room of the Salem Custom House was one attraction, but he admitted an even more direct commitment to writing the story in seeking atonement for his Puritan ancestors, who "made themselves conspicuous in the martyrdom" of witches and Quakers.

> I know not whether these ancestors of mine bethought themselves to repent, and ask pardon of Heaven for their cruelties; or whether they are now groaning under the heavy consequences of them, in another state of being. At all events, I, the present writer, as their representative, hereby take shame upon myself for their sakes, and pray that any curse incurred by them—as I have heard, and as the dreary and unprosperous condition of the race, for many a long year back, would argue to exist—may be now and henceforth removed.

Thinking broadly about these issues, one can see in Hawthorne's work both a primitive and a sophisticated stress on problematic moral values, and this has something to do with the power of his effects. There is in the first place a bluntness in posing the questions appropriate to a pioneer effort in democratic living. The challenge of socialization is bare and fundamental. In the American democracy the temperament of judgment was such that it was as if the first principles of moral collaboration had to be examined all over again. Like writers of the Old Testament, Emerson and Thoreau communicated an inspired relationship with nature, a divine expression that harmonized with an equally religious egocentricity. Hawthorne felt it his function to teach the lessons of association and counteregotism. These seemed values in the first position of discovery, as if a society were indeed in the unique condition of creating itself.

An imagination like that of Hawthorne, unembarrassed by ideological necessities, was best equipped to deal with such themes. Was it easy to affirm that the arbiter of all judgments was the individual conscience, and that a community existed, by a kind of miracle, as the sum of such individuals? It was easier for democracy, reacting against its own anarchic strain, to assert the dominant rights of the community, particularly as they were implicit in the egalitarian ideal, the familiar logic flowing from the fact that only a restrictive community could enforce such equality. The Puritan ancestry made salvation center in the individual soul, but it also made heavy demands in the name of collective righteousness, or an abstract virtue that was only visible in the congregation of saints. The Anglo-Saxon yeoman farmer thought he was sure of his individual sovereignty, but the growth of secular institutions pressed the American democracy with the force of the political consensus, as well as the impersonal choices of the marketplace and the collective discipline of the new industries.

These were complex problems and they needed the resources of metaphor, if not allegory, to be best understood. The effect was endearingly archaic and wonderfully lucid as they translated themselves in the delicate moral sensibility of Hawthorne. There was no interest in a choice among alternatives, or in a straightforward ideological criticism. The point to be stressed is that issues that were in the province of enthusiasts on behalf of nature, and social engineers on behalf of reason and science, prophets on behalf of humanity, and reactionaries on behalf of historic order, were brought by Hawthorne back to the elementary clarifications of the moral dialogue. The sophisticated aspect of his themes, as well as the evidence of his creative imagination, is felt in the way he kept contradictions alive. The values of his society were contested half-truths until they underwent a somewhat mysterious transvaluation, which was effected in his hands through the dramatic process of gaining higher levels of recognition and sympathy. He called this a "humanizing" of character and institutions, and it is this which works to the conclusion of *The Scarlet Letter.*

To be "humanized" in Hawthorne is to be saved; that is, quite clearly, to be saved from destructive contradictions. In the case of Goodman Brown, though he renounces the "Devil," he is ironically a man lost by his knowledge of contradictions. He knows the breach between the inner self and public respectability. All the people of his life are implicated in the shame of this knowledge, the old women, the minister, the solid citizens, his father and mother, and his wife, Faith. Because he cannot resolve that issue of the moral dialectic, Brown descends into isolation and distrust; he lives the rest of his life as an austere Puritan, but only increasing his barren despair. To be saved from this fate, or properly "humanized," would have required the ultimate grace of sympathy, which clearly in that context would be a moral translation of the sense of human fallibility. Basically Goodman Brown's failure is in his inability to lose the standpoint of the self. He has not felt forgiveness for himself or those closest to him, and this is because he sees the world in his exterior judgment and not in a participatory identification with it. In that sense he loses the one value the Devil's community meeting in the forest might have given him.

Nature and Humanity

"O exquisite relief" is her exclamation as Hester tears off her badge in the forest and both of the lovers at their rendezvous feel the joy of their sudden liberation. Hester is brilliant as the exponent of this command from life. "What we did had a consecration of its own," she says. Her beauty at this point is imperious and absolute, and nature is making its great and rightful claim against conscience.

D. H. Lawrence had good reason to believe that Hester was an invention that threatened to carry Hawthorne's book out of his control. At times she seems almost contemptuously beyond the law of the community and the moral and spiritual needs of her lover. She submits to them as though despairing that any man could reach her level of emancipation. Such is the strength of life in her that even in the last act she seems to stand to one side and not take her share in that "triumphant ignominy" and repentance. Her moral isolation is real but she almost seems successful in it. For her the "balance between heart and mind" has indeed been upset, but she is able through force of character to take each extreme in its turn and make it vital. She is the woman of passion, great in her natural life, the temptation in Dimmesdale's life. Later, in her years of punishment, she turns to cold thought, and her intelligence seems more truly revolutionary and experimental than that of Chillingworth, which is strained by the spirit of revenge.

It is possible to conclude that Hester, like Chillingworth, is a lost soul, a casualty of the severe conflict, who spends the rest of her life disengaged from humanity and only partially touched by that "sympathy" which has had such profound effects on Dimmesdale and Pearl. Maternal passion binds Hester to the story on behalf of Pearl, and something similar has developed from her earlier passion for Dimmesdale. These two she might have taken with her to any form of exile, and herself survived, although they both cannot take her invitation. She therefore surrenders them, Dimmesdale to his victorious confession and his death, Pearl to humanity, symbolized by the graces of old Europe and her conventionally idealized marriage. It is significant in the epilogue that Hester separates herself from Pearl and returns to her cabin at the margin of the American settlement. Here Hawthorne speaks of her still seeking penitence, but she becomes the saintly confidante and helper for others in trouble, particularly the women in women's sorrow. Perhaps the implication is that she is beyond penitence. She has transformed the isolation of sin to the isolation of virtue, and she is not *in* the community but somewhere at its side, supporting it.

These are speculations warranted by complex, perhaps unresolved elements in Hawthorne's imagination, and indicate he was serious in examining a marginal human freedom. Like Zenobia in *The Blithedale Romance*, Hester's will matches the vitality of her impulses, she becomes a prophecy of emancipation, and Hawthorne is obviously entranced by her. On the other hand, her existence, in its wasted gifts and unused possibilities, is the sign that Hawthorne wrote a tragedy, not a moral sermon. Her self-reliance was based on the hypothesis of rare strength, and whatever her own suffering, the consequence for others would be moral insecurity, neurosis, the decay of the community, the disintegration of selves. As if knowing this, Hester gives herself up to sacrificial and remedial acts. In a sense the vitality of passion itself leads her to assent to human needs.

Dimmesdale and Pearl are her moral dependents, one might say, and they demonstrate the barrier to a natural freedom. In their lives it is clear that such freedom destroys the coherence of the personality in the world. The invitation to escape drives Dimmesdale even further toward disorientation and madness. As he walks back to the town, after their meeting in the forest, he cannot recognize himself nor can he recognize the people he meets, except in violently deranged and reversed roles. Everything becomes a phantom of his psychological misery and his past experiences. "To the untrue man, the whole universe is false,— it is impalpable,—it shrinks to nothing within his grasp." The true world is revealed as dependent on the moral communion of men.

Accepted as one of Hawthorne's framing ideas, this is the most important point of difference with Emerson and Thoreau. To achieve coherence of being was for them the success of a lyrical self-reliance. It was something gained only in self-communion, or when nature speaks in a sublime ventriloquism. Nature here might substitute for God, though in actual fact, as Emerson put it, it was more like "the ass on which the Saviour rode." A personality explores itself within its own ambience, speaks *from* itself as though the world spoke from within. For Hawthorne such affirmations are suspect, they are "impalpable." Alone in nature, reduced not elevated by its singular freedom, the human personality is unmoored, and the incoherence affects not only itself but the intelligibility of the real world.

It is quite clear that Hester's and Dimmesdale's original act could not remain isolated and self-reflecting. It is now chiefly felt in its direct consequences in the lives of others. Chillingworth is exhibited as a primary victim. His life becomes deformed by their adultery and his obsessive response to it. This clear case of moral causality is the basis of their relationships and their final destinies. Chillingworth confronts the two lovers; they face him as they face themselves in their own making. Inevitably he moves in to live with Dimmesdale, and inevitably he must take passage on the same ship which would take them to England.

Similarly Pearl insists on being acknowledged by both Dimmesdale and Hester. The scarlet letter must be returned to its place on Hester's breast, and Dimmesdale must accompany Pearl in public acknowledgment to the scaffold. This is an insistence on the responsibility of acts, as if to say no relationship is credible unless that responsibility is avowed. In communicating that point Pearl may be allegorical to an extreme, but she is an expression of a moral realism nevertheless. She dramatizes the full sequence of moral cause and effect. What she is in her character is exactly what was present at her conception, and by her sign Hawthorne insists that there is nothing gratuitous or inconsequential in a moral event.

Pearl is specifically the child of nature. She lives outside, but just outside, the moral community. "Hath she any discoverable principle of being?" "None—save the freedom of a broken law." She thereby expresses the unordered possibilities of nature or human nature without a "principle of being." She is described in her wild, unearthly beauty; she has tenderness and a capacity for love but also a great malice and an appetite for torment. The genius of the perverse is in her and she cannot distinguish among intense experiences. But she does have a need for definition; she seems to be looking for her formal being. She therefore demands that Hester resume wearing the badge of sin and that Dimmesdale give her intelligible life by acknowledging her. She has been born outside the community and yet she is the one to claim it—and to lead her mother and father back toward it from their planned escape.

In this struggle to become human Pearl might illustrate an implicit challenge to Hawthorne's transcendental contemporaries. Thoreau and Emerson were unwilling to make such a distinction between what is human and what is of nature, not because they cared less for a humanizing principle but because they insisted on it absolutely. All their assumptions proceeded from the ground that "Nature must be viewed humanly to be viewed at all." But that discovery was primary, a prerequisite for their positive beliefs. Hawthorne dramatized such a discovery and conceived its negative contrast, an inhuman nature, an inhuman life. Thoreau's words in his journal have more relevance for Hawthorne's writing than his own. "If I have no friend, what is Nature to me? She ceases to be morally significant."

To become human, the tremendous project of moral culture which marks Hawthorne's work, is not the same thing as seeing the world in human terms. It requires, rather, the making of sharp distinctions. In "Roger Malvin's Burial," for instance, the forest is described in language stamped by the human experience enacted there. The shadows among the trees emanate from Reuben's consciousness as he leaves his father-in-law to die, and they remain the projection of his guilty memory. However, this story, more clearly than others, helps define Hawthorne's concept of nature as the unredeemed wilderness. In one stress it is everything that is outside or indifferent to human existence and human valuations. In another it is the projection of the unknown and uncontrolled areas of the human psyche. In other words, in nature and in human nature there exists a boundary between that which is "humanized," which constitutes, like a frontier settlement, a charted area of recognition and communication, and that part which is unexplored and dangerous, where one can be lost. With a temperament sharply resembling that of Joseph Conrad (who spent his early lifetime as a traveler to new worlds), Hawthorne described man as a pioneer who civilizes a relatively small space in the world and in his own consciousness. The rest is dark, and in moral terms, when not empty, utterly ambiguous. The moral enterprise consists largely of the ability to define the margin and resist its encroachment. Humanity becomes a cause *against* nature, and against the unredeemed substance of original human nature. When nature in this sense is met by the single man, it is the place for the terror felt at the margin. So in "Roger Malvin's Burial" the chief infliction is that of dying alone, and, suggestively, Reuben's guilt for leaving Roger is felt with superstitious power, as if, in effect, he had violated the aboriginal law of the human community. This point is the more stressed by the fact that the choice was hopeless; Roger's death was certain and to stay with him would almost certainly have cost the young man's own life.

The diabolism Hawthorne imagines in his writing is based on the possibility of a world which can no longer be expressed through the human conscience. When that conscience is troubled or seems to be losing its hold on reality, the original elements of nature are transformed into the scene of the macabre, the nightmare. In "Young Goodman Brown," the night woods, where the demon presides over his festivals, are the antithesis to the daylight of routine Puritan compulsions. His young wife, Faith, pleads with Goodman Brown, "Stay with me tonight." At the devil's orgy, however, she is heard surrendering to the nature that is strong within her.

> There was one voice of a young woman, uttering lamentations, yet with an uncertain sorrow, and entreating for some favor, which, perhaps, it would grieve her to obtain; and all the unseen multitude, both saints and sinners, seemed to encourage her onward.

What then is this "faith" which had enjoined her husband to stay with her? It is an appeal to transcend such truthful revelations, urging him to keep faith with man.

Similarly, transgression when it comes is not against God or nature but against man. Hawthorne's Faustian characters, accepting diabolism, have not invaded the sphere of the devil, firelit as some passages are, and God is notable chiefly by his absence. The affront is to man, a violation of his interest, and Gothic and surreal as the atmosphere of their sins may be, that is the way Hawthorne makes us see Ethan Brand, Rappacini, Aylmer, and Chillingworth. He was more successful than he thought in combining the "Actual and the Imaginary" (the writing problem he put to himself in "The Custom House"), for the "Actual" is represented as the verifiable human interest, which is visible like a true talisman amid the smoke and fantasy of his alchemical laboratories.

The Democratic Faust

Reading Hawthorne, one usually begins with modest expectations, his own light tone of "romanticizing" and his lucid simplicities making their effect, and only gradually becomes aware of a surprising strength of implication. Like Melville, though with less strain as well as less grandeur, he is wrestling with big themes, issues we can call cultural, affected by the premises of belief and the actual adventures of the civilization of his time in America. Glauco Cambon, a student of American literature writing with the advantage of a European perspective, recalls Goethe and speaks of the American Faust. Goethe's genius, like that of Locke and Rousseau, seemed either to spring from the myth of the new world or to be its creator. To Cambon, the American writers were Fausts, though it might be more accurate to say that they examined Faustian experiences, as described in these first words of Cambon's study of American poetry.

> The Founding Fathers of American literature are embodiments of Faust, the prototype of Western man, who, having rejected the burden of his cultural past, finds himself confronted by a horizon of unknown possibilities. Experience is his only guide, and the demonic drive, the quest for a new formula beyond the shattered old ones ("in the beginning was the deed"), can also be said to characterize the spirit of these iconoclastic prophets to whose homeland old Goethe yearningly looked when, in one of his "Xenien" poems, he praised America for being free from the fetters of European history.[1]

European romantic literature, the Byronic tradition, the Gothic fantasia, provide their own versions of Faust's demonic drive, but Goethe is actually the best model for the seriousness and moral realism that characterize the work of Hawthorne and Melville. It may be that the American Mephistopheles offered very close and realistic temptations. In America the Faust story deepens itself because the old formulas of life were not shattered and remade in some atmosphere of restless decadence but in the actual context of revolutionary change and the clear urgencies of the new world. At the same time, if the old Goethe could have read the work of Melville or Hawthorne, he might have felt sobering modifications in that praise of America for being "free from the fetters of human history."

These may be useful ideas in dealing with the characteristic hubris of Hawthorne's scientists and magicians, whose laboratories are otherwise dark and Gothic enough. They feel licensed to invade nature, and certainly their work tends to transgress against humanity. But their resources are clearly those of humanity, and the sin is secular, democratic, bound within the paradoxes released by the idea of freedom. The imagination and the intellect are the instruments of libera-

---

1. *The Inclusive Flame* (Bloomington: Indiana University Press, 1965), p. 3.

tion, but what does it mean to be free, to act for the imagination? In briefest summary, it might mean the unrestricted pursuit of perfection as well as power in the world. The imaginative intellect, as in the example of Aylmer in "The Birthmark," develops within itself a disastrous impatience with what is human. That overcharged alchemist believed in the "quest of the universal solvent by which the golden principle might be elicited from all things vile and base." The logic of his search led him to classify his wife, Georgiana, with these inferior things, and so condemn her even before he destroyed her in his actual experiments.

It is not difficult to locate the serious basis of Hawthorne's treatment of the demonic intelligence. To abstract, to generalize, to imagine perfection, came finally to threaten Georgiana in her intrinsic, personal being. If this remained unacknowledged, the danger was released. Even a barren man of evil intelligence, like Chillingworth, understood that his existence depended on a relationship with people he hated rather than the autonomous power of his science. There was then no knowledge or power divorced from the effects of either love or hate.

A story like "The Birthmark" translates the breach between man and nature into a contest between the imagination and reality. The ideal images in the brain resist the given dross of the real world. But that dross of the real world includes human realities and persons. The imagination itself is human and so the struggle for perfection is merely a kind of civil war unless it is dominated by human valuations. The intellectual imagination may waste itself in space or, more dangerously, interpose itself in the life of nature or, even more dangerously, depart from the human sphere with the power stolen from nature, as in the discovery made by Aylmer. The humanist self-confidence of Aylmer led to his sin against life. The creative genius of Ethan Brand led directly to self-destruction.

In a poignant fairy tale, "Feathertop," Hawthorne described the creation of a puppet human being by witchcraft and art. But art and intellect can create only the illusion of life. When the young girl is attracted to the handsome scarecrow Feathertop, she has been excited by a thing of surfaces, pleasing her vain imagination. She finally sees him in the mirror for what he is, sticks, rags, and straw, just at the point when she might have made her illusion real by giving him the human kiss. He was barred from life by this failure of sympathy. "Feathertop" is the parable of the man who has not yet become human, as "Ethan Brand" is the story of the man who has gone beyond the human and found a void. The theme is familiar in Henry James, who took even more than Melville from Hawthorne's inspiration. The problem of the imagination is twofold; it must accommodate the moral sense and it must come to terms with the flawed nature of real things. The moral sense, which is confined neither by the realm of the "Actual" nor the realm of the "Imaginary," cannot accept Feathertop as a puppet of sticks and straw, which is to consider him reductively, with the eye of reason. Nor can he remain the shining artifice created by witchcraft; this is to give him over to the esthetic imagination and keep his life an illusion. To be alive he must become human, that is, a combination of flawed reality and aspiration, made whole or supportable by an act of faith.

Hawthorne's imagination is keenest when he touches this verge of living consciousness. It marks life as a precarious gathering together of antagonistic forces. Matter is repugnant to spirit, love is separated from power, the esthete wars with the practical man, reason is divorced from beauty. Only at the center of judgment itself is there a possibility of synthesis. That exuberant fantasy, "Earth's Holocaust," has special value for this topic. The bonfire holocaust features the mood of revolutionary apocalypse, with man burdened by the weight of his history and dissatisfied with all his traditional aspirations. It dramatizes the eternal restlessness of the imagination, a demonic impatience with things as they are; the struggle for perfection begins again and again. The prejudice of some who feed the fire is on behalf of nature. "Is not Nature better than any book?" The prejudice of others is that of the imagination, on behalf of all things new. So the "Titan of innovation" does his work, as the much hated and much loved symbols of civilization go into the fire. A wry observer points out, they will not eliminate death, or what death implies. An even more relevant question is raised when a young girl attempts to throw herself on the fire because she has been brought to see her worthlessness by the general rush toward perfection. She is saved by another observer, but the question remains. All such revolutions must come to terms with residual and irreducible values. The story ends with a recognition of the "human heart," which for good or evil is the source of everything human and will not burn in this fire. It is a "dark-complexioned personage" who says this, and his inference is dark. But the devil's cynicism is accompanied by a subdued human confidence. The emphasis finally is on what we can call the humanist imperative; man transcends all his works and he survives the phases of his history. Hardly heroic, this faith in man is divorced from specific claims and rises from historic failure. The great utopian dreams and revolutionary inspirations have gone into the fire.

Hawthorne's didactic but rich illustration works out as if he realized how much his own culture was dependent on the uninhibited release given to secular hopes. Revolutions are made by the imagination and revolutionary societies live by its impetus (or they do until they are created and reduced into formal being, at which point they become reactionary in the world of the imagination). In America, a conservative response was needed in order to describe the monsters created in the revolutionary imagination: intellectual monsters—abstractions that kill—or esthetic monsters, like the contraption created by Owen Warland in "The Artist of the Beautiful," a mechanical butterfly that broke in a child's grasp. The theme is prophetic in its several facets, looking forward to such literary heirs as Henry James and Wallace Stevens. These both collaborate with Hawthorne to express the insight that the active imagination is both a wealth and a special problem in a democratic civilization.

The imagination sins against experience and truth when it serves the will to power or is made rigid in the bigotry of desire or judgment. But life is multiformed, multivalued, and moves in the flux of reversible values. This vitality of substance is approached, even if with gingerly allegorical means, in all of Hawthorne's writing. Goodman Brown discovers radical, instinctive evil behind the conventional "goodness" of human character. In "Rappacini's Daughter" the process is reversed; the protagonist discovers an essential good existing in depth behind the terrifying surface of evil.

This is a condition that promotes great mistakes. In a revulsion from evil that is really a revulsion from man, Rappacini condemns himself, but above all his daughter, to the desperate defenses of his science. He has inoculated her with evil to protect her against the external danger. But Beatrice is also the victim of the univocal judgments of her lover. To Giovanni, who is the moral explorer in the story, Beatrice and her garden have first exhibited nothing but the ripe surfaces of beauty and goodness. Then the powerful poison in her nature is revealed, and Giovanni succumbs to radical distrust.

Full enlightenment and moral maturity come too late for Giovanni. The third convolution remains; at the core of her identity, Beatrice is good, loving, trustful. But this is not a matter of mere discovery; it is a naming, a choosing, and it could have been redemptive for Beatrice's indeterminate and ambiguous character, as designed by her father. Sympathy could have *given* Beatrice her saving virtue, because virtue, like life itself for poor Feathertop, is an aspect of active relationships and not a fixed possession. It depends on action and response, the exchange between communicants. In that sense evil is the effect of a relationship more than it is a cause or determination. As Beatrice says to Giovanni at the end, "Was there not, from the first, more poison in thy nature than in mine?" Similarly the active evil in the story comes from Rappacini's effort to defend his daughter against it.

The subtlety of Hawthorne's moral psychology is felt in this emphasis. Evil does not exist preceding active relationships, nor is it a force which seizes men like an uncontrollable instinct. It is more like a species of alienation, the felt effects of moral isolation, the fear and suspicion which projects itself into events. Like egotism, evil is disease of the body and mind, a sickness of character. It is curable because character is self-restoring and nourishable in the fertile interchange of human relationships.

The judgment of evil itself can be a kind of intellectual transgression against actual life. It is a sin of the intellectual imagination to form such abstractions, like the similar abstractions of the purely beautiful and the purely good. These categories, which arise from the vulnerability to criticism, tend to violate human reality by intolerance and persecution, by withdrawal and rejection, by rigid obedience to law, and by anarchic self-expression in liberty. Facing such ideal choices and ideal negations, the higher moral consciousness resists them and seeks the human state beyond the polarities of judgment, unenclosed by moral definition. The conclusion is a simple didactic message: all forms of the imagination, moral, intellectual, and esthetic, must be cautioned by humility and give constant deference to life.

How much Hawthorne gave thought to his own theme is made clear in the introduction to *The Scarlet Letter*. Studying himself, he defines the motives of the artist as working restlessly against the excesses of his own imagination. Like Ethan Brand and Aylmer, the artist is capable of upsetting the counterpoise between mind and heart and losing his place in the "magnetic chain of humanity." The most important struggle of the artist's imagination is against itself, toward gaining a new hold on reality, avoiding the hermitage of fantasy, the arid world of "magic moonshine." His aim is consciously addressed to the place where the "Actual and the Imaginary" meet; his main object, Hawthorne says, is to convert "snow images into men and women." This meeting of the "Actual and the Imaginary" he calls a "spiritualiza-tion" of experience. The medium of romance invests the familiar world with strangeness, but moonlight is not enough. A combination of moon-light and firelight, he says, in his own rapt speculation, is necessary to make things human. The moon is the distancing imagination and the fire is the fire of life.

It is probable that critics have not sufficiently appreciated the subtlety of this formula and its direct invitation to a struggle, often unsuccessful, on the part of the artist. Lionel Trilling, for instance, in an essay on Hawthorne makes the point that his work is marred by a sense of guilty omission in the duty to "reality"; because of that diffi-dence he failed to give himself up fully to his own imagination.[2] Haw-thorne himself voiced that diffidence, as in the passage from "The Custom House," and Trilling points with partial justification at the consequent enfeeblement in Hawthorne's work, sometimes expressed in didactic moralizing, which was in part an attempt to bring himself down to the ground from too much imaginative "moonshine." But the conscientious duty to reality and the obligation to seek it out were also the source of Hawthorne's richest themes as well as the center of his dramatic constructions. Hawthorne could not be himself without it, and so one is troubled by Trilling's misgivings, particularly in the context of his discussion where he makes an unfavorable comparison with Kafka. Kafka's inventions have sharper edge, no doubt, but in both cases the imaginative power is meaningful only as the instrument of a complex consciousness of experience. Hawthorne, in a clearer sense, does justice to the psychic panic of fantasy and the *moral* com-pulsion to seek and make known the actual world.

A similar misemphasis, I think, is made by another perceptive critic of his work. Marius Bewley saw Hawthorne's art being abused by his democratic conscience.

> Hawthorne's art is frequently the point at which two conflicting ten-
> dencies in him cross. The conditions of American society repel him, just
> as they had repelled Cooper, and drive him to retreat from society; but
> his democratic social conscience urges him, on the contrary, to take a
> role in society. Naturally enough, he finds that his creative and critical
> impulses inevitably side with the tendency to withdraw that he feels so
> strongly.[3]

2. Lionel Trilling, *Beyond Culture* (New York: The Viking Press, 1965), pp. 179–208.

3. Bewley, *The Eccentric Design*, pp. 117, 135.

In summing up this ambivalence, Bewley says, "It was his American democratic prejudices which provided the corrupting element." This suggests that Hawthorne's latent but frustrated theme was a more vigorous, critical, and self-confident expression of alienation from society. But surely it is not accurate to say that Hawthorne's "creative and critical impulses inevitably side with the tendency to withdraw." Those impulses drew at least half their strength from his sensitivity to the morbidities of isolation, and every strong image of withdrawal, whether of Hester, Wakefield, Ethan Brand, or Rappacini, is founded on the keenest sense of a moral problem. In other words his democratic prejudices did not corrupt or enfeeble his art; acting within his critical and tragic temperament, they offered the reason for being of his work.

What throws judgment off, as it may have in the case of Bewley, for instance, is the stress on personal withdrawal and cultural crisis in the work of Hawthorne's generation, as if the choice was between tragic prophecy and romantic alienation, in each case expressing a despair of society. That has been a favored critical approach to Melville as well as Mark Twain, and the general pressure on its behalf is particularly strong today. But it is a view that needs serious rebuttal. As I argue here and elsewhere, in each of these cases we may be seeing the enacted rites of democratic criticism, accompanied by the appropriate ordeals and reversals, whereby a society renews itself by finding the irreducible basis of its being. The novelty, I think, of democratic culture and the problem it presents for both writers and critics, is that this process of cyclical moulting can look singularly like graphic final destruction; allegiance can look like treachery or withdrawal, affirmation like despair, and all things seem divided fatally like the apparent quarrel between Hawthorne's imagination and his democratic conscience on behalf of the real world.

To return to my original reference, Hawthorne was challenged by the alternations between snow images and real images, the dialectic of moonlight and firelight, which were his images for the process of creation.

> This warmer light mingles itself with the cold spirituality of the moonbeams, and communicates, as it were, a heart and sensibilities of human tenderness to the forms which fancy summons up.

The word "fancy" could stand for all forms of the intellectual imagination, the artifacts not only of genius but those of society, which are in their own way also "moonlight" inventions. These need always to be conditioned by the reality defined as "human." In the specific literary vein, we might accordingly better understand the surreal traits of Hawthorne's writing. His taste for dream images successfully avoids artistic vacuity by the continuing hold on psychological and moral reality, as this might translate what Hawthorne meant by the "heart and sensibilities of human tenderness." But another qualification may be made on this important meeting of the "Actual and the Imaginary." He accused himself of too much "magic moonshine," but in the effective mixture, moonlight fantasies are not mere moonshine after all. Their mystifications are indispensable, they charm and attract, but more important they refine moral simplicities. Although Hawthorne was a psychologist of considerable sophistication, his probing never quite reaches conclusions but respects the impenetrability of human nature. He did not propose theories of the mind; he proposed knowledge and mystery, and that sense of mystery served his largest moral theme. Chillingworth and Ethan Brand were great psychologists but they abused life monstrously. A "human tenderness" is the compensation for limited knowledge, but it is also a defense against those half-truths, whether psychological or political, which seize power over life. One of the brightest inventions of Hawthorne's work was the parable of "The Minister's Black Veil," and the warning against lifting it.

A democratic instinct works in this caution against the abuse of power, specifically against the intellectual forms of power rather than the physical, and as much against the moral as the intellectual. In these areas exist the greatest dangers.[4] This is illustrated in the discovery that the line is not sharp or exclusive between the diabolism of Chillingworth or Ethan Brand and the works of that noble soul and philanthropist, Hollingsworth, in *The Blithedale Romance*. As Zenobia, exposing his masked selfishness in the climactic scene, exclaims, "The fiend, I doubt not, has made his choicest mirth of you." The reformist and the revolutionary are a special problem on Hawthorne's moral

4. These are the instincts of an artist, it may be said, always hostile to flat abstractions, and the obtuseness of formulas. True enough, though in this case I think they support a temperament deeply formed in a democratic culture. Hawthorne's dialectic of the "Actual and the Imaginary" has the significance of a critique of these isolated extremes. Too much respect for the "Imaginary" is like the over-stressed guidance of the moral law, of tradition, of imagined doctrine and imagined ideals. Too much respect for the "Actual" is really the imposition of another kind of law, that of science in one emphasis, and that of historic fatalism in another. Behind it, as a threat, lies the tyranny of fact, the given world. The "realist" can be the most forbidding enemy of a free society, as witness the fearful combinations of utopian and determinist doctrine in authoritarian politics. The problem then of converting "snow images into men and women," becomes immensely significant beyond art.

stage. The virtuous presumption, the utopian wilfulness that would cure human miseries becomes a violent and aggressive form of the manipulative intelligence. The implication in "Earth's Holocaust," for instance, is that such men are the chief agents in the tragic dialectic of innovation and rejection, merciless in the exercise of the narrow judgments of yea and nay. The old conflict of yea and nay will go on, the story suggests; what is characteristic in the emphasis, and characteristic in the moral tradition which Hawthorne helped clarify, is the overriding concern for the *object* of moral judgments, the sense that all moral values were limited and could even be at odds with the human interest.

The actual monsters created by fanaticism or moral enthusiasm are illustrated more decisively in "The Gentle Boy." The Puritans who persecuted the Quakers were inhuman enough, but the complication comes from the greater cruelty (greater in the context) in the fanatic resistance of the Quaker mother and father. The suffering of the little boy from both sides is at the center of the story. The irony of such moral confrontations is almost despairing. "In the meantime, neither the fierceness of the persecutors, nor the infatuation of their victims, had decreased."

Democracy and Tragedy

The tragic theme in Hawthorne's writing seems sometimes to be his response to a vestigial belief in original sin. More relevantly, considering his obsession with moral antinomies, tragedy was the natural avenue of a divided moral consciousness, a "double consciousness" in an un-Emersonian but explicit sense. If men around him were trained, like Emerson, to believe in the predestined moral harmony of the free republic, Hawthorne seemed to have appeared believing that nothing was what it seemed, that virtue bore a snake in its bosom, and, most pertinent to tragedy, that moral judgment must shrink before the veil over the human face. For a temperament so disposed it was a corollary, almost a requirement that freedom should be associated with tragic experience; the model was Prometheus as much as Faust. To define tragedy most simply is to say that it means always the discovery of limits to an heroic enterprise or stance. As such there would necessarily be a tragic component in the moral education of the free man. The great secular optimism of democracy invited that response. More specifically, Hawthorne's best work responded to the condition of a democracy by conducting its search into the limits of freedom, the limits of a communal order, and the real basis of human equality.

The affirmations of the democratic creed no doubt offered important stimuli for developing the dialectical irony that ruled Hawthorne's imagination. That mode of making neat reversals can be illustrated almost at random from his work, as in these two entries from the same page of his journal.

> Curious to imagine what murmurings and discontent would be excited, if any of the great so-called calamities of human beings were to be abolished,—as, for instance, death.

> Would it not be wiser for people to rejoice at all that they now sorrow for, and *vice versa?* To put on bridal garments at funerals and mourning at weddings? For their friends to condole with them when they attained riches and honor, as only so much care added?[5]

These are playfully mordant, but behind them is the urge to gauge life deeply, as he revealed when considering his theme in *The Scarlet Letter.* In the chatty, deceptively light discussion of "The Custom House" he attempted the description of natural happiness in a man constructing his life primarily on the basis of contentment with his dinner. Concededly a narrow definition of happiness, yet it served the general prejudice in Hawthorne's mind. He foreclosed interest in the man by deciding that he lacked a soul, for which a deep discontent, if not suffering, is required.

The Scarlet Letter itself has for its theme the life history of that "soul." It comes to its luminous existence by suffering the strong antinomies of the novel. Hester and Dimmesdale are divided from each other in the public acknowledgments of saint and sinner, though they are in love by their real affinities. Pearl, an uncivilized natural force, waits to become human, but meanwhile expresses the perverse disorder of her first condition. At the same time the Puritan community sharpens itself to inhuman bigotry in applying the law. These are the antinomies of tragic suffering, and they must approach resolution or the moral life of man is hopeless.[6]

5. *The American Notebooks*, vol. 18 of *The Complete Writings of Nathaniel Hawthorne* (Boston: Houghton Mifflin, 1903), pp. 30, 31.

6. In this respect, perhaps the best introduction for reading *The Scarlet Letter* is "The Maypole of Merrymount." Here pagan meets puritan in the most acute stage of conflict, with Endicott and his men armed and ready to slay for virtue, the pagan celebrants quite clearly vulnerable to their judgment. The young couple, lord and lady of the May, support each other in this crisis and transcend the murderous antinomy. Even Endicott recognizes their role and sends them forth without punishment as a kind of symbol of moral maturity, built upon the meeting between conscience and nature.

The question to be answered was the old one of suffering itself. It could be the instrument of God's teaching and the purgatorial gateway from this life into heaven. But could it be the support of social unity and a secular faith? And how was it consistent with the ideal of freedom? At the moment when human misery comes to the foreground, it seems that in its presence freedom appears a selfish fantasy or a terrifying irrelevance. This was one of the great issues of nineteenth-century thought, as attested in such classic expressions as that of Dostoevsky's Grand Inquisitor or the general revolutionary attack on bourgeois liberalism.

It was indeed a topic for the tragic imagination, and Hawthorne dealt with it in an unpretentious intellectual style which does not suggest the actual profundity of his theme. Freedom set the stage for tragedy; that idea was as much in his mind as it was in Melville's. But it was implicitly the necessary condition for the existence of a "soul." No number of contented dinners could do its work in that respect. Hawthorne's tragic imagination seized a further principle, basic to the challenges of the democratic ideal. This principle was that pain, not happiness or innocence, was the natural ground of human communication and the support of human communities.[7] In the forest, when Dimmesdale and Hester imagine their escape, they are almost free, almost happy. But Pearl, Chillingworth, the Puritans, all block their path. This is not by a tyranny of conscience or a compulsive obedience to the law. When Hester and Dimmesdale mount the scaffold, they are together in a profounder sense than in the forest, and *all* are together—the husband, the child, the lovers, the people, the place, in effect the whole moral world and its contradictions. In this sense the

---

7. An entry in the notebooks suggests a kind of sociology of suffering. Hawthorne speculates as follows:

> A new classification of society to be instituted. Instead of rich and poor, high and low, they are to be classed, First, by their sorrows: for instance, whenever there are any, whether in fair mansion or hovel, who are mourning the loss of relations and friends, and who wear black, whether the cloth be coarse or superfine, they are to make one class. Secondly, all who have the same maladies, whether they lie under damask canopies or on straw pallets or in the wards of hospitals, they are to form one class. Thirdly, all who are guilty of the same sins, whether the world knows them or not; whether they languish in prison, looking forward to the gallows, or walk honored among men, they also form one class. Then proceed to generalize and classify the whole world together, as none claim utter exemption from either sorrow, sin, or disease; and if they could, yet Death, like a great parent comes and sweeps them all through one darksome portal,— all his children (*The American Notebooks*, pp. 28–29).

social bond is forged, not broken, by suffering, and it is a bond which has no significance except as approached by those who have known or practiced freedom. Pearl, the chief beneficiary of the testamental act on the scaffold, is the emblem of the theme; she is the vital spirit of instinct and life captured within the mold of humanity.

The narrative is most explicit on this point. Moral suffering is an initiation into the state of being human. It gives privileges of membership according to its intensity and the proportionate awareness gained. Hester's scarlet badge becomes "the taper of the sick chamber." "She came, not as a guest, but as a rightful inmate, into the household that was darkened by trouble." It is this forced acknowledgment which gives her the great moral advantage she has over both Dimmesdale and Chillingworth. In real terms the climax of Hester's struggle ends with her first day on the scaffold. From that point on she grows in character and strength.

Both Dimmesdale and Chillingworth have tried to conceal rather than enact their commitments in the open world, and the result is to triple the burden in private. Chillingworth in a particular stress of pride as well as vengeance has refused the role of victim-husband. His dehumanization begins here, and from this point his unrestrained intelligence carries him to diabolism. Though Chillingworth has become all mind, hardly capable of the proper instinct of revenge, he cannot break his ties with these people and this place. He and the others remain bound together, though it is a terrible inversion of the moral community.

The human community is, it seems, a necessity beyond rational or practical justification. It is partly for this reason that Hawthorne dramatizes the failure of a great intelligence, like that of Chillingworth. The latter is a curiously modern villain. He is not in love with evil, and he is not morally vindictive in the wish to punish it; he is skeptical and fatalistic, bitter in his response to experience, curious about the operations of human character, and eager only to aid the natural laws of suffering as they affect his victims and himself. In a word he is a pessimist who respects only his knowledge of the world, to the point of supporting its demonstrative proofs.

Chillingworth is like a black shadow opposed to the Emersonian optimism. The answer to him must meet him on his own ground in this abusive and absurd commingling of humanity, united apparently only in mutually inflicted suffering. What makes a true community, with its beneficent values as well as its tragedies? This is not a matter for detached intelligence, and Hawthorne makes his characteristic stress on the action of the "heart" and on "sympathy." Sympathy has a tragic meaning, however, which departs from the traditional romantic emphasis; it is not a fountain of easy sentiment, but a response to antagonisms which seem impossible to resolve. Tragic sympathy thrives where the world's problems seem hopeless, when as in the argument of Hegel, the ethical substance is divided within itself. The ethical dialectic of democracy becomes relevant to tragedy at this point. Sympathy stands for a kind of transcendent good faith, the last appeal, as it might be put, in the face of irremediable conflict. As the action of the "heart" it solves nothing in the entanglement of interests, yet it is a mute, unarguing affirmation of unity, the context itself of the community's survival.

Hawthorne's tragedy in its ultimate scene is a kind of ritual exaggeration for a tolerance or sympathy which could be present in the most placid and mundane event. In this respect the tragic vision is linked to the ideal common sense of a people which perceives existence in such a way as to refute the categorical distinctions, moral or otherwise, which are most often the armament of bigotry and oppression. It might be described as the way in which the community takes possession of experience. It is significant that Hawthorne tends to stress the polarity in events precisely when those events or experiences are most visibly public. In this way the rose bush grows against the wall of the jail. Hester's scarlet insignia is a beautiful red design against the drab background of her Puritan dress. On the scaffold, carrying Pearl, she presents the image of the Madonna simultaneously with that of the degraded woman. Insofar as the tragic protagonist embodies this mixture of terms, the common man of a democracy finds his way to him not in order to bring heroes down but to confirm a moral equality in the nature of what is human.

The last emphasis is on the tableau of saint and sinner finally united on the scaffold. The dramatic search of the novel is toward a way of *including* Hester and what she represents in every significant expression of life, not merely in transvaluing her sin or conducting her toward redemption. "Felix culpa" is the ground of all equality, and the key to this is in the act of recognition when the community's moral spokesman unites himself with Hester. If a redemption is involved here it is as pointedly that of the community as that of the protagonists themselves.[8] It is notable for instance how Hawthorne pauses to describe the variants in type, dress, and origin among those who are witnesses to the final drama. Before all these the dignity and moral force of their best man has just been established in his Election Sermon. Before them he now reveals himself and accepts his disgrace. In what sense can we say that the democratic imagination is at work? Knowing the *possibility* of a moral excellence, one discovers its opposite as an equal possibility. To fuse these possibilities is to universalize and reconcile mankind. To do otherwise is to categorize men in a moral inequality, the most dangerous, by far, of all forms of inequality because it is usually the ground for defending inequality. The final object of the democratic aspiration is to find an uncategorized humanity.[9]

As Aristotle emphasized, tragedy treats the misfortunes of a man who is ultimately discovered to be a man like ourselves. This is sometimes not adequately considered in a view of the parallel Aristotelian point that the tragic fall is a fall from high place. This precisely, how-

8. One special emphasis of Hawthorne's book comes from his characterization of the life of that early American community. Puritans though they were and religious, their inclinations seem bent not toward God so much as a congregation of piety formed of themselves. Their interests, the problems they recognize, are moral not spiritual; they have everything to do with the interaction of person and person, individual and society, but hardly anything to do with the religious dialogue with God. It is not God, for instance, who can help Dimmesdale, that devout man. This is demonstrated clearly by the conclusion of the story, where whatever could appear as "grace" or the salvation of sinners requires the fusion of public and private experience, or what could be called the redemption of the person in the community, the community in the person.

9. Democratic equality in this view is primarily a moral principle and not simply a sociological or political term. It cannot be adequately described or fulfilled on the extrinsic plane of prestige and possessions. It must be defined intrinsically as a form of moral parity and communion. The conclusion can follow that a system of economic and social equality may not be a system of moral equality at all, but its opposite, if it depends on the allowance from the strong to the weak, or the wise to the ignorant.

I would propose that the American tradition, whatever its flaws in other measures of equality, has tried to put moral equality first, and rightly so, in the interests of a democracy. This involves the primary assumption of the right of each man to judge his own interests. These may be misconceived, in terms of a "false consciousness," but the right to judge *that* must also remain intact. It follows that the various rights of free speech, dissent, personal involvement, and the contestant franchise are primary because they are the rights which express a moral equality. If this is what men claim, no amount of well-distributed euphoria in a perfectly just state can substitute for it. This is not to say that poverty is not degrading or economic justice is a trifle. But the authoritarian relief of those evils, whether violent or paternal, is even more degrading in the democratic ethic.

ever, is the best way to stress the equality of men. Tragedy organizes a treatable concept of the universal, and the tragic response, which Hawthorne called sympathy, is its binding solvent. A viable concept of the universal admits the dialectic of its being. This is what the tragic action has manifested most clearly. No simple moral definitions are now possible, and one might usefully say that if there is any class of judgments which tragedy purges most cleanly it is that of categorical prejudice. As Hester and Dimmesdale are united on the scaffold, they reverse and exchange values. Dimmesdale is seen as the culprit, Hester is the saint. Then they move together again in the common shape of the human.

That humanity is a collective symbol. The final scene on the scaffold is an enactment of the sense of community, precisely in the Greek sense when the spirit of the polis was renewed in the communal rite of tragedy. This gives the classic ring to Hawthorne's novel, as well as its deep affinity to the spirit of the early American democracy. After Dimmesdale's inspired sermon, a great cry from all present touches the depth of communal experience. Led by the guiltiest and most secretive man present, all men have sensed their common nature. It remains only for the last act of acknowledgment to arouse that sympathy for themselves, now mingled with sympathy for others, which confirms a community.

Emerson would understand Hawthorne at this point, though he might not appreciate the difficult road of getting there. As Hester and Dimmesdale stand together they support a marriage of spirit and nature, the life force in one, the clarifying conscience in the other. With appreciation and dismay the will to be free has had its full recognition, and so has the demand of the communal order. Meanwhile the intellectual devils of disbelief, the knowledge of contradictions, the awareness of unacceptable depths in both nature and man, make a symbolic retreat with Chillingworth, whose purposes stand defeated. A retreat, that is, because in tragic terms there is no coherent or explicit moral victory. Similarly the community is "humanized," thereby transcending its own abusive and simplistic laws. But this does not predict a new formula of laws. To be "humanized" is to reach a luminous consciousness, a moral readiness or sympathy which is a temperament in human relations, but not a definition of what they should be. Understanding Hawthorne's term this way makes it singularly appropriate to the needs of democratic society.

In this context it is a stronger surprise to recall Richard Chase's judgment that the American writers of this generation were willing to abandon moral questions and ignore the scene of man in society.[10] It was not his view alone, of course. Representing the dominant judgment, H. B. Parkes remarked:

> What is lacking in their [Poe's, Hawthorne's and Melville's] framework of experience is any sense of society as a kind of organic whole to which the individual belongs and in which he has his appointed place.[11]

The problem may be reflected in that last phrase; to have an "appointed place" and all that goes with it, the securities, the obligations, might itself obstruct the deeper view of "the spectacle of man in society." The Americans saw this in crisis, not in terms of the harmonic qualities of a civilization at its center, but at its margin, where the danger is tragic, where society, as well as man, can be lost. *The Scarlet Letter* illustrates this perfectly, and Emerson perhaps less clearly. The margin in his case is transcendental, bordering on God, or universal spirit, to which man ascends from his engagement with society and history. The classic American writers were so deeply concerned with the problem of society and of human relations within it, that they treated it on the largest ground, as a religious culture would treat relations with its God. It is in this emphasis that one can understand Hawthorne's use of terms like "Felix Culpa" and the "triumphant ignominy" of Dimmesdale's martyrdom. It could be argued that such borrowed modes of redemption limit the tragic realism of Hawthorne's work. But his "Felix Culpa" does not transcend the human state. It penetrates as deeply as possible within it, accepting what it finds, and the proper heroism of a man, the self-definition of the tragic protagonist, characterizes the conclusion a good deal better than the affirmations of Christian martyrdom. Even so, it seems by strong compulsion a triumph of renewed belief, universal in its inclusiveness. The definition of tragic effect in this case must be modified to include the frame

10. See my discussion in chapter 1, above.

11. H. B. Parkes, "Poe, Hawthorne, Melville: An Essay in Sociological Criticism," *Partisan Review* 16 (February 1949): 159.
    The rebuttal made by Q. D. Leavis to Parkes is worth repeating, since it makes what I think is the appropriate claim for Hawthorne's work. "It is precisely those problems, the relation of the individual to society, the way in which a distinctively American society developed and how it came to have a tradition of its own, the relation of the creative writer to the earlier nineteenth century American community, and his function and how he could contrive to exercise it—the exploration of these questions and the communication in literary art of his findings—that are his claim to importance" (Q. D. Leavis, "Hawthorne as Poet," *The Sewanee Review* 59 [1951]:183).

of what one might call a democratic morality drama, superimposed upon the essentials of tragic experience.

With that firmness of resolution we have come through to where
Emerson and Thoreau began their own panegyrical assurances. Theirs
is a belief by faith whereas Hawthorne invokes a humanist belief by
works and action. In effect Emerson and Thoreau won their way to
synthesis by fiat of the mind and in spiritual contemplation. In Thoreau's case a religious integration, expressed in the common language
of man and nature, was necessary before he could make a statement for
freedom, where freedom is exercised in the welcome of nature, which
is itself a community. We might put it that Hawthorne has a kind of
second thought on behalf of freedom, a maturing and correcting
thought. The self is not formed in withdrawal and independence, within its own mirror, or within its private dialogue with nature. It is formed
in a dramatic meeting with that which *opposes* the self, as in the paradigm of tragedy. These encounters could convey a sense of the community sternly demanding its old right from individuals, and of
individualists, in their turn, intoxicated by resistance. The terms
suggest that only tragedy could deal with the full pitch of such oppositions. If his life was indeed some sort of unifying testament, as was
Dimmesdale's, the tragic protagonist could then be a true democratic
personage, who was inclusive, as Emerson and Thoreau made the person inclusive, and yet inspired a reverence for final distinctions. This
democratic hero has gained a "soul," fired in the ordeal of contention.

What he most clearly inspires, however, is a form of consciousness
which we call tragic. This resembles the Emersonian transcendental
consciousness in important respects, much as it differs in others. They
both supply the means of detaching moral judgments from the limited
alternatives of choice, or from their objectification in events. Both are
perspectives to one side, which keep the conscience in reserve, never
wholly committed to fixed agents of belief or the seeming completeness
of truth. In this way the Puritan community was taught to condition
its view of its saint, Dimmesdale, the social outcast, Hester, and their
transgression of its laws. Better than the mode of Emerson, the tragic
consciousness includes the possibility of a faith "beyond skepticism,"
disciplined in the knowledge of contradictions.

With a lucidity that parallels Tocqueville, Hawthorne exposed a
system of values that criticized each other, and for that reason we can
see the relevance of his work to a traditional wisdom of democracy.
He created an open dialectic of values, open in the sense that they re-

sist the intervention of a combining formula. The cost of this liberality of insight is considerable pain, appropriate on the stage of tragedy, but its reward is critical insight. The integrating core is a consciousness capable of regarding with respect the great moral enthusiasms which are at war in the democratic system. The affirmative idealism of Emerson suggested that no sincere and authentic man can move into discord with his community, if it is an enlightened and authentic community. But in the view of Hawthorne's tragedy this is a question-begging idealism. Affirmations begin with the ruin of such hopes, on the pillory of community life. God proved his mercy, Dimmesdale says, "by bringing me hither, to die this death of triumphant ignominy before the people." The traditional Christian reward in punishment is implicit in these words, but something more. A "triumphant ignominy before the people" was most simply the recognition of moral equality among men. But in subtler reach, it could as well be called a "triumphant irony," an irony that has met the deepest source of contradiction and survived in a moral consciousness. This, one has reason to say, may be the richest ground of spirit for a democracy. It has purged itself of monopolistic terms of judgments. A man has fallen, a world of judgments has fallen in what seems the greatest confusion, and yet the reason for faithful being is made secure. In this case surely there is application for what John Dewey brought from "the final word of Emerson's philosophy, the identity of Being, unqualified and immutable, with Character." On that basis, a clear and invulnerable humanism, the struggle of contingencies resumes. But the terms of conflict are themselves enriched. The figure of Hester Prynne lives strongest after the drama, for in her the passion of a democracy is renewed toward both its gods, or rather those unperfected deities that Plato called daimons, the daimon of an unsatisfied freedom and the daimon of an unsatisfied justice.

6/ Melville
"One Royal Mantle of Humanity"

A Democratic Dignity

Captain Ahab, megalomaniac, dictator of his ship, is the democratic hero fallen from grace. He is the evil genius of freedom because of his determination to test his personal power to the limit, to act always in a challenge to life that holds back nothing, and as though one were put into the world to seek mastery of it.

It is a universal response to Melville's book to feel its epic qualities, particularly in the sense that it shapes the legendary frame of American experience. The analogies of this experience with Captain Ahab's voyage are clear. At the center there is one stressed dramatic event: man facing the unexplored world, summoning the largest range available to his own choice and action. The psychological prologue could be described in the way Ishmael prepares for the Pequod's long and indeterminate voyage. He feels, he confesses, a tormented energy and curiosity. Pulled by his own strength, he rushed toward his meeting with that monster of immanent existence, "one grand hooded phantom, like a snow hill in the air."

> With other men, perhaps, such things would not have been inducements; but as for me, I am tormented with an everlasting itch for things remote. I love to sail forbidden seas, and land on barbarous coasts. Not ignoring what is good, I am quick to perceive a horror, and could still be social with it—would they let me—since it is but well to be on friendly terms with all the inmates of the place one lodges in.

What is telling here is Ishmael's remark that he could "be social" with a horror, "would they let me." There is a pioneering bravado in such words, but also the wry premonition of defeat. This is not Captain Ahab speaking, of course; he would not be social with a horror.

In his case the appeal has turned to hatred, and the difference is fundamental, appropriate to the contrasting roles of Ishmael and Ahab in the story. Ishmael is still the good American; he remembers that he must live in this place, whatever he finds in it. But his anticipation of a "horror" is a way of describing the atavistic impulse of the voyage. Ahab is an Old Testament warrior; his prophets surround him, among them Bildad and Peleg, whaling-captain oaths mingling with Scripture. The savage trappings of Peter Coffin's inn, "a heathenish array of monstrous clubs and spears," and Queequeg the cannibal add to the omens for a journey backward to the starting point of human history. Everything will be in question in Melville's book; the theme will pursue the problematic origin of any religion, any metaphysics, and that of comprehensible humanity itself.

The democratic hero of Melville's imagination has been thrown again into the mouth of the Leviathan. He repeats a primitive experience and, as a free man, is doomed to repeat it eternally. Americans at least could see themselves in this way. In one of the most pregnant of his remarks on the literature of a democracy, Tocqueville said that a democratic writer would have a distinctive vision of man because metaphysical man in his primary being was his only subject. The emphasis is worth repeating in his own image, as the prototype of a democratic literature.

> Man springs out of nothing, crosses time, and disappears forever in the bosom of God; he is seen but for a moment, wandering on the verge of the two abysses, and there he is lost.[1]

This finds a rich echo in what was later to come from American writers in the first period of literary renaissance, and nowhere does it have better application than to Melville's book. In a clear sense Tocqueville's passage repeats the subject of Ahab's recurrent brooding, and Ahab himself might sum up his final desperate awareness before he dies, in the stress on the words "wandering between two abysses," "disappears forever," and "is lost."

To tell the story of the Pequod required the fullest imagination of those "abysses" which surrounded life. His theme compelled Melville to produce an articulate awe and terror, to suggest the quality of an "aboriginal awfulness" as he put it.

> Though we know the sea to be an everlasting terra incognita, so that Columbus sailed over numberless unknown worlds to discover his one

1. Tocqueville, *Democracy in America*, p. 80.

superficial western one; though, by vast odds, the most terrific of all mortal disasters have immemorially and indiscriminately befallen tens and hundreds of thousands of those who have gone upon the waters; though but a moment's consideration will teach, that however baby man may brag of his science and skill, and however much, in a flattering future, that science and skill may augment; yet for ever and for ever, to the crack of doom, the sea will insult and murder him, and pulverize the stateliest frigate he can make; nevertheless, by the continual repetition of these very impressions, man has lost that sense of the full awfulness of the sea which aboriginally belongs to it.

To invite this knowledge can create a spiritual revulsion which shakes the world. Ahab does indeed, "Consider the subtleness of the sea. . . . Consider, once more, the universal cannibalism of the sea; all whose creatures prey upon each other, carrying on eternal war since the world began."

The point of these images is to isolate the human ethic within the universe. Melville's deepest sustained theme is a challenge to anthropomorphic illusions, and even that soul of equanimity, Queequeg, voices it in its simplest terms. He and another sailor have been fighting off sharks which are attacking a captured whale, and they observe the remarkable ferocity that survives in them, though wounded or dead, "by a sort of generic or Pantheistic vitality."

> They viciously snapped, not only at each other's disembowelments, but like flexible bows, bent round and bit their own; till those entrails seemed swallowed over and over again by the same mouth, to be oppositely voided by the gaping wound.

Queequeg makes a judgment which could speak for Ahab.

> "Queequeg no care what god made him shark. . . . wedder Fejee god or Nantucket god; but de god wat made shark must be one dam Ingin."

This questioning of God is reinforced by the echoes of the Job story (as rendered in vaudeville parody, for instance, in dialogue between Stubb and Flask) which emphasize God's peculiar agreement with the Devil to torment mankind. Captain Ahab, with his capacity for moral revulsion, might reasonably decide that the world actually belongs to the Devil, or that Devil and God are the same. Thus Ahab calls up Fedallah, the demonic figure from the hold of the ship, to be his servant. The significant fact about Fedallah is that he is a follower of Zoroaster and believes in a dual universe, unresolved in its conflict between the forces of good and evil. This is a doctrine whose function for Ahab is to emphasize that forms of "pantheistic vitality" rule the world and that the principle organizing it is conflict, not harmony, a conflict whose ultimate expression is the battle between man and nature.

The superstitious whalemen think Moby Dick is ubiquitous and immortal and that he is something like a god. Cases are cited of the actual worship of the whale, and in one vivid example his skeleton has become a temple, the bones overgrown with palms and grasses. Ahab, however, understands that the whale is not a god, but the antithesis of what a god can be. In the whale's profundity of meaning the gods themselves have drowned, and his secret would "make an infidel of Abraham." That the whale is malign is a most frequent and expressive aspect of Ahab's obsession. But deeper than that he senses the speechless ignoring void, and his preference may be to inhabit it with his demons. If the whale indeed represents some sort of god, his anterior attributes are parodied in another personification, the Carpenter-God, whom Ahab calls "leg-maker" and "man-maker."

> "Art not thou the leg-maker? Look, did not this stump come from thy shop?"
> "I believe it did, sir; does the ferrule stand, sir?"
> "Well enough. But art not thou also the undertaker?"
> "Aye, sir; I patched up this thing here as a coffin for Queequeg; but they've set me now to turning it into something else."
> "Then tell me; art thou not an arrant, all-grasping, inter-meddling, monopolizing, heathenish old scamp, to be one day making legs, and the next day coffins to clap them in, and yet again life-buoys out of those same coffins? Thou art as unprincipled as the gods. . . ."
> "But I do not mean anything, sir. I do as I do."
> "The gods again. . . ."

In this rare moment of ironic reflection Ahab has forgotten the demon spirit whose "right worship is defiance." But the carpenter suggests all the more significantly the source of his torment, as in the following passage which describes the wooden builder in a universe of wood.

> For nothing was this man more remarkable, than for a certain impersonal stolidity as it were; impersonal, I say; for it so shaded off into the surrounding infinite of things, that it seemed one with the general stolidity discernible in the whole visible world, which . . . ignores you, though you dig foundations for cathedrals.

That "general stolidity" is the worst of the gods, but in the face of it, Ahab's defiance becomes most meaningful, even sane, as he asserts himself and his cause in the fatal contest.

In the midst of the personified impersonal, a personality stands here. Though but a point at best; whencesoe'er I came, wheresoe'er I go; yet while I earthly live, the queenly personality lives in me, and feels her royal rights.

To record this is to modify that version of Ahab which sees him as a Promethean figure committing gigantic hubris, or as the protagonist of a self-assertive ideal of freedom which has turned into megalomania. That conception of Ahab describes him as an unusually strong man, maddened by the limits to his strength. He is the archetypal leader of men in a series of expeditions which exploit and master nature until he is finally challenged by the resistance of the fatal white whale himself. From what else does his passion to transgress limits spring? It is emphasized that Ahab has the special majesty of a hero, a king among men. A regal dignity, yes, but as it becomes clear, this hero has been selected from the "kingly commons."

> Ahab, my captain, still moves before me in all his Nantucket grimness and shagginess; and in this episode touching Emperors and Kings, I must not conceal that I have only to do with a poor old whale-hunter like him.

The ordeal which he magnifies in his monomania is a common denominator of human fate, as simply universal as death. It is not that Ahab feels the insult offered to great men who wish to exceed the common lot. It is rather the insult offered by an omnipotence which recognizes no courage, no motive, no quality, but annihilates the minimal significance which is human. In the face of this power all human distinctions are irrelevant; it was not Ahab's greatness that was challenged, though his greatness arose from that challenge.

To mistake this is to misread Melville's book; to stress a diseased egotism, like that of Roderick Elliston in Hawthorne's story or even the power drive of Ethan Brand, is to emphasize a pathology and leave unclear the tragic and universal theme of Melville's book, as well as its specific references to the moral premises of democracy. That these were at stake in Melville's mind is as clear as his words can make it in a remarkable peroration on the subject of human courage, dignity, and the rights of personality.

> It is a thing most sorrowful, nay shocking, to expose the fall of valor in the soul. Men may seem detestable as joint stock-companies and nations; knaves, fools, and murderers there may be; men may have mean and meagre faces; but man, in the ideal, is so noble and so sparkling, such a grand and glowing creature, that over any ignominious blemish in him all his fellows should run to throw their costliest robes. That immaculate

manliness we feel within ourselves, so far within us, that it remains intact though all the outer character seems gone; bleeds with keenest anguish at the undraped spectacle of a valor-ruined man. . . . But this
august dignity I treat of, is not the dignity of kings and robes, but that
abounding dignity which has no robed investiture. Thou shalt see it
shining in the arm that wields a pick or drives a spike; that democratic
dignity which, on all hands, radiates without end from God; Himself!
The great God absolute! The centre and circumference of all democracy!
His omnipresence, our divine equality!

If, then, to meanest mariners, and renegades and castaways, I
shall hereafter ascribe high qualities, though dark; weave round them
tragic graces; . . . then against all mortal critics bear me out in it, thou
just Spirit of Equality, which has spread one royal mantle of humanity
over all my kind!

I think there can be no doubt that this passage reflects the quickening
point of Melville's inspiration. "The fall of valor in the soul" is a terrible event, it leads to nothing less than the disintegration of the personality. Valor is the support of dignity, that is, a "democratic dignity."
Equality requires this self-respect, for men would otherwise divide
into those who take possession of others and those who surrender themselves. (The carpenter's world is a rather good description of a totali-
tarian universe.) Such self-respect requires the affirmation of courage,
for to lose courage is implicitly to lose the claim to independent being,
in respect to nature and in respect to man.

We know that democracy and its moral dilemmas, particularly
the problem of human equality, obsessed Melville at the time he was
writing *Moby Dick*. His mood was almost defiant on the subject as he
wrote to Hawthorne.

There have been those who, while earnest in behalf of political equality,
still accept the intellectual estates. And I can well perceive, I think, how
a man of superior mind can, by its intense cultivation, bring himself, as
it were, into a certain spontaneous aristocracy of feeling,—exceedingly
nice and fastidious,—similar to that which, in an English Howard, conveys a torpedo-fish thrill at the slightest contact with a social plebian.
So, when you see or hear of my ruthless democracy on all sides, you may
possibly feel a touch of a shrink, or something of that sort. It is but nature to be shy of a mortal who boldly declares that a thief in jail is as
honorable a personage as Gen. George Washington. This is ludicrous.
But Truth is the silliest thing under the sun.[2]

2. *The Letters of Herman Melville*, ed. Merrel R. Davis and W. H. Gilman
(New Haven: Yale University Press, 1960), pp. 126–27.
    The passage from Melville's letter reflects Hawthorne's own interest in forms
of intellectual aggrandizement. The "intellectual estates" will always question dem-

This affirmation, which sounds desperate, bringing a thief in jail to stand with George Washington, is a reflection of his theme in *Moby Dick*. The savages and exiles, "the renegades and castaways," of the Pequod's crew are the evidence of his "ruthless democracy," but it is the contest with the whale itself which demonstrates the basis of equality. In simplest terms, men are equal before the ultimate strength of nature, equal before death. Courage distinguishes the personality in that universal struggle, and truly it can compare thieves to George Washington, for all the more refined distinctions of behavior and physical and intellectual capacity have been swept away. But then, one might ask, is this equality limited to the brave and are cowards beyond acceptance? The fatal point, of course, is that courage links with strength, and strength is the factor in oppression and inequality. Melville faces this naturalistic logic in his book; it is the way in which Ahab turns from the champion of man to become tyrant of his ship. The issue is so strong in Melville's mind that he introduces cowardly Pip, the cabin boy, in scenes with Ahab which are almost sentimental in their appeal of the weak to the strong. But before that point is reached, the men of the Pequod match each other in their manliness, vie in the exercise of courage, which must be understood, as I have said, as the aboriginal virtue because it is equated with survival as well as self-respect.

Courage then, the universal manliness, marks out the equality of the men on board ship, but as distinctions progress we see that this primitive ethic establishes a hierarchy. The harpooners, Daggoo, Tash-

---

ocratic equality, perhaps unanswerably, and it would be plausible that both the popular folklore and the sophisticated culture of a democracy would warn against the misuse of intellect. The appeal to the "heart" as against the "intellect," to sympathy as the guide of knowledge, is part of the moral conditioning of democracy, a necessary premise for its existence.

The problem was deep and had ramifications for Melville. The confession of his "ruthless democracy" makes it possible to conclude that in writing *Moby Dick* he brought into balance for a long creative moment the forces which fought in his mind for assent or yielded to disbelief. That the balance was tense is evidenced by an afterthought in the same letter to Hawthorne. "It seems an inconsistency to assert unconditional democracy in all things, and yet confess a dislike to all mankind—in the mass. But not so,—But it's an endless sermon,—no more of it."

If this was uncertainty it has been reflected by his critics, some finding, like D. H. Lawrence, that Melville's strongest note was a revulsion from humanity. Apart from the merits of his case, which I discuss later in this chapter, one speculates that some measure of misanthropy must associate with the practice of democracy and may even be an ingredient of its value system. Translating this distrust for "mankind in the mass," the American democracy drew up its own safeguards.

tego, and Queequeg, are distinguished by their courage, because they are savages and understand natural survival. This upsets civilized distinctions, but immediately their natural superiority imposes a new order of rank; they are the harpooners, "squires" of the ship. The "knights" distinguish themselves in their turn. Starbuck's courage is a civilized and refined principle, daring, even noble, in its exercise of limited aims in the whale hunt, but basically prudent and refusing unnecessary risks. Stubb is sensual in his courage, as with everything else. He enjoys his courage as he does eating a whale steak. Flask is simply the unintelligent fighting terrier whose courage is reflexive.

Ahab is imperial in his courage, the most desperate and most sophisticated case, willing to approach the margin and test himself as if he could force a total revelation of his manhood and his life. He is described as a man of bronze, fixed and fearless, brought to the pitch of his unsurrendering will. If he is so greatly and destructively himself, it is because he has been challenged and understands the challenge. He has been struck by lightning and carries the scar down the length of his body. He has lost a leg, he is old and worn; in other words, if he survives at all he survives by the force of "valor in the soul." His judgment has come to a crucial point; in a universe run by "cricket players, ye pugilists (ye deaf Burkes and Blinded Bendigoes)" his courage is the only faculty that has relevant use.

But the courage (or dignity) that was exacerbated becomes madness. "I'd strike the sun if it insulted me," Ahab cries. "Who's over me?" The loss of his leg does not have fragmentary meaning; it means everything, for the autonomy of his body in a naturalist world is essential to the autonomy of character. An emasculating injury, the obvious Freudian reading would say. That is true, but perhaps in a less reductive sense than is usually meant. The word "insult" is the key to understanding. Ahab faces the possibility of seeing in himself "the undraped spectacle of a valor-ruined man." He suffers from humiliation on the heroic level of response, and it is this which gives him a "tragic grace."[3]

3. A significant affinity between the work of Dostoevsky and Melville is felt here. That contemporary on the other side of the world was also stressing humiliation as a metaphysical and psychological theme in a universe without God. Ahab might well have understood the remark of one of Dostoevsky's minor characters who says, if God does not exist, how can I be a captain then? More to the point, the specific pathology of Dostoevsky's "underground man" is based on the insult offered him by that "stone wall" of indifferent nature which confronts any man with enough consciousness to see it and reject mere animal complacency. Melville uses the same image

To conceive Ahab as the hero of tragic democracy, we must think of an original confidence, not unlike Emerson's, which supported his vigorous freedom on the open seas. This good faith has been amputated by the white whale. To understand this original confidence it is necessary to recall the words "man in the ideal, so noble and so sparkling, such a grand and glowing creature." It is necessary also to oppose to that ideal the "universal cannibalism of the sea." Ahab, contesting the "outrageous strength" and "inscrutable malice" of the whale, implies a defense of that ideal of man. And for that reason he thinks only of a great "insult" and thinks obsessively of retaliation, blow for blow.

> "Talk not to me of blasphemy, man; I'd strike the sun if it insulted me. For could the sun do that, then could I do the other; since there is ever a sort of fair play herein, jealousy presiding over all creations. But not my master, man, is even that fair play. Who's over me?"

We are dealing with a tragedy, and in tragedy a great claim on life turns toward a great and destructive mistake. Ahab cries that he would pit himself against "all truth with malice in it." His suffering has brought him to believe, however, that malice is in "all truth." Ahab goes toward the mouth of Leviathan as though his death is necessarily murder, and so he offers murder in turn, even in his last gesture. He has made the shark principle exclusive in nature, and has become the shark, or killer whale, himself. But the narrowness of choice is his, not that of nature. On the third day of the chase, at the last interval before final destruction, Moby Dick is seen swimming in full velocity, not toward the ship, but in the opposite direction. Starbuck cries,

> "Oh, Ahab . . . not too late is it, even now, the third day, to desist. See! Moby Dick seeks thee not. It is thou, thou, that madly seekest him!"

There have been details to stress that the whale includes much more than fatal strength and malice. From his substance comes light and food, as Stubb, in the plain human bravado of survival, demon-

---

in exactly the same sense. "If man will strike, strike through the mask! How can the prisoner reach outside except by thrusting through the wall? To me, the white whale is that wall, shoved near to me. Sometimes I think there's naught beyond. But 'tis enough."

Of course the more direct analogy in Melville's writing to the sullen inversions of the "underground man" is Bartleby, who in explicit effect, spends his life and dies facing the "stone wall."

strates in eating a whalesteak by the light of the whale-oil lantern. The whale's substance is comfortingly familiar and ubiquitous, as emphasized in a reference to the whalebone in women's corsets. Such a witty surprise is beyond Ahab's capacity; he has lost his balance, particularly in the sense of maintaining some anchorage in the mundane world. Of course the right balance is not cheaply won. When the Pequod encounters the amazing herd of whales called the Grand Armada, it must pass through an outer circle of extreme commotion and violence. But within the circle the whalemen find the center which is called a "sleek," "a smooth, enchanted surface, an enchanted calm." Here they find the women and children of the host, in a great brooding nursing peace.

In the complex development of the theme, the whale has the widest meaning of fatality, but his intransigence is qualified. It has been pointed out that no man could ever see the full shape of the living whale. In that sense he must be formed by the vision in each man's mind. If the whale is fate, he enacts the judgment chosen by those who confront him. It is clear in the final action that Ahab's death is more suicide than murder. Fedallah, his demonic partner, is last seen wrapped in his harpoon rope and fastened to the back of the whale. Ahab himself is pulled into the sea by the uncoiling of his own launched weapon.

The irony in the final complication is that Ahab does have a form of the freedom he so desperately claims. He cannot strike the sun, nor can he overcome the whale, whose strength is really represented by the certainty of death. However, he does have a limited human freedom which allows him to choose the form of his death and also the form of his living. It is in that arena of human freedom that Ahab is culpable, where his choices have meaning. In accepting his freedom as metaphysically absolute, he is exercising it against a master he cannot defeat, and it has become despair. Aggrandizing against nature, he has turned his last-ditch individualism into an aggrandizement against the human community. Starbuck points out,

> "He would be a democrat to all above; look, how he lords it over all below!"

This is a democratic mistake, a democratic sin. He has turned his own passionate will to live into a war of life against life. In so doing he makes himself into the tyrant dictator of his ship with power over other men's lives. Implicitly, what Ahab does not see is that he is restricted to a moral freedom which is exercised in that interval "on the verge of two abysses" which Tocqueville described. Knowledge, power—these are limited by the walls of the abyss, but there is yet the inner circle or, simply, the lonely ship itself and its community. This human community is Ahab's chief victim. He knows that at the end, and he knows what he is losing. In a last speech to Starbuck, he says, after describing his forty years of making war "on the horrors of the deep,"

> "Close! stand close to me, Starbuck; let me look into a human eye; it is better than to gaze into sea or sky; better than to gaze upon God. By the green land; by the bright hearth-stone! this is the magic glass, man; I see my wife and my child in thine eye."

Quite specifically Melville has described humanity as an island shelter surrounded by the "horrors of the deep." Nantucket is the paradigm of all land communities. With instruction from Ahab's own words, we give attention to all signs and effects which point to "a sympathy from the green country without" as a countertheme to monomania, isolation, and death. When Melville wrote Hawthorne to say "I have written a black book and have felt purged and cleansed in the process," he perhaps meant to say that *Moby Dick* was no more despairing than any genuine tragedy, and that purgation was available within the book as well as in the writing of it.

That the dialectic in *Moby Dick* is tragic is not difficult to illustrate. What is fascinating to observe are the manifestations of a vision of American history, with the dialectic outlining a struggle within the democratic ideal. For instance, one is impressed by the symbolic universality, the cosmopolitanism of the Pequod's crew. It is an international society including "a deputation from all the isles of the sea and all the ends of the earth, accompanying old Ahab in the Pequod to lay the world's grievances before that bar from which not very many of them ever come back." The bypassing of racial barriers is more impressive than the national representations. Tashtego, the Indian, Daggoo, the Negro, and Queequeg, the South Sea cannibal, are put into command over the polyglot but essentially European crew. The fact that the chief officers are American is not inconsistent with the theme. They are first of all islanders, from either Nantucket or Martha's Vineyard. But as Americans they are universalist at the start, and have transcended their ancestral origins. Therefore they lead into the future, whether toward success or catastrophe. But Melville's book is a drastic medicine for typical American optimism. The Pequod's enterprise resembles a renewed effort to build the Tower of Babel, inspired by a demonic leader. There is implicit violence and anarchy in the mixture of the ship's company itself, to be observed in the Walpurgis Night scene when the crew gets drunk on both rum and Ahab's murderous incitements. Certainly the ship falls easily under the tyranny of intrinsic strength, Ahab's primordial force of character. The Pequod finds its unity in greed and its driving impulses in violence. These are the adventures and trials of a universalist society, stripped of coherent moral traditions, experimenting with freedom in an unexplored savage world. As historic vision it is tragic, but the generations of American experience could no doubt testify to its pertinence.

In the profoundest sense the tragic dialectic records the misadventures of naturalism as secular doctrine. Melville exposed the positive faith in nature to its extreme reversal, challenging Emerson and the deepest original assumption of the democratic tradition. But in so doing he transformed and revived the humanistic affirmations which were the complement of that assumption on behalf of nature. It is fair to say that Ahab's hatred of the whale reads like an inverted and poisoned pantheism. It is implicit that in one stage of Ahab's life the whale might have been his god, and that his earliest voyages were more joyful affirmations of his manhood. In any case he has ventured by compulsion far out from the "green land," "the bright hearthstone," (of forty years, he tells Starbuck, he has spent three ashore), and he has chosen to live in the element of what he calls his "sacramental" experience. He cries to the corpusant flames at the masthead during a storm,

> "Oh! thou clear spirit of clear fire, whom on these seas I as Persian once did worship, till in the sacramental act so burned by thee, that to this hour I bear the scar; I now know thee, thou clear spirit, and I now know that thy right worship is defiance."

In his madness he speaks for a supreme rejection of his god, though he himself is still a prisoner. "Leap! leap up, and lick the sky! I leap with thee; I burn with thee; would fain be welded with thee; defyingly I worship thee."

Believing in himself, he must feel hatred in this worship. "In the midst of the personified impersonal, a personality stands here." The old questions surround him; how could one claim freedom, or the rights of the personality, or rights of any sort, without the friendly support of nature? Self-reliance, was it suicidal or heroic? Natural virtues, courage and self-assertion, did they lead to victory, or even survival? Tragedy marks the limits of such striving, as nature writes the answer to such questions. Ahab tested nature as well as himself to such an extreme that one hardly knows what he wants or what his victory could be. Before it ends in his death, the question shifts; allegiance, response, meaning, are not to be found in nature and are transferred elsewhere.

There are two important effects with final resonance as the pages of *Moby Dick* close with a view of the whirlpool ocean after the Pequod sinks. One is the echo of Ahab's last speech, "Nor white whale, nor man, nor fiend, can so much as graze old Ahab in his own proper and inaccessible being." This defiance is figured in the last event with the sight of Tashtego's arm flashing from the sea to continue pounding the pennant to the mast. The other emphatic sign is the bobbing, spinning life buoy, Queequeg's coffin, which now saves the life of the only survivor, Queequeg's friend, Ishmael.

> The black bubble upward burst; and now, liberated by reason of its cunning spring, and, owing to its great buoyancy, rising with great force, the coffin life-buoy shot lengthwise from the sea, fell over, and floated by my side. Buoyed up by that coffin, for almost one whole day and night, I floated on a soft and dirge-like main. The unharming sharks, they glided by as if with padlocks on their mouths, the savage seahawks sailed with sheathed beaks. On the second day, a sail drew near, nearer, and picked me up at last. It was the devious-cruising Rachel, that in her retracing search after her missing children, only found another orphan.

Ishmael is a meaningful survivor. To expound this conclusion it is necessary to observe not Ishmael so much as Queequeg, whose coffin saves him. Melville needed a survivor of the Pequod's doom for much deeper reasons than to account for the narration. We remember that Jonah was thrown up from the belly of the monster to preach God's message. As Melville renders the story of Jonah, it is clear that the prophet sinned against man rather than against God and for this reason was thrown into the mouth of the whale. Jonah never denied God but refused his command to preach to mankind. When he confesses his responsibility to the sailors, he asks them to throw him overboard to save themselves, and when they do the storm subsides. This is the first step in Jonah's regeneration. But first he must be swallowed by the whale, that is to say, endure his isolation from man and God.

Ishmael is chosen for life, but it is Queequeg's friendship which offers life; his affective bond with Ishmael has been sharply singled out, contrasting with Ahab's apocalyptic hunt for death. From the beginning Queequeg has been the counterpoint to Ahab's stark theme. He is a hideously tattooed savage, a cannibal, a pagan, but he is also the son of a king. He is first an object of fear, prohibited from intimate contact. But as a friend, accepted as a friend, he is almost motherly in tenderness. When the crew is assigned, his courage and skill make him one of the "squires" on the ship, raised above the rest. From the "aboriginal awfulness" of nature, Melville chooses a primitive to dramatize human excellence, but with nature *and* an alien civilization as his context, Queequeg is surrounded by ambiguities of judgment.

When Ishmael meets Queequeg at the beginning of his adventures, what is taking place, very obviously, is a test of moral communication across the greatest distance possible. The cannibal, grotesque in his manners and appearance, presents the question to the democratic belief in a universal humanity, a "divine equality." Ishmael passes this test; he makes his choice when Queequeg is offered as his bed partner in the New Bedford inn. But Queequeg is much more than a clean and sober cannibal. He concentrates in himself that "august dignity" which Melville made the theme of his rhapsody on democratic man. We are prepared for the seriousness as well as the humor in the suggestion that Queequeg looks very much like George Washington, cannibalistically developed.

Queequeg's coffin saves Ishmael; we then remember Queequeg's own earlier confrontation with death, when falling ill with a fever, he orders his coffin from the ship's carpenter. A whim, a matter of pathos, but this is meant to say that in dying Queequeg remains in command of himself. He insists on being laid in the coffin for trial. " 'Rarmai' (it will do; it is easy), he murmured at last, and signed to be replaced in his hammock." The parallel and the contrast is with Ahab, whose struggle with the white whale is his own long struggle with death. Queequeg can accommodate himself to death for reasons that pertain to his generosity of soul as well as his pagan stoicism. Early in their friendship Ishmael observes Queequeg's remarkable self-collectedness.

> There was something almost sublime in it. Here was a man some twenty thousand miles from home, by the way of Cape Horn . . . thrown among people as strange to him as though he were in the planet Jupiter; and yet he seemed entirely at his ease; preserving the utmost serenity; content with his own companionship; always equal to himself.

Again the contrast with Ahab, another man of strength, is effected. Both men refuse to cringe before the world, but Ahab is tormented and never "equal to himself," since his pride requires an effort to overwhelm the world or its master. Queequeg is at home everywhere, whereas Ahab is a lost man, who finding his great opponent, "pitted himself, all mutilated, against it."

Queequeg's ordering of his coffin has a further complication of meaning. He does not die after all, but rallies from his sickness, and the coffin will not be needed. Upon questioning, he asserts it was his will not to die.

> and thereupon, when some expressed their delighted surprise, he, in substance, said, that the cause of his sudden convalescence was this;—at a critical moment, he had just recalled a little duty ashore, which he was leaving undone; and therefore had changed his mind about dying; he could not die yet, he averred.

That "little duty ashore" seems very suggestive, particularly if one remembers the general opposition between sea and land, and Ahab's (as well as Starbuck's) evocation of the "green country" of the home island. Queequeg therefore does not master his death as Ahab might imagine that victory. Indeed he admits that although mere sickness could not kill him, something like "a whale, a gale, or some violent ungovernable unintelligent destroyer" might.

The reader is entitled to conclude that "the little duty ashore" implies that survival is connected with the quotidian life. In "savage" Queequeg's case this is a domestication of the natural man, an ethical use of his great strength. That point is made in the early episodes when Ishmael and Queequeg consort together in great sociability, and wild Ishmael becomes civilized by a savage.

> I felt a melting in me. No more my splintered heart and maddened hand were turned against the wolfish world. This soothing savage had redeemed it.

The point is further emphasized in the episode describing a "cutting in." Queequeg dances gingerly on the revolving body of the dead whale, surrounded by sharks in the water, and secured only by the "monkey rope" or lifeline fastened to Ishmael on the deck of the ship. If Queequeg falls, they fall together, unless Ishmael stands fast, and so, "Queequeg was my own inseparable brother."

It has been designed that one should save the other. Ishmael survives in order, like Jonah, to tell the secret of his survival. Perhaps it was that secret which was noted among the hieroglyphs of Queequeg's tattooed body, later carved on the coffin-like buoy.

> And this tattooing, had been the work of a departed prophet and seer of his island, who, by those hieroglyphic marks, had written out on his body a complete theory of the heavens and the earth, and a mystical

treatise on the art of attaining truth; so that Queequeg in his own proper person was a riddle to unfold; a wondrous work in one volume; but whose mysteries not even himself could read, though his own live heart beat against them; and these mysteries were therefore destined in the end to moulder away with the living parchment whereon they were inscribed, and so be unsolved to the last.

"Unsolved to the last," but the point has been made. Ahab's metaphysical riddle has had an answer, though it could not divert a tragic conclusion. A mystical treatise has been tattooed on Queequeg's body, but we are entitled to think that it is only the treatise of the body itself.

That Queequeg exists in the "calm collectedness of simplicity" suggests that he is in touch with the secret in the sense that he does not aspire to be more than himself, master more than himself. He asserts only humanity. He exists by a centripetal principle, moving inward toward himself as a stable center, while all the rest may be dark and unintelligible. This stability is conditioned, however, by the image of precarious balance, the "monkey rope." Queequeg's collectedness is related to his ability to unite with Ishmael and other men. By forming a community he quells violence and domesticates nature, even as he domesticated death by placing food and drink in his coffin, and interrupted death in order to finish "a little duty ashore."

Queequeg's god is a figurine he keeps in his pocket. On first seeing Yojo, Ishmael thinks, "we are all somehow dreadfully cracked about the head." Yojo is a comically diminished god, but there is something in him or in Queequeg's relation to him that strikes us, particularly in the contrast with Ahab's volcanic thought and feeling. Queequeg carved him from wood himself, and when he prays he places him on top of his own head. The suggestion is clear; Yojo's chief significance is that Queequeg made him and worships him. This value increases enormously when Ishmael, out of friendship and good-natured communication with the savage, worships Yojo as well. The point is elaborated when Queequeg joins Ishmael in his attendance at the Christian church. Their comradeship is the support for any sign of faith they use or ritual they practice; they, as men, transcend their beliefs, are more meaningful than their gods. Queequeg is unforgettable when after the twenty-four hours of Ramadan in complete immobility, he rises stiffly on his legs, replaces the toy god in his pocket, and returns cheerfully to his daily routine of living.

The general response to Melville's book might very well depend on a view of this episode. If men's gods are indispensable, then the irony here is merciless and humanity is pathetic. But if Queequeg truly seems to have absorbed the best virtues he gives to Yojo, then the superstition alone is pathetic, and mankind becomes taller, with a dignity like that of the cannibal. The issue is fundamental, as it was in Melville's mind, but there is striking disagreement among critics in judging it.[4] Alfred Kazin, for instance, observed that "the meditation on the whiteness of the whale . . . becomes an uncanny attempt to come to grips with nature as it might be conceived with man entirely left out; or, what amounts to the same thing, with man losing his humanity." This is an accurate but partial insight, for it takes no account of the tragic theme stressed in that loss of humanity, or of the countertheme which reestablishes it in the last scenes. Kazin concludes by saying that

> The only thing left to man, Melville seems to tell us, is to take the span of this magnitude . . .
> And it is this, this poetic power, rather than any specifically hu-

4. Newton Arvin's sanely brilliant study of Melville should be noted in this summation of great moral alternatives in *Moby Dick*. He deals with Ahab's "tragic error" in a sense that resembles but differs significantly from Greek tragedy, as well as the Christian dialectic of the sin of pride.

The alternative to Ahab's egoism is not, then, the ideal of "Nothing too much," nor is it a broken and a contrite heart. On one level it is an intuition that carries us beyond morality, in the usual sense, into the realm of cosmic piety; on the usual ethical level, however, it is a strong intuition of human solidarity as a priceless good. Behind Melville's expression of this, one is conscious of the gravity and the tenderness of religious feeling, if not of religious belief; it came to him in part from the Christian tradition in which he had been nurtured. The form it took in him, however, is no longer specifically Christian; as with Hawthorne and Whitman, it was the natural recoil of a sensitive imagination, enriched by the humanities of romantic idealism, against the ruinous individualism of the age. It is Melville's version of Hawthorne's "magnetic chain of humanity," of Whitman's "manly attachment": so far, it is an essentially humanistic and secular principle (Newton Arvin, *Herman Melville* [New York: William Sloane, 1950], p. 181).

I endorse his findings in my general theme that stresses the secular humanism of Melville and his contemporaries. I am equally indebted to F. O. Matthiessen, most respected of all critics of the classic American writers. He observed that Melville ". . . also learned what Keats had, through his kindred apprehension of the meaning of Shakespeare, that the Heart is the Mind's Bible. Such knowledge was the source of the passionate humanity in Melville's own creation of tragedy" (F. O. Matthiessen, *American Renaissance* [New York and London: Oxford University Press, 1941], pp. 513–14). Arvin and Matthiessen were the first to clarify the rich and coherent moral tradition of American writing, and their work will remain indispensable for a long time.

man one, this power of transcription rather than of any alteration of life that will admit human beings into its tremendous scale . . . that makes up the greatness of the book.[5]

D. H. Lawrence, with more emphasis, defined Melville's sea urge as an escape from humanity.

Never man instinctly hated human life, our human life, as we have it, more than Melville did. And never was a man so passionately filled with the sense of vastness and mystery of life which is non-human.[6]

Again, with due respect to Lawrence's forthright intuitions, the effect is that of a work half-read. Melville was indeed the writer who in his time went furthest across the border that marks a human sensibility, but the adventure in the end highlights unforgettably the need to return home. Rachel still seeks her children, and that should supplement the note which Kazin expresses when he relates a very sharp but incomplete perception. "Narcissus was bemused by that image which 'we ourselves see in all rivers and oceans,' and this, says Ishmael, when he is most desperate, is all that man ever finds when he searches the waters—a reflection of himself."

The problem, I think, comes from the difficulty of holding the ground of Melville's dialectic. To see Melville so drastically dismantling a traditional anthropocentric view of nature, leads perhaps directly to the judgments expressed by Lawrence and Kazin. The debate actually was with basic optimistic assumptions of the American democratic tradition, as if to say that since Jefferson and Emerson were so rich with humanist affirmations, it was probable to conclude that Melville was a consistent nay-sayer, anxious, as Lawrence put it, to be washed clean by the sea "of the leprosy of our humanity." The text which could support that particular judgment is of course *The Confidence Man*. Marius Bewley does indeed make the later book, as well as the entanglements of *Pierre*, the basis for inferring that Melville was profoundly disillusioned by American democratic civilization, and that this disillusionment was inseparable in his mind from the metaphysical rebuff of God and nature: "the very texture of the American universe revealed the way it had been betrayed by God. Democracy existed only in ruthless competition, and God, who alone might have redeemed it, was unequal to the task."[7] However, Bewley

5. Alfred Kazin, *Contemporaries* (Boston: Little, Brown, 1962), pp. 33, 38, 40.

6. *American Literature*, p. 197.

7. Bewley, *The Eccentric Design*, p. 191.

makes the important distinction between *Moby Dick* and the later work, and admits that the former, by a tremendous effort, did succeed in introducing "order into his moral universe" and so give form to his experience and his art. One agrees, but Bewley may ignore the fact that democratic ideals were again being given their test, and that their affirmations were strong enough to meet disillusionment in the mysterious balance of this success. I would rephrase Bewley's sentence to make the point. "Nature existed in ruthless competition, and there likely is no God; but man, alone, might redeem the world, if he were equal to the task."

In theme there is everything in common between *The Confidence Man* and *Moby Dick*.

> If next to mistrusting Providence, there be aught that man should pray against, it is against mistrusting his fellow man.[8]

In the writing of tragedy the point of view is always dangerously near to nihilism and moral defeat. Bewley describes *The Confidence Man* as a response to "a tragic confusion in which good and evil were indistinguishable." That may indeed be what Melville felt and wrote. But the source of it was not far from the moral realism, a tragic realism, which informs the pages of *Moby Dick*. A closer look at *The Confidence Man* suggests that the cynicism in it is purgatorial. The failure in *The Confidence Man* is the failure of life featured by comedy, which can be just as serious as the failure in tragedy. American humor, as Mark Twain was about to demonstrate, flourished in the folklore of skepticism. The comedy was partly relief, but to invade the furthest margins of distrust was also a tempering of democratic faith, which must be founded on a moral realism or is in peril. This special effect is notable in *Billy Budd*, as I discuss it in the later pages of this chapter, and I think we can say that faith is as paradoxical in that story as cynicism is in *The Confidence Man*. But on the ground of paradox, moving as if by Emerson's injunction "beyond skepticism," Melville created the most resonant and stirring legend of American humanism in *Moby Dick*.

Rachel's Children

Ishmael originally saw his voyage as an alternative to suicide. This mood is not long stressed in the view we actually have of him, and even before the voyage he does not seem to be a man close to despair. The point has effect, however, when Ahab is introduced, for it

8. *The Confidence Man* (New York: The Grove Press, 1949), p. 26.

is Ahab who actually faces the voyage in this way. I think we can say that Ishmael was diverted from suicide and all it implies before he even embarked. He walked into the jaws of the whale when he entered the public room of the Spouter Inn, owned by Peter Coffin. Surrounded by emblems of the whale hunt and of death, Ishmael descends into the netherworld, and there he finds the nether-principle of life, an actual cannibal, with whom he spends the night—in a kind of marriage—as he says. It turns out that Ishmael never slept better in his life. "The man's a human being, just as I am." After that, and as a minor consequence, Ishmael shares his religion with the savage, the two peaceably attending the Christian church together as if they were immune from the apocalyptic violence of Father Mapple's sermon.

Captain Ahab has gone to the last boundary of exactly such a religious and metaphysical storm as was endured by Jonah and preached by Father Mapple. He has gone too far, as he acknowledges himself. "There is a wisdom that is woe, but there is a woe that is madness." In going so far he was able himself to recognize precisely that alternative to suicide which was expressed in the friendship between cannibal and Christian. Ahab looks into the "magic glass" of a human eye, as Starbuck makes his last appeal to him, and acknowledges wife, child, "green land" and "bright hearth-stone." And it is Ahab who, reached in human feeling by the mad little black boy, Pip, says, "Lo! ye believers in gods all goodness, and in man all ill, lo you! see the omniscient gods oblivious of suffering man; and man, though idiotic, and knowing not what he does, yet full of the sweet things of love and gratitude." This preference for man over God is the sum of Ahab's long indictment, but it is also the germ of that countertheme of man supporting man which grows in Melville's book as the battle with the whale continues. It could be said that Ahab pulls the old gods down with him when he dies, all of them, "the Fejee god or Nantucket god," Fedallah's fire god and the carpenter god of wood. What is left is the figure of a man afloat in the ocean, Ishmael, supported by his friend Queequeg's coffin.

Ahab himself cannot accept that kind of rescue. This is made sufficiently clear as he puts away the invitations from Starbuck and Pip, and even more so in his refusal to help the captain of the *Rachel* search for his lost son. This is the same ship which later is destined to pick up that allegorical orphan, Ishmael. Confronting only gods and antigods, Ahab, like Wakefield and Ethan Brand, has made the fatal voyage into the nonhuman universe.

It is clear indeed that Ahab has developed a revulsion from humanity. His ambitions have been too great, his comparisons too high. Even after the final appeal made by Starbuck, Ahab dismisses him contemptuously, coupling him with Stubb, the one an example of the conventionally pious and craven man who survives by avoiding great risks, the other a philistine cynic who cannot see the seriousness of that woe which is either madness or wisdom. The major human test Ahab fails, however, is his relationship with the little coward, Pip, though here he was most tempted to turn from the hunt of the whale. Ahab has built too much on the self-affirmations of courage to know how to deal with weakness. The moral is clear. Challenging the gods, he has sought to replace them. Courage is almost everything, but it is not enough to make man human.

When Ahab dies flinging his lance at the whale, he wins a great respect. "Nor white whale, nor man, nor fiend, can so much as graze old Ahab in his own proper and inaccessible being." This is a defense of that "valor in the soul" which, in Melville's theme, was the basis of the "divine equality" of men. But the grand parable needs to be completed; the meaning of a democratic dignity and equality has to go further. Cowardice is human too. Though Ahab's courage marks the center of his individual being, cowardice may be the force acting for the human community. Little Pip was abandoned by the "creative libertines" of this world. And for this, seeing "God's foot on the treadle of the loom," he has gone mad. But the point is made that the two madnesses, Ahab's and Pip's, could have made each other sane. Their sympathy could have restored the real world, because the real world is a moral, not a metaphysical, creation. "Let me look into a human eye; it is better than to gaze into sea or sky; better than to gaze upon God."

Melville has absolute control of his theme and he is determined to exhibit a world stripped of metaphysical support. Most of the negative statement has been pointed to religion, but science at its marginal limits, a frustrated curiosity, a futile empiricism, has been introduced to complete the circle of failure. Cetology, the busy documentation of the whale and its habits, does not lead out of ignorance, any more than the extracts from his reading offered by the "sub-sub-librarian" as a prologue to the book. The more facts and random speculations are accumulated, the more it becomes apparent that the whale remains a mystery. Industrious as the men of the Pequod are in their craftsmen skills, when they see the giant squid or the mouth of the shark they touch metaphysical bottom. Here all civilized languages and reason are broken. The aboriginal awfulness reigns, like that of sea storms, which, paralleling the old flood of Noah, engulf "baby man bragging of his science and skill." It is no surprise to find Ahab eventually calling on Fedallah and the powers of darkness.

Dismissing his best science and skill, as when he dashes his quadrant, "vain toy," to the deck, Ahab's monomania of hatred has become the inversion of religious belief. But this defiance, no more than surrender, will not call up the whale's image from the deep and fix his meaning. Moby Dick is not one thing, nor is he two, in a Parsee-like conception of good and evil at war. The indeterminacy of his meaning is reflected by the fact that the whale is both hunted and hunter, both victim and victor. His only real god-like traits are that he is ubiquitous and that his substance is immortal. Otherwise he has many contrasting roles. Men feed on him and in the end he engulfs them. He dies as an old and ulcerated whale; he dies also in gallant battle, and finally he doesn't die at all and escapes into his immortality. He is everything knowable, both science and religion make his bones familiar relics, and yet his brow remains pleated with a riddle.

Against this background of mystery, the human drama with its very specific meanings plays itself out. The drama is founded, I believe, on the secular premises of the democratic experience which produced it. If Ahab is a democratic hero it is not because of the gratuitous will to conquer nature and prove his strength. Rather the unexplored and resistant power of nature marked a line where he could not go, the "personality" struggling against extinction within the "personified impersonal." Therefore it challenged the premise of his freedom. It was at best a prudent, conditioned freedom, like that of Starbuck, or mindless, like that of Stubb. The theme of the tragedy is that nature cannot satisfy Ahab in this respect. The problem is, what will satisfy him? God once gave favor to men by his special consideration. A secular naturalist faith later suggested that nature itself was submissive. But this faith excited courage and the will to freedom only to throw men back on the ultimate limits of human strength.

The teaching of Emerson should always be remembered by those who read Melville, as F. O. Matthiessen perfectly demonstrated in his study of contrasts between the two. Emerson for instance announced, "No law can be sacred to me but that of my own nature." On this principle Ahab founds his own sense of what needs to be defended. But if we add another Emersonian thought we see precisely where

Ahab's ordeal begins. "He [man] is sure that his welfare is dear to the heart of being." For Emerson this anthropomorphic tenderness was the basis of the coherent universe. Perhaps this was true for Captain Ahab before he found that the "heart of being" had become the "monomaniac incarnation of all malicious agencies." The world in the "colorless all-color of atheism" surrounds Ahab, the universe of "heartless voids and immensities."

It might have some meaning, if whimsical, to say that Ahab is a transcendentalist and American democrat gone berserk. It is not the orthodox Christian god he has lost (he didn't begin with enough humility for that), but the great god of nature himself with those "linked analogies" which were affinities and reassurances meant for man. Such a voyage as that of the Pequod should have been conducted in the transcendentally optimistic vein, a voyage into the "heart of things" and a prosperous return. The rage of Ahab might be that of a man who has taken the great gamble of naturalistic confidence and lost. What was freedom without Emerson's metaphysical guarantee, the assurance that nature deeply accommodated it? Destructive, shark-like, cannibalistic Ahab, asserting himself in defiance, was proving a kind of freedom which Emerson must have sensed as an alternative and a threat.

As with his contemporaries, Melville's questioning of nature must be understood from the perspective of the frontier. In the lives of his sailors he approximated the experience of contemporary and traditional American frontiersmen. In a sense his own experience of going to sea paralleled the old experience of the immigration from Europe. Behind him was the bankruptcy of his family, their fall from high place in the established civilization of old New York.

That intellectually, like his contemporaries, he had high expectations for nature was indicated by his early books. *Typee* was an experiment in the naïve school of Rousseau naturalism. *Omoo* describes the ruin of a happy natural community where the white man's civilization brought along his corruption. *Mardi* describes a more general disillusionment, a romantic criticism of life based on the frustrated quest for the "lost paradise." The work of Hawthorne which he read at this point probably saved him from silence, or from further essays in mere elegiac and pessimistic romanticism, like *Mardi*. What Hawthorne gave him was a grasp of the tragic theme, and made it possible to eject the metaphysics of innocence from his own mind. This required, more clearly and completely than it did for Hawthorne, a total reconsideration of his view of the relation between man and nature.

The complexity of his state of mind and the direction in which he was moving can be found in his letters to Hawthorne at this time.

> There is a certain tragic phase of humanity which, in our opinion, was never so more powerfully embodied than by Hawthorne. . . .
>
> There is the grand truth about Nathaniel Hawthorne. He says No! in thunder; but the Devil himself cannot make him say *yes*. For all men who say *yes*, lie; and all men who say *no* . . . they cross the frontiers into Eternity with nothing but a carpet-bag,—that is to say, the Ego.[9]

The image interestingly recalls Tocqueville's similar evocation of the view of man in a democratic poetry.

> Man springs out of nothing, crosses time, and disappears forever in the bosom of God; he is seen but for a moment, wandering on the verge of the two abysses, and there he is lost.[10]

Carpetbags and lonely egos suggest *The Confidence Man*, which might be described as Melville's own surrender to "No," though its effect was not thunderous.

In any case the dialectic of yea and nay must be kept in mind for understanding Melville in his maturity. There are several magnificent apostrophes in *Moby Dick*, among them the call to man's "august dignity" and "divine equality," but perhaps the following passage from the earlier work, *Mardi*, can express the nourishment of democratic idealism in Melville's work and the way it laid a basis for the tragic pathos in *Moby Dick* and elsewhere.

> King Noah, God bless him! fathered us all. . . . All of us have monarchs and sages for kinsmen; nay, angels and archangels for cousins; since in antediluvian days, the sons of God did verily wed with our mothers, the irresistible daughters of Eve. Thus all generations are blended, and heaven and earth of one kin . . . the nations and families, flocks and folds of the earth; one and all, brothers in essence—oh, be we then brothers indeed! All things form but one whole; the universe a Judea, and God Jehovah its head. Then no more let us start with affright. In a theocracy, what is to fear?[11]

Such inspiriting values of Emersonian humanism remained to motivate the writing of Melville's great book. Whatever his defeat Captain Ahab is still the champion of human self-reliance. What, as

9. *The Letters* . . . , pp. 124, 125.
10. Tocqueville, *Democracy in America*, p. 73.
11. *Mardi* (New York: Albert and Charles Boni, 1925), p. 10.

he confronts them, are his options? He can surrender to a blank but overruling fate and be, like other men, the unnoticed victim of a thousand random contingencies. On the other hand, without hope for victory he can make his challenge, and by the gestures of opposition, assert his independent existence. Ahab's sense of identity has become inseparable from conflict and therefore entails his own destruction The third option is offered by Starbuck and Pip, that retreat to an island humanity in its self-preserving bond. But for Ahab this is a demeaning retreat, and he sees in Starbuck what is there, a cautious settling for half-gains, expressed by his professional courage in killing whales when they can provide his modest wants—a little light, enough food, the income from the voyage.

Ahab's cause is more honorable than that, more serious than that. He is resisting, as he says, a retreat beyond the point where he can claim a personality. This means an ordealistic demand on all his own strength. But in his isolation, power has become self-consuming. His response to challenge has had only the effect of shifting all the power to the other side. The more Ahab fights his single cause the more he arouses the overweening strength of the universe. It is like awakening a quiescent beast, and what has tempted that beast is Ahab's own strength.

Yet Ahab's death remains eloquent. It demonstrates that the defense of personality takes place beyond pragmatic as well as metaphysical justifications. Ahab's claim wins a great respect, I have proposed, and perhaps that is all that can be said for it. Tragedy seems the proper ground for assent, if only because it has purged illusions and reduced values to something intrinsic in human action. At the scene of tragedy all values seem absolute and at the same time conditioned, but conditioned in such a way as not to detract from their effective strength. Ahab's death indicates that his cause has meaning only in the human context, but that is where it returns and is justified. The tragic sense of freedom deals with its defeat but this is its ethical conditioning. In nature man is not free, but all purely egocentric concepts of freedom push man, denuded of his strength, into nature. Freedom is a human phenomenon, where will answers will, choice meets choice. Entering nature on nature's terms, man is reduced to nature and dehumanized. He fights like the shark, but even his last personal cry for his being is lost as the great wave passes over him.

But survival is not the point. Scarred like a great tree, Ahab bears "the regal dignity of some mighty woe." This regality is only the apotheosis of the "kingly commons" but it is the greater dignity for that reason. Democracy needed tragedies to prove the universality of its heroes and their right to represent man. All classic tragedy treats the fall of human greatness only to bring it back to greatness. And only tragedy could survey the contradictions which Melville conceived in the human struggle for freedom. Whether lost in great oceans or bound in communities, democracy's hero remains aware of his singular being and is jealous for its sake, as Ahab was madly jealous, against the encroachments of nature and man.

Ahab, Bartleby, and Billy

It would be plausible to read "Bartleby the Scrivener" as social criticism; the setting is Wall Street and the man is the palest of the imprisoned office clerks who could symbolize human alienation in modern bureaucratic and technological society. But most would agree that this would be as limited a reading as the same emphasis would be for Kafka. It has been reported by several critics, chief among them Lionel Trilling and Richard Chase, that American writers of the classic period had little interest in social realism, the depiction of life styles and manners, the analysis of specific social conflicts. The mistake, as I have said elsewhere, is to extend this judgment too far, in suggesting that the theme of their work is not man in society. This is precisely the most actively considered theme of Emerson, Thoreau, Hawthorne, Melville, and Whitman, but they write in terms of the *first* questions which associate with this theme and not the last. That is to say they write as if the problem of living in society had just been offered to men who were otherwise morally and intellectually complete. These were the men of the myth of America, stepping onto the soil of a new continent and preparing to establish a new society. As such they had no social experiences to describe but they did indeed have the most intense interest in the first principles of social relationships.

In this respect "Bartleby" is as much a legend for the primordial stages of human intercourse as *Moby Dick*, and as much as the latter its "social" theme is deeply intermixed with the metaphysical. This is true despite the fact that the scene is not the high seas and the personages are not the great beasts of nature and man in an atavistic contest with them. Bartleby is best understood as an inverted Captain Ahab; crushed into a small office space and now entirely deprived of either the will or the freedom to act, he nevertheless faces the same metaphysical wall or barrier to human freedom. Bartleby has lost more than a leg; he is barely left alive, but he is still capable of a muted, frozen rebellion. His inertia is as stubborn as Ahab's exertion; he won't be moved, he won't work, he won't be helped. "I would prefer not to," replaces "I'd strike the sun if it insulted me," but it is reasonable to see the parallel.

Certainly Ahab, after his address to the "Carpenter-God," would understand the hints of a grim education which Bartleby received working for the Dead-Letter Office. Those letters which never reach their destination are the chorus for another Job-like reproach, and Bartleby makes it, facing the wall outside the office window, and the wall of his prison as he dies. The prison is almost a melodramatic postscript to a life whose main feature is empty and pointless routine. Bartleby's world seems to have been ordained by a master whose intentions or interests are best characterized by the dry unreadable jargonized legal documents which Bartleby has been set to *copy* for the duration of his life. His home, it appears, is only that barren office in which his duties are performed. Anticipating his use of Captain Vere in *Billy Budd*, Melville puts special significance into the role of Bartleby's employer, the lawyer and original author of the documents. Like Vere he is a kind of surrogate god or providence who is nonplussed by his own creature, man. He says now and then, to cover his confusion and his random sense of guilt, that despite this or despite that, he found Bartleby "a useful man to me." That remains until Bartleby's refusals are complete and he must forcibly evict him. (It is characteristic for Melville to add another touch. The lawyer is a Master of Chancery, a sinecure position with no meaning or function, but he is quite resentful because it is about to be abolished.)

When Bartleby's refusals begin, it is with the small step of refusing to read what he has written. This actually may be the crucial point of his rebellion for he is thus exposing the possibility that the world's document is meaningless. Copying it would be something like an act of automatic life, like breathing or eating, but it does not pay much honor to the draft.

The subtlety of Bartleby's defiance lies in the effect of indicting his master and his fate. He will die in the principle by which he has been forced to live. Life faces a dead wall; he will do so. Man is a mechanically driven creature; he will be so. And yet finally he must say no, like Ahab. Again he is more subtle than Ahab. "I would prefer not to" is a reduction of the will past hopelessness to inarticulate passive resistance. "He was a man of preferences rather than assumptions."

In the walled space of his existence, Bartleby, like Ahab, preserves a salient dignity. When the lawyer interrupts him in the early morning, he sends him away until he can dress and put away the meager personal articles in the bedroom-office. "I am occupied," he says. In his silence as well as his refusals, he keeps his independent though empty being.

But yet he does cling to the lawyer's premises, and he must in the end be pulled from the scene of his desiccated life and work. He dies finally before another wall, in the New York Tombs. Even as this is said the implications are clear. So other men live in their prison of life and the inhospitable universe. But more directly he means to haunt the lawyer's remorse. His protesting spirit seems to demand something from men and God, the more terribly as it seems unreasonable, silent, and stubborn. He has already understood the negatives of the Dead-Letter Office, but still he remains in his metaphysical prison, like the shadow in some universal conscience. "I know where I am," he says finally, peered at, from the jail windows, by "murderers and thieves."

"He's asleep, ain't he?"
"With kings and counselors."

"Bartleby" has a major role to play in the understanding of Melville's richest, sustained theme. Reflection at this point would show the sharp contrast but also the significant affinity with the later portrait of Billy Budd, as this in turn relates to Ahab. The pantheon in Melville's mind became complete; he had created three demigods of his fictional imagination. If we search for the stimulus we may find it in the image of "a certain tragic phase of humanity" that he found in Hawthorne's work and which he described as follows.

We mean the apprehension of the absolute condition of present things as they strike the eye of the man who fears them not, though they do their worst to him,—the man who, like Russia or the British Empire, declares himself a sovereign nature (in himself) amid the powers of heaven, hell, and earth. He may perish; but so long as he exists he insists upon treating with all Powers upon an equal basis. If any of those other Powers choose to withhold certain secrets, let them; that does not impair my sovereignty in myself; that does not make me tributary. And perhaps, after all, there is *no* secret.[12]

12. *The Letters*, p. 124.

These sentences, I believe, describe what was strongest in Melville's inspiration to write. With Ahab, Bartleby, and Billy Budd the sovereignty of a man is asserted against those rival powers and their secrets, and progressively in each case the secret diminishes in proportion to the increasing weight and significance of the man, until we are left finally with that sovereignty and no other.

Reading *Billy Budd* brings these revelations to focus, revelations that are clearest when Ahab and Bartleby are kept strongly in mind. It could seem, for instance, that Billy was drawn carefully as an exact contrast for both Ahab and Bartleby. Where Ahab was monomaniacal and obsessed, Billy is perfectly at ease with himself, with men, and with nature. Ahab was determined to defend his independence as if everything were at stake on that point; Billy does not seem aware, like an infant, of the demarcation between himself and the world. "Of self-consciousness he seemed to have little or none." Basically, the mark of Bartleby is the total silence and isolation in which he lives. In a sense Billy is as passive as Bartleby, but one is the passivity of total acceptance whereas the other is that of a man transforming his weakness into a reproach, his nonresistance into a defiance as uncompromised as that of Captain Ahab. These two have reacted to blows and indifference. Billy, however, like a moral sun, seems to generate his own good nature and good will, and doing so transforms the world he accepts. It is stressed how far this generosity goes; he accepts impressment, he accepts the military order which rules the ship, he accepts the persecution of Claggart up to the margin where resistance becomes a reflex on behalf of self-preservation, and finally he accepts and affirms his own punishment at the hands of Captain Vere. One is entitled to ask, did Melville write *Billy Budd*, so much later in his life, as an answer to the challenges of Captain Ahab? Ahab had become a demon, Lucifer-like, a wild unleashed spirit of rebellion. "Rebelling against all above," he was a "tyrant to all below." He was a demon of the democratic conscience. In *Billy Budd*, as if it were a sequel, Melville chose the exactly right historic setting, the reactionary years of Bonaparte, the naval wars and mutinies, to frame the large moral and spiritual problems of revolution.

It is a particular emphasis that everything in Billy's world received his good-natured or stoic acceptance *except* revolt and mutiny. Even his fatal response to Claggart was an uncontrollable revulsion from the charge of rebellion. This is Billy's obsession to oppose that of Ahab. He is compelled by a will for human harmony to the point where tyranny changes its nature when applied to him. Without being weak or cowardly (he is demonstrably not that but is the "Handsome Sailor," unique for his courage, beauty, and strength) he is dominated by a spirit which accommodates to any human order, whatever its peculiar form or motives, *because* it is a human order. He is profoundly and innocently the conservative, where Ahab and Bartleby are proportionately subversive at the deepest level.

Tragic irony, which equates with moral complexity, arises from the fact that Ahab drags himself and everyone else down to destruction in the blind moral impasse of his rebellion. The equal paradox is that Billy, with all his good faith and willingness to serve the established order, is the victim of that system in its evil reflexes. He is the victim first of a kind of disciplinary sadism run berserk in Claggart, who represents the pathology of the police principle in his duty as master-at-arms of keeping order on board ship. Billy is chiefly, however, the victim of Captain Vere's inexorable reactionary logic applied in that time of mutiny and revolution. When Billy ends his life with the cry of "God bless Captain Vere," blessing his judge and executioner, the implications must be taken with full seriousness and with closest attention to Melville's lifetime theme of questioning the human and metaphysical order.

Everything depends on how the death of Billy is read, and on how the model world which Captain Vere rules is understood. Billy has been impressed into the naval service and taken from his ship, the *Rights-of-Man*. In leaving that ship, he innocently cries, "And goodbye to you too, old *Rights of Man*." The cry is echoed ironically when he calls out later, at his death, "God bless Captain Vere!" The two pronouncements converge in the complex meaning of Billy's story. There is no question but that he represents in the first case a distinct instance of the reasons for which revolutions are fought. It is further clear that at the time he is hung Billy might have aroused the whole crew to mutiny, and perhaps saved his own life, with a repetition of the first cry. He refrains and instead directs his blessing to Vere. He has saluted each cause at its moment of failure, the cause of liberty at the time he is impressed, and the cause of Vere's martial order at the time when it must destroy its favorite sailor, the tenderly loved "son" of Captain Vere.

The significance of his martyrdom is stressed by Billy's identification with the "Handsome Sailor," a ghostlike but vivid image which recurs in Melville's work. In *Moby Dick* he is perhaps best represented by that abortive figure in the story, Bulkington, but he also appears in the reflections cast by Steelkilt, the Erie Canal man who commits mutiny, as well as in the shadow cast by Ahab himself, from his youth, so to speak. Queequeg represents the same human champion figured as universalist man and savage. The culminating figure, as an image of human excellence, is of course Billy Budd, but he is best understood on the ground of the earlier expressions. For instance, Jack Chase, in *White Jacket*, exhibits the same gathering together of human values. "He was loved by the seamen and admired by the officers; and even when the Captain spoke to him, it was with a slight air of respect." In fact the ability to appreciate him is what marks the line between good and evil, faith and despair. "There was such an abounding air of good sense and good feeling about the man, that he who could not love him, would thereby pronounce himself a knave." It is clear, from such expressions, as well as the longer development in *Billy Budd*, that the "Handsome Sailor" was a man who reflected for other men their best sense of themselves. When he provokes envy, for instance, it is by that mysteriously antihuman and diabolical response projected by Claggart (or by Radney against Steelkilt). And yet he is a superior creature; "But Jack, he was better than a hundred common mortals; Jack was a whole phalanx, an entire army."

The effect is to say that the "Handsome Sailor" is universal in his humanity, and superior at the same time. He is, significantly, a democratic hero in another sense. In his various embodiments he is associated with revolutionary action, with mutiny, and the over-throw of authorities. When Jack Chase deserts ship, he goes to defend a democratic revolution in Peru. Steelkilt and Billy Budd are directly connected with mutiny on board ship. Bulkington is a mysteriously restless personage, who cannot tolerate life on shore; he is, perhaps, as I've suggested, a figure from Ahab's youth, committed to self-assertion and rebellion, though destined to be a ship's captain. The tension between resistance and conformity dominates the long development of the theme, a point which fulfills expectations for a democratic hero. In the last complete incarnation, Billy Budd cheers for the "Rights of Man," but also dies affirming Captain Vere. Similarly of Jack Chase it is observed, "Though bowing to naval discipline afloat; yet ashore, he was a stickler for the rights of man, and the liberties of the world." Later, after his desertion, when he is recaptured by his old captain, he accepts that authority.

"Your most devoted and penitent captain of the main-top, sir: and one who in his very humility of contrition is yet proud to call Captain Claret his commander," said Jack, making a glorious bow, and then tragically flinging overboard his Peruvian sword.
"Reinstate him at once," shouted Captain Claret.[13]

In these effects Melville communicates a charged ambivalence of virtues, heroic individualism and self-respect on one side, and on the other the peculiar ability, in a given instance, to assent to authority. If this projects the ideal man of a democracy, we cannot say that anywhere, not even with *Billy Budd*, does Melville fully describe the terms for such a character and community. But that is not the point, which is, rather, an interest in the opposed forces and claimant values which test character and society, and which find their clearest expression in tragedy.

The tragic design in *Billy Budd* requires a clear understanding of the role of Captain Vere. He serves, I think, a double role on the two levels of the human and metaphysical orders of power. In precise illustration he serves as analogue as well as direct agent for both the English king and the world's God. Like Claggart himself, who is so clearly performing for the devil (God's master-at-arms), Vere plays the role of authority in a system of mysterious discipline which overrides intrinsic justice, compassion, and even the private conscience of Captain Vere himself. There is one hint in the effect made as Captain Vere announces the action by which Billy was tried and condemned: the sailors listened as though to a "Calvinistic text."

Vere's justice is designed for a system of war and for confronting the constant threat of mutiny. It is a primitive justice, like that of Jehovah, but particularly Calvinist in its strain, because it regards men as dangerous and guilty of an original trespass which continually threatens renewal. The French Revolution and the Great Mutiny of the British fleet now compel a strict and watchful discipline. This law of the angry Father, administered by his demonic policeman, Claggart, aims to keep his subjects in automatic obedience.

To understand the alternative that appears in Vere's mind, one must contemplate not the "rights of man" or liberty, but the kind of vengeful and savage disorder which in *Moby Dick* is expressed as latent in nature, the principle of the shark. Such bleak alternatives are what outrage the mind of Captain Ahab. He rebels against mechanical

---

13. *White Jacket*, in *Romances of Herman Melville* (New York: Tudor Publishing Company, 1931), pp. 1116–17, 1119–20.

authority, the incomprehensible police rule of the universe. He cries out for the inalienable rights of his "personality." But he is also outraged by the shark and the destroying whale. That natural anarchy which brought death was as much an insult as the mindless Carpenter-God who offered him another leg. Rebellion becomes his choice, even though rebellion summons the murderous power of nature which he hates. With his freedom to oppose the world all he has left, he fights murder with murder, terror with terror. But it is for such rebellions that Captain Vere's justice was designed.

Discipline is a better word here than justice. God's rule may have no better reason for being than to keep order. On the human plane, Vere's system of martial law suggests the ordinary authoritarian compulsions of rule. The threat of anarchy makes the accurate judgment of guilt or innocence impossible. Rather in extreme cases, as in the story, innocence and guilt go down together in the exigencies of the overt act and overt discipline. To illustrate this there is the pointed irony of the official naval gazette version of the story, describing a patriotic servant of the king killed by the nefarious William Budd. This bespeaks in full the philistine world of conventional loyalties and formal law which fixes the case in its simplistic terms. These are calculated to teach by example, and they are only the public expression of what Vere has rationalized in his more sophisticated fashion.

This reading of *Billy Budd* is supported by recalling pertinent aspects of "Benito Cereno." Here the extremes are clearer, opposing a decadent authority to mutinous savagery. Captain Delano, the American interpreter of these events, emphasizes his perception of the faded decrepit rule of the Spanish captain, Cereno. It is less easy for him to understand the cruelty of disorder and rebellion, good American that he is. He is disposed to be optimistic and sentimental about the nature of primordial man, as he sees the Negro in the story, and he hopes for the improved design of civilized systems, of ships and ships' captains, and the world in general. Cereno is an interesting variation on the theme of Vere: an enfeebled and conquered Vere, remembering his former rule and grandeur, and forced to mimic his old acts of power. Vere is strong, Cereno is weak, but they both are expressive of the fact that the human orders they represent are humanly deficient. This is surely Melville's strong democratic bias at work. However, "Benito Cereno" is an incomplete allegory in the sense that although a savage natural rebellion has been crushed, and an invalid social discipline destroyed, there is nothing to take their place. The story is at the crucial mid-point or at the climax of questioning whereby the hypothet-ical democrat, modestly represented as he is by Captain Delano, surveys the alternatives of savage nature and a decadent or inept civilization.

These dichotomies were consistently in Melville's mind, and the variant roles he gives his sea captains enforces their oppositions. Captain Vere recalls not only Captain Cereno but also Captain Ahab. The ship's order has become compulsive repression in the crisis that Vere recognizes, just as Ahab with the same conviction accepts anar-chic self-assertion as the means of declaring himself. But that military law which requires Billy's death is like the blood cannibalism of the sea; who can comprehend it except as the universe's expression of an inexplicable hostility to man?

Vere and Ahab, two sea captains, each adopt opposing principles as the rule of life but both miss widely the secret of man. Ahab has rebelled against all rule and has descended into the abyss of his desper-ate freedom. He has found an enemy in everything external to himself. But is order then so unyielding an external force to which men are sacrificed? Vere as much as says so in addressing the court-martial. Recognizing that the officers had been deeply moved by Billy's natural or intrinsic innocence, he emphasizes that their allegiance is not to "Nature" but the "King," the "King" being the name for that ab-stract authority which could supersede everything else in their lives as officers of the state. The "King's" authority is not traced; it is absolute, suggesting in the multileveled complexities of Melville's writing that he has more in mind than the authority of social institu-tions. Vere himself suggests that it goes beyond human comprehension and appeal, "For that law and the rigor of it, we are not responsible. Our vowed responsibility is in this: That however pitilessly that law may operate, we nevertheless adhere to it and administer it." Stressed this way, it seems to approximate the pure force or discipline in events, a principle of necessity strong enough to match Ahab's instinctive protest, or his volcanic will.

In either case humanity has been set aside, as it was when Ahab left the lost children of the *Rachel* and pursued his natural freedom and destruction. But the interesting equivalence between the two forms of dehumanization is made by Vere himself, when he says, "We proceed under the law of the Mutiny Act. In feature no child can resemble his father more than that Act resembles in spirit the thing from which it derives—War." This is the basis of the fascinating affinity between the two sea captains, the one the "shaggy Nantucket whale hunter" released to the primeval violence of ocean and whale, the other, the tightly buttoned king's officer restraining natural chaos by the superior violence of his discipline.

The necessitarian and abstract justice of Captain Vere cannot examine the heart and conscience of Billy, cannot distinguish deeper motives and values. If Vere represents the rule of God or king, it is Billy who must give *him* his moral education. "Something healing" takes place in the private interview between the two after sentence has been passed. But which of the two required most healing has been made clear in the context. It is to Vere, ruler of the ship, more than to the assembled men of the ship's company, that Billy directs his unexpected words, "God bless Captain Vere," which are implicitly forgiveness, and his last assent. Salvation is reversed; it is offered to the superior intelligence or power that administers to human limitations.

This conclusion makes it a misreading of the implication of Melville's text to treat Billy as an analogue of Christ, Son of God, fulfilling his redemptive interest in man. Literally and truly Billy is the "son of man." Billy's death proposes with some irony that man has always been the source of his own salvation and has redeemed or converted his gods to humane purposes. If Billy is a saint there is nothing supernatural about him. On the contrary, when Billy is approached by the chaplain with the last comforts of religion, the latter is made to recognize their irrelevance in this case; "futile to all appearance were his efforts to bring home to him the thought of salvation and a Saviour."

In other words nothing stands for value or faith in the scene of his death except Billy. When the ship's crew has echoed Billy's dying cry for Captain Vere, they look only at Billy and "Billy alone must have been in their hearts." As for God, where is he? Captain Vere soon after takes his death wound in battle with a French ship called the *Athéiste*. Melville makes his point with the choice of that name, and he makes it further when he describes the last words heard from Captain Vere, "Billy Budd." The threat of mutiny has subsided, simultaneously as the *Athéiste* is overcome and Captain Vere dies; the war eventually ends. The meaning is expansive. Rebellion dies when the universe loses its old master. Perhaps Vere acknowledged this with Billy's name, and has released to men the moral responsibility for their lives.

The parable is humanist and democratic. It could illustrate D. H. Lawrence's theme in his view of an American myth, "Henceforth be masterless," though too much in that direction would be misleading. Martyred Billy has put a tragic question to all systems of authority, human or divine. The Mutiny Act, like an expression of the larger postlapsarian universe, assumed that men had a bias for destruction which only the most consistent and severe discipline could control. Captain Vere concentrates his whole sensitive intelligence on this point. He was "a man resolute to surmount difficulties even if against primitive instincts." For Vere the rebellion released the original violence, an abyss over which human civilization poised itself; in the face of this violence, the "rights of man" were sentimental and beside the point. Billy has the same absolute revulsion from mutiny, but not the same contempt for the "rights of man." If democracy is at stake then, it is not on behalf of a natural and innocent freedom. And yet the calculated sadism of Claggart, the logical discipline of Vere, have broken themselves upon Billy's real innocence and good nature. What then proposes itself as an alternative to repression and anarchy?

Billy is not an intellectual critic, nor is he the symbol for an intellectual criticism of social repression and natural liberty. He is an exponent, in purest form, of the affective response to irreconcilable human experiences, that response which Hawthorne called "sympathy." Sympathy is not mere good nature in this case, but the abiding will to exchange the human interest, despite such despairing entanglements as those which call for Billy's death. This affirmation both criticizes and transcends the alternatives of subversion and repression. It has a detached standpoint but also supports faith, and this is indispensable to a democracy which proposes to be free of the compulsions of disorder and the compulsions of authority. Like Billy's words it is a communication that reaches across passion, reason, and utility, across murder and the law. It is finally a moral reserve that is necessary in a loose and dialectically balanced democracy. Billy is detached from his own death; that is perhaps a unique heroism, but in principle it resembles an Emersonian detachment which was based on happier assumptions. Emerson could lift himself above "irreconcilables," not because he knew so definitely a transcendent place to stand, but because the effort itself was rewarding and illustrated character. Character is the whole issue; in Melville only personality is transcendent, and he carried it logically to the tragic extreme.

Billy gives and attracts sympathy, but in his case it is an emanation more solid and mundane than Christ-like compassion. Perhaps in the last refinement it is merely the expression of his inner balance and moral health, as in the case of Queequeg. It seems certainly to be an accessible and simple human faculty. And yet, when it appears, man's shackles fall off as irrelevant and gratuitous. The sympathy that comes from within is the security that supports freedom. At the same time it binds men together more firmly than any other force within their codes. Billy has ordained the death of the world's severe master by demonstrating to him that he was no longer necessary. The good ship *Athéiste* had little more to do.

The luminous but complex allegory, which features a metaphysical politics, proposes that man's liberty is linked to his emancipation from old but respected gods, as well as his moral evolution. But the latter requires a knowledge of what is quintessentially human, that is, to use D. H. Lawrence's acute response to Whitman's idea of democracy, the announcement of a humanity supported "not by anything but just itself." To affirm this is the ultimate revolution, and with it false gods indeed must go. But that image of man excludes self-love and self-aggrandizement; it does not require a practical victory, as this instance of tragedy illustrates; its realization is in the image of Billy for the ship's company when "Billy alone must have been in their hearts, even as he was in their eyes."

The scene points a challenge to Captain Vere's first assumption, the one which ruled his action, as when he says, "with mankind, forms, measured forms are everything." Vere has made himself such a form in his discipline, and assumes the surrogate identity of the state and even, in the context, of the world's more distant Master. But he is a man too, and educated in his humanity by the tragic action. The genius of this narrative calls for the movement of Vere and Billy from levels of abstract allusion to intrinsic and personal revelations. In Vere's case this is brought to climax in his last interview with Billy before his execution. It is an emotional experience which Melville treats as if it demanded privacy from the reader.

> He was old enough to have been Billy's father. The austere devotee of military duty letting himself melt back into what remains primeval in our formalized humanity may in the end have caught Billy to his heart even as Abraham may have caught young Isaac on the brink of resolutely offering him up.

This records the indispensable tragic effect, as these figures of conflict, playing roles in an abstract antinomy, "melt back into . . . primeval . . . humanity." It is only on this level that the communication at the end of the story is intelligible, as it is effected on three sides—Billy, the ship's crew, and Captain Vere. In that respect it achieves the kind of deep chorus which is sounded in the pillory scene at the end of *The Scarlet Letter.*

But in the rare strength of Melville's story this organ-like note of dramatic unity is accompanied by uneasy and diverse implications of meaning. The problems which were brought to crisis have not been put at rest. For instance, Vere has represented the formal state in its justice, but because he is a man, and a greatly just man, he recognizes that the exceptional case in justice, reflected in Billy's intrinsic innocence, is not really exceptional. Before the necessity of laws, every man shares to some extent in Billy Budd's innocence. In other words the laws are a blunt instrument, administered justice is always in some measure injustice. Melville, I think, is pursuing a democratic dilemma, to be recognized by a democratic criticism, that the social form cannot be enclosed with perfect moral justifications. In a sense one could argue that democracy, with its rejection of authoritative moral justifications, requires that every man perform Billy's act of forgiveness, "God bless Captain Vere," in sacrificing some measure of personal interest and some measure of ideal justice in adhering to the state.

An unforgiven Captain Vere is suggestively the dangerous tyrant, the bigoted ruler. The mutinous growl from the sailors at the end of the story could be released to direct revolt and anarchy. However, Billy's shout does not imply a surrender to power, but an act of gracing it, endowing it with superior sanctions. This can only be in the form of a tragic communication. Perhaps the American writer of the nineteenth century sensed the need for "boundless sympathy" in his state, a remedy for the looseness of democracy as well as the coldness of its power. Above all, and this is the crux of the matter, sympathy could act in the place of fear, and that indeed would be a superior endowment for the institutions of power.

Such a "mistake" as that made in the execution of Billy Budd might destroy all good faith at the basis of any community. Billy reverses that threat, but it is not his innocence which is redemptive. If that were the issue, mutiny itself might be justified. Certainly there would be no need to "bless" Captain Vere. What communicates to the sailors and to Vere himself is the ethical meaning of Billy's generosity, his own good faith. It is neither his innocence nor his defiance, but that capacity for ethical assent which finally releases his old master, Captain Vere. It is indeed the condition for men's freedom.

But this freedom is not fulfilled, nor is it reconciled with justice. The brutal logic of the Mutiny Act does not in itself command respect. It is visible that Billy's last gesture has been added to a mixture of reactionary violence and revolutionary skepticism. Things will never be the same, Captain Vere is truly dead. Yet his necessities are alive and will always be resummoned against license and anarchy. In a democracy, one remembers the death of Captain Vere painfully, with vestiges of guilt and renewed rage against his discipline. Billy was after all a secular saint; no one can, like him, *bless* Captain Vere. But Billy was "in their hearts." And the fact that Captain Vere in particular was struck hard by Billy's last words remains impressive. There is a passage from a letter to Hawthorne which reflects the inspiration of this scene, written so many years later: "we incline to think that God cannot explain His own secrets, and that He would like a little information upon certain points Himself. We mortals astonish Him as much as He us."[14]

14. *The Letters*, p. 125.

7/Whitman
"Song of the Answerer"

"The priest departs, the divine literatus comes." Walt Whitman would only briefly have shocked his contemporaries with this claim in "Democratic Vistas" if they grasped his meaning. When he said, "Literature in our day . . . has become the only general means of morally influencing the world," his words indicate a significant source of power in the great nineteenth-century generations of American writing.[1] Emerson and Melville accompany Whitman here, and how serious and aspiring their concerns were, it seems to us now, made diffident by a century of moral defeat and by a tradition of twentieth-century writing which has been notable for its covertly anti-democratic spirit and its revulsion from humanist pretensions. That is not a contrast to pursue at this point, but the reference is worth making because it is only recently that Whitman has been given revived and increased respect. That is to say, admired as he has always been, the patronizing note was rarely absent, and this expressed the sense of a monumental crudity of purpose, precisely in the aspect of his work in which Whitman took his mission as a "literatus" seriously. No one can treat "Democratic Vistas" as only a gloss on his political sentiments and general ideas; it is a clear statement of intention which molds his life as a poet and adds in its own

1. Nineteenth-century Russian literature exhibits fascinating parallels, and it is on this issue of the moral interest that the analogy has most point. The critic V. G. Belinsky, whose position as forerunner and guide for Russia's golden age resembles that of Emerson in important respects, made pronouncements that compare exactly with the words of Whitman: "all our moral interests, all our spiritual life have hitherto been and will, still for a long time to come, be concentrated in literature: it is the vital spring from which all human sentiments and conceptions percolate into society." Writers had become priests indeed if Belinsky could say, "Literature was for our society a vital source even of practical moral ideas" (V. G. Belinsky, "Thoughts and Notes on Russian Literature," in *Belinsky, Chernyshevsky, and Dobrolyubov, Selected Criticism*, ed. Ralph E. Matlaw [New York: E. P. Dutton, 1962], pp. 7, 9).

right to the major literature of democratic thought. To read it is to discover that Whitman could do justice to a great idea, one of the fertile ideas which breed poetry by their moral complexity and not by the mere strenuous impulse of faith.

As he wrote the essay, Whitman was asking the dramatic historic question, in time with post-Civil War disillusionments, what did democracy offer beyond its rejection of old forms of oppression? Assuming it gave freedom, did it teach the free man what to do with it? These were questions of Emerson and Thoreau, but Whitman was even more urgent, as if failure were very close.

> I say that our New World democracy, however great a success in uplifting the masses out of their sloughs, in materialistic development . . . is, so far, an almost complete failure in its social aspects, and in really grand religious, moral, literary, and esthetic results.

His poetry generally conceals what Whitman felt in this respect, but reading the essay is to make the appeal in the poetry stronger.

> Never was there, perhaps, more hollowness at heart than at present, and here in the United States. Genuine belief seems to have left us. The underlying principles of the States are not honestly believ'd in (for all this hectic glow, and these melodramatic screamings), nor is humanity itself believ'd in. What penetrating eye does not everywhere see through the mask? The spectacle is appalling.[2]

On this basis Whitman was a democratic revivalist, and his consciousness of a problem, "like a physician diagnosing some deep disease," belongs also to his younger contemporaries, Mark Twain and Henry James.

In his approach to the "disease," Whitman did not pursue specific symptoms with invective, but strove to locate the roots of the old faith. He recognized the dispersion or fragmentation of aims, "small aims, or no aims at all, only to kill time," and the dominant distraction of making money. These filled a vacuum; given an aimless freedom, action becomes trivial and debased.

Therefore Whitman searched again for the moral inspirations of democracy. He states for himself what was essentially the problem of Emerson. The burden of the latter's meditation was to assert faith in a morally solid, spiritually coherent universe, and still present perfect independence to its parts. The enthusiastic hopes and radical negatives

2. "Democratic Vistas," *Complete Poetry and Selected Prose*, ed. James E. Miller, Jr. (Boston: Houghton Mifflin, 1959), p. 461.

of freedom, liberating a series of contradictions, seemed to require transcendental forms of metaphysical support.

The plausible answer to this need was stated succinctly by Tocqueville twenty years or so before the first edition of *Leaves of Grass*. Tocqueville saw pantheism as an effort to meet the political and moral premises of democracy.[3] With this insight Tocqueville caught one of the paradoxes which made his work a great perceptive document in American social criticism. He noted the obsession with unity which arose from the fragmentation of values in the revolutionary acts of liberation; this concern for order, which, as he put it, was "embarrassed by [the] primary division of things," put an ambiguous gloss on the major premise of individual freedom. Pantheism made it possible to recognize and praise the cosmos simultaneously with the recognition of the microcosmic fragment which reflected it; the part *was* the whole, but as Tocqueville perceived, such an intellectual victory was reversible and could look rather like a total surrender. This kind of euphoric and confused self-extinction was probably what Tocqueville had in mind when he went on to say, "Against it [pantheism] all who abide in their attachment to the true greatness of man should combine and struggle." It is legitimate to attach the emotional trance and the moral passivity of pantheism to many of the lines written by Emerson and also by Whitman, but it cannot be left as the final judgment. The philosophic and moral energy of both writers in particularly luminous moments was dialectical, and being so they were as aware in their own way as Tocqueville was of the state of tension in which the double values of freedom and moral unity would lead their existence.

Whitman in his essay thinks first of the task of the poet to provide unifying identities. The American and democratic poet confronted truly great diversity: "races, far localities, . . . the States, with all their variety of origins, their diverse climes, cities, standards, and so forth."

> Subjection, aggregation . . . is impossible to America; but the fear of conflicting and irreconcilable interiors, and the lack of a common skeleton, knitting all close, continually haunts me.

This is blunt and revealing; "the fear of conflicting . . . interiors, and the lack of a common skeleton" unites Whitman with his contemporaries. Could Melville have said more to explain his writing of his "black book," *Moby Dick*, or Hawthorne for his parables of demonic

3. Tocqueville, *Democracy in America*, p. 33.

or neurotic isolation? More germane, Whitman's text recasts the memory of Emerson's gracefully protean principle of cosmic unity, to which he seemed to retreat from the shock of pluralistic experience. The imagination must find order at all costs, but here was its challenge, one of the most serious in the history of culture, when moral unity was proclaimed, spontaneously as it were, and based only on the free action of individuals who were committed to selfhood as an immutable principle.

It is not surprising that Whitman acknowledged a theme of contradiction. He said that democracy found its idea of origin in conceiving the "singleness of man." But he consequently goes on to say that the larger unity must be "provided for. Only from it, and from its proper regulation and potency, comes the other, comes the chance of individualism. The two are contradictory, but our task is to reconcile them."

He invokes the two-sided moral demand as follows.

> Not that half only, individualism, which isolates. There is another half, which is adhesiveness or love, that fuses, ties, and aggregates, making the races comrades, and fraternizing all. Both are to be vitalized by religion (sole worthiest elevator of man or State), breathing into the proud, material tissues, the breath of life. For I say at the core of democracy, finally, is the religious element. All the religions, old and new, are there.

But this religion was an ultimate politics which activated and held together a system of balanced forces.

> For to democracy, the leveler, the unyielding principle of the average, surely join'd another principle, equally unyielding, closely tracking the first, indispensable to it, opposite (as the sexes are opposite), and whose existence, confronting and ever modifying the other, often clashing, paradoxical, yet neither of highest avail without the other, plainly supplies to these grand cosmic politics of ours, and to the launch'd forth mortal dangers of republicanism, today, or any day, the counterpart and offset whereby Nature restrains the deadly original relentlessness of all her first-class laws. This second principle is individuality, the pride and centripetal isolation of a human being in himself—identity—personalism . . . the principle itself is needed for very life's sake. It forms, in a sort, or is to form, the compensating balance-wheel of the successful working machinery of aggregate America.

Like Emerson, Whitman pursued unity and found dialectic on his way. Whether one stressed conflict or compensation, the thinking conceived opposite values and accepted antithesis in the nature of things. The purpose of the mind and of moral action was synthesis, but meanwhile the real health of the moral sensibility was indicated in the acceptance of pluralist and combative terms. The democratic dialectic emphasized a value *process* in place of a value structure, and thereby tried to combine the movement of continuous conflict and criticism with an equally continuous basis of assent. And this, if not the pain of it or its invitation to tragic action, was what Whitman seemed to see clearly in his prose manifesto of belief.

How lighthearted Whitman's initial statement of a double faith seems to be.

One's-self I sing, a simple separate person,
Yet utter the word Democratic, the word En-Masse.

One might think that there ought to be a greater distance between those two lines. To propose contradictory values and accept them both is not by itself to make a dialectical system. Did the simplicities of the popular democratic myth capture Whitman and prevent his imagination from taking the sophisticated values of his subject, those he himself proposed in "Democratic Vistas"? His verse certainly does not thrive in the confrontation of opposites, the crisis of alternatives, and the strategy of a conversion of terms. In major respects, Whitman's own optimism, or the strain to express an initial subsuming act of faith, defeated his poetic theme in its dramatic possibilities. We might sometimes wish we had received from him a long narrative poem which matched the range of experience in *Moby Dick* and *The Scarlet Letter*. To make a dialectic of values convincing requires dramatic enactment, a serious passage through difficulty; in the most forbidding sense this approximates tragedy, as both Melville and Hawthorne approached tragedy. In his essay Whitman spoke of "mortal dangers" for the tensions held in balance by democracy, the turning between adhesiveness and independence. In his verse, however, there is no sense of danger whatever.

Of course no one is going to talk about Whitman as a tragic poet, and if the better analogy is with "epic," it is idle to imagine a different sort of epic poet appearing in America's nineteenth-century ferment. As Randall Jarrell said warmly, "One Whitman is miracle enough." He goes on to say in marking the failure of comparisons

It is Homer, or the sagas, or something far away and long ago, that comes to one's mind only to be dismissed; for sometimes Whitman *is* epic, just as *Moby Dick* is, and it surprises us to be able to use truthfully this word that we have misused so many times. Whitman *is* grand, and elevated, and comprehensive, and real with an astonishing reality, and many other things—the critic points at his qualities in despair and wonder, all method failing, and simply calls them by their names.[4]

One could be moved to agree with this but, despite Jarrell's abjuration of critical method, still ask how that astonishing sense of reality makes itself felt. The essence of this quality is, I think, the effect of a living and moving world; it comes from the dominance of life metaphors in Whitman's verse, the dialectic of nature, one might say, appearing within the frame of affirmations. The strongest source of vitality in Whitman is erotic; his theme is communication and his metaphors are sexual. This enables him to express life as action and at the same time point to its unassailable, biological source of unity.

Two stanzas from "Song of Myself" offer the clearest example of the sexual metaphor in this use. Whitman defines two identities, two "I am"s, one of which is the particular person, surrounded by "trippers and askers," "the people I meet," involved in contingencies, "dinner, dress, associates, looks, compliments, dues." But there is another which stands apart.

> Apart from the pulling and hauling stands what I am,
> Stands amused, complacent, compassionating, idle, unitary.
> Looks down, is erect, or bends an arm on an impalpable certain rest,
> Looking with side-curved head curious what will come next,
> Both in and out of the game and watching and wondering at it.[5]

He stresses spectatorship in the overlooking "I am," but its principle is both detachment and universality, "existing both in and out of the game." There is immunity in the words "amused, complacent, idle" and the stress on "looking down." Here is the appearance of the Over-Soul, revealed in its invulnerable self-sufficiency. This wider self is meant to be inclusive, complete; when Whitman calls it the soul, as in lines from "Starting From Paumanok," he calls the contingent personal self the body. But this gives him his clue and in "Song of Myself" he launches into a vividly erotic passage which does everything possible to break through the immunities of the "over-self."

> I believe in you my soul, the other I am must not abase itself to you,
> And you must not be abased to the other.

4. Randall Jarrell, *Poetry and the Age* (New York: Alfred A. Knopf, 1953), p. 131.

5. "Song of Myself," *Complete Poetry*, p. 27.

Loafe with me on the grass, loose the stop from your throat,
Not words, not music or rhyme I want, not custom or lecture, not even
the best,
Only the lull I like, the hum of your valvèd voice.
I mind how once we lay such a transparent summer morning,
How you settled your head athwart my hips and gently turn'd over upon
me,
And parted the shirt from my bosom-bone, and plunged your tongue to
my bare-stript heart,
And reach'd till you felt my beard, and reach'd till you held my feet.

Swiftly arose and spread around me the peace and knowledge that pass
all the argument of the earth,
And I know that the hand of God is the promise of my own,
And I know that the spirit of God is the brother of my own,
And that all the men ever born are also my brothers, and the women
my sisters and lovers,
And that a kelson of the creation is love,
And limitless are leaves stiff or drooping in the fields,
And brown ants in the little wells beneath them,
And mossy scabs of the worm fence, heap'd stones, elder, mullein and
poke-weed.[6]

This is the essential Whitman. Is it an autoerotic scene, or the
sexual meeting of two "among all the men and women ever born"?
It doesn't much matter, although the onanistic implications serve his
theme better. This is the communication between soul and body, the
two ideas of self bound together, both universal and particular. On
this ground love cannot be distinguished from self-love. Self-love is a
primary principle, as if when this universe began there was only the
single person, who knew how to appreciate himself and therefore was
complete. The act of love in Whitman is immediately universal; it
hardly passes through the medium of the private experience. The
sexual partners remain anonymous, they come and go in a series, or
they are, as in this case, the elements of an erotic organism which has
its mate everywhere and in everybody. The act of love is understood
as the "procreant urge" of all the world, the life force itself.

Have you ever loved the body of a woman?
Have you ever loved the body of a man?
Do you not see that these are exactly the same to all in all nations and
times all over the earth?

6. Ibid., pp. 27–28.

Conception becomes the sign as well as the instrument of immortality.

> A woman's body at auction,
> She too is not only herself, she is the teeming mother of mothers,[7]

Love is the fathering and mothering of all time.

> Through you I drain the pent-up rivers of myself,
> In you I wrap a thousand onward years,[8]

Love is the basis of ultimate explanations, as in the following lines.

> My Comrade!
> For you to share with me two greatnesses, and a third one rising inclusive and more resplendent,
> The greatness of Love and Democracy, and the greatness of Religion.[9]

As the poet who thus announced his three great themes to be Love, Democracy, and Religion, Whitman was under the compulsion to teach that love and democracy were the structural elements of his natural philosophy. For Whitman they were the life-energy of human relationships. Accordingly his erotic theme has concreteness but is generalized; it accompanies the moral implications of love and democracy. Passion if not subdued is quite definitely sublimated. Sex as a metaphor verifies the interflow and interpenetration of values to which communication in an organic democracy addresses itself.

"Calamus," his most specifically erotic series of verses, speaks to the point in proposing that love is reassurance for the "doubt of appearances."

> Of the terrible doubt of appearances,
> Of the uncertainty after all, that we may be deluded,
> That . . .
> May-be the things I perceive . . .
> . . . are only apparitions . . .
> . . . .
> To me these and the like of these are curiously answer'd by my lovers, my dear friends,
> When he whom I love travels with me or sits a long while holding me by the hand,
> When the subtle air, the impalpable, the sense that words and reason hold not, surround us and pervade us,
> Then I am charged with untold and untellable wisdom, I am silent, I require nothing further,

7. "Children of Adam," *Complete Poetry*, p. 75.
8. Ibid., p. 77.
9. "Starting From Paumanok," *Complete Poetry*, p. 19.

I cannot answer the question of appearances or that of identity beyond
    the grave,
But I walk or sit indifferent, I am satisfied,
He ahold of my hand has completely satisfied me.[10]

It is rather remarkable to see Whitman express in these lines the
exact meaning of an ontological humanism, in the effect that is stressed
with greater emphasis by writers of a different temperament, Hawthorne and Melville. The term ontological is useful to indicate the
resort to humanity as a support against the metaphysical uncertainty
of the ground for one's being. Whitman is as explicit as it is possible to
be in summing this up, although elsewhere as a rule he does not record
much of "the terrible doubt of appearances," or "the uncertainty after
all, that we may be deluded." In these respects he resembles Emerson
a great deal more than Melville. But he confesses the urgency behind
the Emersonian reassurance, and in this case, and throughout his
poetry, the form of reassurance is comradeship. To make certain of
metaphysical place, of reality, requires the hand-hold of lovers and
friends, and once this is received, "I require nothing further." It is an
"untellable wisdom," and in that respect it directs itself not only toward
the dramatic symbolism of Hawthorne and Melville, but also to the
aphoristic and oracular style of Emerson. The source of wisdom is
properly a matter of intuition and inspiration, because it is implicitly
unegalitarian to devise a "system" with its appended definitions and
restrictions. "Life only avails," Emerson said, and "it resides in the
moment of transition from a past to a new state, in the shooting of the
gulf, in the darting to an aim." Similarly when Queequeg, like the
others aboard ship, is challenged to expound on the esoteric final
mysteries engraved on the South American coin which Ahab had
embedded in the mast, he points mutely somewhere in the direction
of his thigh and goes on his way.

If in the last recourse character was reality for Emerson, the
body, known intimately and loved, is the substratum reality in Whitman's verse. Let us be religious, Whitman says, about these first things.

The man's body is sacred and the woman's body is sacred,
No matter who it is, it is sacred—is it the meanest one in the laborers'
    gang?
Is it one of the dull-faced immigrants just landed on the wharf?

10. "Calamus," *Complete Poetry*, pp. 88–89.

Each belongs here or anywhere just as much as the well-off, just as much
    as you,
Each has his or her place in the procession.

(All is a procession,
The universe is a procession with measured and perfect motion.)[11]

The body is sacred, "No matter who it is, it is sacred"; the first fact
in experience, which is a natural fact, is absolute in value. In evoking
the laborer and the immigrant Whitman does not appeal to compassion, or to generosity, but to an unarguable premise. Pursue nature
far enough, base essential thinking on nature, particularly as men
have bodies, and the principle by which men share value in each
other's eyes becomes clear. So Whitman can write in one of his great
moments.

> Undrape! you are not guilty to me, nor stale nor discarded,
> I see through the broadcloth and gingham whether or no,
> And am around, tenacious, acquisitive, tireless, and cannot be shaken
>   away.[12]

This theme enforces the point that the discussion of nature
which the nineteenth-century Americans conducted was a struggle
on behalf of anthropomorphic faith. Men could support their equality
as well as their kinship if they could declare a revered common source
in nature. That all men had organic bodies could be made as reassuring
and unifying as the belief that all men had immortal souls. Men indeed
had souls, both Whitman and Emerson asserted, these souls were
manifestations of the common soul which inhabited nature, but the
evidence of equality had to be made more explicit than that. (Certainly
this was true for Whitman; one could guess what small fragments of
overt equality might satisfy Emerson, who felt that the meaningful
universe was most of all a function of thinking and seeing.) To be
equal only in the realm of soul would be a reminder of that postponed
equality in heaven by which Christianity had reassured believers. A
belief in nature seemed necessary for a secular democracy in order to
transfer its hope for equality to this world. Tocqueville assumed this
when he speculated that pantheism was the appropriate general
philosophy of a democracy. But no "pantheist" had yet dealt with the
ultimate biological dramas of life as forthrightly as Whitman. The

11. "Children of Adam," *Complete Poetry*, p. 74.
12. "Song of Myself," *Complete Poetry*, p. 29.

contemplative and "transcendental" naturalism of Emerson and Thoreau seems a genteel evasion in contrast. The fact that Whitman took these themes up so strongly is an index of his determination to prophesy as the newly arrived democratic poet.

The body was a great democratic agent; what could do more to challenge aristocratic assumptions? Death, in fact, was the strongest affirmation of likeness and unity, if that was what one was looking for. If men were not exactly equal as sexual bodies, they surely were in the coffin. The life cycle in its most obvious sense was confirmed by death, always a reminder that the whole was greater than its parts, and that lives come and go but their common substance remains.

This calls up the sense of the moral danger in pantheism which Tocqueville expressed. One moves as closely as possible to nature; the consequence could be a harsh, morally callous set of life values, or they could take the tone of hedonistic irresponsibility, an equally cruel pattern of indulgence and selfishness. The god of nature is not necessarily a god of moral injunctions or, to put it more clearly, he is not necessarily human in temperament. The ingenuity of the humanist and secular poet, the democratic poet announced by Whitman, is greatly taxed in extracting moral values from nature, but that is his mission, whatever ambiguities might lie in his success.

Such ambitious affirmations are at work in his two great poems on death. The effort is very strong indeed. In "Out of the Cradle Endlessly Rocking" the poet's vocation itself is taught by the bird who sings, mourning his dead mate.

> O you singer solitary, singing by yourself, projecting me,
> O solitary me listening, never more shall I cease perpetuating you,
> Never more shall I escape, never more the reverberations,
> Never more the cries of unsatisfied love be absent from me.

Here is the predicament from which poetry arises. The love for the mate, confronted with loss, is a supremely keen life situation in which all action, thought, as well as the poet's songs are rooted. To live is to sing, to express love or the need for love. But the final word in the song, the goal of its singing, is death. It is a determined apotheosis, whatever else it is; all issues are resolved in it, all needs and hungers and the greatest of aspirations.

> The word final, superior to all,
> Subtle, sent up—what is it?—I listen;

It is the sea that answers,

> Delaying not, hurrying not,
> Whisper'd me through the night, and very plainly before daybreak,
> Lisp'd to me the low and delicious word death,
> And again, death, death, death, death,

This is the redemptive final act of the naturalist religion. Here in the ocean of death each fragment of life receives its welcome.

A large part of the human temperament must be frustrated by such offerings of relief. The brutal and ambiguous implications remain with a vision of the body which is chiefly operated by the sexual power, or of life as it is dissolved in the great natural continuities of dying and being born. In the American literary and intellectual tradition we see recurrently this dangerous invitation to a power above the personality and beyond the sanctions of the civilized community itself. Sex may be a sign of the eternal unity and commingling of man, but in its concrete significance it does not necessarily have that quality and it may have in fact the opposite meaning. It requires the poet to generalize such values, and Whitman understood this when he called for a priesthood of poetry. But to handle these matters freely, to engage without restraint in a worship of nature, has threatening possibilities. The end may be the same as Captain Ahab's hatred. Both give themselves up to a power in nature which divorces itself quite easily from any of the important aims of human life. The ancient effect of such submissions to the natural process was to undermine the ground supports of the collective human order. To love death without conditions, to worship its power, may be the same as the worship of life, but both such terms press against the moral defenses of life and may sacrifice men to nature. This again is what Tocqueville meant when he spoke of the dangers of pantheism, and it points to the source of strain in the treatment of nature in American writing. Perhaps it also locates the strain in the American social order, in its serial preoccupations with violence and the myth of total, or orgiastic, experience.

A somewhat different tone is available to Whitman when he writes his elegy for President Lincoln. This death is not abstract, nor is it a small integer among the daily thousands who join death. Here the democratic hero beyond parallel appears, and he dies the martyred death. Now if ever the opportunity occurs to humanize the meaning of death and raise it above the naturalistic reduction. To a large extent this happens in the great poem by Whitman. For one thing the sorrow itself is a theme in this rare instance, and the grief is the more clearly human for being personal and concrete. In the same effect, that grief unites humanity. Men assemble at the funeral procession and recognize each other in the greatest of all signs of common experience.

> Over the breast of the spring, the land, amid cities,
> Amid lanes and through old woods, where lately the violets peep'd from the ground, spotting the gray debris,
> Amid the grass in the fields each side of the lanes, passing the endless grass,
> . . . .
> Coffin that passes through lanes and streets,
> Through day and night with the great cloud darkening the land,
> . . . .
> With processions long and winding and the flambeaus of the night,
> With the countless torches lit, with the silent sea of faces and the un-bared heads,
> With the waiting depot, the arriving coffin, and the sombre faces.[13]

The sympathy aroused by death now records the traditional elegiac compensation. If death brings to great intensity the love one felt for the man dead, there comes in the surplus of feeling a surprising reward which endows life with the appreciations which are the antithesis of death. Accordingly in Whitman's poem he moves from grief to a celebration of the rich swarming landscape of spring.

> Pictures of growing spring and farms and homes,
> With the Fourth-month eve at sundown, and the gray smoke lucid and bright,
> With floods of the yellow gold of the gorgeous, indolent, sinking sun, burning, expanding the air,
> With the fresh sweet herbage under foot, and the pale green leaves of the trees prolific,

But to contemplate nature's richness is not enough. Whitman's strongest note is sustained in the idea of human comradeship.

> Then with the knowledge of death as walking one side of me,
> And the thought of death close-walking the other side of me,
> And I in the middle as with companions, and as holding the hands of companions.

At this climax death becomes the "strong deliveress," the "dark mother" who must be welcomed.

> *Lost in the loving floating ocean of thee,*
> *Laved in the flood of thy bliss O death.*

13. "When Lilacs Last in the Dooryard Bloom'd," *Complete Poetry*, pp. 233–34.

Is this the joy of recognizing the unity of men, or the affinity with nature? The terms cannot be distinguished any longer.

> Yet each to keep and all, retrievements out of the night,
> The song, the wondrous chant of the gray-brown bird,
> And the tallying chant, the echo arous'd in my soul,
> With the lustrous and drooping star with the countenance full of woe,
> With the holders holding my hand nearing the call of the bird,
> Comrades mine and I in the midst, and their memory ever to keep, for the dead I loved so well,
> For the sweetest, wisest soul of all my days and lands—and this for his dear sake.

The death of Lincoln aroused a poignancy of feeling which clarified the naturalist doctrine. It called forth in Whitman the strongest part of his sensibility, which clung so firmly to the immanence of life. This was a daring adventure he conducted; he invaded an area which men had always surrounded with the most fervent antinaturalistic concepts. Both sex and death had always received the intensively sublimated process of civilized thought. They were the messages most threatening from nature. For Whitman himself it was necessary to make a renewed effort in their moral conversion. By going as far as possible into the realm of nature, his imagination seized the one term available for a reconciliation with nature. He never for a moment drops it; every reference to the body and to natural experience is dressed with the accommodations of sympathy, kinship, or the moral recognition of equality. In nature, as in society, that principle attacked the forces of instinctual anarchy and aggression at their source, and it conditioned the dread fact of physical extinction.

The gregarious spirit expresses the first gesture of humanity, even when Whitman announces his intention to "celebrate and sing myself." He says, "Camerado, this is no book,/Who touches this touches a man." The phrase is taken from Emerson, but as in the case of that strangely impersonal personality, what in his verse is discovered about Whitman the singular man? The fact is that Whitman does not write personal lyrical poetry but something one could describe as public poetry, or a political and religious poetry which is meant for a communal service.

It is visible to all readers, eventually, that the first-person protagonist is a generalized person and has a dual function. There is a quick and constant shifting of reference from the particular to the collective protagonist. The pronoun "We" would have been inadequate for Whitman's purposes; it would indicate an abstract, relatively lifeless, quantitative identity which is not at all what he wants. The democratic "We" is really a transcendental "I," strong in its sense of fused being. Whitman has imagined a universal first person, projected from the multiple lives of the crowd, so that the people will again have a drama of personal salvation. In that respect the dual terms of a community worship are satisfied, to be one among many and part of many; nothing more clearly demonstrates the dialectical urgencies which Whitman acknowledged in "Democratic Vistas."

Whitman's egocentric hyperbole is a device of self-transcendence and his manner of self-assertion is extreme in order to make effective the escape from self. This is not a paradox merely, but an effort to justify discrete existence in a worship of the universal.

> Having pried through the strata, analyzed to a hair, counsel'd with doc-
>   tors and calculated close,
> I find no sweeter fat than sticks to my own bones.
>
> In all people I see myself; none more and not one a barley-corn less,
> And the good or bad I say of myself I say of them.
>
> I know I am solid and sound,
> To me the converging objects of the universe perpetually flow,
> All are written to me, and I must get what the writing means.
>
> I know I am deathless,
> . . . .
> I know I am august,
> I do not trouble my spirit to vindicate itself or be understood,
> I see that the elementary laws never apologize,
> . . . .
> I exist as I am, that is enough.[14]

In such passages extravagant self-assertion moves into its opposite term. The self enlarges in its own praise only to become dissolved in organic spirit. But this is reversible; "In all people I see myself," and thus the poet aims to subdue the collective abstraction. By translating it into the personal term he morally transforms it. Through such acts of the imagination, as Whitman explicitly understood, the democratic experience becomes fundamental or, in his language, religious.

There remains a poetic and dramatic problem. Such great ambitions tend to develop to quietism, or a diffuse, abstractly considered mysticism. The effort to achieve inclusiveness may cancel particulars

14. "Song of Myself," *Complete Poetry*, p. 38.

out. There is a generalized frame of unity but it has no distinguishable form. At the worst extreme the quick elevation from concrete references weakens the sense of reality in Whitman's verse, and its values are sometimes reduced to the incantatory effect of his rhythms, with rhetoric doing the work of perception and feeling. The effect, reminding us of Emerson, is the failure to satisfy the dramatic sensibility. After the first appearance of the microcosm in its self-sufficient meaningfulness, what is there left to do except add lists of objects, events, people, incidents which multiply the single case? The sacrifice is made of the dramatic sensibility because of the lack of a dimension for change as well as the absence of the actual singularity of characters and experiences. This is a great paradox, that a dialectical principle, very self-conscious as it was, should overlook drama itself. Whitman's poetry is open-ended, if not formless, additively becoming one large poem whose writing is never done because its elements are a series and not a structure. The only way to close is by saying good-by, as he did three different times, in the closing verses of the three last editions of *Leaves of Grass* published in his lifetime. The democratic poet, champion of equality and respectful of numbers, has not only the right but the obligation to repeat himself.

However, the effect of monotony is not frequent or overbearing. To return to Whitman is to be stimulated by him again, loud, discursive, and repetitious as he may be. One reason for this, as I've suggested, is the overlay of the personal protagonist which freshens the interior abstraction. Another is the effect of what I have called public poetry. The audience is in his verse, implicitly, standing as listeners, and this suggestive dialogue may do service for dramatic structure. The orator speaks in one voice, but what is at issue is a public experience which men can only feel as they imagine an audience.

Whitman distinguishes himself clearly from the truly egocentric or narcissistic voice in poetry. In the hundred years since his time we find much better examples of poets talking particularly to themselves, or to the ideal reader who is sufficiently abnegating to lend himself to the unparalleled degree of idiosyncrasy and self-assertion in modern verse. This exhibition of personality, enthralling as it might be, is not Whitman's note; we are not overpowered by a sensibility whose chief interest is to bring us into a rich, exclusively private world. Whitman seems to reach the reader in *his* world, or to break barriers between all private worlds. The direct address to the listener is fresh and invigorating like good public oratory; it has a generosity of emotion whose basis seems to be the assumption that every man shares the poet's experience, as well as his capacity for experience.

In the broader sense one might see here the still unreconciled dimensions of the public and private life in a democracy. Twenty or thirty years ago, the voice of Whitman seemed too much like the bellow of the politician, or the evangelist, or the salesman; the poetry had the sloganizing abstraction of such speech, and after a little of it one felt starved for the subtler excitements of the personal sensibility. Now the need is different; the vogue of poetry readings, of coffee house recitations, the "amateur" style and discursiveness of much contemporary verse may tell us something of this awakened need for the communal experience of poetry.

It is precisely the problem of reconciling the public and private life that concerns Whitman. If he adopts a public personality and speaks from a platform, he is not satisfied to remain there. The general address concentrates with the sudden emergence of the counter-protagonist, the singular "you" who is always there, who is represented by the reader. The lines, "this is no book,/Who touches this touches a man," should also recall the lines which follow immediately.

> (Is it night? are we here together alone?)
> It is I you hold and who holds you,
> I spring from the pages into your arms—decease calls me forth.[15]

This is not his luckiest formulation, but the power of Whitman's verse indeed counts on this impulse leaping from his pages. It is a drive toward intimacy, erotic in its figurative language, making unembarrassed address to strangers.

The effect is characteristic in his lines entitled "To You," which speak to everyone unknown who feels his anonymity. It is to say, whoever you are, I have found you, I know you.

> Whoever you are, now I place my hand upon you, that you be my poem,
> I whisper with my lips close to your ear,
> I have loved many women and men, but I love none better than you.[16]

This is meant as a dialogue of writer and reader. Reading the poem is taking part in it. It is a poetry to invade privacy, vulgar even and not always ingratiating, but full of the idealized good nature and mute brotherhood of crowds. The looseness of the verse, its volubility, its

15. "So Long," from "Songs of Parting," *Complete Poetry*, p. 349.
16. "To You," from "Birds of Passage," *Complete Poetry*, p. 171.

stops and starts, are appropriate to a rage for communication. Whispering and shouting, and making a great turbulence, but finding its way directly to the reader—

> O I have been dilatory and dumb,
> I should have made my way straight to you long ago,
> I should have blabb'd nothing but you, I should have chanted nothing
> but you.
> I will leave all and come and make the hymns of you,
> None has understood you, but I understand you,
> None has done justice to you, you have not done justice to yourself,
> None but has found you imperfect, I only find no imperfection in you.

The voice is ecstatic, and it follows the bolder strategies of seduction.

> O I could sing such grandeurs and glories about you!
> You have not known what you are, you have slumber'd upon yourself
> all your life,
> . . . .
> I pursue you where none else has pursued you,
> . . . .
> The shaved face, the unsteady eye, the impure complexion, if these balk
> others they do not balk me,
> The pert apparel, the deform'd attitude, drunkenness, greed, premature
> death, all these I part aside.

To be pursued where none other has pursued—but not toward an exclusive and self-centered intimacy. The spirit is humane, generous, unexploiting. Growing from the root of self-esteem, the reassurance is there for all men.

> There is no endowment in man or woman that is not tallied in you,
> There is no virtue, no beauty in man or woman, but as good is in you,
> . . . .
> No pleasure waiting for others, but an equal pleasure waits for you.

This love reaches toward equality, not aggrandizement. Its good can be shared among many, but it is still selective and gives reassurance to the singular "You."

The imagined goal is clearly not possession but the achievement of empathy. The poet is satisfied with speaking, bodily touch is only one figure of his speech. What he wills most strongly is to share minds, to move across distances of time and space and say, I was there, where you are, or I will be there, like you, therefore knowing you. Crossing on the ferry between Brooklyn and Manhattan, Whitman projects himself into worlds and identities.

It avails not, time nor place—distance avails not,
I am with you, you men and women of a generation, or ever so many
    generations hence.
Just as you feel when you look on the river and sky, so I felt,
Just as any of you is one of a living crowd, I was one of a crowd.[17]

Empathy is the concrete emotion of the principle of equality and
takes it beyond the abstract principle of justice. It is not impulsive or a
matter of generosity in one current of emotion. Whitman is not only
caressing the subjective fantasy of the reader, but addressing himself
to the projected higher self which inhabits both the protagonist I and
the protagonist You. Nevertheless the personality is not allowed to
escape, the hyperbole is meant to work. "None has understood you,
but I understand you." By this we see better what is meant by a
"public poetry." He is able to make an emotional appeal resting on two
poles of reference, addressed to the "over-self" and yet answering the
needs of the separate person, oppressed by his loneliness and insignifi-
cance. The crowd, given a voice and a soul, speaks to the person,
made lonely in the crowd. This, we are certain, is a democratic poetry.

It is really to human weakness that Whitman speaks, and not to
the self-inflation of individualists. He is truly the first of democratic
poets in his will to break through the anomie of single individuals and
lift them from it. In that sense his work is, in Newton Arvin's phrase, a
"statement of the psychological costs of individualism" as much as
that of Hawthorne's. Rather than justify and release egocentricity, or
actual narcissism, his larger effort is to circumvent individualism or
reduce its penalties. Whitman's real intent, like that of Emerson, is to
achieve so deep a sense of organic community that it is then simultaneous with the sense of self-hood. Self-liberation in Whitman becomes
the instrument of moral recognition among men. The acts of freedom,
the phenomena of diversity, the range of possibility, are all proofs of a
living common identity.

The democratic sensibility, in its authentic state, in this way
builds everything on the experience of empathy. The universe may be
welcomed but it also must be held together, and so this verse-writing
Paul Bunyan, braggart and boaster in the very special American
sense, will brag for everyone. The simple principle of his writing is
this, "In all people I see myself." This is not merely a matter of mutual
flattery. What gives moral balance to Whitman's idealization of
likeness is his power to make forgiving recognitions. He strips down to

17. "Crossing Brooklyn Ferry," *Complete Poetry*, p. 116.

disgraces and inferiorities in order to find the common ground of human personality.[18] In "Song of Myself," everyone is invited to the feast.

> This is the meal equally set, this the meat for natural hunger.
> It is for the wicked just the same as the righteous, I make appointments with all,
> I will not have a single person slighted or left away,
> The kept woman, sponger, thief, are hereby invited,
> The heavy-lipp'd slave is invited, the venerealee is invited;
> There shall be no difference between them and the rest.[19]

To be democratic in spirit is to be perfectly generous; it is to forgive before the need to forgive has appeared, and again after the most oppressive failure.

> With music strong I come, with my cornets and my drums,
> . . . .
> I beat and pound for the dead,
> . . . .
> Vivas to those who have fail'd![20]

The "daimon" or god of equality will join consciousness with any experience. A poem that is direct in this theme is "Song of the Answerer" and there the "Answerer" is specifically the protagonist of a universal acceptance.

> The insulter, the prostitute, the angry person, the beggar, see themselves in the ways of him, he strangely transmutes them,
> They are not vile any more, they hardly know themselves they are so grown.

"Answering" in this way, in "Song of Myself," the poet expresses his identification with convicts, with handcuffed mutineers, a "youngster taken for larceny," a cholera patient at the last gasp with people

18. The point of view here recalls Melville-Ishmael making his passionate affirmation of "democratic dignity." "But were the coming narrative to reveal, in any instance, the complete abasement of poor Starbuck's fortitude, scarce might I have the heart to write it; for it is a thing most sorrowful, nay shocking, to expose the fall of valor in the soul. Men may seem detestable as joint stock-companies and nations; knaves, fools, and murderers there may be; men may have mean and meagre faces; but man, in the ideal, is so noble and so sparkling, such a grand and glowing creature, that over any ignominious blemish in him all his fellows should run to throw their costliest robes." Whitman's address to the guilty and degraded also recalls Melville's exuberance in writing to Hawthorne, declaring that "a thief in jail is as honorable a personage as Gen. George Washington."

19. "Song of Myself," *Complete Poetry*, p. 37.

20. Ibid., p. 37.

retreating from him; as if overwhelmed by these vicarious experiences, he seems to stop short for a moment. He recovers from the memory of suffering as if the strength itself that he needs were the product of the sharing of consciousness. The climax of this moral power is passionately asserted.

> To anyone dying, thither I speed and twist the knob of the door,
> Turn the bed-clothes toward the foot of the bed,
> Let the physician and the priest go home.

> I seize the descending man and raise him with resistless will,
> O despairer, here is my neck,
> By God, you shall not go down! hang your whole weight upon me.[21]

Passionate enough to break the cold surface of abstractions, and yet this protagonist, it is important to remember, is the collective person, and his energy is the moral energy of the democracy in its inclusiveness, its will to accept everyone.

The aim, however, is to dismiss the need for forgiveness.

> Showing the best and dividing it from the worst age vexes age,
> Knowing the perfect fitness and equanimity of things, while they dis-
> cuss I am silent, and go bathe and admire myself.[22]

Here there is a reserve of detached judgment to which he, like Emerson, could retreat. He restores himself with the "equanimity of things" by going back to himself. The true home of the universal, this is a point at which to rest. One is reminded again of his lines,

> Apart from the pulling and hauling stands what I am,
> Stands amused, complacent, compassionating, idle, unitary. . . .
> Both in and out of the game.

I doubt if these could have been written by anyone but a disciple who had deeply read his Emerson. "Complacent and compassionating"— the words are an illustration of a crucial moral balance, a dialectical fervor. It is in precise effect what Emerson meant by the "double consciousness." Was it not immensely important to remain "both in and out of the game," the democratic game where no victory could be absolute? That reserve is indispensable in the moral arena which excludes bigotry, or total possession by an idea, a passion, a person, or a party. All the more reason for compassion to be available if complacency marked its own borders.

Still it must be said that "complacency" would seem to be the

21. Ibid., p. 57.   22. Ibid., p. 26.

most foreign of all terms in a sympathetic response to experience. The traditional religious drama of suffering involved a full share in the error and pain of its being, and the relief of a transformed experience when protagonists and participants are brought to the knowledge of good. There is no "double consciousness" for Christ on the cross, or for his followers below the cross. There the moral unity of men is meant to be absolute, including every sincere person with the whole of mankind.

To be "both in and out of the game" is a revolutionary concept in ethics. It proposes a quality of self-consideration, a detachment, which conflicts with that merging of self and community which tradition put highest, whether in utopian secular terms or in salvationary religion. Is it ethical never to give oneself up totally to any ethical enterprise? Yes, if one stresses the repressiveness of a unitary ethical system, its tendency to abuse that part of life which it cannot enclose. Yes, again, if one remembers the civil war of ethical systems which strain against compromise and are repelled by the means of reconciliation. Purity and consistency have always been moral ideals. Against this, what is the gain for risking passivity, insensitivity, detachment? The apocalyptic moralism of recent years would make a quarrel with Emerson and Whitman more than ever in this respect.

The Emersonian fortress of the self can seem to refuse human access. The effect of the same determined equanimity is probably what many remember with most dissatisfaction in their reading of Whitman. The effect is more "out" than "in the game"; like his master, Emerson, he seemed to call upon his faith in a law of compensation so quickly that his proclaimed willingness to face the world becomes suspect. One begins to distrust his catalogs of experience, to the extent that the more detail he provides the less we give our attention. Like Emerson, he is accused by the modern consciousness of a lack of moral maturity; certainly he loses something for readers accustomed to observe ordealistic experience and the stoic manner which is its product. And yet, if optimism is his ambience it does not contain only static affirmations. He is embodied in the world of action, and more certainly than Emerson he spoke not so much for things as they are, or as they *must* become in the abstract definitions of progress, but for the world as it might be re-created by a moral passion. In that sense his poetry itself is one of the acts by which compensation arrives. The dramatic role is supplied by his mode of empathic response, the "Song of the Answerer." That "answerer," who is a creator, acts in an open world, a pluralistic and complex reality. Whitman may cheat us of suspense when he speaks of the "ultimate equanimity of things," but the need for such assurance accompanies the responsibility as well as liberation he gives to man at the center of the living world. The joy of his assertions is made equal to a moral energy.

In a poem with bravura intellectual aims, "Chanting the Square Deific," Whitman invented a four-sided complex to represent the ultimate deity, whose final, or squaring line, was provided by man, the "breather." But he awards one side of the square to Satan; room must be made for the genius of evil.

> Aloof, dissatisfied, plotting revolt,
> Comrade of criminals, brother of slaves,
> Crafty, despised, a drudge, ignorant,
> . . . but in the depths of my heart, proud as any,
> Lifted now and always against whoever scorning assumes to rule me,
> . . . .
> Defiant, I, Satan, still live, still utter words, in new lands duly appearing, (and old ones also,)
> Permanent here from my side, warlike, equal with any, real as any,
> Not time nor change shall ever change me or my words.

Defiant Satan is given a role which serves life by maintaining resistance, by exploring the multiple sources of rebellion and dissatisfaction, by harboring criminals and slaves as if they were a permanent caste in the created world. As criminals, they would be the agents of disorder, or, as slaves, the images of submission and oppression, and it is a moral realism which conceives their permanent presence in the world. And yet they become a part of something large enough to contain them. Will there remain words for criminal and slave in a true democracy? Whitman is careless of that question. Whatever these identities may be or become, a power acts upon them nevertheless, a spirit of inclusiveness, making them "equal with any," "real as any."

The willingness to include criminals in the democratic census, so to speak, might record the effect of moral nearsightedness, as if it were an effort to convert Satan. This shallow innocence is what some readers name and find repellent in both Whitman and Emerson, more so in the first than in the latter because of Whitman's more bumptious enthusiasm. This is an understandable reaction. But a fuller reading may see the point of view as quite sophisticated, as a matter of maturity and not innocence, when placed in the terms of the "double consciousness," properly understood. The latter implies a continuous moral reserve which is maintained in the face of the obvious need to commit judgment and choose between right and wrong. This reserve is not merely on behalf of a spiritual immunity of the individual. It is based first on the sense of the truly inclusive human community, whose unity transcends all the instances of moral failure. Most important, that reserve of uncommitted judgment works to keep alive the ethical limits of judgment. It proposes that "comrade of criminals, brother of slaves" are subordinate terms, subjugated to that passionate respect for humanity, "permanent here from my side," which is the labor of Whitman's communication.

The problem for the "democratic priest" was to discover whether equality was more than a legal standard, whether it had actual moral substance and was an active spirit motivating men. As Tocqueville understood, the problem of equality in its public compulsions was the chief one facing democracy. Until it was solved, liberty itself would have uncertain justification, if not a compromised state of being. As for "fraternity," that was an ideal that could live with distinctions and even thrive on them. It was only equality that could supply the *democratic* bond of unity, with the assumption that somewhere all differences, wickedness and goodness, strength and weakness, success and failure, met on a level of human affinity, difficult as it was to locate.

The rare, even unique quality of Whitman's statement comes from his power to express self-affirmation with zest and support it by an equally strong moral sensibility. As I have said, almost every line of Whitman's verse is simultaneously an act of self-assertion and an act of communication. In the sense of public poetry the person conquers his isolation by speaking, for as he speaks for himself he speaks at once for the likeness of his listeners as well as to their response. The recognition of likeness is not a dramatic event, or a change of consciousness brought by dramatic experience, as in the active, narrative forms of Melville and Hawthorne. Whitman is much closer to Emerson in this respect, to a world in which moral insights are as natural and inevitable as any other phenomena. However, where energy is expressed in Emerson's writing, it is truly on behalf of self-recognition, or the recognition of the "Universal Mind." With Whitman, in the contrasting effect, the impulse of his writing turns toward the dialogue, directed toward awakening response. Where Emerson's faith is pure, where he expects a spiritual meeting of consciousness with consciousness which really would leave both words and acts behind, Whitman's spirit is intense and personally melioristic, "I seize the descending man and raise him with resistless will,/Hang your whole weight upon me." The clue to the distinction is reflected in the role given to erotic energy in Whitman's verse. The body is active and reproductive in communication, and this describes a natural world which grows or is lifted into its ideal possibilities, unlike the pictorially conceived, static nature celebrated in Emerson's roving "Eyeball."

Accordingly there is nothing more natural than moral sublimation. "I am he attesting sympathy," Whitman wrote as the expressive climax of his sense of being alive.

> I have said that the soul is not more than the body,
> And I have said that the body is not more than the soul,
> And nothing, not God, is greater to one than one's self is,
> And whoever walks a furlong without sympathy walks to his own funeral
> drest in his shroud.[23]

Things meet in this world as equals, and they are accordingly set free. Each member of the world can presume to face God in that spirit. But if the "self" is now at the center of the universe, in effect displacing God, it carries a great responsibility. Quickly the destructive possibility appears, and as quickly it is foreclosed. The self is borne to its own death immediately, unless it retains "sympathy," a moral force completely identified with life. This is a world which men inhabit, and by Whitman's clear meaning it is a world which does not exist without their presence.

In his essay on Whitman, D. H. Lawrence expressed the deeper notes of the ambivalent attraction which led him to write his book on the American classics. Whitman's themes of self-affirmation and erotic pantheism resembled his own, and were for both of them a new religion. Lawrence acknowledged this after much sharp puncturing of the inflated images of Whitman's rhetoric of democracy. In the poet, for instance, "I behold a rather fat old man full of a rather senile, self-conscious sensuosity." He stamps without mercy on Whitman's cherished concept of a democratic emotion. "Walt becomes in his own person the whole world, the whole universe, the whole eternity of time." "Song of Myself" is the song of the "All One in One Identity, like the Mundane Egg, which has been addled quite a while." Lawrence mocks,

23. Ibid., p. 66.

Oh, Walter, Walter, what have you done with it? What have you done with yourself? With your own individual self? For it sounds as if it had leaked out of you, leaked into the universe.[24]

Typically, however, after howling him down, Lawrence confesses that Whitman was a great poet, "the one pioneer," and that he was a great moralist, like the other classic Americans.

He was a great leader. He was a great changer of the blood in the veins of men.[25]

He more than anyone illustrated what Lawrence meant when he said on the first page of his book, "There is a new voice in the old American classics." A new doctrine of life was preached by Whitman, despite the fact that even in his case it was diluted by Christianity, versions of love and charity which Whitman couldn't shake off. It was also made bathetic by the popular sentimentality of "democracy, en masse," a merging in the "Allness" while the soul leaked out. Nevertheless, it was the basis for a new morality, a new relationship among men. The essence of it was Whitman's doctrine of "sympathy." Sympathy was not love, Christian or other. It was a species of recognition, of "feeling with," not "feeling for," Lawrence says. It was a way of discovering one's own life simultaneously with the lives of others, a kind of realistic as well as mystical communication among comrades. Lawrence expands on this experience, and it seems the climax of his whole book, the one positive achievement of democratic literature.

This is Whitman's message of American democracy.
The true democracy, where soul meets soul, in the open road. Democracy, American democracy where all journey down the open road. And where a soul is known at once in its going. Not by its clothes or appearance. Whitman did away with that. Not by its family name. Not even by its reputation. Whitman and Melville both discounted that. Not by a progression of piety, or by works of Charity. Not by works at all. Not by anything but just itself. . . . Democracy: a recognition of souls, all down the open road, and a great soul seen in its greatness, as it travels on foot among the rest, down the common way of the living. A glad recognition of souls, and a gladder worship of great and greater souls, because they are the only riches.[26]

No one among the American writers achieves quite that level of intoxicated vision, not even Whitman. The tone is different, modified by distance, even withdrawal, as in Whitman's own words, "Apart

24. *American Literature*, p. 245.

25. Ibid., p. 254.   26. Ibid., pp. 263–64.

from the pulling and hauling stands what I am . . . compassionating, idle." But Lawrence's mystical comradeship, though the *wrong* tone for the Americans, helps clarify the range of effects that centered on such revelations. The "soul," supported "not by anything but just itself," does indeed receive all concern in classic American writing, where a wide area of misadventure and torment as well as affirmation surrounds that demand on human recognitions. The phrase recalls Tocqueville's image of democratic man, crossing alone in his life between two abysses. All the more reason to understand why it was, as Lawrence put it, a "yearning myth," as much desperate as hopeful. Lawrence's mood of apocalyptic communion was wrong for the American democracy, wrong in fact for his own mind, if we are to interpret his later and apparently fixed revulsion from democracy, in becoming one of the great reactionaries of modern literature. The Americans really understood the egalitarian "myth" better than he did and placed the restraints of irony and detached consciousness on those bare confrontations of men. Doing so, they were avoiding the compulsive absolutism, the passion for pure acts of freedom or communion in Lawrence's temperament, an ancient psychic antagonist in the practice of democracy. The distinction is fundamental and illustrates the clarity of a moral tradition which so definitely guarded against either the communitarian or anarchic force of those glad affinities which Lawrence praised.

8/Huckleberry Finn
What It Means To Be Civilized

Huckleberry Finn is a book of disguises, and the greatest disguise and the most successful is that of the author in the person of a semiliterate boy. The force of this style is in its unpretentiousness, and it is effective because it is constantly in implicit contrast with the traditional literary voice, which, like Tom Sawyer, takes what it knows out of books. In this respect Mark Twain was illustrating the thesis of Tocqueville, who observed that a democratic literature would feature a shift from the written to the spoken language.[1] The rivalry between the spoken and written language was the more intense because in America popular culture was not humble, and elite culture was not self-confident. The latter looked in two directions, backwards toward Europe where the impressive literary examples existed, and homeward to the people in town, country, and frontier who had democratic sovereignty.

We sense generally in the American writers of the nineteenth century a hard grip on style which denotes stylistic insecurity, even in the examples of outstanding success, like Thoreau, Mark Twain, and Henry James. These were successful stylists by their peculiar stress upon personality, approaching the extreme of mannerism. In a revealing example of the struggle with style, Melville at his best

1. "American authors may truly be said to live rather in England than in their own country, since they constantly study the English writers and take them every day for their models. But it is not so with the bulk of the population, which is more immediately subjected to the peculiar causes acting upon the United States. It is not, then, to the written, but to the spoken language that attention must be paid if we would detect the changes which the idiom of an aristocratic people may undergo when it becomes the language of a democracy" (Tocqueville, *Democracy in America*, p. 69). That Mark Twain implicitly recognized the demands of a "democratic style" is revealed in his remark on Fenimore Cooper's prose, "he ought to have saved those splendors for a king" (Mark Twain, *Letters From the Earth*, ed. Bernard De Voto [New York: Harper & Row, 1962], p. 140).

achieved a monumental language, though baroque and eclectic in its reflection from the sweeping stream of the English literary past. At his worst, Melville lost control of both his subject and his medium. Hawthorne, in contrast, choosing his limits and staying within them, used almost an anachronistic mode of language, not far from the tone of polite "ladies' fiction" of the nineteenth century. But Hawthorne was especially aware of his problem, and expressed his literary bad conscience in his introduction to *The Scarlet Letter*. Observing the men he found working or loafing in the Custom House, he recognized the challenge of their spoken language.

> Could I have preserved the picturesque force of his [a veteran ship-master] style, and the humorous coloring which nature taught him to throw over his descriptions, the result, I honestly believe, would have been something new in literature.

But the fault, if it was a fault, was general. It is a curious fact that the chief American fiction writers of the nineteenth century appear to be romantic fabulists when viewed in the context of European realism. This is of course a superficial classification, unless, like Richard Chase, we view the writing of romance in a generous perspective and see a heroic literature in the making, precisely when the rest of the world was turning more and more to the dry masterpieces of disillusioned realism. It is true that *Madame Bovary* and *Moby Dick* were published within six years of one another.

If there is a genre of literature which a freshly alive democratic culture tended to make its favorite, the evidence would on the one hand support Richard Chase's judgment and suggest that romance is democracy's first vein. However, this would have to join emphasis with Constance Rourke's implicit finding for comedy, primarily in the roots of folk literature, but spreading deeply in its effect on the formal writing of the century.[2] But comedy and satire could express the self-criticism of the romantic spirit. Imaginative hungers, imaginative aspirations turn naturally to mock-heroic deflation. The belief in freedom, which is a great hope, has several tonalities, some of them contradictory. Primarily it leads to the expansive imagination, as Emerson, Thoreau, and Whitman were expansive, each in his own way dealing

2. Constance Rourke, *American Humor* (New York: Harcourt, Brace and Co., 1931).

Chase recognized this in observing that the American novel engaged "either in melodramatic actions or in pastoral idyls, although intermixed with both one may find the stirring instabilities of 'American humor'" (Chase, *The American Novel*, p. 1).

with the will to possess the world. In their temperamental bias these were the true romantics. The contrasting theme was Hawthorne's and Melville's, in dramas of self-assertion that lost both self and world. But these reversals of freedom were felt like tragedies and had the mature insight of tragedy, and to call Hawthorne and Melville romancers seems a singularly inadequate mode of description. Comedy is a more direct instrument for criticizing great illusions, and it is a matter of wonder that Mark Twain was our only major comic writer of the nineteenth century, though the answer might lie in the division between popular and elite culture, a breach that Mark Twain mastered in only one book.

Men imagining freedom can almost at once taste the effect of romantic experience in its manic and apocalyptic stress. If they view their freedom with a great moral seriousness, their imaginations could pass naturally to tragic themes and perspectives. But to feel free also means to be critical, in the exhilarating extreme of the comic spirit. The strongest real skeptic of the nineteenth-century figures, Mark Twain was also closest to the average life of his time. He gathered rich materials for satire, while his temperament was attracted to comedy. To distinguish it from satire on an approximate scale of effects, comic humor is on one side the spirit of playful revelry, and on the other a more disinterested mode of criticism, purer than satire. All these values can be found in *Huckleberry Finn*, and the deft mixture makes it the major work it is.

A democratic culture feeds the appetite for illusions but also arouses a great appetite for reality; with some educated detachment, the observer in a democracy notices the discrepancy between optimistic presumptions and the radical limits of experience. The necessary daily life is visible everywhere, without much else in view except the mock-heroic dreams of liberated small men, who thereby have flavored their already mean lives with vulgarity and pretense. The levelling instinct of the democratic temperament is irrepressible, and in this respect it would join the comic spirit in finding illusions of superiority loathsome and ridiculous. By old prejudice, men in a democracy would prefer to find most heroic postures fraudulent rather than recognize their serious claims.

Mark Twain's comedy becomes reductive satire in this sense, involving a parody of aristocratic symbols. The disillusioned spirit of democratic satire had its deepest stimulus from the revolutionary destruction of old elites. But turning toward a general cynicism, and

Mark Twain was more than a little of a cynic, this strain of democratic comedy would be designed to prove all men equal in their being scoundrels or dupes. Some of the scenes in *Huckleberry Finn*, particularly those engaging the duke and the king, are a kind of democratic horseplay where the stereotypes of rank are made to roll in the dust. The frauds in their performance of Shakespeare provide a popular form of comic philistinism. The duke playing Romeo, the king playing Juliet, the two smelly clowns give relief from the burden of refined and delicate values. The duke reminds the king not to bray like a jackass when he recites Juliet's speeches. Such reductive comparisons run through Mark Twain's text, though they can leave simpler themes behind and reach Swiftian depths, as in this passage.

> There warn't anybody at the church, except maybe a hog or two, for there warn't any lock on the door, and hogs likes a puncheon floor in summer-time because it's cool. If you notice most folks don't go to church only when they've got to; but a hog is different.

The titles assumed by the down-and-out confidence men are themselves the sign of an ancient and universal confidence game. After the Royal Nonesuch swindle, Jim says, beginning to wonder,

> "Don't it 'sprise you, de way dem kings carries on, Huck?"
> "No," I says, "it don't."
> "Why don't it, Huck?"
> "Well, it don't, because it's in the breed. I reckon they're all alike."

Huck then gives his "innocent" vaudeville version of the career of Henry VIII as a first-class king and rapscallion and ends by saying,

> "All I say is, kings is kings, and you got to make allowances. Take them all around, they're a mighty ornery lot. It's the way they're raised."
> "But dis one do *smell* so like de nation, Huck."
> "Well, they all do, Jim. *We* can't help the way a king smells; history don't tell no way."

This joyful mockery performs a democratic service. They smell remarkably like mortal men, these kings and dukes, and their historic superiority was implicitly the superior ability to fool and cheat the rest of men.

Again, the illustration supports Erich Auerbach's theme that realism in heroic ages of literature conveys itself as comedy.[3] Mark Twain's victory of style and point of view was a success of lasting sig-

---

3. Erich Auerbach, *Mimesis* (Princeton: Princeton University Press, 1953), chap. 2.

nificance for the American stream of modern realism; we hardly need Hemingway's familiar testimony for that.[4] The supple colloquial ease, the appropriateness of response, opened the door to scenes and events which had the authentic flavor of life on the river and shore of the Mississippi central axis of America. Implicitly, the living voice of the young boy invited the search for that reality; it was a poignant reminder of a life that could no longer be overlooked.

Realistic fiction, particularly that of the nineteenth century, was never simply the expression of a wish to portray the actual world. It was moved, to one degree or another, by the spirit of cultural criticism and implied an attack on conventional values, as well as a rejection of the language and subjects of the genteel imagination linked with those values. Literary realism, not to mention naturalism, has always had a subversive bias; what was at stake was the "truth," opposed to the mendacity and irrelevance of established illusions. *Huckleberry Finn* is a complex literary phenomenon because in it are linked the themes of neoromantic pastoral and a strong development of critical realism, both dominated by the comic perspective. It is in fact a particularly expressive example of the harmonious transition between literary temperaments, specifically the familiar nostalgia for child and nature, and that harsher mood which renewed a very old relationship between pastoral and satire. It makes sense to call Huck and Jim the heroes of a pastoral idyll, if it is understood that their great natural virtues serve to expose the flaws of the world they meet. By their language alone they are a testament to authenticity—and this is the lodestone principle of the hero in the realistic novel. The boy and the Negro are so concentrated in their direct responses, so bare and vulnerable, that everything they meet which opposes them tends to take on almost immediately the aspect of the meretricious. The whole "contraption" of civilized life, customs, laws, morals, conventions, ideals, and superstitions is exposed to their candid gaze, as if to imply that what wasn't deceptive in that cumbersome array was at least superfluous. "We was always naked" says Huck, when they were alone on the raft—and their nakedness is their reproach to the life on the shore.

The quarrel between lies and the truth, that is the saga of Huck Finn, as he tells us very early in the story.

4. "All modern American literature comes from one book. . . . *Huckleberry Finn*. . . . it's the best book we've had. All American writing comes from that. There was nothing before. There has been nothing as good since" (*Green Hills of Africa* [New York: Scribners, 1935], p. 2).

I got an old tin lamp and an iron ring and went out in the woods and rubbed and rubbed till I sweat like an Injun, calculating to build a palace and sell it; but it warn't no use, none of the genies come. So then I judged that all that stuff was only just one of Tom Sawyer's lies. I reckoned he believed in the A-rabs and the elephants, but as for me I think different. It had all the marks of a Sunday school.

The last phrase indicates the sizable giant that this little David must overcome. But his weapon is a dangerous one. It is a persistence for the truth which turns his innocence into his justification and his shrewd instinct for survival into a radical skepticism. Huck Finn was persuaded to become "respectable" by being offered the chance to join Tom Sawyer's gang of robbers. He innocently tells us so on the first page of his book, and from that moment on we are forewarned that the respectable world is doomed to relentless self-exposure.

What is to be demonstrated is suggested in the incident in which Jim and Huck encounter a house floating downstream and find that it contains the body of a murdered man. This is Huck's father, as Jim discovers and keeps secret, but the incident has a metaphoric significance. To see what happens in detail within the "house of civilization," the sequence follows with the Grangerford episode.

The Grangerfords live in a very imposing frontier house, which provides, with some acute irony, the furnishings of civilization. There was a "beautiful oil-cloth" table cover which came all the way from Philadelphia. There were books, the Bible, and *The Pilgrim's Progress*, and there were pictures on the wall, "mainly Washingtons and Lafayettes, and battles, and Highland Marys, and one called 'Signing the Declaration.'" Huck notices on a table "a kind of a lovely crockery basket that had apples and oranges and peaches and grapes piled up in it which was much redder and yellower and prettier than real ones is, but they warn't real because you could see where pieces had got chipped off and showed the white chalk or whatever it was, underneath."

This sign of the meretricious associates with the other manifestations of a traditional inheritance. The daughter Emmeline provides a comic exaggeration of mimetic emotions, or the sentimentality of civilization. She is the poetess of death who expresses in caricature the conventionalized ideals and motives which operate most strongly in the lives of the other Grangerfords. She sublimates death as they have sublimated violence and slavery. The fine old gentleman and his sons in their white suits are chivalric emblems. They are the expressive social ideal of their place and time, and their kindness and decency are harmonious attributes. The almost cruel instinct for truth in Mark Twain's book is never better expressed as all this structure of refinement, gentleness, affection, and faith is reduced to the lust to kill. The feud of the Grangerfords and the Shepherdsons is essentially an allegory of war. No one can remember the original cause of the feud, yet both sides show great courage and dignity. They go to church with their guns and they argue doctrinal issues. In the end, the death of Buck and his brothers is an abrupt, destructive challenge which demolishes everything, everything, that is, except the drifting subliminal reality of life on the raft, to which Huck now returns, as though it were a kind of preconscious state.

> And afterwards we would watch the lonesomeness of the river, and kind of lazy along, and by-and-by lazy off to sleep.

That return to aboriginal existence will contrast periodically with the world on shore. The Grangerfords have lived and died by their elaborate illusions, specifically the crystallized prejudice of the feud, which is a fatal disjuncture between the social imagination and reality. The example of the daughter Emmeline's sentimentality is meaningful to a fine point. What the poor girl produces is a poetry for the sake of poetry, and grief for the sake of feeling grief. This is finally the evaporation into nonsense of the moral-esthetic imagination. Tom Sawyer, who plays the games of the imagination, is the more attractive surrogate for the same overwrought and destructive power which dominates the lives of the Grangerfords. That conventionalized sensibility at work is illustrated in the grief of the townspeople at the funeral of Peter Wicks, led by the fraudulent heirs, the duke and the king, in comic hyperbole.

> Well, when it come to that, it worked the crowd like you never see anything like it, and so everybody broke down and went to sobbing right out loud—the poor girls, too; and every woman, nearly, went up to the girls, without saying a word, and kissed them, solemn, on the forehead, and then put their hand on their head, and looked up towards the sky, with the tears running down, and then busted out and went off sobbing and swabbing, and give the next woman a show. I never see anything so disgusting.

As we see, this sentimentality is not harmless, and it plays a key role in the general confidence game which expresses social relationships throughout the book. In this context the life of Huck and Jim on the raft is a kind of magnificent understatement on behalf of trusted experience, cleansing the sensibility of rigid prejudice, confusion, sentimental and meretricious emotions, the "social lie."

The theme so understood enlarges the view of targets for Mark Twain's comic criticism. The slapstick duke and king, when they first appear, echo the folklore of democracy, dealing with its aristocratic enemies and reducing them to comic debility. However, in proof that his comic spirit is catholic, Mark Twain shifts his focus easily from the exploiters to the exploited. As if he had his own aristocratic revulsion to express, the people in the crowd are the objects of exposure, and actually in such scenes a tone of outrage penetrates the caricature.

One such town at which they stop "well down in the State of Arkansaw" seems to be the portrait of pioneering democracy in its utterly joyless aspects.

> Then we went loafing around the town. The stores and houses was most all old shackly dried-up frame concerns that hadn't ever been painted. . . . The houses had little gardens around them, but they didn't seem to raise hardly anything in them but jimpson weeds, and sunflowers, and ash-piles, and old curled-up boots and shoes, and pieces of bottles, and rags, and played-out tin-ware. . . .
> All the stores was along one street. . . . There was empty dry-goods boxes under the awnings, and loafers roosting on them all day long, whittling them with their Barlow knives; and chawing tobacco, and gaping and yawning and stretching—a mighty ornery lot.

This is a place that seems to frustrate every moral and esthetic need. The average man, in a *public* scene, in his aggregate numbers, becomes threatening and ugly. Eventually an aristocrat himself appears, contrasting with the canaille, in the person of Colonel Sherburn. Colonel Sherburn has been publicly insulted by the drunken Boggs, the butt of the crowd, but also in a sense its leader. The boasting, shouting, and jeering express a society made degenerate by its indiscipline.

> By-and-by a proud-looking man about fifty-five—and he was a heap the best dressed man in that town, too,—steps out of the store, and the crowd drops back on each side to let him come.

As he gives Boggs his warning, his cultivated speech contrasts sharply with the idiom of the text as well as the speech of the people. Sherburn fulfills his threat to kill Boggs, and his direct violence seems to be the extreme response of fastidiousness to the general riot and disorder as well as to the personal insult he received from Boggs. This is made clear when the mob collects around Sherburn's porch, threatening to lynch him. When he comes out to confront them alone, his force of character is overpowering.

Do I know you? I know you clear through. I was born and raised in the South, and I've lived in the North; so I know the average all around. The average man's a coward. . . . The pitifulest thing out is a mob; that's what an army is—a mob; they don't fight with courage that's born in them, but with courage that's borrowed from their mass, and from their officers. But a mob without any *man* at the head of it, is *beneath* pitifulness. Now the thing for *you* to do, is to droop your tails and go home and crawl in a hole. If any real lynching's going to be done, it will be done in the dark, Southern fashion; and when they come they'll bring their masks, and fetch a *man* along. Now *leave*—and take your half-a-man with you.

The melodramatic scene lives in its democratic context, but it is not quite a climax and certainly doesn't present a choice of values. The rare individualist like Colonel Sherburn can only express his superiority with a murderous arrogance. Perhaps the moral impasse which such a mob presents can only lead to violence. The lynch spirit is a degenerate response to Sherburn's pride and independence, and his will for murder is in turn the sign of the utter breakdown of a moral relationship between individuals and the crowd.

The theme of violence is always latent; Huck's father indicates its personal and criminal dimension, but the Grangerfords illustrate the extremes to which specifically socialized passions and prejudices can be led. But the more characteristic mode of social conflict is represented by the confidence men, the duke and the king, facing their gulls in the towns. In that world of mean appetites and deceptions there are only the foolers and the fooled, the cheaters and the cheated. The aura of folklore in the narration suggests that deception is indulged for its own sake, receiving ritual attention as a part of survival, but also as a form of practical joking which is the people's entertainment. Huck himself is particularly good at inventing an elaborate story, as when he tells the men looking for a runaway slave that the raft is occupied by his sick father and lets them guess that the sickness is smallpox. Constance Rourke's description of the "Yankee peddler" is pertinent for illustrating the model in American folk humor. This cynical comedy appreciates rascality and opposes the competing forms of hypocrisy against each other. The successful fraud is actually a kind of hero as well as scoundrel, when he has matched his wits against the people and won.

That the people in the collective sense are the victims of the confidence men is only more evidence that society as a whole is run as a confidence game. In cheating the people the duke and the king illustrate how the people act toward each other; their gullibility lies never in their innocence but rather their vices and stupidities, and when they retaliate, as in the Royal Nonesuch affair, they express their limitless appetite for a victim. The duke and the king are rascals but are joined with Jim and Huck on the raft. They too are outsiders who must live by their wits, and it is a case where cynic meets innocent with a cause in common. The alternative to their cast of mind is Colonel Sherburn in his cold and proud misanthropy. Tramps, bums, neocriminals, they live to survive, and doing so they can even win a species of sympathy in contrast with their antagonists of the backwash Arkansas town. Would Emerson find a place for them in his pantheon of self-reliant men?

Huckleberry Finn is a mock-heroic epic of a cultural ambivalence. It is a democratic classic precisely because the antagonist is the people, and the sense of danger which must be relieved comes from them. The single man and the crowd have a troubled intercourse in American writing. This we know, and Mark Twain's spirit is as disturbed as any as he struggles to repel the threat of the "people" and at the same time give dignity or a soul to the plain common substance of what is human. For we know from his text that the average man is not only a coward but a fool, the greatest of fools. His ideals and morals are sentimental fictions, and those who dominate his mean state do so by cheating and deceiving him. The king, who knows how to adapt democracy to his own uses, says at one point,

> "Hain't we got all the fools in town on our side? and
> ain't that a big enough majority in any town?"

This comedy of deception is obviously expressive for a social structure dominated by the techniques of persuasion. The politician and the salesman had dominant place in American public life, and in such a society the comedy comes naturally from the availability of the people to be fooled and the presence of those who live by fooling them. The dismaying sense of a social world where truth does not exist dominates the story. But disillusioned and realistic as the viewpoint is insofar as democratic institutions are concerned, it salvages a humble mode of affirmation which might be expressed in Lincoln's much loved words, so well calculated to comfort a democracy. "You can fool some of the people all of the time, and you can fool all of the people some of the time, but you can't fool all of the people all of the time." One of the people you can't fool all of the time is Huck Finn.

In serial adventures Huck emerges from being fooled or fooling others, and the point of his legend is to transcend fooling. In that emphasis the climax of the book comes when Jim and Huck bind their friendship after Huck's effort to play his practical joke, following their separation in the fog. The episode is revealing on many sides, and in one aspect it is exactly pertinent to my larger discussion since it is founded on the issue of discovering trusted and true identities. Their search for each other in the fog on the river is poignant and dangerous, like almost every other of their adventures, and yet Huck's first impulse on getting back to the raft is to play his joke and convince Jim that nothing had happened, they had both been asleep, and that Jim had done some marvelous dreaming. Jim, in his desperation, interrupts to say,

> Well, looky here, boss, dey's sumf'n wrong, dey is. Is I *me*, or who *is* I? Is I heah, or whah *is* I? Now dat's what I wants to know.

This, as the reader learns, is a thematic statement for the series of concealments, false roles, and disguises through which their journey takes them. The seed of the conclusion to be reached in *The Mysterious Stranger* is here in Jim's summary.[5]

> Well, den, I reck'n I did dream it, Huck; but dog my cats ef it ain't de powerfullest dream I ever see. En I hain't ever had no dream b'fo' dat's tired me like dis one.

Finally the shock of being fooled is administered as Huck points to the rubbish on the raft, picked up in drifting through fog, signs that they were not dreaming. Jim's reproach is the more moving in that context—trash of the real world, trash of deception.

> When I got all wore out wid work, en wid de callin' for you, en went to sleep, my heart wuz mos' broke bekase you wuz los', en I didn't k'yer no mo' what become er me en de raf'. . . . En all you wuz thinkin' 'bout wuz how you could make a fool uv ole Jim wid a lie. Dat truk dah is *trash;* en trash is what people is dat puts dirt on de head er dey fren's en makes 'em ashamed.

5. *The Mysterious Stranger* calls to mind that late work of Melville, *The Confidence Man*, and suggests for both writers that the works of their prime were stimulated in part by inclinations toward an apocalyptic pessimism.
Huckleberry Finn and *Moby Dick* are the more brilliant because of this latency they avert. The alternative possibilities imply the difficult choices of the democratic writer, who faced the extreme test of an extreme assumption on behalf of man. Emerson suggests how inviting it was to turn to an equally conclusive and one-track optimism. Perhaps the beginning of all speculation on traditional American writing takes place with the confrontation of such temperamental contrasts, but proceeds from there to appreciate the unique complexity of the great achievements.

Huck responds to "humble myself to a nigger," and that is his moral redemption, but it is a redemption of the truth as well, a restoring dismissal of both "trash" and dream. "I didn't do him no more mean tricks," Huck says, and it is an end to fooling, so far as these two are concerned. They have founded their community on something "real," and this can only be described as the reality of their friendship itself.

It is a small island for reassurance, but made as firm as possible for that reason. The maneuver of the democratic sensibility is to find its moral heroes in miniature. This has a curious double function, to demonstrate an egalitarian sentiment and at the same time criticize average values. In this enterprise one chooses a hero from below rather than from above, though in either case the threat is from the middle. It suggests the romantic inversion which esteems the presocial or the primitive protagonist. The primitive theme was attractive to the covertly antisocial spirit of European romanticism as its weapon against middle-class culture, just as it called on Faust and Manfred, morbid supermen, as instruments against the same mediocrity.

The greatest individualist affirmations of the American imagination were markedly restricted in their claims, as in the case of Thoreau, who took dominance in a very small place. Noting the great example of Captain Ahab, we can see that the Faustian theme is as sinister as it is tragic in this tradition, and when Melville looked for a protagonist who could arouse universally positive response, he chose the generous and passive Billy Budd. Beyond Huck Finn there is Ahab, or the comic Paul Bunyan, or Natty Bumppo, but these proportions are, one might say, out of Tom Sawyer's head, out of the hungry imagination. Huck Finn is far from all of these; he is the realistic democratic hero, whose purpose is to deflate pretension and strip complacency, for here he is, dedicated as he is to survival, a boy of the most outcast tribe, sleeping in hogsheads.

This is the involution of a democratic paradox. It contains an effort to reconcile divided impulses; to criticize the power (and foolishness) of men in numbers and the degraded character of men in the crowd, and at the same time to avoid creating heroes to contradict the democratic ideal. *Huckleberry Finn* is a book of the people, although at the same time the people are the enemy and must be warded off. It is the people's book because it takes up the humblest and the lowest, the abused and the exploited, and lets these demonstrate the mutual recognitions which define equality. But it is ambiguously the people's book in taking up the social outcast, as he calculates the terms of his independence, like Huck, or must flee for his safety, like Jim. More than the oppression of society or institutions is involved in this flight. Does Huck need to escape Miss Watson more than the wretched and criminal abuse of his father? And yet when two such unregenerate rascals as the king and the duke are tarred, feathered, and ridden on a rail by the town people, Huck observes with his inevitable instinct for judgment, that they "didn't look like nothing in the world that was human," and "it made me sick to see it." In that response Huck again reveals that he is a "third force," as one might put it, beyond a simple allegiance to alienated criminals and aristocrats, and beyond automatic loyalty to the "crowd."

 Huck Finn as a democratic hero is a shrewd agent for survival in the midst of dangerous contradictions. He is resistant and subversive by half-measures, by inner withholding and by convenient evasions, and so he can avoid the open conflict which suggests anarchy, or the opposite surrender which puts an end to his real freedom. Most significantly what Huck stands for is truth, not power, and that being so, what he performs unconsciously is the saving act of criticism in democratic culture. The positive spirit in this criticism, and within the comedy which is the instrument of criticism, is based first on a skeptical resistance that denies foothold to any social bigotry or individual license, and second upon the precarious moral balance which is required to live beyond the reach of the chronic foolishness of the crowd or the chronic destructiveness of the alienated.

To grow deeply serious about Mark Twain's book, as is inevitable, leads to the judgment that *Huckleberry Finn* is another sharply outlined but complex democratic legend which features the purgation and self-renewal of the social order. Huck is demonstrably a frontier Thoreau, who has a ritualistic need for isolation, and whose escape from his social role is dramatized by his false death and funeral. Huck feels particularly good when the people recognize him as dead. He is now free, he is himself, he is alone. He says, looking over his domain on the river island, "I knowed I was all right now." And "I was boss of it; it all belonged to me."

The passage is a minor echo of Thoreau, with a difference.

> When it was dark I set by my campfire smoking, and feeling pretty satisfied; but by-and-by it got sort of lonesome, and so I went and set on the bank and listened to the currents washing along, and counted

the stars and drift-logs and rafts, that come down, and then went to bed; there ain't no better way to put in time when you are lonesome; you can't stay so, you soon get over it.

And so for three days and nights. No difference—just the same thing.

That last phrase has an ominous sound to Thoreauvian anticipations. The point is that for Huck this isolation won't sustain itself; there is really nothing to do and nothing to say (or "write"), until he meets Jim, just at that point in fact in the story. There is no question then that he needs Jim badly, demonstrated by his relief when he finds him. *Huckleberry Finn* is in fact an enormously gregarious book; Huck lives by his adventures with the people in the towns, and his curiosity is directed toward human intercourse, not nature, not even the "great brown god" of the river. Probably no American book published to that time is so filled with actual dialogue in the accents of authentic speech, to stress its dominant interest.

Walden pond was fixed, like the eye of God, but the river flows onward, and that is a suggestive difference. Thoreau was equipped with some transcendental beliefs, and when he went through the process of stripping away the excess baggage of civilized practice he had a religious minimum on which he could count. Huck is a more agnostic or independent soul. His truth, or sense of reality, is not recovered within a new imaginative dress or a cosmological belief. The river-god, as T. S. Eliot called it, offers truth and freedom, and by their periodic return to the river, Jim and Huck are baptized in its spirit. But this ceremony of renewal is altogether modest, reflected in their simplest needs. It is important to remember that Jim wants nothing better than to return to his wife and family, and as for Huck, his freedom is really a kind of hedonist laissez faire, the freedom to do as one chooses, to have passive and casual pleasures, to be comfortable. It is a boy's heaven, and it is also a lazy man's heaven, in which one would only be unsettled by transcendental expectations.

Some suggestive effects visible very early in the story can keep the reader from sentimentalizing the river, or nature, as either a pastoral or transcendental refuge. In the first pages Huck reacts from the oppression of Miss Watson. "Miss Watson she kept pecking at me, and it got tiresome and lonesome." The word "lonesome" is a kind of bridge for another mood that follows. Going upstairs to his room and sitting by the window, Huck pursues his loneliness.

> I felt so lonesome I most wished I was dead. The stars was shining, and the leaves rustled in the woods ever so mournful; and I heard an owl,

away off, who-whooing about somebody that was dead, and a whippo-will and a dog crying about somebody that was going to die; and the wind was trying to whisper something to me, and I couldn't make out what it was, and so it made the cold shivers run over me. Then away out in the woods I heard that kind of a sound that a ghost makes when it wants to tell about something that's on its mind and can't make itself understood, and so can't rest easy in its grave and has to go about that way every night grieving. I got so down-hearted and scared, I did wish I had some company.

At this point Huck feels a terror which engages his superstitions about witches and spiders, about "awful bad signs" and worse luck.

I set down again, a shaking all over, and got out my pipe for a smoke; for the house was all as still as death, now, and so the widow wouldn't know. Well, after a long time I heard the clock away off in the town go boom—boom—boom—twelve licks—and all still again—stiller than ever.

The stillness is suggestive; it is recurrent in the story as a dark note to indicate Huck's disconnection with the world, an effect he feels behind his disguises. Finally the need for some company is answered by a signal from below. "Sure enough there was Tom Sawyer waiting for me."

The sequence has a rhythm that reflects the longer narrative. First there is the reaction from the nagging restrictions of Miss Watson, who would "sivilize" him. But in the withdrawal there is no consistent liberation and relief. At moments like this one there is actual terror. That this is an unbearable condition is clear in the text. In the larger narrative the companion he finds so gladly is Jim, waiting for him on Jackson's Island.

Well, I warn't long making him understand I warn't dead. I was ever so glad to see Jim. I warn't lonesome, now.

There are, in effect, two ways of being "lonesome." One is the reaction to Miss Watson's "pecking," a social persecution, and the other to an alternative stillness, away from everyone, and haunted by the "sound that a ghost makes when it wants to tell about something that's on its mind and can't make itself understood."

It is striking that Huck's withdrawal to the river is presented to others as his death. That is his planned disguise in his first escape, and it has recurrence in the text in several ways. His language reflects the motif, as in punctuating the end of one of their adventures (finding the criminal gang in the marooned boat), he says,

By the time I got there the sky was beginning to get a little gray in the east; so we struck for an island, and hid the raft, and sunk the skiff, and turned in and slept like dead people.

It is suggestive again to note that they sleep during the day, when people are stirring, and are active at night. Or a typical day is like this one,

So we would put in the day, lazying around, listening to the stillness. Once there was a thick fog, and the rafts and things that went by was beating tin pans so the steamboats wouldn't run over them. A scow or a raft went by so close we could hear them talking and cussing and laughing—heard them plain; but we couldn't see no sign of them; it made you feel crawly, it was like spirits carrying on that way in the air. Jim said he believed it was spirits; but I says:

"No, spirits wouldn't say 'dern the dern fog' "

The passage is expressive for that margin they occupy between quotidian reality and the outer "stillness," and it is quite explicit that the "stillness" invites "spirits" and is like that of the grave. In the Wilks episode Huck is a kind of representative of the dead man, Peter Wilks, who himself, as a corpse, maintains a role in the episode, culminating in the final discoveries at his opened grave.

These effects that put Huck into the outer stillness, or disguise him as dead, are not meant, of course, to be portentous, or symbolic. But in the sequence of my general discussion they become necessarily expressive, and illustrate what I call elsewhere an introspective distance, with the personal consciousness marked dramatically in its separation from the world. One can see its relation to the isolation of consciousness which Emerson and Thoreau pursued, as if they were in search of "stillness." There is an even stronger relation to the morbid phases of introspective distance illustrated by Hawthorne's Wakefield and Melville's Bartleby. And finally it is not straining for analogies, I think, to see a connection with Poe's obsession with premature burial and the sentience of the grave. The sequence seems convincingly related to an American obsession, best described perhaps by Tocqueville in one of his remarkable general insights dealing with "individualism in democratic countries."

Thus not only does democracy make every man forget his ancestors, but it hides his descendants and separates his contemporaries from him; it throws him back forever upon himself alone and threatens in the end to confine him entirely within the solitude of his own heart.[6]

6. Tocqueville, *Democracy in America*, p. 106.

Solitude is then an ambiguous value; it reflects transitional needs and can become an infliction. As an experience it cannot be divorced from the reacting need for community. Huck was forced to mimic his death as the only escape from his father, and Miss Watson as well, and later he experiences the extreme effect of this distance as he watches the ferryboat, packed with all the people he knew in his life, come floating close to his hiding place, searching for his body. He *is* dead to them.

> Most everybody was on the boat. Pap, and Judge Thatcher, and Bessie Thatcher, and Jo Harper, and Tom Sawyer, and his old Aunt Polly, and Sid and Mary, and plenty more.

This limbo is his refuge and the starting point for all his adventures; it generates deep relief, an awed silence, and also a considerable fear and loneliness. It is necessary to return to the world from this "death." In a sense the magic talisman of his survival is presented in his guess that loaves of bread containing quicksilver would be floated out to locate his corpse, and this is the bread he eats.

> I says, now I reckon the widow or the parson or somebody prayed this bread would find me, and here it has gone and done it.

That is one link with men, but revival goes farther when he meets Jim. These experiences have been the context for the community which the boy and the Negro establish for themselves. They are, without each other, as though dead. This is the startling and profound theme so clearly expressed in *Moby Dick*, and in Hawthorne's more glancing allegories. *Huckleberry Finn* is not in any characteristic sense a neo-primitive challenge to the oppression of communities. To be a runaway slave has major significance. Jim is a victim, and as such he expresses an implicit criticism of society, but he is not, nor is Huck, an exercise in self-reliant independence. Escape down the river is a strong relief, it provides a paradisal glow, at least until the arrival of the duke and the king, but that eventual effect itself complicates the innocence of life on the raft. Whatever the river may represent, the slow, even sluggish movement of the life stream, the lazy hedonistic inner self and inner body, a place of being naked and being asleep—it is also certain it casts up the murdered man in the drifting house (Huck's own father), and such semicriminal and degenerate refugees as the duke and the king.

The refuge on the river has meaning only in an *active* relationship with life on the shore. The small brotherhood of Jim and Huck on the raft is by its existence an argument against the spoiled community they face. But the point is that they constantly face it, their chief attention is directed toward it. And in the process what they discover is not their independence from the community on shore, but the primary values which might redeem its existence./The stress is on what Jim can mean to Huck and how he will deal with him. Huck's struggle with his formal "Miss Watson" conscience on the issue of turning Jim over to his masters is a comic inversion of the problem on shore. What is wrong there becomes right on the raft, but what is right on the raft is demonstrated in ways that dismiss both the casuistry and the categoric authority of the moral argument which troubles Huck./The instinct which makes him choose to save Jim is founded on a primary, person to person response, and as Huck gives in to his feelings he never sanctimoniously declares that he is right and society is wrong.)

This is fundamental to the spirit of the book. The lack of moralistic presumption in his act is a significant measure to oppose such extreme failures of the social ethic as slavery. When the contest reaches its climax, the concrete substance of Huck's imagination saves him.

> And went on thinking. And got to thinking over our trip down the river; and I see Jim before me, all the time, in the day, and in the night-time, sometimes moonlight, sometimes storms, and we a floating along, talking, and singing, and laughing.

This is a human immediacy, glowing and clear, as Huck senses Jim as a man, beyond preaching and debate. With this awareness he has no more misgivings; it is a recognition like that which concluded his effort at practical joking, when they had been separated in the river fog and current, and when he humbled himself for the sake of his friend's dignity.

Jim's growth to dignity in Huck's eyes is a striking recall of Melville's theme. The correspondence is the more convincing in view of the analogies between the friendship of Ishmael and Queequeg and that of Huck and Jim. Pagan and Christian, savage and civilized, or Negro and white, free and enslaved—these dualities are diagrams of the barriers between civilization and man which must be passed in the search for the higher meaning of both terms.

Further analogies between the voyage of the Pequod and the voyage of the raft are available. No murdering white whale inhabits the river, but it is, as I have pointed out, a drifting, contentless symbol of nature and freedom, one nearer to Melville's hooded phantom in its "colorless all-color" of meaning than to Emerson's Over-Soul. Ishmael confronting an ocean voyage as if it were an alternative to suicide suggests again the subliminal reality of the river, a place to which one escapes, but ultimately a place where one cannot stay and remain alive. As Huck needs to return from his simulated death, so does Jim from his slavery, a human limbo accented by his being a runaway. But in the strongest sense they lay the basis for a return when they recognize each other in the shared experiences of the raft. There is nothing there but a concrete humanity, released from definitions and prejudices. It should be enough for good faith, as Jim makes clear in several comic dialogues which feature his insightful naiveté. In one he condemns Solomon and all his wisdom for failing to appreciate the difference between a whole child and "half a chile." In another he considers the puzzle of Frenchmen who talk French.

> "Looky here, Jim; does a cat talk like we do?"
> "No, a cat don't."
> "Well, does a cow?"
> "No, a cow don't, nuther."
> "Does a cat talk like a cow, or a cow talk like a cat?"
> "No, dey don't."
> "It's natural and right for 'em to talk different from each other, ain't it?"
> "Course."
> "And ain't it natural and right for a cat and a cow to talk different from *us?*"
> "Why, mos' sholy it is."
> "Well, then, why ain't it natural and right for a *Frenchman* to talk different from us? You answer me that."
> "Is a cat a man, Huck?"
> "No."
> "Well, den, dey ain't no sense in a cat talkin' like a man. Is a cow a man?—er is a cow a cat?"
> "No, she ain't either of them."
> "Well, den, she ain' got no business to talk like either one er the yuther of 'em. Is a Frenchman a man?"
> "Yes."
> "*Well*, den! Dad blame it, why doan' he *talk* like a man? You answer me *dat!*"

This is vaudeville, but something more, surely. It enriches Jim's character; he *is* a man, and his concentration on that point establishes the serious coherent meaning of Mark Twain's book.[7]

7. In the most poignant example of Jim's obsession, he declares to Huck that he is rich, he is worth 800 dollars in the slave market of New Orleans. "I's rich now, come to look at it. I owns myself, en I's wuth eight hund'd dollars. I wisht I had de

Appreciating this, one may understand why the raft continues drifting downstream against the logic of survival for Jim, and why an overt and specific escape from slavery is not featured in the text. That may not make it easier for some readers to accept the concluding passages of the book, as this problem is featured in a critical debate which has invited elaborate apology and lingering dissent.[8] To disappointed lovers of Mark Twain's book, the last quarter of the story seems trivialized because Jim's freedom has been compromised by Tom Sawyer's ritual games which cast Jim as comic scapegoat for an extended practical joke, thus reversing Huck's earlier determination to "do him no more mean tricks." After the rich satire that went before, one feels doubly cheated to discover that Jim has actually been freed, gratuitously so to speak, by a last obscure gesture of his mistress, Miss Watson, before she died.

Leo Marx leads the negative in the debate over the conclusion of the book, on the ground that it was a lapse of moral seriousness to return Huck and Jim to the society from which they escaped, both of them submitting to a farcical final adventure which insults as well as defeats their search for freedom. But if I may continue the argument, Marx may be imposing his own moral aspirations when he says.

> Miss Watson, in short, is the Enemy. If we except a predilection for physical violence, she exhibits all the outstanding traits of the valley society. She pronounces the polite lies of civilization that suffocate Huck's spirit. The freedom which Jim seeks, and which Huck and Jim temporarily enjoy aboard the raft, is accordingly freedom *from* everything for which Miss Watson stands.[9]

For Miss Watson one can read the Phelpses, to gain Marx's criticism of the concluding episode.

I suggest that this sharp moral dualism, opposing raft to town, river to shore, freedom to the social morality, is a source of confusion here. Mark Twain's theme need not be stated as Marx put it, and if it isn't, it may not be caught in the inconsistency that Marx claims.

money, I wouldn' want no mo'." The darker irony doesn't conceal the thrust of "I owns myself."

8. Leo Marx, "Mr. Eliot, Mr. Trilling, and *Huckleberry Finn*," *The American Scholar* 22, no. 4 (Autumn 1953): 423–40. Trilling, *The Liberal Imagination.* T. S. Eliot, Introduction, *The Adventures of Huckleberry Finn* (New York: Chanticleer Press, 1950). The essays by both Trilling and Eliot seem to me to hold up very well, and keep their stature as milestones in the recognition of Mark Twain's work.

9. Marx, "Mr. Eliot, Mr. Trilling, and *Huckleberry Finn*," pp. 423–40.

> We are asked to assume that somehow freedom can be achieved in spite of the crippling power of what I have called social morality.

He claims too much for freedom, and he oversimplifies Mark Twain's view of human nature.

> Evil in *Huckleberry Finn* is the product of civilization, and if this is indicative of Clemens' rather too simple view of human nature, nevertheless the fact is that Huck, when he can divest himself of the taint of social conditioning (as in the incantatory account of sunrise on the river), is entirely free of anxiety and guilt. The only guilt he actually knows arises from infractions of a social code. (The guilt he feels after playing the prank on Jim stems from his betrayal of the law of the raft.)

The latter remark simply won't hold. The prank teaches Huck his biggest moral lesson. The guilt Huck feels on the raft is as profound and "natural" as the comradeship which leads him to work against his social conscience in helping Jim escape.

It is this moral point of view of an either/or variety which dominates Marx's criticism and leads him to judge an artistic and moral lapse in the book's conclusion. But he contradicts himself, I believe, with credit to his perception, when he says that the "logic of metaphor," with the raft floating on the irreversible current downstream to the South, carrying two relatively helpless protagonists, leads to the defeat of freedom. "The raft patently was not capable of carrying the burden of hope Clemens placed upon it." Isn't the "logic of metaphor" the author's own logic after all; and whose hope has been defeated? It seems to me that it is more likely Marx's hope in the complicated area of "social morality." I suggest that freedom and a political or social morality may have a different relationship in the book, and in Mark Twain's mind, from the one he considers.

I cite these points, although Marx's argument has considerable plausibility in its own vein, to illustrate a tendency to deal with dialectical issues in the American classics as if they were manifestations of a profound split, not always clearly faced, in a tradition of values, and as if to say that the breach between American aspirations and American practice were a source of artistic and personal demoralization. This has its own applications of truth, of course, and the later life of Mark Twain-Sam Clemens has been presented as good biographical evidence. But *Huckleberry Finn* must be treated as an imaginative achievement, not as a man, or as the material of his biography. I have proposed in my general discussion that a democratic culture, more sophisticated than its critics believe, had its own way of expressing its contradictions, and it was not always the way of spiritual and moral confusion.

Since the issue is remarkably clear in this instance I shall try to face it in these following paragraphs. Some distinctions should be made first. Freedom, insofar as we can say it is a theme of Mark Twain's imagination, might be the name for life on the raft. But the book does not promise that there really is such a condition, permanently free *from* the defects of a civilization or, more broadly, the defects of human relationships. Freedom will coexist with oppression, criminal abuse, anarchic rivalries, and the polite lies on the shore. There never was any possibility of escape down the river. Nevertheless I would agree that Jim and Huck experience something that can be called freedom, if it is properly understood for what it is. Its larger dimension is frankly subjective, it stands for a resistance, a criticism of any given state of society. It cannot be equated with such a state, called "liberated" or "free," for active freedom is based on its independent power to resist and to redefine its opponents. I have proposed that the life on the raft is at the margin of "reality"; it is almost subliminal as a state of consciousness. Its "real" existence depends on the coexistence of the shore. But it should be possible to swim out for the raft when necessary, and in terms of that metaphor it might be possible to define the actual conditions for freedom, but they won't require the disappearance of a blemished "social morality" or assume the purification of social life.

Mark Twain did face a problem in concluding his book and sustaining its tone, but from the point of view of artistic judgment, I think he was more careful than some of his critics, who seem to be wishing for a stronger dose of explicit moralities than the book as such could ever have produced. These protagonists, the Negro and the boy, *do* require the help of luck and fortuitous events; they are not the ones to change society or oppose its dominant values. Throughout we have understood that the world is much too strong for them and that their chief weapons are evasion and escape. The distant act which frees Jim illustrates the random movements of a world too powerful, too thick in its encrusted practices for Jim and Huck to confront it directly, either to win over it or to lose completely to it. To lose completely would be to give up all hope, but Jim and Huck are not the heroes of liberation for a righteous cause. They could not be, without contradicting much richer moral implications. And yet to fall back suddenly into the world of Tom Sawyer, his robber bands and Arab caravans, is inevitably a shock. The future toward which Jim and Huck floated down the river was apparently one of participation in a boy's game, a final mock pantomime of the escape to freedom. Huck joins Tom Sawyer again, and in doing so surrenders to childhood and its irresponsible play-acting, which is a kind of apprenticeship to mature play-acting. On consideration, hasn't this role-playing been the constant feature of the shore world? The narrative provides a series of disguises and false identities, the deceived, the self-deceived, and the calculating tricksters. Emmeline Grangerford and the duke and the king face each other in the empty space filled by their posturing.

The last disguise assumed by Huck has a particular significance. Huck says to himself when he meets the Phelpses (who represent the return to the starting place, the normality of St. Petersburg),

> I was getting so uneasy I couldn't listen good. I had my mind on the children all the time; I wanted to get them out to one side, and pump them a little, and find out who I was.

To find out as he does that he has been mistaken for Tom Sawyer is a happy result.

> But if they was joyful, it warn't nothing to what I was; for it was like being born again, I was so glad to find out who I was.

This was his destined role, to become Tom Sawyer. Tom himself is the role player with confidence and style; he can impose his imagination on the world and share in the general fantasy of role-playing. He has the worldly skill, and this is perhaps why Huck must finally impersonate him, in order to close the story. But it is *only* a role, one final comic disguise. The real Huck Finn has been established and cannot be forsaken.

The original contrast between Tom and Huck is put forward again in these final scenes. Tom is given entirely to the ritual imagination, he allows reality to take care of itself, the forms are everything. Huck, as always, cares for concrete objectives. As they argue over the method of digging Jim out and Tom says that it would be "immoral" to use picks when the form requires "case-knives," Tom finally agrees that they could pretend they were using case-knives, and Huck is prompt in endorsing the reasonable solution.

> Picks is the thing, moral or no moral; and as for me, I don't care shucks for the morality of it, nohow. When I start in to steal a nigger, or a watermelon, or a Sunday-school book, I ain't no ways particular how it's done so it's done. . . . and I don't give a dead rat what the authorities thinks about it nuther.

Tom is willing to use "pretending" when he has to, but he insists that "right is right, and wrong is wrong, and a body ain't got no business doing wrong when he ain't ignorant and knows better." Tom lives in a fantasy which resembles the fantasy of culture itself, the world of books, rules, laws, ideal fictions. He is willing finally to confess that it is make-believe, but *he must have it as such.* He expresses what he feels and what he needs earlier with Huck when the latter had proposed a sensible and simple plan for escaping with Jim.

> *Work?* Why cert'nly, it would work, like rats a fighting. But it's too blame' simple; there ain't nothin *to* it. What's the good of a plan that ain't no more trouble than that? It's as mild as goose-milk. Why, Huck, it wouldn't make no more talk than breaking into a soap factory.

All this illustrates how ethical principle and ritual form are turned into comic grotesques at the end of the book. But this is deeply consistent, for it was a ritualized morality which endorsed Jim's slavery and imposed the farce of a bad conscience on Huck for helping his escape. These forms are not only an encumbrance, but a positive menace to "real" needs, "real" feelings. Tom's fantasy of an escape is a bookish and romantic rebellion as conventional as the coded form of slavery. When Tom says "right is right, wrong is wrong," he immediately throws doubt on those emphatic distinctions, and suggests that the powerful righteousness which might have acted on Jim's behalf in another book had no comfortable place in this one. In a sense, the place where Jim and Huck have met is beyond such formulations, whether they work for Jim or against him. Knowing this perhaps, they can tolerate Tom's nonsense, which caricatures and properly expresses the absurdity of the adult world.

But this is a serious unseriousness. Tom may have a point when he says, "it's too blame' simple," and he may be expressing more than the ideal need for moral distinctions or the superficial need for style. It is meaningful to say that the life on the raft must come to an end for many reasons, but among them is the fact that the undressed simple hedonism of such living has a languishing interest. We are made to feel the inertia, perhaps the pointlessness of nature, divorced from human or civilized complications. As Huck himself said for his stay alone on the island. "And so for three days and nights. No difference—just the same thing." Idyllic naturalism is not the theme, whatever the protest against the idiocy of life on the shore.

Again it is important to remember the drift of the river to the South. The escape was tentative, their freedom is neutral or merely receptive. The things that are evil on shore are washed into it and swept away; the river itself simply moves. It accepts everything but also reduces everything to lesser significance. Literally the river leaves behind the death of Boggs, the arrogance of Sherburn, the honor-loving and death-loving Grangerfords, the shabby duke and king. It carries its unyielded values, the *reserve* for living established by Jim and Huck, a form of the inner consciousness, but that is all. The refugees must finally come to terms with living on the shore, and the last episode engages with the process by which this can be done.

The conclusion seems to be that to become a man in the world is to become the dual identity which absorbs both Tom and Huck. One plays the game, conforms with a flourish, or rebels with an equal display of style, but meanwhile there remains Huck, aware of the truth, critical of deception. Remembering Whitman's words, it is to be "both in and out of the game." The end of the story suggests that the real Huck Finn, the boy of innocence, shrewdness, and truth, must live in a world of disguises and complicated prevarications. He has simulated death to find reality but, as he says, he must become Tom Sawyer in order to be born again. This is a classic emphasis, the testimony to the fragility of the external order in American life. The *looseness* of this civilization dramatizes the fact that all men live "both in and out of the game," and part of the personality (if not the best part), is a detached and critical sensibility.

The conclusion presses home the clear reason for this. Sally and Silas Phelps are good and kind people, yet they practice the bad values of their society. They are the parental figures, eternally a problem for the young and truthful spirit. They must be teased, humored, and circumvented, but they cannot be finally overturned, because in a sense they are the only possible authorities; they are, in effect, the "people," and there is no one else who can invite faith or give support. Huck's father, the duke and the king are long gone, hopeless scoundrels that they turned out to be. No, finally, only Silas and Sally remain, and the trust is in general luck and their latent kindness, because there is nothing and no one else to trust.

Perhaps this is too bitter a pill to swallow in the context of the book itself. It is impossible to argue to anyone's full satisfaction that the book's ending is *not* an artistic flaw. The ground shifts for social and moral issues, like that of slavery, and these issues are treacherous in their effect on literature. There is no question that the elements which composed Jim's portrait in *Huckleberry Finn* could not be used today. An atavistic social consciousness, like that of the Phelpses themselves, seems to have written the concluding portion of the book. To think of a Negro slave as a *boy* in heart and mind, which is basically what Jim is again at the end, is repellent, if it seems to reveal the moral blindness which was at the source of the original evil. But a whole people lived by that illusion. How is it that Mark Twain, who exposed so much, did not expose this?

The answer is partly that the "boy" is his own protagonist. The struggle with society is conducted at that level of the boy's dream of freedom, the "pecking" of laws and codes, a juvenile conscience, a delinquent happiness, and the sad but necessary return to clean clothes and good manners. A very strong tradition put the Negro into that mold, or rather made it acceptable—to see him that way, and even see slavery as not radically distinct from the prison which encloses childhood. The book returns to that view, almost helplessly, as if it had no other recourse. Mark Twain was not on the way of writing tragedy, or tragic satire, though his subject suggests such treatment the minute one glances away from his own context. To follow the distinction, one can say that he was consistently dealing with comedy, in which a kind of festive celebration is usually made of the marriage of incompatibles. Huck returns to the Widow Douglas, Jim to an ambiguous freedom in a slave society. Such agents, as comic agents, have to be treated lightly in their original break from the social order. The "boy" is a good protagonist in that respect. The return, however, is also lightly treated; it is not a close reconciliation, but something as quizzically detached as Huck Finn's role-playing at the end or as indefinite as his promise to "light out for the Territory," because Aunt Sally wants to "sivilize" him and he has been "sivilized" before.

This indefiniteness of conclusion should be some comfort to questioning readers who object to Jim and Huck's final fate. The book illustrates better than most what strains of contradiction existed and required reconciliation in the American consciousness. The closest parallel in this respect is with Melville's *The Confidence Man*. The issue in both books remains the question of whom to trust. The Phelpses and Aunt Polly seem unworthy of trust. None of the people on shore, including the warm-hearted Mary Jane Wilks, seem worthy, particularly when their sentimentality and piety make them so vulnerable to a world of "confidence men." In Melville's book the simplemindedness of trust and the universality of deception seem to play themselves out to an impasse. They become equally unattractive and dangerous, but the effect is neither satiric, in a serious or neotragic vein, nor comic. It leads to a stalemate in a book which reads as if it baffled Melville's resources of judgment. But perhaps this means that he carried the problem of "confidence" to a level where it resisted all resolutions. In dealing with humanity, confidence will nest with betrayal forever, until the day of doom. But in Melville's book one is not allowed to come down on the side of righteous anger or satiric destruction. These people are not Yahoos, and they require a different perspective. Cynicism is as vulnerable as faith, but they cancel each other out, and this is a position that might defy the resources of art. In *Huckleberry Finn* too much has been given us in favor of Huck and Jim to stay at that point of irresolution. They remain alive, attracting sympathy, even while they join Tom Sawyer's absurd play or the Phelpses' compromised world. The point has been, and this is the classic American emphasis, to go to the margin of "confidence" in man and civilization— and come back.

The problem is that of a moral criticism pushed to its limits. In the writing of Hawthorne and Melville, when they were most in control of their themes, this opened the way to tragedy. But Mark Twain was not any more sentimental than they were. A democratic criticism naturally turned in the end to the Phelpses, the good people, who serenely maintain the institution of slavery. This is what the limits of a democratic criticism mean; it stops here in the sense that it can take no higher standpoint, not in the intervention of a better sort of people, nor in the intervention of good rulers, nor of God. But the criticism must stand firm. Mark Twain's comedy required the subtlest weapons which would avoid destruction to the Phelpses, while assailing the radical evil of their society. The effort reveals the inner restriction of democratic satire. It cannot be revolutionary and absolute. The target is not a class (not in Mark Twain's view certainly), nor a ruler who can be eliminated from existence or consideration. The target is the people. The evil the people do, and can always do, must be exposed; their power to do evil, that is, their sovereignty, must be defended. Such is the paradoxical and difficult task of the moral critic in a democracy.

Certainly what was needed was not a bigotry of judgment or a blueprint for a new society. There is rather the creation of that small, *inner* community on the raft, while on shore the greater community was being subversively exposed. The wisdom achieved begins simply with the ability not to be fooled completely, or all the time. The counterattack is not that of righteousness; it is more subtle than that, and also more humane. That superior community of the raft has meant one thing at least, that the intrinsic values of community can survive their generalized abuse. The exposure of cheating and corruption is merciless, the people in crowds are mean and ugly, deception and disguise rule all social relationships, and yet the mode of comedy is forgiving, if only because it has discovered a haven from the world it exposes. That haven is the ironic consciousness, another pattern of Emerson's double consciousness, which never gives itself up totally to its high assumptions and never totally to its low discoveries. That consciousness is in two places at once, on the river and on the shore, and because it is, it is never entirely at the mercy of a danger coming from one or the other. I tend to think that here we touch the special moral gift of a democracy, which thrives, like a useful antigen, on its own self-division and incoherence. Its name may be good humor, an ultimate generosity; its spirit is in Mark Twain's book.

We know that Huck Finn will not "light out for the Territory." He has indeed been civilized for good by Tom Sawyer and the others, and that's just as well, for Tom and the Widow Douglas, for Silas and Sally and Jim, and also for Huck himself. But his enlightened consciousness, extended brilliantly for the length of the book, has outdone that of Tom Sawyer, for Huck Finn lives in the civilized imagination of his society.

9/ Henry James
Conscience and Freedom

Eliot's remark that James had a mind so fine no idea could violate it has become a part of his legend. By this sign he became a hero of the modern sensibility; the best writers of our century exhibit the same exaggerated faculties of perception, discrimination, and nuance. Joyce and Proust are the peers of James and he belongs in their world, so much so that one might forget his link with his proper ancestors, Hawthorne and Emerson. Certainly no writer was more gifted in searching the perspectives of irony, more skeptical, accessible, and lucid in his view of experience than James. But there is a difference, and I propose that its source lay in his American origin, the influence of the writers who most affected his youth, and the fact that his formative career belongs to the humanist nineteenth century.

Modern writing seems to have been obsessed with proving that the sensible judgment is superior to all the real possibilities of experience. In this world observation is irony, and criticism accompanies every insight. There is something eventually forbidding and hopeless about this truth in the work of Joyce and Proust. Their standpoint was criticism, but it was criticism from the point of view of demigods who were no longer human. Fallen priests, fallen aristocrats, they had become artists, in the cruel modern sense.

The fineness of James's mind may have been a barrier to ideas, but it was not fatal to a curious, almost anachronistic survival of the moral interest which approximates Hawthorne's allegorizing themes. It is phenomenal, in fact, that he made this consistent with the subtle, convoluted pattern of his fiction. He is the master of the ambiguous turn of events and the reversal of moral expectations. But in struggling to describe this, critics are pointing to the intense treatment of life and action. His characters are in the toils of conscious experience.

The emphasis is on consciousness but not on mere subjectivity, though it is accepted that James conducted some of the first great experiments in modern perspective techniques. What is truly modern in his work is that he pictured the ordeal of consciousness, which is that of making firm approaches to a real world and the real people in it. The threat of solipsism is an intellectual, esthetic, and moral problem for James, and the fact that it is the last is an attribute of his place in the American tradition, notably in the inheritance of Hawthorne. The highly developed mind, the highly developed imagination—these are vulnerable to the solipsism of pride, the sin of egotism. No matter how far James goes in his study of the sensibility in its transcendent refinements, the obsession which accompanies him is the moral form of experience, or the way in which knowing and dealing with an external world is essentially a moral problem. Like Hawthorne before him he dramatized an experience in which there was only one resort against solipsism, and that is a communication between persons, the failure of which is dramatized most explicitly in the "The Beast in the Jungle."

In the larger volume of James's work, that story, and a few others here treated, like "The Madonna of the Future," "The Real Thing," and "The Aspern Papers," are remarkably expressive in illustrating his major themes, particularly for the interests I stress, problematic reality in the dialectic of the imagination, problematic innocence (or evil) in the dialectic of judgment. James was beyond all writers in his ability to render these "ambiguities," in a more involved sense than even Melville proposed, but anchoring that uncertainty was a deep sense of human pathos. In his case one could define this as the hunger for experience opposed to the terror of its revelations, as in the spring of the beast.

The Real Thing

Caroline Spencer, in the early short story, "Four Meetings," is an archetype among Jamesian protagonists, the victim of the starved imagination. The swindle that cheated her was in part engineered by her own great desires, though the selfishness of her "artist" cousin is both an ironic parody of what the greed for experience can do as well as the proper devil raised by her own vulnerability to deception. The imagination serves and defeats the hunger for life, and this is the doubly vital energy which propels the Jamesian universe. The cousin himself exhibits that ripeness of appetite as he slowly masticates an apricot while explaining to the narrator how he meant to absorb Caroline Spencer's life earnings. A similar hunger is the motive force for the great selfish agents of James's fiction, including Gilbert Osmond and John Marcher. It can arouse the cruelty in nature, as it can be the source of victimization for those made vulnerable to selfishness in others. But the search for life is also the basis for the deep sensitivity and ultimate wisdom exhibited in such superior victims as Isabel Archer, Lambert Strether, and Milly Theale. This is faintly suggested by the drab and timid Caroline Spencer when she obtains her experience of Europe in giving what she has to her cousin and his woman, the parasitical relic of the old world who came to live with her. In this respect she reminds us of Milly Theale, another dreamer who was strangely victorious in offering her loss to the gain of others. The blindness of Marcher, the awareness of Milly Theale, these are responses to the hunger for experience which converge at exactly the same point, the impingement on the lives of others, or on the craving for life in others. The imagination may cheat universally but there is a rich secret in that experience; the center from which dreams arise is the place of knowing oneself and becoming known to others. Caroline makes herself known, a little like Tina in "The Aspern Papers," to the unresourceful if not insensitive narrator of "Four Meetings." In life she met not her own desires but the greed in others that parodied them. Perhaps for this drab shadow of herself she makes her unacknowledged sacrifice.

The American is the especial victim of the imagination because his "reality" is so barren; that is the crude judgment of the way the theme works in James's fiction. But there is always something stronger, more positive on behalf of the American in James's actual consideration of the theme. "You've the great American disease," a morbid appetite for color and form at any price, the narrator says almost as soon as he meets Caroline Spencer. She admits that what she has "is a kind of craziness. It kills any interest in things nearer home—things I ought to attend to." To be an American, James said elsewhere, was a special condition, a "complex fate." But no evaluations remain from his findings except the sympathetic interest with which he located the free force of life itself. Like great clowns and comedians, the American character in James communicates the pathos of his vulnerability. The frustrations are keen but so is the mark of the readiness for living.

This obsession with the search for life characterizes his own exposition of the principles of his fiction. In "The Art of Fiction," his strongest critical pronouncement, he said of the novel that "the only reason for [its] existence . . . . is that it does attempt to represent life," and that "A novel is in its broadest definition a personal, a direct impression of life."[1] The problem of the artist was to find what *does* represent life. That this was not easy and that it led to interesting complications is illustrated by one of the most suggestive of his shorter writings, "The Real Thing."

The protagonist is an artist searching for the best models to help him illustrate a book with an upper-class scene. The particular irony in this story is that he is misdirected by the "real thing" itself, represented by Major and Mrs. Monarch, genteel folk, who are in life exactly what the painter wishes to portray in his art. The question in the story evolves, *are* they the "real thing," if they can become so lifeless in the copy made of them? The given truth blocks the way to a discovered truth. Major and Mrs. Monarch are too much the "real thing" to arouse the imagination, which apparently has the primary role in presenting what is called "the sense of life."

The point made by the story is that the pathetic couple are not the "real thing" at all, but only a copy, an imitation. They are formed as an elaborate cliché and they have not sufficient life in themselves to transcend it. The real thing is discovered for what it is in Miss Chum, the cockney model, who is not anything definite so much as she is alive in her capacity to suggest other things. The discrepancy between what she is and what she might be, and her mimetic capacity to bridge those terms, is the basis of her power of suggestion; it is the sense of her life itself as the heightened awareness of the artist might deal with it.

The "real thing" is particularly misconceived as the way in which life freezes in convention, routine, and stereotype. Such things halt the imagination rather than give it its start. The imagination is aroused by a subject moving in transit between one possibility and another. The cockney girl and the Italian servant can shape the forms of an elegant lady and gentleman. By the reverse process Major and Mrs. Monarch descend at the end of the story to serving tea for the artist and the successful models. This is more than a note of pathos, or if it is pathos, it is that of the volatile dialectic of life in which forms shape themselves and disintegrate. One should add that Major and Mrs. Monarch become quite "real," win a victory over their own artifice,

1. Henry James, *The Art of Fiction and Other Essays* (New York: Oxford University Press, 1948), p. 8.

when they descend in the social scale. That movement acknowledges their humanity.

"The Real Thing" is a lesson in freedom as well as art, for it describes the power of self-transcendence, life breaking through life in its traditional forms, criticizing its stale and rigid obediences, complicating it, reimagining it. That is the artist's awareness, but it parallels what we might call the democratic imagination, which moves like Miss Chum from poverty to riches, from drab veracity to histrionic longings, which becomes *something*, whatever it would be. That is the hopeful aspect, but the democratic imagination is sensitive also to the ironies and implicit tragedies of reversed status. The servants in the story become the lady and gentleman, and the actual lady and gentleman become servants. The curious irony here, which might seem cold, is that they do this *willingly*, not only because they desperately need something to do, but because the accumulated useless rituals of their previous existence make them apt for the role. This reversal of roles reveals the awesomeness of the "real thing," the violence of its movement, the intangibility of its substance, for which the personal imagination and civilization as well can supply only transient forms.

In the last effect, Major and Mrs. Monarch didn't want to starve. This is an emergence of the real "real thing," in the stoic clarity with which Melville might conceive it. Behind all forms there is something overwhelming in nature. In another metaphor used by James, the "real thing" is the great destroyer, a beast in a jungle. Some readers miss that violence in the midst of the superrefinements of scene, situation, and character, but it is there unmistakably, to such effect that James ranks among writers of authentic tragic temperament.

Support for this interpretation of James's theme is found in the close connection elsewhere in his fiction between the activity of the imagination and its power to hurt or increase life. The artist gains the power to render the sense of life. But life itself is a free and vulnerable process, in which the imagination acts to promote this, renounce that, desire, reject, and choose. The imagination in life finds itself in a nest of contradictions, unstable forms, unstable relationships. Its compensation is its power to experience and appreciate more than one thing, and finally, as in the reward of art, to achieve some frame of judgment founded on a stoic knowledge of contradictions.

On this ground James seems to have concluded, in his stories of artists and writers, that the problems of art and life are the same. That is to say that survival, if not success, in both requires the ability to maintain an openness of relationship between the ideal world of the imagination and the actual world. This is perfectly illustrated in "The Madonna of the Future." "I'm the half of a genius," cries Theobald, the expatriate American painter, "Where . . . is my other half?" He has spent his life contemplating the face of his living model and an empty canvas. He has had a fruitful relationship with neither one. Largely this is because he has failed to distinguish between his ideal Madonna and the pungently flawed Italian woman who inspired him, and because of that he cannot reconcile them either. Obviously the "other half" of his genius exists in the person of the shabby sculptor of pornographic statuettes, the actual lover of his "Madonna." The great Raphael himself, it is understood in the story, made love to his models and sat down to hearty suppers with them. But Theobald is of the "famished race" who refuse to be fed by gross substance. This is their mistake against themselves, against art, and against life. The combination of the two halves of a genius is also the combination of the two parts of an active protagonist in the theater of experience.

The American Child of Nature

James was as explicit as he possibly could be in such stories as "Four Meetings" and "The Madonna of the Future," with their references to "the great American disease" and "the famished race." In this way he presented initial assumptions for considering his treatment of the American theme; among them, it becomes clear, is the classic opposition between nature and culture. In that emphasis *Daisy Miller* is perhaps the clearest American fable in James's work, short enough to be highly visible, simple enough to stress the outline of the large theme.

Daisy stands in the foreground, a touching and contemptible figure, offering a compound of ambivalent substance in herself and ambivalent judgment in the observer. Her major characteristic, or the principle she embodies, is stated very clearly as "having no idea whatever of 'form.'" She herself is all attractive latency, but so open that she is formless and therefore cannot be understood, not even treated with, as Winterbourne found to his pain. "She was composed . . . . of charming little parts that didn't match and that made no *ensemble*."

I doubt if even Winterbourne's confession of guilt and a mistake at the end of the story should be accepted uncritically, despite the emotional relevance of his remorse. He is again sentimentalizing Daisy, as he did earlier in their relationship and as it was a mistake to do.

Giovanelli states that she was "innocent," but that has a formal and ironic meaning, I think. In James's world there is no innocence, no uncompromised natural goodness. Daisy is no more innocent than her brother Randolph, whose caricature accompanies her in our minds with his little boy's appetite for sugar, his ignorant prejudice for everything American, and the sharp angular stabbing movements with his stick, the bony, thin shape of his body. This has the hardness of something implicitly destructive; we sense that what is served by his freedom, or willfulness, is simply the uneducated appetite for pleasure and the innate capacity for violence.

Like Daisy, he is "much more a work of nature than of art" and, like her, he mostly "did what he liked." The more ominous note of human failure enters the story in the figure of Mrs. Miller. The father back home in Schenectady doesn't appear and is hardly referred to, which sufficiently characterizes his role in the lives of his family. The abdication of the mother is stressed, however. She leaves only one strong impression, that of a great vagueness. She lacks mind, she lacks values, she lacks response. Everything descends to an ineptitude which looks like apathy and indifference. The point is adequately made; she has been the moral context for Daisy.

But that is not the full characterization of "America." In contrast to her and at another American extreme, Mrs. Costello, Winterbourne's aunt, is featured by her snobbery and her sick headaches. She is so full of discriminations and rejections that she has nothing left to reject. Her life is a series of sojourns at fashionable stopping places, spent in hotel rooms from which she rarely descends. She has a fierce need for standards, which Mrs. Miller does not, but she has the same barrenness of resources. In contrast to them Daisy is fresh and spirited, lively and mischievous, almost an ideal vision of what it means to be "a child of nature and freedom."

The story is thus a skillful maneuver of positive and negative judgments that attach to all members of the group and reverse themselves. But the center for judgment and the talisman for values is Daisy. In one perspective she is fated to be a martyr of freedom, like the prisoners of Chillon, whose cells she visits, and like the Christians who were thrown to the beasts at the Roman Colosseum. Europe, the scene of rich culture and history, throws into relief the shapelessness of American character, but it also projects itself in the contrast with Daisy's vulnerable humanity. History is pain, corruption, mortality— that is the lesson Rome teaches, and Rome is the fate of Daisy.

What after all is that Roman disease which finally kills Daisy? The martyr, the slave, the prisoner, are the symbols which parallel Daisy's own story. Rome represents a rich and beautiful monument to intelligent choices as well as old unutterable suffering. The past has a great dignity; the triumphal ruins, the scarred majesty of Rome add a counterpoint to accompany Daisy on her path to destruction. The irony is strong and everything in Schenectady and Daisy's being seems reduced to inanity in the contrast. But Rome claims Daisy as its own in the end. The disease that kills her may be its "cynical streets," a poisonous secret in old experience, but the result is to give her some dignity. It could be said she has become human, in Hawthorne's sense.

On one side, however, she is a victim, and her victimization implies a criticism of the prejudice of moral conventions. These latter have a fatally mendacious element, which prohibits sincere impulse and frank existence. They live by suspicion as well as restraint and can become the mentors of evil, not the protection against it. There is a special American dimension to this conflict between nature and civilization. Daisy's chief judges, Mrs. Walker and Mrs. Costello, are Americans themselves, but so devoted to the *sense* of form, that they have nothing but decorum and propriety to recommend to Daisy, an arid basis for the teaching of manners. When Winterbourne objects to his aunt's criticism, remarking that the Millers aren't really "bad," Mrs. Costello responds, "They're hopelessly vulgar . . . being 'bad' is a question for the metaphysicians." She admits that moral values for her have taken a degenerate form. The effect is simpler but very much like the elaboration in James's other work where he deals with such amoral estheticians as the narrator in "The Aspern Papers" and Gilbert Osmond. What is suggested is a barren approach to values, an approach from the outside, as spectators and expatriates, as dilettantes who have taste but little human connectedness, or what Hawthorne would call sympathy. Winterbourne himself is highly uncertain in his own moral composition, a man living between two worlds and at home in neither, attracted to the fresh substance of life in Daisy, repelled by her formlessness and the vague threat of that force of life. When he confesses at the end of the story that he had been doomed to make a mistake, "I've lived too long in foreign parts," he is admitting the cost of being overcivilized.

But on the other side, "the child of nature and freedom" is also exposed to ambiguous judgment. In an interesting footnote to the story provided by James in the preface to the New York edition, a friend accuses him of complicating what was simple.[2] The narrative was the story of a plain, undisciplined, unformed little girl and the disarray such a personage might cause. And this reader protested, "[you] made *any* judgment [of it] quite impossible." James must have been delighted by that remark. And when his reader complains, "Is it that you've after all too much imagination?" other readers might understand how much imagination was needed to be enough. It would be limited imagination to respond on behalf of martyred innocence in this story. It would be simple also merely to review the self-destruction caused by an absolute gaucherie. But the evil here is almost beyond judgment; complacency is impossible, for what is at hand is a tragic ambiguity, as far-reaching as any that Melville and Hawthorne liked to imagine.

To the extent Daisy is innocent and free, she is also fated to be misjudged. The greatest mischief in her life is that she remains unknowable; she might arouse faith, but she cannot support judgment. This is what Winterbourne had failed to see; attractive as pure latency, she wasn't yet anything in herself. And the ironic basis of his failure is the fact that he himself is so little of anything, not like her on the side of nature and freedom, but with the imitative and shallow gloss of civilization.

No matter how trivial Winterbourne's life may seem, nor how coldly sterile Mrs. Costello's judgment, it is not possible to sentimentalize the "child of freedom." She is ignorant, for instance, not merely of the conventional requirements of society, but of the dangerous possibilities in herself. Apart from her charm, perversity is a great feature of her free spirit. Her freedom seems to act chiefly *against* expectations and not *for* anything in herself. "That's all I want—a little fuss," she says at one point in first proposing and then retreating from a boat trip alone with Winterbourne at night. And all her later behavior with Giovanelli seems designed for the fuss it would make in Winterbourne's mind as well as for the shock it would be to judges like Mrs. Walker.

Something more sinister than girlish teasing is suggested in all this "fuss." It is appropriate that the shadow of old pain and suffering is called up at the Colosseum. Daisy "did what she liked," and this sets free more than mere misjudgment but the real chance that she could be seduced, that she might marry a cheap fortune-hunter (though Giovanelli is not merely that) or, as she is finally left to do,

2. *The Art of the Novel* (New York: Charles Scribner's Sons, 1950), pp. 269–70.

sink under the symbolic ancient disease of Rome, which is a composite of human violence and indifferent abuse. Is there a world where Daisy's innocence might have led a protected life? Is it Schenectady? We doubt it. If Schenectady is to have a future, it will resemble the past of Rome.

The American theme which strikes response among many readers makes them perceive Daisy as a critical commentary on the extremes of cultural failure, a barren resourcelessness on one side and an equally barren formalism on the other. This is valid, but the deeper complications of meaning should be stressed. A natural innocence has been violated and misjudged; the fresh impulse to live has gone unappreciated. Something deficient, a kind of predestined failure, has been exposed in conventional forms of action and judgment. And yet the innocent, unjudged life has no intelligible and negotiable being in itself; it must bend to the forms of action and knowledge. Without such forms it is either *vague*, as Mrs Miller is quintessentially vague, or it disintegrates in abuse as Daisy's fate proposes. To be merely natural is to be inadequate for human existence—this is the theme.

James, like his mentor Hawthorne, rejects the choice between nature and culture. They are the two halves of the condition of being, not in harmony yet indispensable to each other, as Theobald, (who in "The Madonna of the Future" worshipped Raphael and painted nothing himself) was in need of that other natural half of his genius. The sophisticated task, the morally educated position, advances only in a finely held consciousness. The task is to see through the irony of contradictions, to understand the violence of nature, to understand the incomprehension and inhibitions of culture. It is like the necessary vision of the artist, the whole genius. The balance is always at strain but the point of leverage nevertheless remains the educated moral judgment. This is another democratic parable in the critical and neo-tragic development first illustrated by Hawthorne and Melville. In its first step, conventionally in fact, the theme criticizes the obtuse tyrannies of cultural forms and exhibits the primary value of the person, equipped with nothing much more than the strong impulse of life. But it is equally critical in its second step, as it exposes the resourcelessness of mere freedom and the destructiveness of nature. This is a consciousness that is revolutionary and conservative at the same time, because on its third level of understanding, it combines negatives and positives in order to safeguard freedom against the threat of order and order against the threat of freedom. These are implicit judgments in the story, though freedom as a degenerate anarchy and order as a degenerate tyranny are so lightly caricatured in the apolitical figures of Mrs. Miller and Mrs. Costello.

"The Unpardonable Sin"

The narrator in "The Aspern Papers" is an idolater who worships the relics of Jeffrey Aspern, dead poet, a shape in his imagination who represents ineffable values. This servant of glory is a high priest of art who has become a literary antiquarian and critic, and his temple is a museum of documents, in this case the missing letters, still in the possession of an ancient survivor, Aspern's mistress. Briefly, the theme of the story is that the narrator worships the dead Jeffrey Aspern at the expense of his human relics, Juliana and Tina Bordereaux, and in ironic caricature of that great love in life and of life which his affair with Juliana represented.

The narrator, like Theobald, belongs to the "famished race." He substitutes symbols for reality presumably because reality has left him hungry. These symbols are the artifacts of his imagination, but also of the highest civilization as embodied in the cultural memory which is great poetry. If we thus let him be allegorized, he is no child of nature like Daisy Miller. He is absent in flesh and life, where Daisy was disturbingly present, though her parts didn't match and made no ensemble; he is the pedant of forms, who himself, for the sake of those abstractions, descends to being nameless in the story. This is passive spectatorship reaching its extreme, for he apparently can do nothing except give himself in parasitic attachment to one who once lived intensely and left the aura of his existence behind.

"The old woman represented esoteric knowledge," he says. She draws him to his ritual worship. "A mystic companionship, a moral fraternity with all those who in the past had been in the service of art." What this idolater is prepared to sacrifice for his idol is made clear. "There's no baseness I wouldn't commit for Jeffrey Aspern's sake." But Juliana wears a mask, and the greater mystery, echoing Hawthorne, greater than anything his "precious papers" could convey, is what lies behind the mask. "Perhaps only a ghastly death's head," is the narrator's thought. It is a sobering thought which conditions his dreams and precedes discovery in the story. One simple truth concealed behind the mask is the existence of two decayed and weak people, subject to his mistreatment.

What the narrator himself discovers as he pursues revelation is a "sarcastic profane cynical old woman," so old as to represent nothing but an utter disenchantment with living. He is chiefly embarrassed by her greed for money, which affronts his genteel and euphemistic imagination, but in this Juliana represents the last force of a reality; it is a concern for survival, that is, Tina's survival. Tina is a faded, pathetic Juliet on that romantic scene, surrounded by Venice and flowers. He could say clearly to himself, "Miss Tina was not a poet's mistress any more than I was a poet." And yet if there is a proper heir to the relics of Aspern, his love letters, it is Tina, a shabby, innocent dreamer all her life, marred with age, already crumbling into the dust of the past. Were the great love poems about such as her? On this point, Jeffrey Aspern smiles ambiguously out of his portrait at the narrator. She at least is stirred directly by feeling. There is a moment at the end of the story when Tina is transfigured and has borrowed the shade of glory. The narrator then whispers to himself, why *not* marry her, but it is already too late, the letters have been burnt. But more than upon her, he has brought the barren fate upon himself. At the end he almost understands the talismanic significance of the papers, or why he was ineligible to receive them.

The narrator has committed the sin of the imagination, not so explicit as Hawthorne's sin of the intellect, but a sin clearly in the same vein of judgment. To be oversophisticated, to love only finely developed images, or the fantasy of the absolute, is to lose touch with "human" reality. These are the people "doomed to make a mistake." The implication, however, is that of an imaginative as well as a moral failure, for the greatest achievement of the imagination is to know the life in others. Daisy Miller put this as a need to be acknowledged; "she would have appreciated one's esteem," is read in her dying message to Winterbourne. The same failure becomes highly visible in "The Aspern Papers" when the narrator refuses at the climax "to unite myself to her [Tina] for life," yet thinks "I might still have what she had." But the papers, or what they represent, cannot be gained by that refusal.

In this respect, to have access to Aspern's art is to have intercourse with humanity. Hawthorne proposed as his theme that those who lack sympathy, affectivity, miss the "real thing." In James, the word "sympathy" would moralize too heavily, but still the moral imagination is his concern. It has fused with the literary imagination which has the goal of achieving a dialectical consciousness, a power to transcend all fixed points of prejudiced knowledge and interest, and in this flexibility of vision to touch the intrinsic stuff of life. In Tina's case, to know her would have been to feel her pathos, a dramatic emotion which arises from her juxtaposition with the glamorous young Juliana, the heroic figure of the poet, or the marvelous scene of Venice. But it would also have meant to recognize the legitimacy of her connection with those images which express sensate living and human desires.

In this emphasis the deficiency in the narrator is something simpler than moral insensitivity; it is the lack of a coarse basic energy for life. Old as she is, Juliana has kept it, as when she deals for money, or as she speaks of the unsweet air of the grave she would soon enter. Jeffrey Aspern himself, we are told, is a hero of the actual world, a natural artist from the young country, free, liberal, not afraid. The kind of poet James had in mind was as much Whitman, perhaps, as Byron. In replying in his preface to the charge of giving an implausible American identity to the great poet, Aspern, he said that he put him on "that side of the modern world . . . bound up with youth in everything else."[3] But there is a historic lesson, even a legend, in his contrast with his disciple, the later American critic, haunting the past, in flight from the commonplace. The irony is that Aspern, who was of life and nature, has become culture.

Art, or culture, has an ironic alliance with the great ambition to live which leads to every eventuality in James's work, sometimes to be defeated by the world, as in the cases of Caroline Spencer and Milly Theale, sometimes to be defeated by itself, as in such examples as Madame Merle and Kate Croy. John Marcher in "The Beast in the Jungle" is the supreme example of the egotism of desire, and in his story he loses more than happiness, fulfillment; he goes beyond the romantic pathos. He loses everything, that is to say, the tangible sense of his own existence.

The case of Marcher is particularly significant because his imagination is described as having no limits. He cannot specify what he waits for because what he wants resists restriction. His vanity or his perversity tends to describe it as a personal catastrophe accompanied by a total revelation of his life's meaning, but we are not to be literal about this, I believe. He might as well have imagined a theatrical apotheosis, like rising into heaven on the wings of angels. The essence is that while he has apocalyptic notions for himself, we know that he

3. Ibid., p. 165.

is self-centered to the verge of madness. The sense of his own existence is the only serious interest he shares with May, and he shares nothing with anyone else. It is absurd but the meaning is clear. This shallowness of substance accompanied by the concentration on himself is the self-defeat of egotism. The paradox is that it has turned all his experience and hunger for experience into purely abstract anticipation.

We are not to forget that Marcher is not merely feeble, a dreamer who plays it safe. In his own way, he is Faustian, or he is an Ethan Brand ready to commit the "Unpardonable Sin." If at the beginning of the story someone had tried to describe his fate as closely as possible to its eventual terms, he would have dismissed it as commonplace. It takes him a lifetime to learn to respect what he has missed. In him the ambition to live is so great that he has a hatred of the common fate. Though no American, he is another of "the famished race," which as a theme now more clearly suggests Tocqueville's as well as James's own observation of the limited subjects for the imagination in the American democracy. Marcher is a fled aristocrat unable to take the common food of the imagination, and is now quite visibly without the old heroic themes, preferring to wait for something else. Such men of aristocratic expectations have only one way to distinguish themselves— by their refusals, or by their fastidious inaction. One is reminded of that more obvious snob, Gilbert Osmond, who gave parties at his palace in Rome for the sake of *not* inviting people. Marcher's problem is his actual lack of talent and color. "As always he was lost in the crowd," it is said of him at a party. He has only his imagination to mark himself out, but only for his own notice, it must be added, and that of May, who has decided to "watch with him."

James might have expected another complaint for an implausibility here. But the story is very much allegorical in its vein, and May, we might say, is the inevitable woman. For good or bad reasons she is Marcher's woman, who doesn't share a choice in the basic matter of what he does with his life, but has chosen him and cannot reject him. As much as he, she lives in terms of the eventual, or the possible, and it takes her almost a lifetime to discover how empty a man can be. The story is bolstered in this respect by a realism touching the dependent status of women, though I think that general as the theme is in James's writing, it serves to dramatize a universal and mutual dependency in human relationships. In much of James's work, the real restrictions on the life of women are combined with the endowment of an exceptional sensitivity to make them ideal protagonists.

Marcher's relation with May has a deeper significance than is first anticipated, in view of the thematic, almost melodramatic, emptiness of their experiences together. It makes possible a remarkable psychological evaluation of the sense of personal existence and inter-personal communication. In the developed allegory the secret which binds May and Marcher is simply the secret of his actual being, his future which will become his identity, and her attraction or curiosity is what in coarser parlance might be called falling in love. To tell his secret to her, as he does, realizing later that she is the only person who aroused the desire to do so, is to invite intimate communication in the universal way. Unfortunately this is the way he has trapped her, perverted and abortive as the telling of the secret is.

His great "secret" then is a metaphor for his selfhood presented as the sense of his own fate in the world. In a perceptive passage James describes how May has moved into his life.

> What it had come to was that he wore a mask painted with the social simper, out of the eyeholes of which there looked eyes of an expression not in the least matching the other features. This the stupid world, even after years, had never more than half-discovered. It was only May Bartram who had, and she achieved, by an art indescribable, the feat of at once—or perhaps it was only alternately—meeting the eyes from in front and mingling her own vision, as from over his shoulder, with their peep through the apertures.

This description touches the rare poignance of such a meeting, destined, as we know already, to futility. "Half-discovered," behind his mask, Marcher illustrates the introspective distance familiar in Hawthorne, indeed an "Americanism" that has its variants in Thoreau, Poe, and Mark Twain. Poe's morbid themes suggest James at more than one point. The struggle to live in Ligeia is only more explicitly ghoulish than the shadowy life of Marcher. Huck Finn, of course, is a boy of disguises and, in his own way, he is as sustained a private person as Lambert Strether or Milly Theale.

The psychological depth of James's story is further verified in the long elaboration of the "beast" metaphor. A lifetime of waiting for what? Surely not just the hothouse fantasy of a neurotic, incapac-itated man. An allegorical sense of beleaguered personal being, as compelling as in the story of Bartleby, is recorded in this long waiting. Expecting the future is what men do while they live; it marks their own sense of their lives. The effect at the end of the story is that when Marcher thinks he no longer has anything to expect, his sense of discrete being and his will to live depart from him. Most remarkably James achieves in this fairly brief narrative an important effect of the full passing rhythm of a lifetime.

Marcher's notion that he waits for a strange fate is essentially an eccentric form of the normal belief in a personal destiny. The principle is representative in Marcher precisely because it is uncommitted to particular ambitions, unwilling in fact to admit to naive or foolish conceit, but nonetheless a secret conviction that something special, quite inevitable, pertains to oneself. May has suggested, "You want something all to yourself—something nobody else knows or *has* known." His sense of singularity supports the sense of expectation, a readiness to go from day to day in a kind of vague but uninterrupted hope that the Big Thing is to happen, that which will justify everything and explain everything.

Beyond the awareness of the secret there is the sharing of the secret. It is really the long and usually silent communication with May which has given Marcher the bare definition of his existence. He has only the abstraction of an identity, and with May, only the skeleton of communication, but they exist and keep him going. It is a tribute to James's brilliant irony that he could conceive it this way. Expectancy keeps Marcher alive while the deeper gift of life is offered and refused. A refusal is worse than death, it seems; what is at stake is a justification for himself, for May, for everyone. For this reason the eyes of judgment can glare at him, as they do from the bereaved man he meets in the cemetery in the last scene.

The spring of the beast, a teleological metaphor, discovers for him that his real fate was to be "something that includes all the loss and all the shame that are thinkable." The "loss" and the "shame" refer, first, directly to May, whose love was offered but not taken, or rather taken for granted and not answered. But it was his own loss after all, and a larger shame, appropriate to an "Unpardonable Sin." The wider reference is seen by May, who does not mourn at all for herself. The "loss," if it means the frustration of experience, is treated sternly, with precise concentration on the destructive paradox implicit in Marcher's greed. It is impossible to sentimentalize at any point on the fact of mere "loss." It is not the failure of life itself, but of a man's obligation to live it and share common existence with others.

The story is another essay on "the psychological costs of individualism" (returning to Newton Arvin's remarkably pertinent phrase), in the tradition of that theme in American writing. The cultivation of personality is forced to a destructive extreme in order to find its tragedy. A man so obsessed becomes a nonbeing in the excess of his pursuit of his unique being. For Marcher's ambition, James says in the preface, there was "no damnation deep enough, no bliss sublime enough." The excess leads him to a perfectly quiet passivity. And passive egotism, it is suggested, is the worst kind. It is indifferent to success or failure, to specific goods and values; it only wants something vivid enough to feel justified. That is to say, it is indifferent to any value except self-magnification. Thus Marcher has been perverted on the deepest ground of moral judgment.

James here illustrated the life cycle of personal freedom, exercised entirely in the imagination, with Marcher being given complete leisure to concentrate on himself. He begins and ends with his own great hunger. The "famished race" are those who violate their own hungers. They live in the legends they have imagined at the expense of the "reality" for which they starve. To clarify the theme with Tocqueville's point, the democratic imagination had lost structure and substance, that of the rich normative imagination of caste and class, of birth and prerogative and duty, of discrimination and value. The famished ones will find their substitutes. Theobald, Caroline Spencer, the Aspern narrator, as well as Marcher, have this in common. They illustrate a kind of homeless aristocratic principle, devoted to ideal forms, consciously or unconsciously repelled by the actual world. They endure disillusionment as if in a world experiencing revolution; everything falls to pieces around them, they lose the signs of their aspiration, but what emerges before them is not only the strong reality which could not be repressed, but their own guilt toward it.

The ordeal of the hungry imagination suggests the relevance of James's treatment of the theme of failed art. The artist who *works*, unlike the dreaming Theobald, has a form of what James in another context called a "double consciousness," describing Lambert Strether, a Yankee who could plausibly echo Emerson's term. This consists of the power to grasp the richness of forms, create the world of possibility, and yet be so rooted in the given life that there is a constant interchange, never a separation. The double consciousness redeems good artists but it is also redemptive in life. In James, it must be understood, art is always the metaphor for life. Or put in another way, they converge in the great discipline of consciousness. Thus when James gave himself the goal of capturing the "sense of life" as a critical theorem for fiction, he was expressing a wider preoccupation. "The

Beast in the Jungle" stresses that to miss the sense of life can mean much more than the inability to write a good story or novel. James is proposing a theme supported in the context of his whole work, that the sense of reality is a *moral* sense. The meeting of man with man makes a world and it is, implicitly, the only world.

The last passages of the story touch a parallel with Captain Ahab, though Marcher's more barren vanity makes him shrivel in the comparison. The excess of self-consciousness leads to the knowledge of the whale, though the whale is an impasse of knowledge, as Ahab admits when he cries "strike through the mask" and "thrust through the wall." The fact that James chose the "beast" for his metaphor suggests that he too sensed an aboriginal violence at the heart of the mystery. But in his story the theme has more specifically the function of a moral criticism, as in Hawthorne.

An entry in Hawthorne's notebooks, noticed by James in his little book on Hawthorne, has immediate bearing.

> I used to think that I could imagine all passions, all feelings, and states of the heart and mind; but how little did I know! . . . . Indeed, we are but shadows; we are not endowed with real life, and all that seems most real about us is but the thinnest substance of a dream—till the heart be touched. That touch creates us—then we begin to be—thereby we are beings of reality and inheritors of eternity.[4]

It is precisely that discovery of an ontological humanism which, as a theme, enters and reenters the pattern of James's own work. I use the term to recall its reference to Whitman's address to "the terrible doubt of appearances," in "Calamus."

> I cannot answer the question of appearances or that of identity be-
> yond the grave,
> But I walk or sit indifferent, I am satisfied,
> He ahold of my hand has completely satisfied me.[5]

This simple experience is, as Whitman goes on to say, the "base and finalé too for all metaphysics," or as Hawthorne put it, the "touch [which] creates us." There was a fruitful relationship between James's continuous concern with the problems of artistic creation and this view, which he shared, of a morally functional, creative consciousness in men. The "method of Henry James" is the exhibit of a rarely unified

4. *Hawthorne* (London: Macmillan, 1887), pp. 53–54.

5. "Calamus," *Complete Poetry*, p. 88.

sensibility, and he gave himself up to his art with a clear conscience, one that Hawthorne might have envied, because it was at once, without distinction, the deeper consciousness active in life.

The Double Consciousness

The largest community of shared experience is tangibly expressed in James's writing by the sensibility which responds to monuments, art objects, landscapes, houses, all the relics and signs of a civilization. The visit to Weatherend, the rich old house in the English country-side, is the prologue to "The Beast in the Jungle." The beautiful ob-jects in the house represent stored experiences, and their existence points toward that shared experience which eludes Marcher, a man of no little esthetic sensibility. Hawthorne was preoccupied with the same paradox. The artifacts of a high civilization contain the revelatory essence of human experience. But the essence is deceptively simple and can elude the overcultivated imagination or intellect.

When this theme in James's writing seems to convey a criticism of America's civilization, it is not restricted to the terms of cultural nostalgia. The barrenness of the American landscape is not the major point at issue. It is true that we remember Woollett, the Newsomes' Woollett in *The Ambassadors*, for the meagerness of its capacity for experience. Woollett isn't sure it ought to enjoy life. But that uncer-tainty is not derived from the cultural poverty of a young country, so much as it is based on an imaginative, moral, and intellectual mis-take. The empire of the Newsomes was built by a trivial manufactured article, so trivial that it never gets mentioned in the novel. That point stresses its lack of concrete meaning. It is an abstraction, really, an abstraction interchangeable with that of money itself.

The conflict between values and the abstraction of value is con-cisely illustrated in an episode at the beginning of the novel. Frustrated by the conversation of Strether and Maria Gostrey on the streets of Europe, or by his inability to share in their discriminations and ap-preciations, Strether's aboriginal American friend, Waymarsh, rushes into a jewelry store and makes a great purchase. Strether calls this the exercise of Waymarsh's "sacred rage." The money he possesses is his power and defiance, it is his freedom and equality, and it remains per-fectly abstract. It dissolves all distinctions except one. To have money means that he is as capable and as much in command of experience as anyone else, the more so to the amount that he has it. The real poverty of America, it is implied, comes in the substitution of such abstractions for experience, whether they are wealth, power, success, happiness, freedom, equality, et cetera. These are all signs rather than realities and the irony is that their abstraction (like Marcher's abstraction of his life) is rooted in hunger, or a "sacred rage." The cold, philistine Newsomes are as much the members of a famished race as Theobald, the Aspern narrator, or Gilbert Osmond.

This split between power and value is clearly illustrated by the divorce between what Mrs. Newsome has come to represent and the money empire built up to support her. She is a fearsome bluestocking, patroness of the arts, moral arbiter, the judge of manners and the conscience of her civilization. But all her enterprises are founded on a history of swindling; her father and her husband were business pirates of the type which dominated the second half of the nineteenth century.

It is powerlessness, on the other hand, which defines Strether. He has chiefly the capacity for appreciations, and he brings these to a kind of climax of martyrdom in the story. The novel concentrates on this split between power and appreciations. Strether lacks the means if not the will to enact his sophisticated judgments. He performs only as an intermediary; he suffers, but vicariously. In no other modern novel has a passive protagonist reached such heights of moral involvement. But in James this is not merely the pathos of the antihero. It emphasizes the division between action and judgment, but it also attests that the key problem is a failure of the moral imagination, and this is not Strether's failure but that of others. At the beginning of the narrative Maria Gostrey observes Strether's role as outsider, as one of the company of failures who "are out of it," and she includes herself in that company. In the same passage Mrs. Gostrey herself adds, "thank goodness, would you be a success today?" But the meaning is more serious than she imagines at that point, and so also is it true that the greater failure is not that of those who "are out of it" but those who are "in it"—Chad, Mrs. Newsome, and Mme de Vionnet. Strether's moral superiority is specific, it is expressed in the dramatic climax of the novel, and it rests on his ability to develop the gift, ruefully called a burden, of the "double consciousness." The term repeats Emerson, without awareness on James's part, I would guess, but it expresses James's special position toward his American protagonist, viewed in his Yankee background and both hobbled and ennobled by a refined and scrupulous imagination that Emerson could respect.

Very early in *The Ambassadors* Strether finds himself entertaining two contradictory responses to his friend, Waymarsh: "he both wanted extremely to see him and enjoyed extremely the duration of delay," and this is considered a premonition of the complexity of his experience in Europe. It is really a revelation of the complexity of his own mind.

> He was burdened, poor Strether—it had better be confessed at the outset—with the oddity of a double consciousness. There was detachment in his zeal and curiosity in his indifference.

A bit later he confesses to Maria Gostrey,

> I'm always considering something else; something else, I mean, than the thing of the moment. The obsession of the other thing is the terror. I'm considering at present for instance something else than *you*.

There is always the knowledge of something else, and this, one thinks, is the essence of the Emersonian hero, a man quite sincere in his practice of freedom. In reading James it is appropriate to pause and appreciate the general reference of this principle. The fact that the "double consciousness" is available to cross-referencing could be illustrated by the following passage from *Walden*.

> With thinking we may be beside ourselves in a sane sense. By a conscious effort of the mind we can stand aloof from actions and their consequences; and all things, good and bad, go by us like a torrent. We are not wholly involved in Nature. I may be either the drift-wood in the stream, or Indra in the sky looking down on it. I *may* be affected by a theatrical exhibition; on the other hand, I *may not* be affected by an actual event which appears to concern me much more. I only know myself as a human entity; the scene, so to speak, of thoughts and affections; and am sensible of a certain doubleness by which I can stand as remote from myself as from another. However intense my experience, I am conscious of the presence and criticism of a part of me, which, as it were, is not a part of me, but spectator, sharing no experience, but taking note of it; and that is no more I than it is you. When the play, it may be the tragedy, of life is over, the spectator goes his way. It was a kind of fiction, a work of the imagination only, so far as he was concerned. This doubleness may easily make us poor neighbors and friends sometimes.[6]

This is a most expressive statement of an effect, a dramatic principle, and an explicit concern in American writing which has preoccupied me deeply in this book. Thoreau's description could also stand as a prologue to *Huckleberry Finn*, in ways I have stressed, the division of Huck's life between river and shore being an example of how he

6. *Walden and Civil Disobedience*, p. 93.

lives outside himself "in a sane sense." The life as spectator, with "the presence and criticism of a part of me," has meaning for Hawthorne's characters who live behind veils, or know that doubleness, that remoteness from themselves as well as others which Thoreau talks about, though it may be psychically different in tone and a theme of suffering, as it is eventually in the case of Strether.

My general point, however, has been that this dramatic self-awareness has significance as a mode of being in a democratic culture. The function of that "criticism of a part of me" has particular importance in a system of divided or partial loyalties. No identity can be inclusive, and no act or event can fully absorb or be identified with consciousness. There is always something left out, perhaps a spectator, perhaps, when aroused, an antagonist, but persistently a reserve of criticism and judgment. In James this is the soil of life and freedom, and all his curiosity bears upon adventures in that realm.

F. O. Matthiessen argued that James's concentration upon "consciousness" had a spiritual or neoreligious basis.[7] It pointed toward the achievement of a "humane consciousness," which renewed the synthesis of religion and politics which his father, Henry James, Sr., had attempted. The significant phrase Matthiessen used in the title of the final chapter of his book on James is "The Religion of Consciousness." This has its deep link to the Emersonian aspiration, as Matthiessen points out. A consciousness, in this sense, is beyond philosophy or ideology. It is rather a state of moral readiness and awareness, engaged always in the *process* of judgment and set free from the points of abstract prejudgment.

Strether in *The Ambassadors* is such a hero of consciousness, to a supreme degree. At the start of his adventures, made vulnerable by his intelligence and imagination, he is ready to pass from one world to another, from his own to that of Chad and Mme de Vionnet. To be in transition, to be free, is to find out contradictions. Strether's experience is replete with them. For instance, connected with him are two Americans abroad, Waymarsh and little Bilham. The one has worked all his life, feels only the "sacred rage" and a revulsion at the sight of anything differing from what he has always known. This includes anyone enjoying himself, or not sacrificing himself, though of course the word sacrifice does not belong in his lexicon. The words work, success, and duty do.

7. F. O. Matthiessen, *Henry James: The Major Phase*, (London and New York: Oxford University Press, 1944), pp. 131–51.

Bilham on the other hand has found the paradise of the "famished race." He is there, in the promised land of the imagination and the esthetic sensibility, and he is determined to enjoy it. He will *do* absolutely nothing, Maria Gostrey says, and in this he is more American than anybody.

A mere hedonism would not attract Strether, he has too much character for that. He transforms the principle of Bilham's life into something ideal when he locates Chad Newsome. It is of utmost importance to understand what Strether *thinks* he sees in the Chad who has been so transformed by Europe. He asks himself for instance at their first meeting, why should the way a man enters a theatre box mean so much, conceding that Chad miraculously had learned how.

In the further description of Strether's response, it is apparent that a high manner means more to him than grace or polish. It implies a power to make the best of life, to conduct it toward its fulfillment. It is this mingling of the power to appreciate and the power to control which most attracts Strether. Chad was outstanding for his ability to arrange things, he was so eminently a man of experience, "a man to whom things had happened and were variously known." Chad in other words seems to illustrate the successful combination of the two extremes in Waymarsh and Bilham. He has the power and he has the knowledge. He can turn his hand in any direction, toward Woollett or Paris, and remain strong, a prince of life.

Chad illustrates an exorbitant ideal, as Faustian as any in Hawthorne's range, as hungry for power over life as Captain Ahab himself. This tells us more about Strether than it does about Chad himself, of course. We see better the direction of his imagination as we observe his reaction to Gloriani, the triumphant artist. The artist of great achievement illustrates the power to make an order of things, and as a man and artist he has extended the capacity for appreciations to their limit. But forecasting his own full development of insight later in the novel, Strether has a sudden disturbing grasp of what this might carry with it. He notes "the deep human expertness in Gloriani's charming smile—oh the terrible life behind it!" Why terrible, one might think? The hint comes again, more strongly, as Strether watches Gloriani and the Duchess, a famous woman of the world, in conversation. He admires these two magnificent creatures but catches the waft of the jungle, something covertly tigerish.

The education of Lambert Strether is the education of the free man, and its chief theme is the ordeal of freedom, that is to say, the questioning of commitments, the questioning of culture. Strether is not fortunate with talents and opportunities, but he does have preeminently the power to choose. He is in the first place examining his origins, though he will also be forced to examine that "terrible life" in Gloriani. The society represented by Mrs. Newsome is so strained that one also senses something "terrible" within it. In one aspect it resembles a temporary shelter thrown up against the frontier. It is rigid, fierce, and detailed in its rules of conduct, but that only reveals its primitive state, and it functions like an army at war. If it is innocent and ignorant, it is also afraid. That is the basis of its superstitions and prejudices. Good and evil must be sharply defined in emergencies and in new conditions. The Newsomes never had the leisure to follow the curious and complex routes indicated by the behavior of Mme de Vionnet.

The Newsomes think of depravity when they consider Europe, but everything proves them wrong to Strether, particularly the Gloriani garden party. This world was not licentious, not besotted by the pleasure of the senses. It was served by the highest intelligence, by the instinct for order, by mastery. Its highest altar is found eventually in Mme de Vionnet's apartment. And here, as James chooses his words very carefully, Strether finds "an air of supreme respectability." The ultimate fine values have been reached by generations of intelligent experience. How could anything here be bad in terms of Boston values, or any values? It would have first to be coarse and that was impossible.

Strether is not superimposing taste on morality but morality on taste. In his innocence he is saying to himself, how could anyone who knew and could choose so well what was beautiful, commit a bad action, which was ugly? In a sense, he is Emersonian in believing that once the discrimination of the good was put to work it could only go on from good to better, for goods were all related.

The clue for understanding him is that he maintains, always, a passionate belief in the power of the imagination. In Woollett he saw the lack of imagination, the banality, the prejudice, the ignorance— and once he had broken his tie of duty nothing could bring him back to a preference for *that*. In Europe or in Mme de Vionnet he saw life fully created by the imagination, satisfying it, and yet deeply the composite of experience from the inherited centuries. This was indeed an American dream, a kind of reversal of the Edenic expectations of the first travelers to the new continent. The esthetic imagination in

Strether has suddenly been liberated to join the moral imagination which judged in the American, pragmatic way—the good is the successful mastery of all contingencies, a practice of the finest harmony of life.

It is therefore easy to persuade Strether at this point that the relationship between Chad and Mme de Vionnet must be a "virtuous attachment." Illustrating one classic extreme for Americans, he had chosen civilization as the highest good, as others might have chosen nature, and therefore he must believe that immorality was associated with vulgarity and coarseness, and that a superior civilization meant a superior morality. In these circumstances, the sudden waft of the jungle to his senses at Gloriani's party has special poignancy.

Strether needs to see things made of a piece and this is why these sudden discords shake him. He has not yet gained the demanding and difficult "double consciousness." For instance when he sees Mme de Vionnet in church at Notre Dame, with every manifestation of actual worship, he asks himself quickly how such a woman could come to church if she weren't *really* innocent. "You and your Boston reallys," Bilham says to him.

At this point Strether reflects another American obsession, a classic emphasis, with his insecure sense of the real world. Considering that we deal here with "Boston reallys," it might be useful to recapitulate. The questioning of reality had its traditional ground in the rawness of the new world, a theme important in James' own response to his native land. The instability of refined values, the uncertainty of the assumptions for choosing them, were effects of the historic experience of immigration, and they were experienced in reverse, so to speak, in James's own lifetime of expatriation. His sensitive American travelers, most notably Isabel Archer and Lambert Strether, are pioneers in old Europe, filled with curiosity, high scruple, and an unlimited capacity for disillusioning experience. The deepest force behind these "Boston reallys" was a temperamental response to the practice and ideal of freedom. It enforced the trial of choice for the American protagonists, most emphatically in the case of Isabel Archer, who was given by her author every chance to meet the "requirements of her imagination," as her benefactor, Ralph Touchett, put it. Strether is at the same time older and more innocent; his crisis is graver. He possesses almost nothing but a fine conscience and an even finer imagination; it is the others, Chad and Mme de Vionnet, who have the experience. But his conscience is joined with their freedom, and as an extreme case, he lives in an agony of suspended judgment, questioning facts and values to the end of his story.

If Boston put "really" to great use, that reflected its dilemma, and Strether's. For instance, Bilham at one major turning point asks Strether the following question. If the "real" relationship of Mme de Vionnet and Chad *passes* for a "virtuous attachment," isn't that enough? If it is good, or shows as good, what else does he want? The wisest people accept the "vain appearance." This is a practical wisdom that seems to have passed over a thin borderline to cynicism, and Strether indeed wants more than that. It is true that his search has led him to face the "appearance" of things apart from the abstractions of moral prejudgment. He cannot believe that all the good he sees in Chad, in Mme de Vionnet, in their lives, could flow from something evil. But it is not an accident that he should see more, as at the country inn where he discovers them in the blunt exposure of a lovers' weekend. His moral curiosity would not rest with a first or second look at the *vain* appearance of things, and perhaps this deeper wisdom has told him all along that the answer to his question—is the relationship between Chad and Mme de Vionnet good or bad?—could not be answered by the bigoted "bad" of Mrs. Newsome, or by the partly seeing, generous "good" of his own first reactions, or by the semicynical and ambiguous "good" of Bilham.

The permutations of Strether's mind on this question provide the basis of the story—and they form a perfect illustration of the growth of a double consciousness. At one point he romanticizes richly and sees the pair illustrating a great moral uplift based on the renunciation of their physical love for each other. This is the Boston or "puritan" inverse side of the coarser dogmatic assumptions of Mrs. Newsome. But it is almost simpleminded and not really his own thinking. What he really hopes to find is even more ambitious in moral terms. At their first meeting, looking at a sudden reflected impression from Chad, he thinks that he must be an "irreducible young Pagan." This comes as an alternative to his very first impression that he was a great gentleman. But then the thought inevitably arrives that it was possible to be both a pagan and a gentleman. It was possible to be free, fully released to life, and good.

It is an old dream but quite typically American at that, and Strether is taking the traditional moral journey. He must first escape the prejudices of Woollett, a narrow morality which is all abstract form and no substance. In reaction he wants to see full experience;

he would preach, as he does to Bilham, for those who *live* their lives, and at least support them in the attempt. But experience in his mind is ruled by the god of beauty, if not by the prohibitory gods, and therefore he must loathe the possible brutality of a natural freedom, the promiscuity, the violence, the unintelligence, and the ugliness. He wants two things; he will not have one without the other—a freedom that is satisfied and a great order in experience. He thinks he sees in the episode of the two lovers a high civilized form that held nothing back and did not fight against life. At this point he does not have to use the word "adultery" and that vulgar question has been transcended. He is not in a trance—but he is certainly in a willing state of belief. He is trusting what he feels and sees, he has dismissed abstract and conventional discriminations, a truce has been declared in the old war between nature and civilization. Is it any wonder that Strether feels like sacrificing himself for the cause of Mme de Vionnet?

The rest of the novel is Strether's education into ambiguities. James uses a striking illustration for the climax of Strether's illusions as well as the process of disillusionment. At the river side, just before he is made to confront Chad and Mme de Vionnet as ordinary illicit lovers spending an ordinary illicit weekend together, Strether contemplates the landscape before him and sees it as a painting by Lambinet which at one time in his youth he had almost bought and which he had always regretted losing. This is the climax of Strether's hungry will to believe. The actuality of the world in that country scene has entered into the painter's composition. There is no disparity between art and life, judgment has corresponded with fact, value has immanence, appearance is not "vain." The rest that happens that day is like a disintegration of the elements of the painting, and the emergence of chaos.

The will to believe was strong but it had to overcome incongruities, strange hints, the recurrence of bad possibilities. There has been more than one waft from the jungle. The most forceful instance is in the fate of the daughter, Jeanne, who resembles those other pale victims, Pansy Osmond and Milly Theale.[8] Strether confronts a revelation

8. The stress on this sort of victimization in James's work is the surest evidence of his attraction to the theme of the abuse of freedom and power. Densher and Kate Croy are particularly magnificent tigers in the jungle; their vitality is made an almost indisputable claim in the context of Milly Theale's illness. Gilbert Osmond's abuse of his daughter is an interesting contrast, based as it is on a more sadistic depravity which arises from his excessive cultivation rather than his superior energy. But in either

that Jeanne is probably in love with Chad, that Chad may be responding, and that the mother is deeply frightened and jealous. When finally Chad himself is brought to find a husband for Jeanne and marry her off, the issue is almost open between Strether and Mme de Vionnet. He feels something anciently cold in all this: the facts, if they were facts, would be as cruel as anything his imagination could bear. It is characteristic that he should be brought around again to her side by the expression of Mme de Vionnet's own terror and need.

The hints of this intrinsic violence have been deft and frequent enough. We recall the striped tigers in their jungle, at Gloriani's party. The vivid presentation of victims has made Strether question those masters of experience. The metaphor of violence returns when he visits Maria Gostrey's apartment, filled with her beautiful treasures, where "the lust of the eyes and the pride of life had indeed their temple." She too, like Mme de Vionnet, is a queen of the experienced life. But her shrine, it is observed, is "as brown as a pirate's cave."

These insights are lasting; they are part of Strether's moral education which lead him beyond the fragmentation of the Lambinet landscape. He is fated to be a moral dialectician throughout the novel in his passage from insight to insight. The Newsomes, on the other hand, and Chad must be included among them, the Newsomes, Strether says, "shut their eyes to each side of the matter, in order, whichever side comes up, to get rid of the other." This is a precise way of summing up. In this respect, as a dialectician, he appeals first to the function of the imagination—and for this reason Mme de Vionnet wins her initial victory over Mrs. Newsome in his mind. Mme de Vionnet "took all categories by surprise" and yet she remained a masterpiece of civilized order. In Woollett, however, he observes to Mrs. Gostrey, there were only two types of people, male and female. Perhaps there was only one. In his ultimate outraged protest he calls Mrs. Newsome "a whole moral and intellectual being or block," and as he says to Maria Gostrey, "you've got morally and intellectually to get rid of her." The key to understanding her is given us. "She has no imagination." The crystallizing of judgment in prejudice is a failure of the imagination. But so, it is eventually observed, is it also true that Chad, the irreducible young pagan, has no moral imagination.

The Ambassadors is significant in the American tradition as an

---

case the existence of the victim serves to condition refined values as well as vital power. Between these imperatives of culture and nature, the victim makes her moral claim on judgment.

essay on the difficulty of constructing a moral civilization. James recognized and implied clearly that the shadow of Mrs. Newsome was spread over American history and society. But so was the more furtive, irresponsible figure of her son, conceived as a liberated hedonist. The superiority of Mme de Vionnet is based on the actual richness of her experience, she rises beyond the callowness of both son and mother— but the true superiority is Strether's. He has the imagination to view and go beyond the opposite sides of the moral equation, but it requires first a clash, the blood of conflict in the dialectic of freedom. It is here that moral maturity begins.

It is not easy to sum up what Strether knows in his many-sided understanding of the matter. He has sensed or guessed that Chad and Mme de Vionnet might really be hideous, not as Sarah Pocock has conventionally defined them, but as in a powerful mixture of reasonable and graceful practice and tigerish self-interest, they sacrifice Jeanne. The appetites find their prey, they make victims. And the close view of animal appetites in action is never pleasant.

The scene at the river is the crucial revelation, and it is possible to wonder at Strether's shock. He has already conceded the probability of an affair and it played a role in his judgment on behalf of the lovers. But this was theoretical, and Strether was determined to be a consistent moral empiricist. He had decided not to judge what he couldn't know, certainly not on behalf of abstract and conventional prejudice. "He had dressed the possibility in vagueness." And didn't he judge in their favor when he saw the *good* consequences of whatever existed between them? Now he knows, actually and empirically, in terms of other effects and consequences.

What shocks Strether is not the mere fact that they are having an adulterous weekend. His horror comes from the manner, not the abstraction, of the event. This is illustrated as he jumps to his feet and shouts to them when they make their first gesture of concealment. The wish for secrecy shocks him, and afterward, the embarrassment, the humiliation, the lack of *form* for dealing with the truth. It is the first time he has seen her at a loss, while Chad almost brutally leaves everything to her. It is a fall from the sublime; "the pity of its being so much like lying," he feels. Strether finally considers that he is glad that they went through the charade of dinner together and the trip back to Paris, keeping the pretense that they had only been out for the day, rather than draw him into their confidence on their own terms.

It might be argued that this awkward deceit was only the required response to Strether's provincial naiveté and that "their own terms" were sufficiently dignified or emancipated to withstand shame in their own world. In other words they had to play a special game for Strether's sake. The answer to this, I think, is that the deceit they used was not only a violation of the supposed candor of their friendship, but also a confession on their part that the terms they used for this affair were not morally adequate terms. They may have had the language of passion, but this was for each other. They may also have had the worldly and cynical terms appropriate to Mrs. Barrace and the confidential closets of Parisian society, but these were not the terms for Strether either. The conclusion is that the two lovers were genuinely ashamed when exposed to full observation by Strether. Among the complex reasons for this is the specific guilt in their affair associated with the treatment of Jeanne; however, the latter was more the effect than the substance of the moral license to which they were committed. There simply *were* no terms to satisfy Strether in this affair, even though his moral sensibility had gone far beyond Woollett prejudices. It could be put that it was the Lambinet landscape, not Woollett, which could not contain the two lovers.

It is the failure of an adequate form that hurts Strether, a disorder which exposes moral defeat and a great humiliation. The humiliation of Mme de Vionnet is the key point. He had hoped for much from this artist of experience, who could translate life into distinguished values, and above all keep her mastery over events. Her failure and distress are real. It is the point upon which to measure all the moral enlightenment Strether receives.

The humiliation is a great theme, but the cruelty is even stronger. The sacrificed victims surround the lovers, Jeanne, Strether himself. Mme de Vionnet makes him play out the drama of choices before Chad's sister, Mrs. Newsome's latest ambassador, and doing so she unhesitatingly gives Strether up to her own interests, taking everything, his future, his Woollett. Everything, that is, before he was able to offer it himself, though he was certain to do so. (For emphasis in the scene, Strether sees himself, a loser and a failure, overwhelmed by these two women who knew so well what they wanted.) A violence in life has been liberated and the greatest victim is Mme de Vionnet herself. In the most complete view of her vulnerability in the affair with Chad, he sees her finally as Madame Roland on the scaffold. Around her is the "smell of blood." The French Revolution is an apt metaphor for the moral chaos and disruption he senses. Strether has the "view of something old, old, old, the oldest thing he had ever personally touched."

The mixture of humiliation and violence continues as a kind of potent tragic draught that must be taken to the end. In the final scene, in the fear of Chad leaving her, Mme de Vionnet collapses in tears, and Strether sees her like "a maidservant crying for her young man." Her suffering is barbarically simple after all. Beyond the immediate pain, what she fears is as automatic as death; the young man will one day, and probably soon, leave her. The beautiful and aging woman has found herself subordinated to the inevitable, ordinary fate. No wonder she says to Strether that "we bore you."

It is no wonder also that the old moral conscience in Strether recovers and rebels. It protests on behalf of salvaging some dignity. He feels the need to know "that somebody was paying." He will pay, if no one else will, so "that they were at least not all floating together in the silver stream of impunity." This is a protest for some discipline, a restraint against the disintegration he has experienced in himself as well as the others.

Renunciation, sacrifice, prohibition have renewed psychological understanding and moral meaning in this treatment. In one sense they become simply the overwhelming desire to say no to the violence of the will, the appetites, an animal determinism. But in another aspect, sacrifice seems to be invoked on behalf of everyone, for a lessening of pain, for the bringing together of what can be saved in life itself. Strether has sacrificed himself so that Mme de Vionnet will not be destroyed. Later he asks Chad to make a corresponding sacrifice of his own freedom or changing desires. And if Mme de Vionnet ever could rise from the "scaffold" on which she presently suffers, she too might be asked to sacrifice. Moral action must still demand renunciation and prohibition when it is focussed on the reality of suffering and not the mere abstract categories of right and wrong. It is pain that makes these demands for renunciation, not prejudice, and Strether, after discovering the pragmatism of pleasure, or beauty, has now stumbled on this truth.

It has become implausible, and he knows it, to turn to Chad for a sacrifice. He warns him, nevertheless, after anxiously seeking him out and waiting for him all one night, that he would be a criminal to leave Mme de Vionnet, that he has a duty, that he owes her everything. But is this plausible for Chad? As Strether recognized earlier, he was a creature formed to please others—but first of all himself. He was not formed for duties, certainly not for sacrifice. That is not even an argument of Mrs. Newsome for his return; she is too shrewd and callous to make such arguments to her son. Rather she dangles Mamie Pocock and a fortune in front of his eyes. The only true moralist here is Strether. Chad dances a kind of jig in front of him, and in ominous effect. Strether sees him again under the light of a street lamp, and again, implicitly, as the "irreducible young Pagan." This time Strether must come to the conclusion of that insight. A form of license produced him and the principle of license is what he must follow. He was a man of the world who knew thoroughly well how to live in it, and habitually he has done it by leaving the painful tasks to others. The sobering question becomes this one—and to it the novel has led. *Can* one live well in the world without compelling the pain, the sacrifice, the whole substructure of dolor that Strether now sees supporting Chad's graceful jig? And then the question becomes, how does one divide this cost, and whose is the moral responsibility for it?

Like his mother, in his own way, Chad lacks imagination, and Strether makes that point. "It isn't his father in him that troubles me," he says elsewhere. Like his mother, he follows one track, though it be the track of pleasure. In the form in which he is finally seen, Chad provides the most ominous note of critical judgment on American civilization that we find in the novel. Weaned from his provincial inherited system of values, he cannot make a full response to Mme de Vionnet. The rich offering of Mme de Vionnet's life, impressed by the intelligence and appreciations of centuries, becomes for this new man from the West not much more than the mere world of pleasure. This conveys the brutal necessity to pursue further enjoyment, and he manifests himself as the opportunist in life, much less attractive than the irresponsible pagan. The fact that he seriously considers taking his mother's offer—returning to the business and developing the advertising branch of it—are further signs that his values are superficial, except those of power and pleasure. In the end, he resembles those money pirates, his father and grandfather, except that the refined instruments he can employ are perhaps doubly corrupting, the manipulations of advertising, his new metier, contrasted with the more forthright operations of trade. If he goes back he will work by the sign of the meretricious.

This is the most disconcerting of Strether's discoveries. Throughout he has had a curiously deep though detached relationship with

Chad, his surrogate for living. He first worships him and then he becomes his conscience. Of all the agents in the drama, only Strether seems to have an adequate moral imagination; it begins with his capacity for appreciations and it ends with his despairing sense of a stalemate in conflicting values. He has above all the gift of empathy— so important in the moral structures of American writing from Hawthorne's typical expression of it to Whitman's. So much so that hardly any experience occurs to Strether that isn't vicarious, whether pleasure or suffering. The man of moral imagination exists between two worlds, or between himself and his communicants, and that is one thing it must mean to be, in Whitman's words, "both in and out of the game." But still the curious question remains for readers of the novel, where does this leave Strether, in his own life?

In view of what has happened and who he is, there isn't the slightest possibility of a glib resolution. There never is in James; resolutions in the ordinary sense are beside the point. However, it is possible to think of Strether as a defeated, hopeless man. "I am not in real harmony with what surrounds me. . . . I take it too hard," he says at the very end to Maria Gostrey. In this way he explains his refusal to take up her own offer. In actual fact, of course, if he has been greatly attracted to any woman, it has been to Mme de Vionnet, but the further conclusion might be that his will to live has been broken, his sense of human relationships has become so abrasive that he is incapable of carrying them further.

William Troy made a similar observation for the concluding episodes of *The Portrait of a Lady*, where Isabel Archer faces "the terror of experience, which at the end she rationalizes in terms of moral obligation."[9] In Strether's case the moral obligation is certainly expressed and behind it lies the "terror of experience." (He feels as if he were going to die. "It amused him to say to himself that he might for all the world have been going to die—die resignedly; the scene was filled for him with so deep a deathbed hush, so melancholy a charm.") But the conjunction is interesting and needs development. Strether's disappearance into a kind of limbo, neither in Woollett nor in Paris, follows a consistent realism in the pattern of his passivity and nostalgia. He has done little and asserted hardly anything for himself. In one sense his future belongs with Chad and Mme de Vionnet in Chad's eventual act of cruelty and Mme de Vionnet's eventual loss.

9. William Troy, *Selected Essays*, ed. Stanley Edgar Hyman (New Brunswick: Rutgers University Press, 1967), p. 60.

Why should he suddenly emerge into his own life? He has *had* his experience, to the end of the inevitable cycle. Once the Lambinet landscape is shattered, if he knows anything he knows there are no happy endings, no reestablished visions of harmony.

We could return at this point to Richard Chase's most valuable perception, "the putative unity in disunity" that he thought characterizes the form of the American novel. This may be expressed in the undefeated principle of judgment which Strether carries with him wherever he now goes. It hasn't restored completeness to life, much less vigorous hope, but it is nevertheless a great gift, that unresting, responsive moral imagination (which is the real profit of a double consciousness). There are those who act—Mrs. Newsome, Chad, Mme de Vionnet—but whatever forms their lives take, Strether has supplied the perspective for knowing them. It is the criticism of a noble conscience, and it has realized itself within the jungle, among its magnificent beasts.

He says something at the end to Maria Gostrey that is not easy to appreciate, since it seems so much like straining at a scruple, beyond any beneficent effect to anyone, least of all himself. He tells her he is now bound by a minimal principle; "not, out of the whole affair, to have got anything for myself." He will not serve his own interest at all while the interests of so many others had been touched by his actions and judgments. He is referring to the renunciation of Mrs. Gostrey's offer of an alliance, under whatever obscure or conventional form it might take. It is clear that this is not heroic martyrdom; it is not a great love or even a great need that he is renouncing. But the renunciation compels him and is meaningful nevertheless. Is it a scruple of unselfishness to challenge a world where so much was done out of self-interest? Is it a form of atonement for Chad? Is it a final revulsion from the arena, shared by its humiliated victims and its striped beasts?

These answers are not quite satisfactory. In any case it is not easy to conclude that Strether is accepting defeat. His wish "to have gotten nothing out of it" for himself expresses his concern for a form of disinterestedness in moral action, as indispensable to good faith. The grandiose illustration could indeed be taken from instances of martyrdom, but it is not necessary. In the end perhaps the renunciation means that his restless conscience, tested continually by his freedom, moves always to the frontiers of judgment and transcends his "interests." It would be inconsistent for Strether to consign himself to any condition, particularly one identified with "Europe," a contestant among value systems in the novel. It would be equally inconsistent for him to solve his own dilemma, when he could not help Mme de Vionnet. The *structures* of the moral life are only fallible; the havoc that is accomplished in the conventional territory of moral judgments, like that ruled over by Mrs. Newsome, has been made manifest in the story. There is no salvation *in* life. But there is a civilized grace of judgment which is indispensable to freedom, and it is for the condition of free men that James's moral drama has any meaning.

Strether is not quite dead, but his own life does not propose any new steps that can be imagined by the reader. The pause, or this equivocal finality, is as necessary as the death in tragedy and has something of the same function. It serves to memorialize a state of consciousness, not of events, a moral premise, one could say, not a conclusion, and before any uses can be taken from it. This has remarkable pertinence for the open moralities of a free civilization. It puts the function of the critical conscience first, always by one step removed from absorption in the shifting action of life itself. Strether's conscience seems to have been exercised to such a fine point that it suggests complete withdrawal. Not so, it has breathed life and the appreciation of it into the novel. It has criticized life and affirmed it, but in the process it has achieved its highest visibility as an unprejudiced conscience. This may be the most realistic definition of his freedom, or a description of where its weight falls and its justification lies. If he has acted, it was to achieve the general sense of failure and make some refusals for himself. But everything has been allowed Strether in the rights of choice, of criticism, of immune judgment, while he honors his commitments as he can, in the meaningful sense of the Emersonian "double consciousness."

Index

Abrams, M. H., 25 n, 26–27, 90
Adams, John, 4, 30–31, 31 n
Adams, Samuel, 4
Adventures of Huckleberry Finn (Twain), 225–52; artistic and moral inconsistency of, 244–45; as comedy, 229, 233–34, 250, 252; and community, 251–52; and *The Confidence Man*, 250–51; and critical realism, 229; as democratic classic, 234, 236–37; and Emerson's "double consciousness," 252, 273; and freedom, 244–47; and pastoral, 229; style of, 225
Ahab, Captain, 46, 96, 131, 209, 236, 270; and Bartleby, 184–87; and Billy Budd, 186–89; and Captain Vere, 192–93; challenging God, 161–62, 170, 178; challenging nature, 170–71, 180–81, 183, 191; contrasted with Queequeg, 172–73; in defense of personality, 166, 170–71, 180, 183, 191; as democratic hero, 159–60, 163, 167–68, 180, 184; and freedom, 113, 168, 180, 183, 192; and the human community, 169, 179; as suicide, 113, 178, 192; as tragic hero, 167, 170–71, 175 n, 183; as tyrant, 165, 168, 170
The Ambassadors (James), 271–87; and American cultural poverty, 271–72; and artistry of experience, 275,
282; conscience and freedom in, 275–78, 283–87; and the dialectic of freedom, 279, 279 n, 281; and the "double consciousness," 277, 287; and the experience of Europe, 273, 276; and ideal consciousness, 274, 287
American Constitution, 2, 5, 30, 43, 57
American fiction, xviii; and Chase's theory of romance, 39–40; form of, 286; interracial friendships in, 9; and the social theme, 40–41. *See also* American literature
American Indians, 9; in D. H. Lawrence's view of Cooper, 104–5
American literature: disorder as an esthetic rule of, 38–39; incoherence of, and culture, 38–41; and the opposition of culture and nature, xi; and social realism, 184. *See also* American studies
American myths of genesis, 2–3
"American Scholar, The" (Emerson), 7, 68
American studies, 2
Anderson, Sherwood, 21
Arendt, Hannah, 5, 12; *On Revolution*, 2 n, 31, 31 n, 35 n
"Art of Fiction, The" (James), 255–56
"Artist of the Beautiful, The" (Hawthorne), 144
Arvin, Newton, 77, 175 n, 216, 268

Pearl, character of, 129, 132, 136–39, 150–53

Pequod, 26, 37, 159, 160, 168, 171, 181, 242; crew of, 165, 169, 170, 179

Perry, Ralph B., 13

"Philosophy of Composition, The" (Poe), 115

Pioneers, The (Cooper), 107–10

Plato, 14, 51, 158

Platonism, 47

Poe, Edgar Allan, 20, 22, 40, 113–28; and his American contemporaries, 113–14, 118, 123, 124–26; and crime, 120–21, 125; and Faustian intelligence, 121; and the guilt of civilization, 125, 126, 128; on Hawthorne, 114; and James, 267; Lawrence's, D. H., judgment of, 104, 113, 127; and natural and psychic mystery, 117, 117 n; and the temperament of decadence, 115, 119–20, 122–28; and the theme of death, 115, 116, 116 n, 118, 120, 240; and Thoreau, 114, 118, 123, 124, 128

———, works of: "Berenice," 119, 120, 122; "Black Cat, The," 125; "Cask of Amontillado, The," 125; "Colloquy of Monos and Una, The," 116 n; "Eleanora," 119; "Fall of the House of Usher, The," 122–25; "Imp of the Perverse, The," 125; "Ligeia," 118; "Morella," 118; "Ms. Found in a Bottle," 117; "Murders in the Rue Morgue, The," 120; "Philosophy of Composition, The," 115; "Premature Burial, The," 116

Pope, Alexander, 24

Portrait of a Lady, The (James), 21, 285

Pragmatism, American, 30 n

"Premature Burial, The" (Poe), 116

Promethean protagonist, xi, 163

Prometheus, xvii, 149

Proust, Marcel, 253

Prynne, Hester, character of, 11, 129, 132, 134, 150, 151, 154, 155, 157–58; moral isolation and commit-

ment of, 136–38, 147; as public servant, 133, 152

Puritan(s), 3, 29 n, 35; ancestors, 5, 36; ancestors of Hawthorne in Salem, 134; and democrat, 67; in Hawthorne's work, xvii, 136, 149, 150, 151, 153, 154 n, 157; settlers, 1; tradition of, 135

Puritanism, 36

Quakers, 134, 149

Queequeg: and his god, 161, 174, 175; relationship with Ishmael, 9, 46, 106, 113, 171–74, 178, 242–43; as savage, 160, 166, 169; as universal humanity, 171–73, 189, 194, 206

Rahv, Philip, 24, 124

"Rappacini's Daughter" (Hawthorne), 144

"Real Thing, The" (James), 254, 256–57

Reich, Charles, xiii

Renaissance, concept of nature, 15 n; legends of new discovery, 14

Revolution: American, 2; and decadence, 126; democratic, x; and dialectic, 28; French, 5, 24, 25, 190, 282; and guilt, 126; and humanism, xii; and paternal order, 127; Protestant, 127; and the romantic imagination, 24–27; as theme of "Benito Cereno," 15–18; as theme of *Billy Budd*, 187; theories of the American, 31–32

Rimbaud, Arthur, 26

"Roger Malvin's Burial" (Hawthorne), 139–40

Romance, and American fiction, 39–41. *See also* Chase, Richard

Romanticism, 24–27; English, 45; European, 141, 236; and freedom, 227; and revolution, 24–27, 90

Rourke, Constance, 226, 233

Rousseau, Jean Jacques, 36, 38, 126, 141, 181

Russian literature, of the nineteenth century, xix, 39, 198 n